James VI and I united the crowns of England and Scotland. His books are fundamental sources of the principles which underlay the union. In particular, his *Basilicon Doron* was a best-seller in England and circulated widely on the Continent. Among the most important and influential British writings of their period, the king's works shed light on the political climate of Shakespeare's England and the intellectual background to the civil wars which afflicted Britain in the mid-seventeenth century. James' political philosophy was a moderated absolutism, with an emphasis on the monarch's duty to rule according to law and the public good. Locke quoted his speech to parliament of 1610 approvingly, and Hobbes likewise praised 'our most wise king'. This edition is the first to draw on all the early texts of James' books, with an introduction setting them in their historical context.

CAMBRIDGE TEXTS IN THE
HISTORY OF POLITICAL THOUGHT

═══

KING JAMES VI and I
Political Writings

CAMBRIDGE TEXTS IN THE HISTORY OF POLITICAL THOUGHT

Series editors

RAYMOND GEUSS
Lecturer in Social and Political Sciences, University of Cambridge

QUENTIN SKINNER
Professor of Political Science in the University of Cambridge

Cambridge Texts in the History of Political Thought is now firmly established as the major student textbook series in political theory. It aims to make available to students all the most important texts in the history of western political thought, from ancient Greece to the early twentieth century. All the familiar classic texts will be included but the series does at the same time seek to enlarge the conventional canon by incorporating an extensive range of less well-known works, many of them never before available in a modern English edition. Wherever possible, texts are published in complete and unabridged form, and translations are specially commissioned for the series. Each volume contains a critical introduction together with chronologies, biographical sketches, a guide to further reading and any necessary glossaries and textual apparatus. When completed, the series will aim to offer an outline of the entire evolution of western political thought.

For a list of titles published in the series, please see end of book.

KING JAMES VI and I

Political Writings

EDITED BY

JOHANN P. SOMMERVILLE

University of Wisconsin, Madison

CAMBRIDGE
UNIVERSITY PRESS

Published by the Press Syndicate of the University of Cambridge
The Pitt Building, Trumpington Street, Cambridge CB2 1RP
40 West 20th Street, New York, NY 10011–4211, USA
10 Stamford Road, Oakleigh, Melbourne 3166, Australia

© Cambridge University Press 1994

First published 1994

Printed in Great Britain at the University Press, Cambridge

A catalogue record for this book is available from the British Library

Library of Congress cataloguing in publication data

James I, King of England, 1566–1625.
[Prose works. Selections]
Political writings / James VI and I; edited by Johann P. Sommerville.
p.   cm. – (Cambridge texts in the history of political thought)
Includes bibliographical references and index.
ISBN 0 521 44209 5. – ISBN 0 521 44729 1 (pbk)
1. Political science – Early works to 1800.
I. Sommerville, J. P., 1953– . II. Series.
JG153.J3   1994
321'.6 – dc20   94–2385 CIP

ISBN 0 521 44209 5 hardback
ISBN 0 521 44729 1 paperback

Contents

Preface and acknowledgements

In recent years there has been a substantial growth of interest in the history and literature of Jacobean England. Amongst the most important texts produced in that period were the writings of King James VI and I himself. Harvard University Press published *The Political Works of James I*, edited by Charles Howard McIlwain, in 1918. That volume has become quite a scarce book. Moreover, an examination of the text which McIlwain printed reveals a number of peculiarities. In James' longest work, the *Basilicon Doron*, marginal comments or summaries which were included in early editions were omitted by McIlwain. He based his edition of James' writings on a single source – the king's *Workes* of 1616 – and he introduced a good many misreadings into that version. For instance, on a surprisingly large number of occasions he strangely read the long 's' of seventeenth-century script as an 'f'. In consequence, such non-existent words as 'trustieft', 'Papifts', 'feueritie', 'iustneffe', 'aduife', and 'feruants' are scattered through his edition.

The present volume is intended to present more accurate texts of James' writings than McIlwain made available. Where appropriate, the *Workes* of 1616 has been used as copy-text, but in every case it has been compared with other early versions of the king's writings. McIlwain made no attempt to track down James' sources. I have traced the sources of most direct quotations, but have not tried to verify or decipher all the references in James' writings. To do so would have increased the size of this book substantially. Many of the references occur in *Basilicon Doron* (which cites 110 classical works in its margins), but they are often too imprecise to be verified (a good discussion of these references is in Craigie 1944–50, 2: 93–105). Unlike McIlwain's book, the present edition includes a glossary – which gives the meanings of obscure words used by James – and select biographical notes identifying some of the people whom the king mentions. It also provides translations of all non-English passages.

For reasons of space, two of the works included by McIlwain have been omitted here. These are *A Premonition to all Christian Monarchs, Free Princes and States* of 1609, and *A Remonstrance . . . for the Right of Kings, against Cardinal Perron.* The *Remonstrance* was first published in French in 1615. The later English translation was not made by James, and the original French was written by Pierre Du Moulin, though it undoubtedly expressed the king's views. Both the *Premonition* and the *Remonstrance* are important works, but their central arguments against papal political claims were already set out in *Triplici Nodo, Triplex Cuneus. Or an Apologie for the Oath of Allegiance,* which was first published in 1608, and which *is* reprinted below. McIlwain included no works belonging to the last years of James' life. The present edition contains texts of two important late writings: *A Meditation upon the 27th, 28th and 29th Verses of the 27th Chapter of Saint Matthew* (1619), and *His Maiesties Declaration, Touching his proceedings in the Late Assemblie and Conuention of Parliament* (1622).

It is now more than seventeen years since I began to work on Jacobean political thinking. In those years I have learned much from more friends and scholars than there is space to thank here. My understanding of James and his ideas has been particularly influenced by Paul Christianson, Tom Cogswell, Richard Cust, Sir Geoffrey Elton, Peter Lake, John Morrill, Linda Levy Peck, Conrad Russell (Earl Russell), and Quentin Skinner. I am very grateful to Dr Peter Blayney of the Folger Shakespeare Library for bibliographical advice about James' writings and especially about *Basilicon Doron.* The staffs of the British Library, Cambridge University Library, the Folger Shakespeare Library, and Memorial Library here in Madison deserve thanks for their courtesy and efficiency. Especial thanks are due to the National Endowment of the Humanities and to the Graduate School of the University of Wisconsin-Madison for providing me with funding which made possible my researches at the Folger Shakespeare Library.

In the introduction and notes to this edition, dates are old style unless otherwise indicated, but the year is taken to begin on 1 January; an exception is that Jacobean books are sometimes referred to by the date given on the title-page rather than the date of publication (for example the *Workes* of 1616 is frequently mentioned; it is dated 1616 on the title-page, but was actually published early in 1617). Square brackets in the notes indicate editorial material. This edition follows the sixteenth- and seventeenth-century texts on which it is based in matters of spelling, punctuation and capitalisation. Indentations after headings have been retained. Material in the margins of the original editions has been transferred to notes. The sources which have been used for each of the works printed below are listed in the first note to that work. In addition, readings from the 1619 Latin *Opera* (STC 14346) are occasionally given in the notes. In James' text, contractions have been silently expanded. Books referred to in editorial matter were published at London unless otherwise indicated.

Abbreviations

B.L.	British Library.
Boderie	Antoine le Fèvre de la Boderie, *Ambassades en Angleterre*, 5 vols., [Paris], 1750.
Bowyer	*The Parliamentary Diary of Robert Bowyer 1606–1607*, ed. David Harris Willson, Minneapolis 1931.
C.J.	*Commons Journals.*
Craigie 1944–50	James Craigie, ed., *The Basilicon Doron of King James VI*, 2 vols., Scottish Text Society, third series, vols. 16 and 18, Edinburgh 1944–50.
H.M.C.	Historical Manuscripts Commission Reports.
L.J.	*Lords Journals.*
PP10	*Proceedings in Parliament 1610*, ed. E. R. Foster, 2 vols., New Haven 1966.
Rushworth	John Rushworth, ed., *Historical Collections*, 7 vols., 1659–1701.
S.R.	*Statutes of the Realm*, ed. T. E. Tomlins *et al.*, 11 vols., 1820–8.
SRP1	*Stuart Royal Proclamations volume 1: Royal Proclamations of James I*, ed. James F. Larkin, C.S.V., and Paul L. Hughes, Oxford 1973. References are to proclamation number.
STC	*A Short-Title Catalogue of Books Printed in England, Scotland, & Ireland and of English*

	Books Printed Abroad 1475–1640, first compiled by A. W. Pollard and G. R. Redgrave, second edition, revised and enlarged, begun by W. A. Jackson and F. S. Ferguson; completed by Katharine F. Pantzer, 3 vols., 1976–91.
Willson 1944–5	David Harris Willson, 'James I and his literary assistants', in *Huntington Library Quarterly*, 8 (1944–5), 35–57.
Winwood	Sir Ralph Winwood, *Memorials of Affairs of State in the Reigns of Queen Elizabeth and King James I Collected Chiefly from the Original Papers of Sir Ralph Winwood*, ed. E. Sawyer, 3 vols., 1725.
Wormald 1991	Jenny Wormald, 'James VI and I, *Basilikon Doron* and *The Trew Law of Free Monarchies*: the Scottish context and the English translation', in Linda Levy Peck, ed., *The Mental World of the Jacobean Court*, Cambridge 1991, 36–54.

Introduction

James VI and I was one of the most influential British political writers of the early modern period. His *Basilicon Doron* was a best-seller in England and circulated widely on the Continent (the details are discussed in Wormald 1991, 51–2). It was translated into Latin, French, Dutch, German, Swedish and other languages (a list of early translations in Craigie 1944–50, 2: 153–78, 188–90, includes thirty-eight items). The book was frequently quoted by political writers. So, too, were James' other works, and especially his speech to parliament of 21 March 1610. John Locke quoted this speech at length and approvingly. He referred respectfully to James as 'that Learned King who well understood the Notions of things' (*Two Treatises of Government*, second treatise, section 200). Thomas Hobbes likewise praised 'our most wise' King James (*Leviathan* chapter 19, final paragraph). Despite the major differences in their political thought, both Hobbes and Locke were able to praise James, for the king combined absolutist principles with an emphasis upon the monarch's duty to rule according to law and in the public good. The king's political philosophy was a nuanced, moderated absolutism. To understand his principles it is useful to look at the circumstances in which he developed them.

In 1566 Mary Queen of Scots gave birth to James. A year later she abdicated in her son's favour. This abdication had been forced upon her by powerful nobles allied with Protestant preachers. The queen tried to recover her throne in 1568, but her supporters were defeated and she fled to England. There she was placed under house arrest and in 1587 was executed for plotting against the English queen, Elizabeth. In his early years, King James was educated by

George Buchanan, one of the most famous classicists of the age. Buchanan was also an outspoken critic of royal absolutism. Like the leading Scottish reformer John Knox, Buchanan argued that a people may take up arms against a ruler who fails to promote the true religion. He held that in Scotland wicked kings had commonly been called to account by their subjects – a theme that featured strongly in his lengthy Latin history of Scotland (*Rerum Scoticarum Historia*, 1582), and in the pithy dialogue *De Jure Regni apud Scotos* (1579). Both these works were dedicated to James.

When the king grew up, he came to reject the ideas of Buchanan, Knox, and like-minded authors. He also took steps to combat the claims of such presbyterian leaders as Andrew Melville, who held that James was accountable to the church in moral and religious matters. Modern scholarship on Scottish history has emphasised the political competence of the adult James VI. The king efficiently and systematically increased royal power at the expense of the nobility and of the presbyterian church. In 1603 he inherited the crown of England on the death of Queen Elizabeth.

Mary Queen of Scots had been married to King Francis II of France. Her mother was Mary of Guise. In the later sixteenth century the Guise family took a leading part in the civil wars which afflicted France for more than thirty years. They advocated the rigid enforcement of Roman Catholicism, and the violent suppression of Protestantism. In the course of these wars, both Catholic and Protestant theorists came to argue that it was legitimate for the people to take up arms against a monarch who ruled tyrannically – for example, by failing to support the true religion. Catholics also sometimes claimed that the pope had the authority to intervene in the affairs of states, and to depose heretical monarchs. In 1585 Pope Sixtus V interfered in French affairs by excommunicating Henry of Navarre, the Protestant heir to the throne. Pius V issued a bull deposing Elizabeth I of England in 1570, and a number of Catholics plotted to assassinate her in the following years. In France, both Henry III and Henry IV (the former Henry of Navarre) were murdered by Catholic fanatics. A group of Catholic gentlemen plotted to blow up James and parliament in the famous Gunpowder Plot of 1605.

James' early experiences in Scotland alienated him from the thinking of such men as Knox and Buchanan. He also vigorously rejected

Catholic theories which legitimated the use of force by subjects against their sovereigns. Like many of his contemporaries, he looked to strong monarchical power to prevent religious civil war and maintain order. He held that kings possess a monopoly of political power, which they derive from God alone. Active resistance to monarchs is always sinful. If our king commands us to do things which contravene the law of God, we must disobey him, for we should always obey God rather than man. But if the monarch calls us to account for our disobedience, we should meekly accept whatever punishment he inflicts upon us. Kings, James argued, had a duty to rule in the public interest and (except in cases of necessity) to abide by the law of the land. But no one had the power to coerce them into performing these duties.

In 1598 the first edition of *The Trew Law of Free Monarchies* was published. It came out anonymously, but the fact that it appeared from the press of Robert Waldegrave, the king's printer, served to indicate royal authorship or at least endorsement, and the book was known to be by the king long before it was included in James' collected *Workes* of 1616 (Alberico Gentili, *Regales Disputationes Tres*, 1605, 18–19). *The Trew Law* warned against the 'Sirene songs' of people who praised or excused rebellions (p. 62). In Scotland, said James, ignorance of true political principles had long been responsible for 'endlesse calamities, miseries, and confusions' (p. 63). His purpose in writing was to 'lay downe . . . the trew grounds' of political duty 'without wasting time vpon refuting the aduersaries' (p. 62). He made it clear which adversaries he had in mind, inveighing against 'seditious preachers in these daies of whatsoeuer religion, either in this countrey or in France' (p. 71), and convicting the French Catholic League of responsibility for a 'superstitious rebellion' which had resulted in 'the great desolation of their whole countrey' (p. 82). Basing his case on Scripture, reason and history, the king argued that subjects must obey their monarch's 'commands in all things, except directly against God' and that they could never actively resist him (p. 72). The *Trew Law* is commonly seen as the most vigorously absolutist of James' writings. But it already placed considerable stress on the duties of rulers. A prince, he said, 'cannot iustly bring backe againe to himself the priuiledges once bestowed by him or his predecessors vpon any state or ranke of his subiects' (p. 80). Moreover, 'a good king will . . . delight to rule his subiects by the lawe' (p. 75). Monarchs, in short, should honour their commitments and abide by their laws.

It was also in 1598 that James completed his most famous work, the *Basilicon Doron*. This book was written in Middle Scots. The original manuscript, in the king's own hand, still survives (B.L. Royal MS 18. B. xv). Seven copies of an Anglicised version of the work were secretly printed by Waldegrave in 1599, and distributed to James' relatives and friends. Even before the book was printed it had come to the notice of the presbyterian minister Andrew Melville, who had seen a copy of the manuscript. He very much resented some of the king's remarks about the Scottish presbyterian clergy, and disagreed with James' claim that monarchs are empowered to supervise the affairs of the church within their realms. Melville drew up a list of eighteen objections to *Basilicon Doron*. These criticisms were presented to the ecclesiastical synod of Fife in September 1599 by John Dykes. Before the synod could formally censure the book, James intervened, ordering the arrest of Dykes – who fled into exile. In England, some people took exception to passages in the book which seemed to suggest that the king desired vengeance against those responsible for his mother's execution, and also to a number of James' comments on puritans. In 1603 a revised edition of the work was published with a long preface in which the king responded to both of these objections (further details on the points made in this paragraph are in Craigie 2: 6–17).

Basilicon Doron is a book of advice purportedly written for James' son and heir Henry, to whom it was dedicated. Advice books for princes were a conventional literary genre in the sixteenth century and earlier. The king was certainly familiar with a good deal of this literature, from which he borrowed freely (a fuller discussion of the literary antecedents of *Basilicon Doron* is in Craigie 2: 63–87). Enlightening his four-year-old son was probably not his only purpose in writing the book. One possibility is that he wrote it mainly for his own amusement (Wormald 1991, 49). Another notion is that he hoped from the first that the work would be widely read. In the preface to the 1603 edition he records how the book circulated 'contrary to my intention and expectation' (p. 4), but in corrupt texts; so he was forced (much against his will) 'to publish and spread the true copie thereof, for defacing of the false copies that are alreadie spread'

(p. 5). It was a commonplace in James' day for authors to allege that they had been forced reluctantly into publication – and so to indicate that they were not motivated by love of fame or lucre. The king had two added incentives for making this kind of claim. First, some people thought it beneath the dignity of a monarch to publish books (in his preface to James' *Workes* of 1616, James Montagu, Bishop of Winchester, found it necessary to rebut this suggestion at length – sigs. b2b-c4a). Secondly, it is arguable that the king wanted to convince himself and others that his books were demanded by the public because of their literary merits (and this would help explain why the *Trew Law* and later *Triplici Nodo* were published anonymously: James hoped the works' contents would be enough to win them public approval).

Basilicon Doron is a book of practical advice rather than abstract theory. It assumed the principles of the *Trew Law* without bothering to prove them. It took for granted that the king alone was to make all final decisions on foreign and domestic policy, and it laid particular emphasis upon his supremacy in ecclesiastical affairs. Much of the advice which the king gave was intended to strengthen the position of the monarchy in Scotland. He repeatedly attacked presbyterian thinking because he held that it undermined the authority of the monarch, and he criticised heritable sheriffdoms for much the same reason (p. 29). Though James did not mention Machiavelli, he was careful to reject Machiavellian teachings, for instance insisting that one king should keep the promises he makes to others (p. 32). He referred to neo-stoicism – which had recently become fashionable through the efforts of Justus Lipsius and others – only to condemn it. As in the *Trew Law*, James stressed the duties as well as the powers of kings. A good king, he said, would think that 'his greatest contentment standeth' in the prosperity of his subjects, and would regard 'the common interesse [i.e. interest]' as 'his chiefest particular [interest]' (p. 20). A tyrant, on the other hand, would pursue his own advantage at the expense of his subjects' welfare, 'by inuerting all good Lawes to serue onely for his vnrulie priuate affections' (p. 20). Even against tyrants, rebellion was unlawful, but it was very likely to occur (p. 21), and God was certain to inflict harsh punishment upon wicked rulers (p. 21).

More than twenty years after penning *Basilicon Doron*, James planned to write another work on 'the office of a King' (p. 232). This book never materialised, but in his *Meditation* of 1619 on Matthew 27: 27–9 James did commit to paper some preliminary reflections which he intended to serve as the basis for the larger treatise. As in his earlier writings, he argued that kings are God's deputies, accountable to Him alone (pp. 238, 241); that they are responsible for the spiritual as well as the temporal welfare of their subjects (p. 237); and that the people's prosperity is the king's greatest felicity (p. 239). Once again, he stressed the duties as well as rights of monarchs, dwelling on the onerous cares of kingship (pp. 239, 249), and urging that a ruler should not stretch 'his royall Prerogatiue but where necessitie shall require' (p. 249).

At the beginning of the *Meditation* on Matthew, James remarked that he was 'weary of Controuersies' (p. 229). Between writing *Basilicon Doron* in 1598 and dictating the *Meditation* to his favourite Buckingham in 1619 the bulk of James' literary labours consisted of controversial works targeted at Roman Catholics. After the Gunpowder Plot, the English parliament enacted new legislation against Catholics, including a statute 'for the better discovering and repressing of popish recusants' (3 & 4 Jac. I, c. 4; S.R. 4: 1071–7). This Act contained a new oath, renouncing the pope's claim to be able to depose kings and release subjects from allegiance to their sovereigns. Any recusant who twice refused this oath – which came to be known as the Oath of Allegiance – was liable to the penalties of *praemunire* (loss of goods and imprisonment during the king's pleasure). The Act was passed on 27 May 1606 (L.J. 2: 445) and printed on 25 June (Boderie 1: 177). On 12 September Pope Paul V issued a breve which forbade Catholics to take the oath and he repeated the prohibition in a second breve of 13 August 1607. Meanwhile, the Archpriest George Blackwell – leader of the English Catholic secular priests – had been captured. On 3 July 1607 he was persuaded to take the oath (*Mr. George Blackwel ... his Answeres vpon sundry his Examinations*, 1607, 15–18). News of this reached Rome, and on 18 September the famous Catholic theologian Cardinal Robert Bellarmine wrote to Blackwell denouncing the oath. By 25 November James was at work on a reply to Bellarmine (H.M.C. Salisbury 19: 343–4). In February 1608 the book, which included responses to the two papal breves, was published by the royal printer under the title *Triplici Nodo, Triplex Cuneus. Or an Apologie for the Oath of Allegiance.*

Though *Triplici Nodo* came out anonymously, its royal authorship was widely known and it soon drew replies from Bellarmine and from the leading English Jesuit Robert Parsons. The king now prepared an answer to these two works, entitling it a *Premonition of his Maiesties, to all most Mightie Monarches, Kings, free Princes and States of Christendom*. In April 1609 this new book was issued along with a revised version of *Triplici Nodo* – of which the king now acknowledged authorship. The *Premonition* dealt not only with the papal deposing power but also with more narrowly religious matters, and it included a profession of faith by James and a section in which he attempted to prove from Scripture that the pope is Antichrist. In the years after 1608 a great many works were written in favour of and against the Oath of Allegiance. Participants in the controversy included the great Jesuit theologian and philosopher Francisco Suarez, the poet John Donne, and the churchman Lancelot Andrewes. Works connected with the dispute were published throughout Europe. In France the question of whether kings could ever be deposed or killed became highly topical when Henry IV was assassinated by a Catholic fanatic in 1610. At the French Estates General of 1614–15, the third estate proposed that it should be declared a fundamental law of the land that kings may not be deposed. This suggestion struck at the papal deposing power, and it was (successfully) resisted on behalf of the clergy by the eminent churchman Cardinal Du Perron. The Cardinal's speech against the third estate's proposal was published at Paris in 1615 under the title *Harangue faicte de la part de la chambre ecclésiastique*. His arguments, which were intended to justify the deposing power, conflicted with the position that James had adopted in his writings on the Oath of Allegiance. The king replied to Du Perron in a work entitled *Déclaration du Sérénissime Roy Iaques I . . . Pour le Droit des Rois & indépendance de leurs Couronnes* (1615). This book was first published in French but was soon translated into English. Although the work was ascribed to James on the title-page, it is certain that it was written with considerable assistance from the Huguenot Pierre Du Moulin (Willson 1944–5, 51).

The *Premonition* and James' reply to the speech of Du Perron added details to the case against the papal deposing power set out in *Triplici Nodo*, but did not really revise it. For this reason, and for considerations of space, the two later anti-papal works have been omitted from this edition. Bellarmine's letter to Blackwell argued that Catholics could not take the Oath of Allegiance because to do so entailed denying the pope's spiritual powers. The English oath of supremacy, which had been enacted by parliament in 1559 and which office-holders were required to swear, asserted that the monarch was supreme over ecclesiastical affairs within England. According to Bellarmine, the Oath of Allegiance was just a disguised version of the Oath of Supremacy, for both oaths denied the pope's supremacy over the church. From the cardinal's point of view, this claim was valid since the pope would not have effective power to govern the church in the spiritual interest of Christians if he were unable to intervene in temporal affairs – for instance, by deposing heretical monarchs. James, like other Protestants, did not believe that the pope had any power over the church. But he insisted that the question of the pope's ecclesiastical supremacy was irrelevant to the Oath of Allegiance, which was concerned solely with civil matters. To say that the pope could not depose monarchs was to deny him only temporal and not spiritual or ecclesiastical power. The Oath of Allegiance was, therefore, very different from the Oath of Supremacy, and there was no good reason why conscientious Catholics should refuse to subscribe to the former document. In *Triplici Nodo* James attempted to prove that Scripture and the writings of the church Fathers require subjects to obey their rulers and not the pope in all temporal matters. Challenging Bellarmine's reading of ecclesiastical history, the king argued that the pope's claim to be able to depose civil sovereigns had no foundation in early Christian tradition.

James entrusted the prosecution of the Gunpowder Plotters to the attorney-general Sir Edward Coke. In 1606 he appointed Coke to the important and lucrative office of chief justice of the common pleas. Seven years later the lawyer was moved to the rather less rewarding though prestigious post of chief justice of the King's Bench. Coke wrote a famous series of law reports in which he expressed attitudes towards royal power which differed sharply from the king's own views. According to Sir Edward, the prerogatives of the monarch in England were defined by the common law of the land. Coke held that in some sense the judges derived their powers from the king, but that James could not himself act as a judge. The king did, indeed, possess great natural gifts, he said; judges, however, required not mere reason but 'artificial reason' which could be acquired only by long years spent in the study of the law. In Coke's opinion it was the judges of the common law courts who were to decide just what prerogatives the king had. They were also to define the limits of the jurisdictions of England's various courts. In addition to the common law courts there were also church courts, chancery, and Civil (or Roman) Law courts. Coke argued that the common law was the supreme form of law in England; the jurisdictions of other courts were subordinate to those of the common law. Sir Edward frequently issued prohibitions which halted cases in church courts or chancery and brought them into the common pleas or King's Bench. In 1616 he went still further. Two swindlers named Glanville and Allen had been acquitted in common law courts and then found guilty in chancery. Coke encouraged them to bring charges of *praemunire* (see glossary) against officials of the chancery court. The judge's conduct in this and other cases not surprisingly alienated the Archbishop of Canterbury, the lord chancellor, and James himself. In November 1616 Coke was dismissed from his position as chief justice. Several months earlier, on 20 June, his actions and attitudes had been roundly attacked by James in a speech delivered before the court of Star Chamber.

The king's speech in Star Chamber did not mention Coke by name. Nevertheless, it was patently intended to criticise the judge's behaviour and opinions. James acknowledged that in settled monarchies kings employed subordinate magistrates as their deputies in judicial matters; but he insisted that they retained the power to act as judges (p. 205). Transparently alluding to Coke's doctrine of 'artificial reason', he remarked that if an interpretation of the common law 'be such, as other men which haue Logicke and common sense vnderstand not the reason, I will neuer trust such an Interpretation' (p. 212). According to James, it was not the common law judges but the king himself who was to determine the boundaries between the jurisdictions of the country's various courts: 'And this is a thing Regall, and proper to a King, to keepe euery Court within his owne bounds' (p. 213). He castigated the notion that a *praemunire* could be issued against the court of chancery, for chancery derived its jurisdiction from the king – and 'How can the King grant a *Premunire* against himselfe?' (p. 215).

Judges, said James, were not to discuss the royal prerogative unless they first obtained the permission of the king or his Council (pp. 212–13). He was happy that the law should grant no more rights to him in his capacity as a private individual than it did to anyone else: 'I desire you to giue me no more right in my priuate Prerogatiue, then you giue to any Subiect.' But the power which he held as king was not to be disputed: 'As for the absolute Prerogatiue of the Crowne, that is no Subiect for the tongue of a Lawyer, nor is it lawfull to be disputed' (p. 214). Just as it is 'Atheisme and blasphemie to dispute what God can doe,' he declared, so 'it is presumption and high contempt in a Subiect, to dispute what a King can doe' (p. 214). It was unjustifiable, he said, 'to meddle with things against the Kings Prerogatiue, or Honour'. 'Some Gentlemen of late', he added, 'haue beene too bold this wayes.' He would take steps to see that they were punished (p. 218). These men were discontented 'with the present forme of Gouernement', 'and in euery cause that concernes Prerogatiue' they felt that they had to 'giue a snatch against a Monarchie, through their Puritanicall itching after Popularitie'. 'Some of them', he noted, 'haue shewed themselues too bold of late in the lower house of Parliament' (p. 222).

James differed from a number of members of the House of Commons on questions of political principle. It would be a mistake, however, to suppose that these differences dominated the king's dealings with his parliaments. As the speeches to parliament printed in this edition indicate, much of what James had to say concerned practical matters of policy and legislation. Moreover, he was generally careful to tone down his grander theoretical claims for parliamentary consumption. The king had no incentive to annoy members, for an unhappy parliament was not likely to vote him generous sums of money. The usual reason why James called parliaments was that he hoped they would grant him taxes. In his first years he also (and unsuccessfully) looked to parliament to enact the union between England and Scotland which he desired. He raised the theme of the union in the speech of 1604, while that of 1607 was largely devoted to this question. In 1605 he touched briefly on the union but was much more interested in the Catholic threat and especially in the Gunpowder Plot, which had been discovered just four days before the speech was delivered.

In 1610 the king hoped to get from parliament not simply a vote of taxes but a long-term financial settlement. The proposal – known as the Great Contract – was that James would give up some of the crown's traditional feudal rights in return for an annual income voted by parliament. In the end the project broke down, but at the time that the king delivered his speech of 21 March this had not yet happened, and he was eager to retain the good will of the House of Commons. In February the attention of the House had been called to a recently published law dictionary entitled *The Interpreter* (Cambridge 1607) and written by John Cowell, a professor of Civil Law at Cambridge. In this work the professor made some trenchantly absolutist statements, for instance asserting that the king 'is above the Law by his absolute power' (Cowell, *The Interpreter*, Cambridge 1607, sig. 2Q1a). The Commons began proceedings against Cowell, but on 8 March James intervened. He did not want a debate on questions of political theory to hold up his financial negotiations with the Commons at this juncture. So he expressed his disapproval of Cowell's doctrines. On 25 March he issued a proclamation suppressing *The Interpreter* (SRP1: 244). It was very vague on just how the lawyer had erred. Cowell's teachings were not very different from the principles which the king himself had enunciated in the *Trew Law* and elsewhere. The Commons were doubtless fully aware of this when they initiated their attack on the professor.

On 11 March 1610 Samuel Harsnett, Bishop of Chichester, preached a sermon in which he adopted views similar to Cowell's, and argued that the king could tax without parliamentary consent. This sermon was criticised in parliament (Rushworth 1: 442). In view of Cowell's case and Harsnett's sermon, James decided that it would be expedient to treat the two Houses to a long speech on 21 March. In this speech he stressed his respect for the common law, and assured his hearers that he had no intention of using 'the absolute power of a King' to alter the existing form of government in England (p. 180). True, kings were 'GODS Lieutenants vpon earth' and were 'accomptable to none but God onely' (p. 181). It was sedition, said James, for subjects 'to dispute what a King may do in the height of his power' (p. 184). A good king, however, would not abuse his power but would rule according to the laws of the land. James distinguished between the earliest times, when kings governed arbitrarily, and later ages when 'Kingdomes began to be setled in ciuilitie and policie' and monarchs 'set downe their minds by Lawes, which are properly made by the King onely; but at the rogation of the people'. In settled kingdoms, rulers had a double obligation to abide by the law, for they swore to do so in their coronation oaths, and even without the oath the office of kingship involved a duty to protect the laws: 'And therefore a King gouerning in a setled Kingdome, leaues to be a King, and degenerates into a Tyrant, assoone as he leaues off to rule according to his Lawes' (p. 183). All good kings, he added, 'will be glad to bound themselues within the limits of their Lawes; and they that perswade them the contrary, are vipers, and pests, both against them and the Commonwealth'. He himself was 'sure to goe to my graue with that reputation and comfort, that neuer King was in all his time more carefull to haue his Lawes duely obserued, and himselfe to gouerne thereafter, then I' (p. 184).

In the speech of 21 March, James stressed his tender concern for the welfare of the people. The love of his subjects, he said, was 'the greatest earthly securitie (next the fauour of GOD) to any wise or iust King' (p. 194), and he declared that 'the hearts and riches of the people, are the Kings greatest treasure' (p. 195). Such comments created a favourable impression, and the speech was well received, though according to one account 'the most strictly religious could have wished that his Highness would have been more spareing in using the name of God, and comparing the Deity with Princes Soveraignty' (John More to Sir Ralph Winwood, 24 March 1610, in *Memorials . . . of . . . Sir Ralph Winwood*, 3 vols., 1725, 3: 141). In later years, a few passages from the speech were frequently quoted, often with the intention of showing that James had favoured limited and not absolute monarchy. Unquestionably, the speech was intended to stress the king's moderation. But the theory it advanced differed in no important respect from what he said in the *Trew Law* and elsewhere. As we have seen, the *Trew Law* recommended that kings abide by the law, though it did not dwell on this point at such great length as the speech. In both texts, moreover, the king alone is made responsible for ensuring that he does in fact obey the law. Subjects might suspect that the ruler is exceeding his traditional powers, but they cannot challenge him, for it is sedition to dispute his prerogative. As James put it in a speech of 21 May 1610 (printed in PP10, 2: 100–7) if 'a king be resolute to be a tyrant, all you can do will not hinder him'. Subjects could never legitimately resist their kings, and so had no choice but to trust them: 'Kings must be trusted' (103–4). The speech of March referred to the fear which some had that the king intended 'not to limit my selfe within' customary 'bounds, but to alter the same when I thought conuenient, by the absolute power of a King' (p. 180). In what followed, James took pains to deny that this was his intention, but said nothing at all to suggest that he lacked 'the absolute power of a King'. Bossuet, the most famous apologist for the absolutism of Louis XIV, later distinguished between arbitrary and absolute government, criticising the former but praising the latter. In arbitrary government there was no law but the king's will (Jacques-Bénigne Bossuet, *Politics Drawn from the Very Words of Holy Scripture*, translated and edited by Patrick Riley, Cambridge 1990, 263). This distinction was much the same as that which James drew between original and settled kingdoms. Indeed, there was little in James' political theory to which Bossuet would have taken exception.

If parliaments refrained from attacking his prerogatives and voted him cash, the king could get on well with them. In 1614 the Commons criticised impositions – extra-parliamentary levies on exports and imports which James had been collecting on a wide variety of commodities since 1608 – and one member delivered an inflammatory speech against the Scots. James dissolved the parliament before it had accomplished anything. When parliament met again in 1621, relations between king and Commons were initially rather more harmonious than they had sometimes been in the past. As the king noted on 26 March, 'the House of Commons at this time haue shewed greater loue, and vsed me with more respect in all their proceedings, then euer any House of Commons haue heeretofore done to mee' (*His Maiesties Speach in the Vpper House of Parliament, On Munday the 26. of March, 1621*, 1621, sig. B1b). In December, however, events occurred which made the king less happy with the Lower House. Prince Henry had died in 1612, leaving James' younger son Charles as heir to the throne. The king planned to marry Charles to a Spanish princess. This project was unpopular because Spain was a Catholic country and because Spanish troops were attacking the Palatinate, a German Protestant state ruled by the Elector Frederick V, the husband of James' daughter Elizabeth. Many people in England felt that the king should give military assistance to his son-in-law and that he ought to break off the marriage negotiations with Spain. The Commons began to debate these matters, though foreign policy and royal marriages were traditionally regarded as topics which fell under the royal prerogative and which parliament could not discuss unless the king specifically invited it to do so. James resented what he saw as an assault on his powers and communicated his views to the Commons. In response, they asserted their privilege of free speech. The king replied by claiming that their privileges were derived from the crown and subordinate to his own powers. He warned them 'to beware to trench vpon the Prerogatiue of the Crowne, which would enforce Vs, or any iust King to retrench them of their priuiledges, that would pare his Prerogatiue and flowers of the Crowne' (p. 261). When the Commons asserted that their privileges were 'their ancient and vndoubted right and inheritance' he responded by declaring that 'the plaine truth is, That Wee cannot with patience endure Our Subiects to vse such Antimonarchicall words to Vs concerning their Liberties, except they had subioyned, that they were granted vnto them by the grace and fauour of Our Predecessours' (pp. 262–3). On 18 December the Commons approved a Protestation setting out their position. On the following day parliament was adjourned. Eleven days later James tore the Protestation out of the Commons' Journal, and on 6 January 1622 he dissolved parliament. Shortly afterwards, he published his *Declaration*, giving his version of the whole affair.

In his youth, James' library had already included the *Six livres de la république* of the French absolutist Jean Bodin. Though the two men diverged sharply on a number of points – including many religious questions – their political theories plainly belong to the same family. Along with Bodin, the king was one of the authorities most frequently quoted by Sir Robert Filmer. Like Filmer – and Bodin – James held that absolute monarchy was sanctioned by Scripture, and also by reason and history. Along with Filmer and Hobbes, the king was one of the most important British theoreticians of absolutism of the early modern period. Written in very lively and pungent prose, his books are also documents of the greatest significance for an understanding of the relationship between literature and political power in Shakespeare's England. Their main subject is power and their author was uniquely placed to write on that subject. Finally, James' writings are of major importance to the study of British history in the years before the Civil War. Whether or not the king's ideas were instrumental in bringing about that war is difficult to determine unless we read his works.

Principal events in James' life

1566	Birth of James (son of Mary Queen of Scots and Henry Stewart, Lord Darnley).
1567	Mary Queen of Scots is compelled to abdicate the Scottish throne in favour of James, who becomes King James VI.
1570	Pope Pius V deposes Elizabeth I.
1582	The Ruthven Raid: James is seized by the Earl of Gowrie.
1583	James escapes from the custody of Gowrie.
1584	Execution of Gowrie.
	The Scottish parliament passes the 'Black Acts', asserting royal power over the church.
1585	Return of Gowrie's supporters from exile in England; they seize James at Stirling.
1587	Execution of Mary Queen of Scots.
1588	The Spanish Armada sails for England.
1589	Assassination of Henry III of France.
	Marriage of James to Anne of Denmark.
1592	Partial repeal of the 'Black Acts', but many Scottish churchmen become increasingly critical of the king, siding against him with Francis Stewart, Earl of Bothwell.
1594	Birth of James' son Henry.
1594–5	Alliance between Bothwell and the rebellious Catholic Earls of Huntly and Errol; defeated by James, they go into exile.

1596–8	Struggle for control over the Scottish church between James and presbyterian ministers; the king largely successful.
1598	James completes a manuscript of *Basilicon Doron* and publishes (without author's name) *The Trew Law of Free Monarchies*.
1599	First printing of *Basilicon Doron* in an issue of seven copies for private distribution.
1600	(5 August) Attempt to seize James by the Earl of Gowrie and his brother, who are killed.
	(19 November) Birth of James' son Charles (later Charles I).
1603	(March) Publication at Edinburgh of a revised version of *Basilicon Doron*.
	(24 March) Death of Elizabeth. James becomes king of England.
	(March/April) *Basilicon Doron* reprinted in London.
	(April) *The Trew Law of Free Monarchies* reprinted in London.
1605	(5 November) Discovery of the Gunpowder Plot of some Catholic gentlemen to blow up the king and parliament.
1606	(27 May) Parliament passes anti-Catholic legislation including a new Oath of Allegiance rejecting the pope's claim to have the authority to depose kings.
	(12 September) Pope Paul V issues a breve condemning the Oath of Allegiance.
1607	(31 March) James delivers a speech to parliament in favour of union between England and Scotland.
	(13 August) Paul V issues a second breve, repeating his condemnation of the Oath of Allegiance.
	(18 September) Cardinal Robert Bellarmine writes to Blackwell remonstrating with him for taking the Oath of Allegiance.
1608	(February) Publication (without author's name) of James' reply to the papal breves and to Bellarmine (*Triplici Nodo, Triplex Cuneus. Or an Apologie for the Oath of Allegiance*).
1609	Twelve Years' Truce temporarily ends war between Spain and the Dutch.
	A revised version of *Triplici Nodo* issued under the king's

name, along with a *Premonition . . . to all Most Mightie Monarches, Kings, Free Princes and States of Christendom.*

1610   (February-March) Negotiations between king and Commons for a settlement of royal finances.
(21 March) James delivers a speech to parliament promising to rule moderately.

1610   (4 May) Assassination of Henry IV of France.

1612   Death of Prince Henry.

1616   (20 June) James delivers a speech in Star Chamber, taking issue with the ideas of the judge Sir Edward Coke on the relationship between royal power and the law, and on other questions.
(15 November) James deprives Coke of his office as lord chief justice of the King's Bench.

1617   (February) Publication of James' *Workes* (dated 1616 on title-page).

1618   Beginning of Bohemian revolt against the Habsburgs.

1619   James' son-in-law the Elector Palatine Frederick V accepts election to the throne of Bohemia.

1620   Reissue, with additions, of James' *Workes.*
Frederick V driven out of Bohemia by imperialist troops.

1621   Renewal of war between Spain and the Dutch.
The Palatinate invaded by Spanish troops.
James summons parliament; the House of Commons discusses foreign policy and the projected marriage of Prince Charles to a Spanish princess; dispute between king and Commons over parliamentary privilege; the Commons draw up a Protestation asserting their right of free speech (18 December); parliament is adjourned (19 December); James tears the Protestation from the Commons' Journal (30 December).

1622   (6 January) James dissolves parliament and shortly afterwards publishes a *Declaration* setting out his reasons for doing so.

1625   (27 March) Death of James.

Bibliographical note

A great deal has been written about James VI and I. In what follows, it will be possible to mention only a small fraction of the large number of important books and articles which discuss the monarch and his reign. The standard scholarly biography of James is D. H. Willson, *King James VI and I*, 1956. Willson plainly detested the king, and his book must be read with caution. A more balanced account, which draws on much recent research, is Maurice Lee, Jr, *Great Britain's Solomon: James VI and I in his Three Kingdoms*, Urbana 1990. Other useful writings by the same author include *Government by Pen: Scotland under James VI*, Urbana 1980, and a historiographical survey entitled 'James I and the historians: not a bad king after all?', in *Albion* 16 (1984), 151–63. Jenny Wormald is currently preparing a full biography of James, and is the author of an important interpretative article: 'James VI and I: two kings or one?', in *History* 68 (1983), 187–209. The classic traditional account of James' reign in England is S. R. Gardiner's *History of England from the Accession of James I to the Outbreak of the Civil War, 1603–1642*, 10 vols., 1883 (the treatment of James runs from the beginning of volume 1 to p. 316 of volume 5). The most important of modern 'revisionist' historians – who have challenged Gardiner's interpretation on a number of fundamental issues – is Conrad Russell. Relevant works by Russell include *Parliament and English Politics 1621–1629*, Oxford 1979, and *The Causes of the English Civil War*, Oxford 1990. A book of essays which take issue with some of Russell's conclusions is Richard Cust and Ann Hughes, eds., *Conflict in Early Stuart England: studies in religion and politics 1603–*

1642, 1989. An older but still helpful collection of essays is A. G. R. Smith, ed., *The Reign of James VI and I*, 1973.

Recent accounts of James' political thought include three essays which approach the subject from different angles and which reach interestingly divergent conclusions. They are: Jenny Wormald, 'James VI and I, *Basilikon Doron* and *The Trew Law of Free Monarchies*: the Scottish context and the English translation'; J. P. Sommerville, 'James I and the divine right of kings: English politics and continental theory'; and Paul Christianson, 'Royal and parliamentary voices on the ancient constitution, *c.*1604–1621'. All three are in Linda Levy Peck, ed., *The Mental World of the Jacobean Court*, Cambridge 1991 (at pp. 36–54, 55–70, and 71–95). The other essays in Peck's collection also contain much useful information on Jacobean thought and politics. There is a great deal of valuable material on James and his thought in the introductions and notes to James Craigie's editions of *Basilicon Doron* (Scottish Text Society, third series, vols. 16 and 18, Edinburgh 1944–50) and the *Trew Law of Free Monarchies* (in *Minor Prose Works of King James VI and I*, Scottish Text Society, fourth series, vol. 14, Edinburgh 1982). C. H. McIlwain's long introduction to his edition of *The Political Works of James I*, Cambridge, Mass. 1918, is especially strong on the debate over the Jacobean Oath of Allegiance. A more recent account of this debate is J. P. Sommerville, 'Jacobean political thought and the controversy over the Oath of Allegiance', unpublished Cambridge University Ph.D. dissertation, 1981.

A good survey of the background to many of James' ideas, and a judicious summary of the king's thinking, is in J. H. M. Salmon, 'Catholic resistance theory, Ultramontanism, and the royalist response, 1580–1620', in *The Cambridge History of Political Thought 1450–1700*, edited by J. H. Burns with the assistance of Mark Goldie, Cambridge 1991, 219–53. Quentin Skinner's *The Foundations of Modern Political Thought*, 2 vols., Cambridge 1978, is a highly important account of late medieval and early modern political thinking; volume 2 in particular contains a great deal of information useful for understanding the ideas of James I. J. P. Sommerville's *Politics and Ideology in England, 1603–1640*, 1986, discusses political ideas and politics under James I and his son; the first chapter – on 'The Divine Right of Kings' – is particularly relevant to James' thinking. J. N. Figgis' *The Divine Right of Kings*, 2nd edn, Cambridge 1914 (reprinted with an introduction by G. R. Elton, 1965) is still well worth reading, though it is only partly on English theorising and has relatively little to say about James. Also useful is Margaret A. Judson, *The Crisis of the Constitution: An Essay in Constitutional and Political Thought, 1603–45*, New Brunswick 1949. Less satisfactory is J. W. Allen, *English Political Thought 1603–1644*, 1938. A good anthology of seventeenth-century English political writings, with a perceptive introduction and commentary, is David Wootton, ed., *Divine Right and Democracy: An Anthology of Political Writing in Stuart England*, Harmondsworth 1986.

In his early years south of the border, James was much concerned with the project for a full union between England and Scotland. Important treatments of this topic are in Bruce Galloway, *The Union of England and Scotland 1603–1608*, Edinburgh 1986, and Brian P. Levack, *The Formation of the British State: England, Scotland, and the Union 1603–1707*, Oxford 1987. A recurring theme in the king's works is the analogy between the ordinary and extraordinary powers of the king on the one hand and of God on the other. This theme is discussed in Francis Oakley, 'Jacobean political theology: the absolute and ordinary powers of the king', in *Journal of the History of Ideas*, 29 (1968), 323–46, and more broadly in *Omnipotence, Covenant and Order: An Excursion in the History of Ideas from Abelard to Leibniz*, Ithaca, N.Y. 1984. James had much to say about religion. Informative writings on Jacobean church history include Kenneth Fincham and Peter Lake, 'The ecclesiastical policy of James I', in *Journal of British Studies*, 24 (1985), 169–207.

In *Basilicon Doron* James counselled his son Henry to ensure that if he wrote anything he should not allow it to be published until it had been 'priuily censured' by experts. The king took his own advice on this point. The best account of how he composed his works, and with whom he collaborated, is David H. Willson, 'James I and his literary assistants', in *Huntington Library Quarterly* 8 (1944–5), 35–57. In addition to the writings printed in the present volume, a number of other works by James are well worth consulting. These include *A Premonition to all Christian Monarches, Free Princes and States* of 1609, and *A Remonstrance . . . for the Right of Kings, against Cardinall Perron* (published in French in 1615, and in English the following year). Both are printed in McIlwain's edition of *The Political Works of James I*, Cambridge, Mass. 1918. James worked very closely with the French Protestant Pierre Du Moulin on the *Remonstrance*, and it is unclear how much of that book was written by the king, though it certainly reflects his opinions. Also of political interest is *His Maiesties Declaration concerning his Proceedings with the States Generall of the United Provinces of the Low Countries, in the Cause of D. Conradus Vorstius* (1612; STC 9233), which was republished in the *Workes* of 1616.

James wrote poetry as well as prose, and some of his poems contain material that is politically interesting. For reasons of space it has not been possible to include any of the poems in this edition. They may be found in James Craigie, ed., *The Poems of James VI. of Scotland*, 2 vols., Scottish Text Society, third series, vols. 22 and 26, Edinburgh 1955–8. An especially relevant item (of which two versions are printed in ibid. 2: 182–91, and a third in James Craigie, 'Last poems of James VI', *Scottish Historical Review* 29 (1950), 134–42, at 136–40) is a reply by the king to a lampoon that circulated in 1622–3. In this poem James expresses his high views of royal power in very bad verse, and declares that Magna Carta 'Came first from Kings' and arose from 'an vniust Rebellion' (2: 188).

Select biographical notes

ALLEN, WILLIAM (1532–94)   An Oxford academic who went to
Louvain early in the reign of Elizabeth I. Allen became a leader of
the exiled English Catholics on the Continent and in 1568 founded
a college at Douai to train English Catholic priests. He was an outspoken critic of the religious policies of Elizabeth and lobbied for
her forcible removal from the throne. In 1587 he published a defence
of the surrender to the Spaniards of the Dutch fort at Deventer by
the English governor Sir William Stanley. James refers to this work
in *Triplici Nodo*. He was made a cardinal in the same year. At the
time of the Spanish Armada of 1588 he wrote *An Admonition to the
Nobility and People of England* encouraging them to oust their heretical
queen.

BALDWIN, WILLIAM (1563–1632)   An English Jesuit who in the first
decade of the seventeenth century was stationed in the Spanish
Netherlands, where he acted as vice-prefect of the Catholic mission
to England. In *Triplici Nodo* James accuses him of complicity in the
Gunpowder Plot. While travelling to Rome in 1610 Baldwin was
captured by soldiers of the Elector Palatine and sent to England.
There he was closely questioned but the charge of involvement in
the Plot was never proved and in 1618 he was released from prison
at the intercession of the Spanish ambassador Gondomar.

BARONIUS, CAESAR (1538–1607)   An Oratorian who in 1593 succeeded Philip Neri as superior of the Oratory. He was made a cardinal in 1596. Baronius was the foremost Catholic ecclesiastical historian of his age. His monumental *Annals* (12 vols., 1588–1607)

surveyed the history of the church up to 1198. James encouraged attacks on Baronius' scholarship but in *Triplici Nodo* cited him to refute a point made by Bellarmine (q.v.).

BEKINSAW, JOHN (*c.*1496–1559)   An Oxford graduate who taught Greek at Paris but later returned to England, where in 1546 he published a defence of the royal supremacy over the church. This book, entitled *De Supremo et Absoluto Regis Imperio* is approvingly referred to by James in *Triplici Nodo*.

BELLARMINE, ROBERT (1542–1621)   One of the foremost Jesuit theologians of his times. Bellarmine was the nephew of Pope Marcellus II and himself became a cardinal and archbishop. His most important work was *Disputationes de Controversiis* (3 vols., Ingolstadt 1586–9) which systematically challenged Protestant doctrines. James refers to it frequently in *Triplici Nodo*, accusing the cardinal of contradicting himself. On 18 September (28 September new style) 1607 Bellarmine wrote from Rome to his old friend the Archpriest Blackwell (q.v.), criticising him for taking the oath of allegiance. Much of *Triplici Nodo* consists of James' reply to this letter.

BINNIUS (or BINIUS), SEVERIN (1573–1641)   A German Catholic theologian and historian who taught ecclesiastical history at Cologne. In 1606 he published at Cologne an edition in four volumes of the decrees of the councils of the church, along with supplementary materials. This work, entitled *Concilia Generalia et Provincilia*, is referred to by James in *Triplici Nodo* to refute a point made by Bellarmine (q.v.).

BLACKWELL, GEORGE (*c.*1545–1613)   An English Catholic priest who in 1598 was appointed archpriest over the English secular clergy by Pope Clement VIII. Blackwell was arrested and imprisoned by the English authorities on 24 June 1607. He was questioned on his attitude to the Oath of Allegiance and persuaded to take it and to write a letter to English Catholics in support of it. Since Pope Paul V (q.v.) had recently condemned the oath in a breve of 12 September 1606, Blackwell's actions represented a major propaganda victory for James. In response, the pope sent a second breve on 13 August 1607, and Bellarmine (q.v.) remonstrated with Blackwell in a letter of 18 September 1607. In *Triplici Nodo* James replied to this letter and to the two breves. Blackwell himself responded to Bellarmine's letter on 13

November 1607, explaining that in taking the oath he did not intend to reject the papal deposing power absolutely, but only to assert that the pope could not exercise it against James in current circumstances. This letter did not please the English authorities. Blackwell was once more interrogated and on 20 January 1608 he was persuaded to write a letter to the English Catholics denouncing the papal deposing power altogether.

BONNER (or BONER), EDMUND (*c.*1500–69)   Bishop of Hereford and then of London under Henry VIII, Bonner was deprived of his bishopric under Edward VI and imprisoned during much of the young king's reign. Under Mary he was restored to his see and became notorious for the active part which he played in the burning of heretics. When Elizabeth became queen he was deprived again and imprisoned. Under Henry VIII he defended the royal supremacy in a preface to the second edition of the *De Vera Obedientia* (1536) of Stephen Gardiner (q.v.). James refers to this preface in *Triplici Nodo*.

BOTHWELL (BOTHUELL) *see* STEWART, FRANCIS

BROWNE, ROBERT (*c.*1550–1633)   An English puritan who with Robert Harrison founded a separatist congregation at Norwich in 1580. In 1582 he published *A Treatise of Reformation without Tarrying for Anie*, in which he encouraged the godly to set up their own congregations outside the church of England. In 1584 he was in Scotland, where he engaged in debate with presbyterians. Browne eventually conformed to the established church and received a benefice, but in his last years he was convicted of nonconformity, excommunicated and imprisoned. James refers to him in *Basilicon Doron*.

BUCHANAN, GEORGE (1506–82)   A Scottish scholar, poet and historian. After teaching in France for many years he returned to Scotland, where he became a vigorous supporter of the Reformation and an outspoken critic of Mary Queen of Scots (q.v.), against whom he published *Detectio Mariae Reginae* in 1571. From 1570 to 1578 he was tutor to James, and it was to the king that he dedicated his *De Jure Regni apud Scotos* of 1579. This book asserted that the king is accountable to the people, who may resist and depose him if he rules tyrannically. In 1582 he published a history of Scotland – *Rerum Scoticarum Historia* – which contained many examples demonstrating the accountability of kings. In 1584 the Scottish parliament ordered that all who possessed copies of *De Jure Regni* or the *Historia* should hand them in to the authorities so that they could be purged of offensive material. James reacted strongly against the political ideas of Buchanan, to whose *Historia* he refers scathingly in the *Basilicon Doron*. In the *Trew Law* James takes issue with ideas broadly similar to Buchanan's.

BUCKINGHAM *see* VILLIERS, GEORGE

CLEMENT VIII, POPE (Ippolito Aldobrandini, 1536–1605; pope 1592–1605) In 1602 Clement attempted to end the dispute over whether a bishop should be appointed to lead the clergy in England (and to replace Archpriest Blackwell, q.v.) by issuing a breve encouraging mutual charity amongst the English Catholics. Paul V (q.v.) refers to this document in his first breve against the Oath of Allegiance (printed in *Triplici Nodo*). In 1600 Clement sent two breves to England (one to the clergy, the other to the laity) advising Catholics to take steps to ensure that Queen Elizabeth would be succeeded by a monarch who was well disposed towards the faith. James mentions these breves in *Triplici Nodo*.

COWELL, JOHN (1554–1611) A civil lawyer and Master of Trinity Hall, Cambridge. The most famous of Cowell's works was a law dictionary entitled *The Interpreter* (Cambridge 1607), which contained a number of passages setting out a very high view of royal power. It also commented scathingly on the medieval common lawyer Sir Thomas Littleton, and argued that current legal practice did not sufficiently recognise the rights of the clergy. In 1610 the House of Commons began proceedings against Cowell's book, but on 8 March the Earl of Salisbury intervened on the king's behalf to end discussion of the matter. James, said Salisbury, had decided to suppress *The Interpreter* since he disapproved of a number of Cowell's opinions and was displeased that the civil lawyer had discussed the royal 'power and prerogative'. James alludes to the affair in his speech of 21 March 1610. Four days later the book was suppressed by proclamation.

DU BARTAS, GUILLAUME DE SALLUSTE, SEIGNEUR (1544–90) A French Huguenot poet whose most famous work is *La Semaine* (1578). James had a very high regard for Du Bartas' poetry, some of which he translated. In 1587 Du Bartas visited Scotland on a diplomatic mission from Henry of Navarre (later Henry IV of France). James quotes Du Bartas and recommends his work in *Basilicon Doron*. He also quotes him, and styles him 'the diuine Poet', in the *Trew Law*.

FISHER, JOHN, BISHOP OF ROCHESTER (1459–1535)   Fisher opposed the divorce of Henry VIII from Catherine of Aragon. He supported Elizabeth Barton, the nun (or maid) of Kent, who predicted a rapid death for Henry if he divorced Catherine and married Anne Boleyn. Fisher refused to take the oath attached to the Act of Succession of 1534, and also refused to acknowledge Henry as supreme head of the English church. The pope made him a cardinal in 1535. Shortly afterwards, Fisher was executed for treason. In his letter to Blackwell of 18 September 1607, Bellarmine portrayed Fisher as a martyr who had suffered death rather than deny the papal supremacy. Replying to this letter in *Triplici Nodo*, James argued that Bellarmine had misunderstood the case and that Fisher was guilty of treason.

GARDINER, STEPHEN, BISHOP OF WINCHESTER (*c*.1497–1555)   An important political figure from the 1530s onwards, Gardiner was a religious conservative who spent much of the reign of Edward VI in prison because of his opposition to Protestant doctrine. Under Mary he became Lord Chancellor. In 1535 he published *De Vera Obedientia*, defending the royal supremacy over the church. James cites this book favourably in *Triplici Nodo*.

HENRY, PRINCE OF WALES (1594–1612)   James' eldest son. The king dedicated *Basilicon Doron* to him. In 1610 he was made Prince of Wales. He died of typhoid in 1612.

JAMES V (1512–42)   King of Scots. His two baby sons died in 1541 and he was succeeded by his daughter Mary (q.v.), who was only six days old. His illegitimate children included James Stewart, Earl of Moray (q.v), and John Stewart (the father of Francis Stewart, Earl of Bothwell, q.v.). Moray was instrumental in the deposition of Mary and became regent for the young James VI, against whom Bothwell later conspired. In *Basilicon Doron* James uses his grandfather's example to argue that divine providence will visit misfortune upon adulterers and their descendants. He also refers to James V's reputation as 'the poore mans King', and records that his heart was broken as a result of his disregard for the nobility – many of whom consequently failed to appear at the battle of Solway Moss (1542), which was therefore a complete victory for the English. In his speech to parliament of 1607, James claims that his grandfather brought the Civil Law from France to Scotland.

KNOX, JOHN (1505–72)   A Scotsman who became a Protestant minister in 1547, and later went to England, Germany and Geneva. In 1558 he published his famous *First Blast of the Trumpet against the Monstrous Regiment of Women* which condemned rule by females as unnatural. During the following year Knox returned to Scotland, where he took a leading part in the Reformation. He wrote a *Historie of the Reformation* of which the first three books were published at London, but most copies were seized and destroyed by order of the Archbishop of Canterbury in 1587. James refers to Knox's *Historie* in *Basilicon Doron*.

LONGLAND, JOHN, BISHOP OF LINCOLN (1473–1547)   An Oxford graduate who became principal of Magdalen Hall in 1505 and Bishop of Lincoln in 1521. He was a staunch opponent of Protestantism but a vigorous advocate of the royal supremacy. In 1536 and 1538 he preached in favour of the supremacy at court. Both sermons were published. James refers to Longland in *Triplici Nodo*.

MARY, QUEEN OF SCOTS (1542–87)   The daughter of James V (q.v.) and Mary of Guise, she became Queen of Scots at the age of six days. In 1548 she was taken to France where she was educated. In 1558 she married the dauphin Francis, who succeeded to the French throne as Francis II in the following year. He died in 1560, and in 1561 Mary returned to Scotland. She married Henry Stewart, Lord Darnley, in 1565 and gave birth to James VI in the following year. Her policies of promoting Catholicism and increasing royal power attracted opposition. In 1567 Darnley was killed, and Mary married the man responsible for his murder – James Hepburn, fourth Earl of Bothwell. She was forced to abdicate, and in 1568 fled to England, where she remained a prisoner until she was executed in 1587 for plotting against Elizabeth. In *Basilicon Doron* James denied having any vengeful intentions against English statesmen on his mother's account, but noted that those who had been constant in their loyalty to Mary had likewise been loyal to himself.

MORAY *see* STEWART, JAMES

MORE, SIR THOMAS (1478–1535)   A noted scholar, famous for his *Utopia* (1516) and other works, More became lord chancellor of England in 1529 but resigned in 1532. He was a fervent critic of Protestantism and refused to support Henry VIII's divorce or the breach with the papacy. In 1535 he was executed for treason. Writing to Blackwell (q.v.) on 18 September 1607, Bellarmine (q.v.) cited More as an example of someone who suffered martyrdom rather than deny the papal supremacy. In *Triplici Nodo* James argued that More was not a true martyr and that it was not for the pope's supremacy that he died.

PAUL V, POPE (CAMILLO BORGHESE, 1550–1621; pope 1605–21) Trained in the canon law, Paul V was a vigorous assertor of papal powers. On 17 April 1606 he excommunicated the doge and senate of Venice for infringing the rights of the clergy, and shortly afterwards he placed the city under interdict. On 12 September 1606 and 13 August 1607 he issued breves condemning the English Oath of Allegiance which parliament had enacted in order to distinguish loyal from disloyal Catholics. In *Triplici Nodo* James prints and replies to the two breves.

PENRY, JOHN (1559–93)   A Welsh puritan who was suspected by the English authorities of responsibility for the scurrilous and outspoken Marprelate tracts which attacked episcopacy. He fled to Scotland in 1590, but was banished by James at the behest of the English ambassador. After returning to England he was captured, convicted of treason and executed in 1593. James refers to him in *Basilicon Doron*.

PIUS V, POPE (MICHELE GHISLIERI, 1504–72; pope 1566–72)   In 1570 Pius issued the bull *Regnans in Excelsis*, excommunicating and deposing Elizabeth I. James refers to this document several times in *Triplici Nodo*, arguing that there is little practical difference between *Regnans in Excelsis* and the breves against the oath of allegiance of Paul V (q.v.).

POLE, REGINALD (1500–58)   A descendant of the Yorkist kings of England, Pole opposed the royal supremacy over the church in the reign of Henry VIII. Under Mary he became a cardinal (1555) and Archbishop of Canterbury (1556). In *Triplici Nodo* James refers to a letter to him from Tunstall (q.v.) in which the latter defended the royal supremacy.

Select biographical notes

POOLE *see* POLE

SANDER (SANDERS, SANDERUS), NICHOLAS (1530–81)   A Catholic cleric and Oxford academic who emigrated to the Continent under Elizabeth. While abroad he wrote a number of works attacking the Elizabethan church and defending papal claims. These included *De Visibili Monarchia Ecclesiae* (Louvain 1571) and *De Clave David* (Rome 1588). In *Triplici Nodo* James took exception to what he regarded as the seditious ideas contained in both of these books, while Bellarmine (q.v.) praised *De Visibili Monarchia* in his letter to Blackwell of 18 September 1607. In 1579 Sander was sent as papal nuncio to encourage rebellion in Ireland and it was there that he died.

STEWART, FRANCIS, FIFTH EARL OF BOTHWELL (1563–1624)   The son of Lord John Stewart – who was himself the illegitimate son of James V. Francis' mother was Lady Jane Hepburn, the sister of Mary Queen of Scots' husband, the fourth Earl of Bothwell. In 1576 Francis was created fifth Earl of Bothwell. He was involved in a number of conspiracies against James during the early 1590s. In 1595 he went into exile. James refers to him in *Basilicon Doron* as an example of what evil consequences result when kings have illegitimate children.

STEWART, JAMES, EARL OF MORAY (*c*.1531–70)   The illegitimate son of James V (q.v.) by Margaret Erskine. In 1559 he led the lords of the congregation in their revolt against the regime of his father's widow, Mary of Guise. Moray became increasingly estranged from his half-sister Mary Queen of Scots (q.v.) after her marriage to Darnley in 1565. He was appointed regent for the infant James VI on Mary's abdication in 1567, and when she escaped from prison in 1568 he took steps to ensure that she would be unable to recover the Scottish throne. In 1570 he was assassinated. James refers to Moray in *Basilicon Doron*, calling him 'that bastard, who vnnaturally rebelled, and procured the ruine of his owne Souerane and sister'.

TONSTAL *see* TUNSTALL

TUNSTALL, CUTHBERT, BISHOP OF DURHAM (1474–1559)   A Catholic in doctrine, Tunstall at first opposed the royal supremacy over the church but later spoke in favour of it. He justified the supremacy in a letter to Cardinal Pole and in a sermon preached before Henry

VIII in 1539 and published shortly afterwards. James refers to these documents in *Triplici Nodo*.

VILLIERS, GEORGE. DUKE OF BUCKINGHAM (1592–1628)   Favourite of James I, who made him Viscount Villiers in 1616, Earl of Buckingham in 1617, Marquis of Buckingham in 1618, and Duke of Buckingham in 1623. He received the dedication of James' *A Meditation upon the Lord's Prayer* (1619) and acted as the king's amanuensis in the composition of *A Meditation upon the 27. 28. 29. Verses of the XXVII Chapter of Saint Matthew* (1620).

ΒΑΣΙΛΙΚΟΝ ΔΩΡΟΝ:[1]
OR
HIS MAIESTIES IN-
STRVCTIONS TO HIS
DEAREST SONNE, *HENRY*
THE PRINCE.

THE DEDICATION
of the booke.
SONET.

LO heere (my Sonne) a mirrour viue and faire,
Which sheweth the shaddow of a worthy King.
Lo heere a Booke, a patterne doth you bring
Which ye should preasse to follow mair and maire.
This trustie friend, the trueth will neuer spaire,
But giue a good aduice vnto you heare:
How it should be your chiefe and princely care,
To follow vertue, vice for to forbeare.
And in this Booke your lesson will ye leare,
For guiding of your people great and small.
Then (as ye ought) giue an attentiue eare,
And panse how ye these preceptes practise shall.
   Your father bids you studie here and reede.
How to become a perfite King indeede.[2]

THE ARGVMENT.
SONNET.

    God giues not Kings the stile of *Gods* in vaine,
For on his Throne his Scepter doe they swey:
And as their subiects ought them to obey,
So Kings should feare and serue their God againe:
If then ye would enioy a happie raigne,
Obserue the Statutes of your heauenly King,

I

And from his Law, make all your Lawes to spring:
Since his Lieutenant here ye should remaine,
Reward the iust, be stedfast, true, and plaine,
Represse the proud, maintayning aye the right,
Walke alwayes so, as euer in his sight,
Who guardes the godly, plaguing the prophane:
  And so ye shall in Princely vertues shine,
  Resembling right your mightie King Diuine.[3]

TO HENRY MY DEAREST
SONNE, AND NATVRAL
SVCCESSOVR.

WHOM-to can so rightly appertaine *this Booke of instructions to*[4] *a Prince in all the points of his calling, aswell generall, as a Christian towards God; as particular, as a King towards his people? Whom-to, I say, can it so iustly appertaine, as vnto you my dearest Sonne? Since I the authour thereof, as your naturall Father, must be carefull for your godly and vertuous education, as my eldest Sonne, and the first fruits of Gods blessing towards mee in my posteritie: and as a King must timously prouide for your trayning vp in all the points of a Kings Office; since yee are my naturall and lawfull successour therein: that being rightly informed hereby, of the waight of your burthen, ye may in time beginne to consider, that being borne to be a king, ye are rather borne to* onus,[5] *then* honos:[6] *not excelling all your people so farre in ranke and honour, as in daily care and hazardous paines-taking, for the dutifull administration of that great office, that God hath laide vpon your shoulders. Laying so a just symmetrie and proportion, betwixt the height of your honourable place, and the heauie waight of your great charge: and consequently, in case of failing, which God forbid, of the sadnesse of your fall, according to the proportion of that height. I haue therefore for the greater ease to your memory, and that yee may at the first, cast vp any part that yee haue to doe with, deuided this Treatise*[7] *in three parts. The first teacheth you your duetie towards God as a Christian: the next, your duetie in your Office as a King: and the third informeth you how to behaue your selfe in indifferent things, which of them-selues are neither right nor wrong, but according as they are rightly or wrong vsed; and yet will serue according to your behauiour therein, to augment or empaire your fame and authoritie at the handes of your people. Receiue and welcome this Booke then, as a faithfull Præceptour and counsellour vnto you: which, because my affaires will not permit mee euer to bee present with you, I ordaine to bee a resident faithfull admonisher of you: And because the houre of death is vncertaine to mee, as vnto all flesh, I leaue it as my Testament and latter will unto you. Chargeing you in the presence of GOD, and by the fatherly authoritie I haue ouer you, that yee keepe it euer with you, as carefully, as* Alexander *did the* Iliads *of* Homer. *Yee will finde it a iust and impartiall counsellour; neither flattering you in any vice, nor importuning you at vnmeete times. It will not come vn-called, neither speake vnspeered at: and yet conferring with it when yee are at quiet, yee shall say with* Scipio, *that yee are* nunquam minus solus, quam cum solus.[8] *To conclude then, I charge you, as euer yee thinke to deserue my Fatherly blessing, to follow and put in practise, as farre as lyeth in you, the præcepts hereafter following. And if yee follow the contrary[9] course, I take the Great GOD to record, that this Booke shall one day bee a witnesse betwixt mee and you; and shall procure to bee ratified in Heauen, the curse that in that case here I giue vnto you. For I protest before that Great GOD, I had rather not bee a Father, and childlesse, then bee a Father of wicked children. But hoping, yea, euen promising vnto my selfe, that GOD, who in his great blessing sent you vnto mee; shall in the same blessing, as hee hath giuen mee a Sonne; so make him a good and a godly Sonne; not repenting him of his Mercie shewed vnto mee, I end, with my earnest prayer to GOD, to worke effectually into you, the fruites of that blessing, which here from my heart I bestow vpon you.*

Your louing Father
I. R.

TO THE READER.[10]

*C*Haritable Reader, it is one of the golden Sentences, which Christ our Sauiour vttered to his Apostles, that there* is nothing so couered, that shal not be reuealed, neither so hidde, that shall not be knowen; and whatsoeuer they haue spoken in darkenesse, should be heard in the light: and that which they had spoken in the eare in secret place, should be publikely preached on the tops of the houses:[11] *And since he hath said it, most trew must it be, since the authour thereof is the fountaine and very being of trewth: which should mooue all godly and honest men, to be very warie in all their secretest actions, and whatsoeuer middesses they vse for attaining to their most wished ends; lest otherwise how auowable soeuer the marke be, whereat they aime, the middesses being discouered to be shamefull whereby they climbe, it may turne to the disgrace both of the good worke it selfe, and of the authour thereof; since the deepest of our secrets, cannot be hidde from that all-seeing eye, and penetrant light, piercing through the bowels of very darkenesse it selfe.*

3

But as this is generally trew in the actions of all men, so is it more specially trew in the affaires of Kings: for Kings being publike persons, by reason of their office and authority, are as it were set (as it was said of old) vpon a publike stage, in the sight of all the people; where all the beholders eyes are attentiuely bent to looke and pry in the least circumstance of their secretest drifts: Which should make Kings the more carefull not to harbour the secretest thought in their minde, but such as in the owne time they shall not be ashamed openly to auouch; assuring themselues that Time the mother of Veritie, will in the due season bring her owne daughter to perfection.

The trew practise hereof, I haue as a King oft found in my owne person, though I thanke God, neuer to my shame, hauing laide my count, euer to walke as in the eyes of the Almightie, examining euer so the secretest of my drifts, before I gaue them course, as how they might some day bide the touchstone of a publike triall. And amongst the rest of my secret actions, which haue (vnlooked for of me) come to publike knowledge, it hath so fared with my ΒΑΣΙΛΙΚΟΝ ΔΩΡΟΝ, directed to my eldest son; which I wrote for exercise of mine owne ingyne, and instruction of him, who is appointed by God (I hope) to sit on my Throne after me: For the purpose and matter thereof being onely fit for a King, as teaching him his office; and the person whom-for it was ordained, a Kings heire, whose secret counsellor and faithfull admonisher it must be, I thought it no wayes conuenient nor comely, that either it should to all be proclaimed, which to one onely appertained (and specially being a messenger betwixt two so coniunct persons) or yet that the mould whereupon he should frame his future behauiour, when hee comes both vnto the perfection of his yeeres, and possession of his inheritance, should before the hand be made common to the people, the subiect of his future happy gouernment. And therefore for the more secret and close keeping of them, I onely permitted seuen of them to be printed, the Printer being first sworne for secrecie: and these seuen I dispersed amongst some of my trustiest seruants, to be keeped closely by them, lest in case by the iniquitie or wearing of time, any of them might haue beene lost, yet some of them might haue remained after me, as witnesses to my Sonne, both of the honest integritie of my heart, and of my fatherly affection and naturall care towards him. But since contrary to my intention and expectation, as I haue alreadie said, this Booke is now vented, and set foorth to the publike view of the world, and consequently subiect to euery mans censure, as the current of his affection leades him; I am now forced, as well for resisting to the malice of the children of enuie, who like waspes sucke[12] venome out of euery wholsome herbe; as for the satisfaction of the godly honest sort, in any

4

thing that they may mistake therein, both to publish and spread the true copies thereof, for defacing of the false copies that are alreadie spread, as I am enformed; as likewise by this Preface, to cleare such parts thereof, as in respect of the concised shortnesse of my Style, may be mis-interpreted therein.

To come then particularly to the matter of my Booke, there are two speciall great points, which (as I am informed) the malicious sort of men haue detracted therein; and some of the honest sort haue seemed a little to mistake: whereof the first and greatest is, that some sentences therein should seeme to furnish grounds to men, to doubt of my sinceritie in that Religion, which I haue euer constantly professed; the other is, that in some parts thereof I should seeme to nourish in my minde, a vindictiue resolution against England, *or at the least, some principals there, for the Queene my mothers quarrell.*

The first calumnie (most grieuous indeed) is grounded vpon the sharpe and bitter wordes, that therein are vsed in the description of the humors of Puritanes, and rash-headie Preachers, that thinke it their honour to contend with Kings, and perturbe whole kingdomes. The other point is onely grounded vpon the strait charge I giue my Sonne, not to heare nor suffer any vnreuerent speeches or bookes against any of his parents or progenitors: wherein I doe alledge my owne experience anent the Queene my mother; affirming, that I neuer found any that were of perfit aage the time of her reigne here, so stedfastly trew to me in all my troubles, as these that constantly kept their allegiance to her in her time. But if the charitable Reader will aduisedly consider, both the methode and matter of my Treatise, he will easily iudge, what wrong I haue sustained by the carping at both: For my Booke, suppose very small, being diuided in three seuerall parts; the first part thereof onely treats of a Kings duety towards God in Religion, wherein I haue so clearely made profession of my Religion, calling it the Religion wherein I was brought vp, and euer made profession of, and wishing him euer to continue in the same, as the onely trew forme of Gods worship; that I would haue thought my sincere plainnesse in that first part vpon that subiect, should haue ditted the mouth of the most enuious Momus, *that euer hell did hatch, from barking at any other part of my booke vpon that ground, except they would alledge me to be contrarie to my selfe, which in so small a volume would smell of too great weakenesse, and sliprinesse of memory. And the second part of my booke, teaches my Sonne how to vse his Office, in the administration of Iustice and Politicke Gouernment: The third onely containing a Kings outward behauiour in indifferent things; what agreeance and conformitie hee ought to keepe betwixt his outward behauiour in these things, and the vertuous qualities of his minde; and how they should serue for trunsh-men, to interprete the inward disposition of the minde, to the eyes of them that cannot see farther within him, and therefore must onely iudge of him by the outward appearance: So as if there were no more to be looked into, but the very methode and order of the booke, it will sufficiently cleare me of that first and grieuousest imputation, in the point of Religion: since in the first part, where Religion is onely treated of, I speake so plainely. And what in other parts I speake of Puritanes, it is onely of their morall faults, in that part where I speake of Policie: declaring when they contemne the Law and souereigne authoritie, what exemplare punishment they deserue for the same. And now as to the matter it selfe whereupon this scandall is taken, that I may sufficiently satisfie all honest men, and by a iust Apologie raise vp a brasen wall or bulwarke against all the darts of the enuious, I will the more narrowly rip vp the words, whereat they seeme to be somewhat stomacked.*

First then, as to the name of Puritanes, I am not ignorant that the style thereof doeth properly belong onely to that vile sect amongst the Anabaptists, called the Family of loue; because they thinke themselues onely pure, and in a maner without sinne, the onely trew[13] *Church, and onely worthy to be participant of the Sacraments, and all the rest of the world to be but abomination in the sight of God. Of this speciall sect I principally meane, when I speake of Puritans;* diuers of them, as Browne, Penry *and others, hauing at sundrie times come into Scotland, to sow their popple amongst vs (and from my heart I wish, that they had left no schollers behinde them, who by their fruits will in the owne time be manifested) and partly indeede, I giue this style to such brain-sicke and headie Preachers their disciples and followers, as refusing to be called of that sect, yet participate too much with their humours, in maintaining the aboue-mentioned errours; not onely agreeing with the generall rule of all Anabaptists, in the contempt of the ciuill Magistrate, and in leaning to their owne dreams and reuelations; but particularly with this sect, in accounting all men profane that sweare not to all their fantasies, in making for euery particular question of the policie of the Church, as great commotion, as if the article of the Trinitie were called in controuersie, in making the scriptures to be ruled by their conscience, and not their conscience by the Scripture; and he that denies the least iote of their grounds,* sit tibi tanquam ethnicus & publicanus;[14] *not worthy to enioy the benefite of breathing, much lesse to participate with them of the Sacraments: and before that any of their grounds be impugned, let King, people, Law and all be trode vnder foote: Such holy warres are to be preferred to an vngodly peace: no, in such cases Christian Princes are not onely to be resisted vnto, but not to be prayed for, for prayer must come of Faith; and it is reuealed to their consciences, that GOD will heare no prayer for such a Prince. Iudge then, Christian Reader, if I wrong this sort of people, in giuing them the stile of that sect, whose errours they imitate: and since they are contented to weare their liuerie, let them not be ashamed to borrow also their name. It is onely of this kinde of men, that in this booke I write so sharply; and whom I wish my Sonne to punish, in-case they refuse to obey the Law, and will not cease to sturre vp a rebellion: Whom against I haue written the more bitterly, in respect of diuers famous libels, and iniurious speaches spred by some of them, not onely dishonourably inuectiue against all Christian Princes, but euen reprochfull to our profession and Religion, in respect they are come out vnder coulour thereof: and yet were neuer answered but by Papists, who generally medle aswell against them, as the religion it selfe; whereby the skandale was rather doubled, then taken away. But on the other part, I protest vpon mine honour, I meane it not generally of all Preachers, or others, that like better of the single forme of policie in our Church, then of the many Ceremonies in the Church of England; that are perswaded, that their Bishops smell of a Papall supremacie, that the Surplise, the cornerd cap, and such like, are the outward badges of Popish errours. No, I am so farre from being contentious in these things (which for my owne part I euer esteemed as indifferent) as I doe equally loue and honour the learned and graue men of either of these opinions. It can no wayes become me to pronounce so lightly a sentence, in so old a controuersie. Wee all (God be praised) doe agree in the grounds; and the bitternesse of men vpon such questions, doeth but trouble the peace of the Church; and giues aduantage and entry to the Papists by our diuision: But towards them, I onely vse this prouision, that where the Law is otherwayes, they may content themselues soberly and quietly with their owne opinions, not resisting to the authoritie, nor breaking the Law of the Countrey; neither aboue all, sturring any rebellion or schisme: but possessing their soules in peace, let them preasse by patience, and well grounded reasons, either to perswade all the rest to like of their iudgements; or where they see better grounds on the other part, not to bee ashamed peaceably to incline thereunto, laying aside all præoccupied opinions.*

And that this is the onely meaning of my Booke, and not any coldnesse or cracke in Religion, that place doeth plainely witnesse, where, after I haue spoken of the faults in our Ecclesiasticall estate, I exhort my sonne to be beneficiall vnto the good-men of the Ministrie; praising God there, that there is presently a sufficient number of good men of them in this kingdome; and yet are they all knowne to be against the forme of the English Church. Yea, so farre I am in that place from admitting corruption in Religion, as I wish him in promoouing them, to vse such caution, as may preserue their estate from creeping to corruption; euer vsing that forme through the whole Booke, where euer I speake of bad Preachers, terming them some of the Ministers, and not Ministers or Ministrie in generall. And to conclude this point of Religion, what indifferencie of Religion can Momus *call that in mee, where, speaking of my sonnes marriage (in case it pleased God before that time to cut the threed of my life) I plainly forewarne him of the inconuenients that were like to ensew, incase he should marry any that be of a different profession in Religion from him: notwithstanding that the number of Princes professing our Religion be so small, as it is hard to foresee, how he can be that way, meetly matched according to his ranke.*

And as for the other point, that by some parts in this booke, it should appeare, that I doe nourish in my minde, a vindictiue resolution against England, or some principals there; it is surely more then wonderfull vnto me, vpon what grounds they can haue gathered such conclusions. For as vpon the one part, I neither by name nor description poynt out England in that part of my discourse; so vpon the other, I plainly bewray my meaning to be of Scottish-men where I conclude that purpose in these termes: That[15] *the loue I beare to my Sonne, hath mooued me to be so plaine in this argument: for so that I discharge my conscience to him in vttering the verity, I care not what any traitour or treason-allower doe thinke of it. And English-men could not thereby be meant, since they could be no traitours, where they ought no alleageance. I am not ignorant of a wise and princely apophthegme, which the same* Queene of England *vttered about the time of her owne Coronation. But the drift of that discourse doth fully cleare my intention, being onely grounded vpon that precept to my Sonne, that he should not permit any vnreuerent detracting of his prædecessours; bringing in that purpose of my mother onely for an example of my experience anent Scottish-men, without vsing any perswasion to him of reuenge. For a Kings giuing of any fault the dew stile, inferres no reduction of the faulters pardon. No, I am by a degree nearer of kinne vnto my mother then he is, neither thinke I myselfe, either that vnworthie, or that neere my end, that I neede to make such a* Dauidicall[16] *testament; since I haue euer thought it the dewtie of a worthie Prince, rather with a pike, then a penne, to write his iust reuenge: But in this matter I haue no delite to be large, wishing all men to iudge of my future proiects, according to my by-past actions.*

Thus hauing as much insisted in the clearing of these two points, as will (I hope) giue sufficient satisfaction to all honest men, and leauing the enuious to the foode of their owne venome; I will heartily pray thee, louing Reader, charitably to conceiue of my honest intention in this Booke. I know the greatest part of the people of this whole Isle, haue beene very curious for a sight thereof: some for the loue they beare me, either being particularly acquainted with me, or by a good report that perhappes they haue heard of me; and therefore longed to see any thing, that proceeded from that authour whom they so loued and honoured; since bookes are viue Idees of the authours minde. Some onely for meere curiositie that thinke it their honour to know all new things, were curious to glut their eyes therewith, onely that they might vaunt them to haue seene it: and some fraughted with causlesse enuie at the Authour, did greedily search out the booke, thinking their stomacke fit ynough, for turning neuer so wholesome foode into noysome and infectiue humours: So as this their great concurrence in curiositie (though proceeding from farre different complexions) hath enforced the vn-timous divulgating of this Booke, farre contrarie to my intention, as I haue alreadie said. To which Hydra *of diuersly-enclined spectatours, I haue no targe to oppone but plainenesse, patience, and sinceritie: plainenesse, for resoluing and satisfying of the first sort; patience, for to beare with the shallownesse of the next; and sinceritie, to defie the malice of the third with-all. Though I cannot please all men therein, I am contented, so that I onely please the vertuous sort: and though they also finde not euery thing therein, so fully to answere their expectation, as the argument would seeme to require; although I would wish them modestly to remember, that God hes[17] not bestowed all his gifts vpon one, but parted them by a iustice distributiue; and that many eyes see more then one; and that the varietie of mens mindes is such, that* tot capita tot sensus;[18] *yea, and that euen the very faces, that God hath by nature brought foorth in the world, doe euery one in some of their particular lineaments, differ from any other: yet in trewth it was not my intention in handling of this purpose (as it is easie to perceiue) fully to set downe heere all such grounds, as might out of the best writers haue beene alledged, and out of my owne inuention and experience added, for the perfite institution of a King; but onely to giue some such precepts to my owne Sonne, for the gouernement of this kingdome, as was meetest for him to be instructed in, and best became me to be the informer of.*

If I in this Booke haue beene too particularly plaine, impute it to the necessitie of the subiect, not so much being ordained for the institution of a Prince in generall, as I haue said, as containing particular precepts to my Sonne in speciall: whereof he could haue made but a generall vse, if they had not contained the particular diseases of this kingdome, with the best remedies for the same, which it became me best as a King, hauing learned both the theoricke and practicke thereof, more plainely to expresse, then any simple schoole-man, that onely knowes matters of kingdomes by contemplation.

But if in some places it seeme too osbcure, impute it to the shortnesse thereof, being both for the respect of my selfe, and of my Sonne con-strained there-unto: my owne respect, for fault of leasure, being so continually occupied in the affairs of my office, as my great burthen, and restlesse fashery is more then knowen, to all that knowes or heares of me: for my Sonnes respect, because I know by my self, that a Prince so long as he is young, wil be so caried away with some sort of delight or other, that he cannot patiently abide the reading of any large volume: and when he comes to a ful maturity of aage, he must be so busied in the actiue part of his charge, as he will not be permitted to bestow many houres vpon the contemplatiue part thereof: So as it was neither fit for him, nor possible for me, to haue made this Treatise any more ample then it is. Indeed I am litle beholden to the curiositie of some, who thinking it too large alreadie (as appears) for lacke of leisure to copy it, drew some notes out of it, for speeds sake; putting in the one halfe of the purpose, and leauing out the other: not vnlike the man that alledged that part of the Psalme, non est Deus,[19] *but left out the præceeding words,* Dixit insipiens in corde suo.[20] *And of these notes, making a little pamphlet (lacking both my methode and halfe of my matter) entituled it, forsooth,* the Kings Testament, *as if I had eiked a third Testament of my owne to the two that are in the holy Scriptures. It is trew that in a place thereof, for affirmation of the purpose I am speaking of to my Sonne, I bring my selfe in there, as speaking vpon my Testament: for in that sense, euery record in write of a mans opinion in any thing (in respect that papers out-liue their authours) is as it were a Testament of that mans will in that case: and in that sense it is, that in that place I call this Treatise a Testament. But from any particular sentence in a booke, to giue the booke it selfe a title, is as ridiculous, as to style the booke of the Psalmes, the booke of* Dixit insipiens,[21] *because with these wordes one of them doeth begin.*

Well, leauing these new baptizers and blockers of other mens books, to their owne follies, I returne to my purpose, anent the shortnesse of this booke, suspecting that all my excuses for the shortnesse thereof, shall not satisfie some, especially in our neighbour countrey: who thought, that as I haue so narrowly in this Treatise touched all the principall sicknesses in our kingdome, with ouertures for the remedies thereof, as I said before: so looked they to haue found something therein, that should haue touched the sicknesses of their state, in the like sort. But they will easily excuse me thereof, if they will consider the forme I haue vsed in this Treatise; wherein I onely teach my Son, out of my owne experience, what forme of gouernment is fittest for this kingdome: and in one part thereof speaking of the borders, I plainely there doe excuse my selfe, that I will speake nothing of the state of England, *as a matter wherein I neuer had experience. I know indeed, no kingdome lackes her owne diseases, and likewise what interest I haue in the prosperitie of that state: for although I would be silent, my blood and discent doeth sufficiently proclaime it. But notwithstanding, since there is a lawfull Queene there presently reigning, who hath so long with so great wisedome and felicitie gouerned her kingdomes, as (I must in trew sinceritie confesse) the like hath not beene read nor heard of, either in our time, or since the dayes of the* Romane Emperour Augustus; *it could no wayes become me, farre inferiour to her in knowledge and experience, to be a busie-body in other princes matters, and to fish in other folkes waters, as the prouerbe is: No, I hope by the contrary (with Gods grace) euer to keepe that Christian rule, To doe as I would be done to: and I doubt nothing, yea euen in her name I dare promise, by the bypast experience of her happy gouernment, as I haue already said, that no good subiect shall be more carefull to enforme her of any corruptions stollen in in her state, then shee shall be zealous for the discharge of her conscience and honour, to see the same purged, and restored to the ancient integritie; and further during her time, becomes me least of any to meddle in.*

And thus hauing resolued all the doubts, so farre as I can imagine, may be moued against this Treatise; it onely rests to pray thee (charitable Reader) to interprete fauourably this birth of mine, according to the integritie of the author, and not looking for perfection in the worke it selfe. As for my part, I onely glory thereof in this point, that I trust no sort of vertue is condemned, nor any degree of vice allowed in it: and that (though it be not perhaps so gorgeously decked, and richly attired as it ought to be) it is at the least rightly proportioned in all the members, without any monstrous deformitie in any of them: and specially that since it was first written in secret, and is now published, not of ambition, but of a kinde of necessitie; it must be taken of all men, for the trew image of my very minde, and forme of the rule, which I haue prescribed to my selfe and mine: Which as in all my actions I haue hitherto preassed to expresse, so farre as the nature of my charge, and the condition of time would permit me: so beareth it a discouery of that which may be looked for at my hand, and whereto euen in my secret thoughts, I haue engaged my selfe for the time to come. And thus in a firme trust, that it shall please God, who with my being and Crowne, gaue me this minde, to maintaine and augment the same in me and my posteritie, to the discharge of our conscience, the maintenance of our Honour, and weale of our people, I bid thee heartily farewell.

OF
A KINGS CHRISTIAN
DVETIE TOWARDS
GOD.
THE FIRST BOOKE.

As he cannot be thought worthy to rule and command others, that cannot rule and dantone his owne proper affections and vnreasonable appetites, so can hee not be thought worthie to gouerne a Christian people,[22] knowing and fearing God, that in his owne person and heart, feareth not and loueth not the Diuine Maiestie. Neither can any thing in his gouernment succeed well with him, (deuise and labour as he list) as comming from a filthie spring, if his person be vnsanctified: for (as that royal Prophet saith) *Except the Lord build the house, they labour in vaine that build it: except the Lord keepe the City, the keepers watch it in vaine;*[23] in respect the blessing of God hath only power to giue the successe thereunto: and as *Paul* saith, he *planteth, Apollos watereth; but it is God onely that giueth the increase.*[24] Therefore (my Sonne) first of all things, learne to know and loue that God, whom-to ye haue a double obligation; first,[25] for that he made you a man; and next, for that he made you a little GOD to sit on his Throne, and rule ouer other men. Remember, that as in dignitie hee hath erected you aboue others, so ought ye in thankfulnesse towards him, goe as farre beyond all others. A moate in anothers eye, is a beame into yours: a blemish in another, is a leprouse byle into you: and a veniall sinne (as the Papists call it) in another, is a great crime into you. Thinke not therefore, that the highnesse of your dignitie, diminisheth your faults[26] (much lesse giueth you a licence to sinne) but by the contrary your fault shall be aggrauated, according to the height of your dignitie; any sinne that ye commit, not being a single sinne procuring but the fall of one; but being an exemplare sinne, and therefore drawing with it the whole multitude to be guiltie of the same. Remember then, that this glister-ing worldly glorie of Kings,[27] is giuen them by God, to teach them to preasse so to glister and shine before their people, in all workes of sanctification and righteousnesse, that their persons as bright lampes of godlinesse and vertue, may, going in and out before their people, giue light to all their steps. Remember also, that by the right knowledge, and feare of God (which is *the beginning of Wisedome,*[28] as *Salomon* saith), ye shall know all the things necessarie for the dis-charge of your duetie, both as a Christian, and as a King; seeing in him, as in a mirrour, the course of all earthly things, whereof hee is the spring and onely moouer.

Now,[29] the onely way to bring you to this knowledge, is diligently to reade his word, and earnestly to pray for the right vnderstanding thereof. *Search the Scriptures,* sayth Christ, *for they beare testimonie of me:*[30] and, *the whole Scripture,* saith Paul, *is giuen by inspiration of God, and is profitable to teach, to conuince, to correct, and to instruct in righteousnesse; that the man of God may be absolute, being made perfite vnto all good workes.*[31] And most properly of any other, belongeth the reading thereof vnto Kings, since in that part of Scripture, where the godly Kings are first made mention of,[32] that were ordained to rule ouer the people of God, there is an expresse and most notable exhortation and commandement giuen them, to reade and meditate in the Law of God. I ioyne to this, the carefull hearing of the doctrine with attendance and reuerence: for, *faith commeth by hearing,*[33] sayth the same Apostle. But aboue all, beware ye wrest not the word to your owne appetite, as ouer many doe, making it like a bell to sound as ye please to interprete: but by the contrary, frame all your affec-tions, to follow precisely the rule there set downe.

The[34] whole Scripture chiefly containeth two things: a command, and a prohibition, to doe such things, and to abstaine from the con-trary. Obey in both; neither thinke it enough to abstaine from euill, and do no good; nor thinke not that if yee doe many good things, it may serue you for a cloake to mixe euill turnes therewith. And as in these two points, the whole Scripture principally consisteth, so in two degrees[35] standeth the whole seruice of God by man: interiour, or vpward; exteriour, or downward: the first, by prayer in faith towards God; the next, by workes flowing therefra before the world: which is nothing else, but the exercise of Religion towards God, and of equitie towards your neighbour.

As for the particular points of Religion, I need not to dilate them; I am no hypocrite, follow my footsteps,[36] and your owne present education therein. I thanke God, I was neuer ashamed to giue account of my profession, howsoeuer the malicious lying tongues of some haue traduced me: and if my conscience had not resolued me, that all my Religion presently professed by me and my kingdome, was grounded vpon the plaine wordes of the Scripture, without the which all points of Religion are superfluous, as any thing contrary to the same is abomination, I had neuer outwardly auowed it, for pleasure or awe of any flesh.

And as for the points of equitie towards your neighbour (because that will fall in properly, vpon the second part concerning a Kings office) I leaue it to the owne roume.

For[37] the first part then of mans seruice to his God, which is Religion, that is, the worship of God according to his reuealed will, it is wholly grounded vpon the Scripture, as I haue alreadie said, quickened by faith, and conserued by conscience: For the Scripture, I haue now spoken of it in generall, but that yee may the more readily make choice of any part thereof, for your instruction or comfort, remember shortly this methode.

The whole Scripture is dyted by Gods Spirit, thereby, as by his liuely word,[38] to instruct and rule the whole Church militant to the end of the world: It is composed of two parts, the Olde and New Testament: The ground of the former is the Lawe, which sheweth our sinne, and containeth iustice: the ground of the other is Christ, who pardoning sinne containeth grace. The summe of the Law is the tenne Commandements, more largely delated in the bookes of *Moses*,[39] interpreted and applied by the Prophets; and by the histories, are the examples shewed of obedience or disobedience thereto, and what *præmium*[40] or *poena*[41] was accordingly giuen by God: But because no man was able to keepe the Law, nor any part thereof, it pleased God of his infinite wisedome and goodnesse, to incarnate his only Sonne in our nature, for satisfaction of his iustice in his suffering for vs; that since we could not be saued by doing, we might at least, bee saued by beleeuing.

The ground therefore of the word of grace,[42] is contained in the foure histories of the birth, life, death, resurrection and ascension of Christ: The larger interpretation and vse thereof, is contained in the Epistles of the Apostles: and the practise in the faithfull or vnfaithfull, with the historie of the infancie and first progresse of the Church is contained in their Actes.

Would ye then know your sinne by the Lawe?[43] reade the bookes of *Moses* containing it. Would ye haue a commentarie thereupon? Reade the Prophets, and likewise the bookes of the *Prouerbes* and *Ecclesiastes*, written by that great patterne of wisedome *Salomon*, which will not only serue you for instruction, how to walke in the obedience of the Lawe of God, but is also so full of golden sentences, and morall precepts, in all things that can concerne your conuersation in the world, as among all the prophane Philosophers and Poets, ye shall not finde so rich a storehouse of precepts of naturall wisedome, agreeing with the will and diuine wisedome of God. Would ye see how good men are rewarded, and wicked punished? looke the historicall parts of these same bookes of *Moses*, together with the histories of *Ioshua*, the *Iudges, Ezra, Nehemiah, Esther*, and *Iob*: but especially the bookes of the *Kings* and *Chronicles*, wherewith ye ought to bee familiarly acquainted: for there shall yee see your selfe, as in a myrrour, in the catalogue either of the good or the euill Kings.

Would yee know the doctrine, life, and death of our Sauiour Christ?[44] reade the Euangelists. Would ye bee more particularly trained vp in his Schoole? meditate vpon the Epistles of the Apostles. And would ye be acquainted with the practises of that doctrine in the persons of the primitiue Church? Cast vp the Apostles Actes. And as to the Apocryphe bookes, I omit them, because I am no Papist, as I said before; and indeed some of them are no wayes like the dytement of the Spirit of God.

But when ye reade the Scripture,[45] reade it with a sanctified and chaste heart: admire reuerently such obscure places as ye vnderstand not, blaming onely your owne capacitie: read with delight the plaine places, and studie carefully to vnderstand those that are somewhat difficile: preasse to bee a good textuarie; for the Scripture is euer the best interpreter of it selfe; but preasse not curiously to seeke out farther then is contained therein; for that were ouer vnmannerly a presumption, to striue to bee further vpon Gods secrets, then he hath will ye be; for what hee thought needfull for vs to know, that hath he reuealed there: And delyte most in reading such parts of the Scripture, as may best serue for your instruction in your calling; reiecting foolish curiosities vpon genealogies and contentions, *which are but vaine, and profite not*,[46] as *Paul* saith.

Now, as to Faith,[47] which is the nourisher and quickner of Religion, as I haue alreadie said, It is a sure perswasion and apprehension of the promises of God, applying them to your soule: and therefore may it iustly be called, the golden chaine that linketh the faithfull soule to Christ: And because it groweth not in our garden, but *is the free gift of God,*[48] as the same Apostle saith, it must be nourished by prayer, Which is nothing else, but a friendly talking with God.

As for teaching you the forme of your prayers,[49] the Psalmes of *Dauid* are the meetest schoole-master that ye can be acquainted with (next the prayer of our Sauiour, which is the onely rule of prayer) whereout of, as of most rich and pure fountaines, ye may learne all forme of prayer necessarie for your comfort at all occasions: And so much the fitter are they for you, then for the common sort, in respect the composer thereof was a King: and therefore best behoued to know a Kings wants, and what things were meetest to be required by a King at Gods hand for remedie thereof.

Vse often to pray when ye are quietest,[50] especially forget it not in your bed how oft soeuer ye doe it at other times: for publike prayer serueth as much for example, as for any particular comfort to the supplicant.

In your prayer,[51] bee neither ouer strange with God, like the ignorant common sort, that prayeth nothing but out of bookes, nor yet ouer homely with him, like some of the vaine Pharisaicall puritanes, that thinke they rule him vpon their fingers: The former way will breede an vncouth coldnesse in you towards him, the other will breede in you a contempt of him. But in your prayer to God speake with all reuerence: for if a subiect will not speake but reuerently to a King, much lesse should any flesh presume to talke with God as with his companion.

Craue in your prayer, not onely things spirituall, but also things temporall,[52] sometimes of greater, and sometimes of lesse consequence; that yee may lay vp in store his grant of these things, for confirmation of your faith, and to be an arles-peny vnto you of his loue. Pray, as yee finde your heart moueth you, *pro re nata:*[53] but see that yee sute no vnlawfull things, as reuenge, lust, or such like: for that prayer can not come of faith: *and whatsoeuer is done without faith, is sinne,*[54] as the Apostle saith.

When ye obtaine your prayer,[55] thanke him ioyfully therefore: if otherwaies, beare patiently, preassing to winne him with importunitie, as the widow did the vnrighteous Iudge:[56] and if notwithstanding thereof yee be not heard, assure your selfe, God foreseeth that which yee aske is not for your weale: and learne in time, so to interprete all the aduersities that God shall send vnto you; so shall yee in the middest of them, not onely be armed with patience, but ioyfully lift vp your eyes from the present trouble, to the happie end that God will turne it to. And when ye finde it once so fall out by proofe, arme your selfe with the experience thereof against the next trouble, assuring your selfe, though yee cannot in time of the showre see through the cloude, yet in the end shall ye find; God sent it for your weale, as ye found in the former.

And as for conscience, which I called the conseruer of Religion,[57] It is nothing else, but the light of knowledge that God hath planted in man, which euer watching ouer all his actions, as it beareth him a ioyfull testimonie when he does right, so choppeth it him with a feeling that hee hath done wrong, when euer he committeth any sinne. And surely, although this conscience be a great torture to the wicked, yet is it as great a comfort to the godly, if we will consider it rightly. For haue wee not a great aduantage, that haue within our selues while wee liue here, a Count-booke and Inuentarie of all the crimes that wee shall be accused of,[58] either at the houre of our death, or at the Great day of Iudgement; which when wee please (yea though we forget) will chop, and remember vs to looke vpon it; that while we haue leasure and are here, we may remember to amend; and so at the day of our triall, compeare with *new and white garments washed in the blood of the Lambe*,[59] as *S. Iohn* saith. Aboue all then, my Sonne, labour to keepe sound this conscience, which many prattle of, but ouer few feele: especially be carefull to keepe it free from two diseases, wherewith it vseth oft to be infected;[60] to wit, Leaprosie, and Superstition; the former is the mother of Atheisme, the other of Heresies. By a leaprouse conscience, I meane *a cauterized conscience*,[61] as *Paul* calleth it, being become senselesse of sinne, through sleeping in a carelesse securitie as King *Dauids* was after his murther and adulterie, euer til he was wakened by the Prophet *Nathans* similitude.[62] And by superstition, I meane, when one restraines himselfe to any other rule in the seruice of God, then is warranted by the word, the onely trew square of Gods seruice.

As for a preseruatiue against this Leaprosie,[63] remember euer once in the foure and twentie houres, either in the night, or when yee are at greatest quiet, to call your selfe to account of all your last dayes actions, either wherein ye haue committed things yee should not, or omitted the things ye should doe, either in your Christian or Kingly calling: and in that account, let not your selfe be smoothed ouer with that flattering φιλαυτία, [64] which is ouerkindly a sicknesse to all mankinde: but censure your selfe as sharply, as if ye were your owne enemie: *For if ye iudge your selfe, ye shall not be iudged,* [65] as the Apostle saith: and then according to your censure, reforme your actions as farre as yee may, eschewing euer wilfully and wittingly to contrare your conscience: For a small sinne wilfully committed, with a deliberate resolution to breake the bridle of conscience therein, is farre more grieuous before God, then a greater sinne committed in a suddaine passion, when conscience is asleepe. Remember therefore in all your actions, of the great account that yee are one day to make:[66] in all the dayes of your life, euer learning to die, and liuing euery day as it were your last;

Omnem crede diem tibi diluxisse supremum. [67]

And therefore, I would not haue you to pray with the Papists, to be preserued from suddaine death, but that God would giue you grace so to liue, as ye may euery houre of your life be ready for death: so shall ye attaine to the vertue of trew fortitude,[68] neuer being afraid for the horrour of death, come when he list: And especially, beware to offend your conscience with vse of swearing or lying, suppose but in iest; for othes are but an vse,[69] and a sinne cloathed with no delight nor gaine, and therefore the more inexcusable euen in the sight of men: and lying commeth also much of a vile vse, which banisheth shame: Therfore beware euen to deny the trewth, which is a sort of lie, that may best be eschewed by a person of your ranke. For if any thing be asked at you that yee thinke not meete to reueale, if yee say, that question is not pertinent for them to aske, who dare examine you further? and vsing sometimes this answere both in trew and false things that shall be asked at you, such vnmanerly people will neuer be the wiser thereof.

And for keeping your conscience sound from that sickenesse of superstition,[70] yee must neither lay the safetie of your conscience vpon the credit of your owne conceits, nor yet of other mens humors, how great doctors of Diuinitie that euer they be; but yee must onely ground it vpon the expresse Scripture: for conscience not grounded vpon sure knowledge, is either an ignorant fantasie, or an arrogant vanitie. Beware therefore in this case with two extremities: the one, to beleeue with the Papists, the Churches authority, better then your owne knowledge; the other, to leane with the Anabaptists, to your owne conceits and dreamed reuelations.

But learne wisely to discerne betwixt points of saluation and indifferent things, betwixt substance and ceremonies;[71] and betwixt the expresse commandement and will of God in his word, and the inuention or ordinance of man; since all that is necessarie for saluation is contained in the Scripture: For in any thing that is expressely commanded or prohibited in the booke of God, ye cannot be ouer precise, euen in the least thing; counting euery sinne, not according to the light estimation and common vse of it in the world, but as the booke of God counteth of it. But as for all other things not contained in the Scripture, spare not to vse or alter them, as the necessitie of the time shall require.[72] And when any of the spirituall office-bearers in the Church, speake vnto you any thing that is well warranted by the word, reuerence and obey them as the heraulds of the most high God: but, if passing that bounds, they vrge you to embrace any of their fantasies in the place of Gods word, or would colour their particulars with a pretended zeale, acknowledge them for no other then vaine men, exceeding the bounds of their calling; and according to your office, grauely and with authoritie redact them in order againe.

To conclude then,[73] both this purpose of conscience, and the first part of this booke, keepe God more sparingly in your mouth, but abundantly in your heart; be precise in effect, but sociall in shew: kythe more by your deeds then by your wordes, the loue of vertue and hatred of vice: and delight more to be godly and vertuous indeed, then to be thought and called so; expecting more for your praise and reward in heauen, then heere: and apply to all your outward actions Christs command, to pray and giue your almes secretly: So shal ye on the one part be inwardly garnished with trew Christian humilitie, not outwardly (with the proud Pharisie) glorying in your godlinesse; but saying, as Christ commandeth vs all, when we haue done all that we can, *Inutiles serui sumus*:[74] And on the other part, yee shall eschew outwardly before the world, the suspition of filthie proude hypocrisie, and deceitfull dissimulation.

OF A KINGS DVETIE IN HIS OFFICE.
THE SECOND BOOKE.

BVT as ye are clothed with two callings, so must ye be alike carefull for the discharge of them both: that as yee are a good Christian, so yee may be a good King, discharging your Office (as I shewed before) in the points of Iustice and Equitie:[75] which in two sundrie waies ye must doe: the one, in establishing and executing,[76] (which is the life of the Law) good Lawes among your people:[77] the other, by your behauiour in your owne person, and with your seruants, to teach your people by your example: for people are naturally inclined to counterfaite (like apes) their Princes maners, according to the notable saying of *Plato*,[78] expressed by the Poet ——

Componitur orbis
Regis ad exemplum, nec sic inflectere sensus
Humanos edicta valent, quam vita regentis.[79]

For the part of making, and executing of Lawes, consider first the trew difference betwixt a lawfull good King, and an vsurping Tyran, and yee shall the more easily vnderstand your duetie herein:[80] for *contraria iuxta se posita magis elucescunt.*[81] The one acknowledgeth himselfe ordained for his people, hauing receiued from God a burthen of gouernment,[82] whereof he must be countable: the other thinketh his people ordeined for him,[83] a prey to his passions and inordinate appetites, as the fruites of his magnanimitie: And therefore, as their ends are directly contrarie, so are their whole actions, as meanes, whereby they preasse to attaine to their endes. A good King, thinking his highest honour to consist in the due discharge of his calling, emploieth all his studie and paines, to procure and maintaine, by the making and execution of good Lawes,[84] the well-fare and peace of his people; and as their naturall father and kindly Master,[85] thinketh his greatest contentment standeth in their prosperitie, and his greatest suretie in hauing their hearts, subiecting his owne priuate affections and appetites to the weale and standing of his Subiects, euer thinking the common interesse his chiefest particular: where by the contrarie, an vsurping Tyran, thinking his greatest honour and felicitie to consist in attaining *per fas, vel nefas*[86] to his ambitious pretences, thinketh[87] neuer himselfe sure, but by the dissention and factions among his people, and counterfaiting the Saint while he once creepe in credite, will then (by inuerting all good Lawes to serue onely for his vnrulie priuate affections) frame the common-weale euer to aduance his particular: building his suretie vpon his peoples miserie: and in the end (as a step-father and an vncouth hireling) make vp his owne hand vpon the ruines of the Republicke. And according to their actions, so receiue they their reward: For a good King[88] (after a happie and famous reigne) dieth in peace, lamented by his subiects, and admired by his neighbours; and leauing a reuerent renowne behinde him in earth, obtaineth the Crowne of eternall felicitie in heauen.[89] And although some of them (which falleth out very rarelie) may be cut off by the treason of some vnnaturall subiects, yet liueth their fame after them, and some notable plague faileth neuer to ouer-take the committers in this life, besides their infamie to all posterities hereafter: Where by the contrarie, a Tyrannes[90] miserable and infam-ous life,[91] armeth in end his owne Subiects to become his burreaux: and[92] although that rebellion be euer vnlawfull on their part, yet is the world so wearied of him, that his fall is little meaned by the rest of his Subiects, and but smiled at by his neighbours. And besides the infamous memorie he leaueth behind him here, and the endlesse paine hee sustaineth hereafter, it oft falleth out, that the committers not onely escape vnpunished, but farther, the fact will remaine as allowed by the Law in diuers aages thereafter. It is easie then for you (my Sonne) to make a choise of one of these two sorts of rulers, by following the way of vertue to establish your standing; yea, incase ye fell in the high way, yet should it be with the honourable report, and iust regrate of all honest men.

And therefore to returne to my purpose anent the gouernement of your Subiects, by making and putting good Lawes to execution;[93] I remit the making of them to your owne discretion, as ye shall finde the necessitie of new-rising corruptions to require them: for, *ex malis moribus bonæ leges natæ sunt*:[94] besides, that in this countrey, wee haue alreadie moe good Lawes then are well execute, and am onely to insist in your forme of gouernment anent their execution. Onely remember, that as Parliaments haue bene ordained for making of Lawes, so ye abuse not their institution, in holding them for any mens particulars: For as a Parliament[95] is the honourablest and highest iudgement in the land (as being the Kings head Court) if it be well vsed, which is by making of good Lawes in it; so is it the in-iustest Iudgement-seat that may be,[96] being abused to mens particulars: irre-uocable decreits against particular parties, being giuen therein vnder colour of generall Lawes, and oft-times th'Estates not knowing them-selues whom thereby they hurt. And therefore hold no Parliaments, but for necessitie of new Lawes, which would be but seldome: for few Lawes and well put in execution, are best in a well ruled common-weale. As for the matter of fore-faltures, which also are done in Parliament, it is not good tigging with these things; but my aduice is,[97] ye fore-fault none but for such odious crimes as may make them vnworthie euer to be restored againe: And for smaller offences, ye haue other penalties sharpe enough to be vsed against them.

And as for the execution of good Lawes,[98] whereat I left, remember that among the differences that I put betwixt the formes of the gouernment of a good King, and an vsurping Tyran; I shew how a Tyran would enter like a Saint while he found himselfe fast vnder-foot, and then would suffer his vnrulie affections to burst foorth. Therefore be yee contrare at your first entrie to your Kingdome,[99] to that *Quinquennium Neronis*,[100] with his tender hearted wish, *Vellem nescirem literas*,[101] in giuing the Law full execution[102] against all breakers thereof but exception. For since ye come not to your reigne *precario*,[103] nor by conquest, but by right and due discent; feare no vproares for doing of iustice,[104] since ye may assure your selfe, the most part of your people will euer naturally fauour Iustice:[105] prouiding alwaies, that ye doe it onely for loue to Iustice, and not for satisfying any particular passions of yours, vnder colour thereof: otherwise, how iustly that euer the offender deserue it, ye are guiltie of murther before God: For ye must consider, that God euer looketh to your inward intention in all your actions.

And when yee haue by the seueritie of Iustice once setled your countries, and made them know that ye can strike, then may ye thereafter all the daies of your life mixe Iustice with Mercie,[106] punishing or sparing, as ye shall finde the crime to haue bene wilfully or rashly committed,[107] and according to the by-past behauiour of the committer. For if otherwise ye kyth your clemencie at the first, the offences would soone come to such heapes, and the contempt of you grow so great, that when ye would fall to punish, the number of them to be punished, would exceed the innocent; and yee would be troubled to resolue whom-at to begin: and against your nature would be compelled then to wracke many, whom the chastisement of few in the beginning might haue preserued. But in this, my ouer-deare bought experience may serue you for a sufficient lesson:[108] For I confesse, where I thought (by being gracious at the beginning) to win all mens hearts to a louing and willing obedience, I by the contrary found, the disorder of the countrie, and the losse of my thankes to be all my reward.

But as this seuere Iustice of yours vpon all offences would bee but for a time, (as I haue alreadie said) so is there some horrible crimes that yee are bound in conscience neuer to forgiue:[109] such as Witch-craft, wilfull murther, Incest, (especially within the degrees of consanguinitie) Sodomie, poisoning, and false coine. As for offences against your owne person and authoritie,[110] since the fault concerneth your selfe, I remit to your owne choise to punish or pardon therein, as your heart serueth you, and according to the circumstances of the turne, and the qualitie of the committer.

Here would I also eike another crime to bee vnpardonable, if I should not be thought partiall: but the fatherly loue I beare you, will make mee breake the bounds of shame in opening it vnto you. It is then,[111] the false and vnreuerent writing or speaking of malicious men against your Parents and Predecessors: ye know the command in Gods lawe, *Honour your Father and Mother*:[112] and consequently, sen ye are the lawful magistrate, suffer not both your Princes and your Parents to be dishonoured by any; especially, sith the example also toucheth your selfe, in leauing thereby to your successors,[113] the measure of that which they shal mete out againe to you in your like behalfe. I graunt wee haue all our faults, which, priuately betwixt you and God, should serue you for examples to meditate vpon, and mend in your person; but should not be a matter of discourse to others whatsoeuer. And sith ye are come of as honourable Predecessours as any Prince liuing, represse the insolence of such, as vnder pretence to taxe a vice in the person, seeke craftily to staine the race, and to steale the affection of the people from their posteritie: For how can they loue you, that hated them whom-of ye are come? Wherefore destroy men innocent young sucking Woluès and Foxes, but for the hatred they beare to their race? and why wil a coult of a Courser of Naples, giue a greater price in a market, then an Asse-colt, but for loue of the race? It is therefore a thing monstrous, to see a man loue the childe, and hate the Parents: as on the other part, the infaming and making odious of the parent, is the readiest way to bring the sonne in contempt. And for conclusion of this point, I may also alledge my owne experience: For besides the iudgments of God, that with my eyes I haue seene fall vpon all them that were chiefe traitours to my parents, I may iustly affirme, I neuer found yet a constant biding by me in all my straites, by any that were of perfite aage in my parents dayes, but onely by such as constantly bode by them; I meane specially by them that serued the Queene my mother: for so that I discharge my conscience to you, my Sonne, in reuealing to you the trewth, I care not, what any traitour or treason-allower thinke of it.

And although the crime of oppression be not in this ranke of vnpardonable crimes,[114] yet the ouer-common vse of it in this nation, as if it were a vertue, especially by the greatest ranke of subiects in the land, requireth the King to be a sharpe censurer thereof. Be diligent therefore to trie, and awfull to beate downe the hornes of proud oppressours:[115] embrace the quarrell of the poore and distressed, as your owne particular, thinking it your greatest honour to represse the oppressours: care for the pleasure of none, neither spare ye anie paines in your owne person,[116] to see their wrongs redressed: and remember of the honourable stile giuen to my grand-father of worthie memorie,[117] in being called *the poore mans King*.[118] And as the most part of a Kings office, standeth in deciding that question of *Meum* and *Tuum*,[119] among his subiects; so remember when ye sit in iudgement, that the Throne ye sit on is Gods,[120] as *Moyses* saith, and sway neither to the right hand nor to the left; either louing the rich, or pittying the poore. Iustice should be blinde and friendlesse: it[121] is not there ye should reward your friends, or seeke to crosse your enemies.

Here now speaking of oppressours and of iustice, the purpose leadeth me to speake of Hie-land and Border oppressions. As for the Hie-lands,[122] I shortly comprehend them all in two sorts of people: the one, that dwelleth in our maine land, that are barbarous for the most part, and yet mixed with some shewe of ciuilitie: the other, that dwelleth in the Iles, and are alluterly barbares, without any sort or shew of ciuilitie. For the first sort, put straitly to execution the Lawes made alreadie by me against their Ouer-lords, and the chiefes of their Clannes, and it will be no difficultie to danton them. As for the other sort, follow forth the course that I haue intended, in planting Colonies among them of answerable In-lands subiects, that within short time may reforme and ciuilize the best inclined among them; rooting out or transporting the barbarous and stubborne sort, and planting ciuilitie in their roomes.

But as for the Borders,[123] because I know, if ye enioy not this whole Ile, according to Gods right and your lineall discent, yee will neuer get leaue to brooke this North and barrennest part thereof; no, not your owne head whereon the Crowne should stand; I neede not in that case trouble you with them: for then they will be the middest of the Ile, and so as easily ruled as any part thereof.

And that yee may the readier with wisedome and Iustice gouerne your subiects,[124] by knowing what vices they are naturallie most inclined to, as a good Physician, who must first know what peccant humours his Patient naturallie is most subiect vnto,[125] before he can begin his cure: I shall therefore shortly note vnto you, the principall faults that euery ranke of the people of this countrey is most affected vnto. And as for *England*, I will not speake be-gesse of them, neuer hauing been among them, although I hope in that God, who euer fauoureth the right, before I die, to be as well acquainted with their fashions.

As the whole Subiects of our countrey (by the ancient and fundamentall policie of our Kingdome) are diuided into three estates,[126] so is euerie estate hereof generally subiect to some speciall vices; which in a maner by long habitude, are thought rather vertue then vice among them; not that euerie particular man in any of these rankes of men, is subiect vnto them, for there is good and euill of all sorts; but that I meane, I haue found by experience, these vices to haue taken greatest holde with these rankes of men.

And first, that I prejudge not the Church of her ancient priuiledges, reason would shee should haue the first place for orders sake, in this catalogue.

The naturall sickenesse that hath euer troubled, and beene the decay of all the Churches,[127] since the beginning of the world, changing the candlesticke from one to another, as *Iohn* saith,[128] hath beene Pride, Ambition, and Auarice: and now last, these same infirmities wrought the ouerthrow of the Popish Church, in this countrey and diuers others. But the reformation of Religion in *Scotland*, being extraordinarily wrought by God, wherin many things were inordinately done by a popular tumult and rebellion,[129] of such as blindly were doing the worke of God, but clogged with their owne passions and particular respects, as well appeared by the destruction of our policie, and not proceeding from the Princes order, as it did in our neighbour countrey of *England*, as likewise in *Denmarke*, and sundry parts of *Germanie*; some fierie spirited men in the ministerie, got such a guiding of the people at that time of confusion, as finding the gust of gouernment sweete, they begouth to fantasie to themselues a Democraticke forme of gouernment: and hauing (by the iniquitie of time) beene ouerwell baited vpon the wracke, first of my Grand-mother,[130] and next of mine owne mother, and after vsurping the libertie of the time in my long minoritie, setled themselues so fast vpon that imagined Democracie,[131] as they fed themselues with the hope to become *Tribuni plebis*:[132] and so in a popular gouernment by leading the people by the nose, to beare the sway of all the rule. And for this cause, there neuer rose faction in the time of my minoritie, nor trouble sen-syne, but they that were vpon that factious part,[133] were euer carefull to perswade and allure these vnruly spirits among the ministerie, to spouse that quarrell as their owne: where-through I was ofttimes calumniated in their populare Sermons, not for any euill or vice in me, but because I was a King, which they thought the highest euill. And because they were ashamed to professe this quarrel, they were busie to look narrowly in all my actions; and I warrant you a mote in my eye, yea a false report, was matter enough for them to worke vpon: and yet for all their cunning, whereby they pretended to distinguish the lawfulnesse of the office, from the vice of the person, some of them would sometimes snapper out well gros-sely with the trewth of their intentions, informing the people, that all Kings and Princes were naturally enemies to the libertie of the Church, and could neuer patiently beare the yoke of Christ:[134] with such sound doctrine fed they their flockes. And because the learned, graue, and honest men of the ministerie, were euer ashamed and offended with their temeritie and presumption, preassing by all good meanes by their authoritie and example, to reduce them to a greater moderation; there could be no way found out so meete in their con-ceit, that were turbulent spirits among them, for maintaining their plots, as paritie in the Church: whereby the ignorants were embold-ened (as bairdes) to crie the learned, godly, and modest out of it:[135] paritie the mother of confusion, and enemie to Vnitie, which is the mother of order: For if by the example thereof, once established in the Ecclesiasticall gouernment, the Politicke and ciuill estate should be drawen to the like, the great confusion that thereupon would arise may easily be discerned. Take heede therefore (my Sonne) to such Puritanes, verie pestes in the Church and Common-weale, whom no deserts can oblige, neither oathes or promises binde, breathing nothing but sedition and calumnies,[136] aspiring without measure, railing without reason, and making their owne imaginations (without any warrant of the word) the square of their conscience. I protest before the great God, and since I am here as vpon my Testament, it is no place for me to lie in, that ye shall neuer finde with any Hie-land or Border-theeues greater ingratitude, and moe lies and vile periuries, then with these phanaticke spirits: And suffer not the principals of them to brooke your land, if ye like to sit at rest; except yee would keepe them from trying your patience, as *Socrates* did an euill wife.[137]

And for preseruatiue against their poison,[138] entertaine and aduance the godly, learned and modest men of the ministerie, whom-of (God be praised) there lacketh not a sufficient number: and by their prouision to Bishoprickes and Benefices (annulling that vile acte of Annexation,[139] if ye finde it not done to your hand) yee shall not onely banish their conceited paritie, whereof I haue spoken, and their other imaginarie grounds; which[140] can neither stand with the order of the Church, nor the peace of a Commonweale and well ruled Monarchie: but ye shall also re-establish the olde institution of three Estates in Parliament, which can no otherwise be done: But in this I hope (if God spare me dayes) to make you a faire entrie, always where I leaue, follow ye my steps.

And to end my aduice anent the Church estate,[141] cherish no man more then a good Pastor, hate no man more then a proude Puritane; thinking it one of your fairest styles, to be called a louing nourish-father to the Church, seeing all the Churches within your dominions planted with good Pastors, the Schooles (the seminarie of the Church) maintained, the doctrine and discipline preserued in puritie, according to Gods word, a sufficient prouision for their sustentation, a comely order in their policie, pride punished, humilitie aduanced, and they so to reuerence their superiours, and their flockes them, as the flourishing of your Church in pietie, peace, and learning, may be one of the chiefe points of your earthly glory, being euer alike ware with both the extremities; as well as yee represse the vaine Puritane, so not to suffer proude Papall Bishops: but as some for their qualities will deserue to bee preferred before others, so chaine them with such bondes as may preserue that estate from creeping to corruption.

The next estate now that by order commeth in purpose, according to their rankes in Parliament, is the Nobilitie,[142] although second in ranke, yet ouer farre first in greatnesse and power, either to doe good or euill, as they are inclined.

The naturall sickenesse that I haue perceiued this estate subiect to in my time, hath beene, a fectlesse arrogant conceit of their greatnes and power; drinking in with their very nourish-milke, that their honor stood in committing three points of iniquitie: to thrall by oppression, the meaner sort that dwelleth neere them, to their seruice and following, although they holde nothing of them: to maintaine their seruants and dependers in any wrong, although they be not answerable to the lawes (for any body will maintaine his man in a right cause) and for anie displeasure, that they apprehend to be done vnto them by their neighbour, to take vp a plaine feide against him; and (without respect to God, King, or common-weale) to bang it out brauely, hee and all his kinne, against him and all his: yea they will thinke the King farre in their common,[143] in-case they agree to grant an assurance to a short day, for keeping of the peace: where, by their naturall dewtie, they are oblished to obey the lawe, and keepe the peace all the daies of their life, vpon the perill of their verie craigges.

For remeid to these euils in their estate,[144] teach your Nobilitie to keepe your lawes as precisely as the meanest: feare[145] not their orping or beeing discontented, as long as yee rule well; for their pretended reformation of Princes taketh neuer effect, but where euill gouerne-ment precedeth. Acquaint your selfe so with all the honest men of your Barrons and Gentlemen,[146] and be in your giuing accesse so open and affable to euery ranke of honest persons, as may make them peart without scarring at you, to make their owne suites to you themselues, and not to employ the great Lordes their intercessours; for intercession to Saints is Papistrie: so shall ye bring to a measure their monstrous backes. And for their barbarous feides, put the lawes to due execution made by mee there-anent; beginning euer rathest at him that yee loue best, and is most oblished vnto you; to make him an example to the rest. For yee shall make all your reformations to beginne at your elbow, and so by degrees to flow to the extremities of the land. And rest not, vntill yee roote out these barbarous feides; that their effects may bee as well smoared downe, as their barbarous name is vnknowen to anie other nation: For if this Treatise were written either in French or Latine, I could not get them named vnto you but by circumlocution. And for your easier abolishing of them, put sharpelie to execution my lawes made against Gunnes and traiterous Pistolets; thinking in your heart, tearming in your speech, and vsing by your punishments, all such as weare and vse them, as brigands and cut-throates.

On the other part, eschew the other extremitie, in lightlying and contemning your Nobilitie. Remember howe that errour brake the King my grand-fathers[147] heart. But consider that vertue followeth oftest noble blood:[148] the worthinesse of their antecessors craueth a reuerent regard to be had vnto them: honour them therfore that are obedient to the law among them, as Peeres and Fathers of your land: the more frequently that your Court can bee garnished with them,[149] thinke it the more your honour; acquainting and employing them in all your greatest affaires; sen it is, they must be your armes and executers of your lawes: and so vse your selfe louinglie to the obedient, and rigorously to the stubborne, as may make the greatest of them to thinke, that the chiefest point of their honour, standeth in striuing with the meanest of the land in humilitie towards you, and obedience to your Lawes: beating euer in their eares, that one of the principall points of seruice that ye craue of them, is, in their persons to practise, and by their power to procure due obedience to the Law, without the which, no seruice they can make, can be agreeable vnto you.

But the greatest hinderance to the execution of our Lawes in this countrie, are these heritable Shirefdomes and Regalities,[150] which being in the hands of the great men, do wracke the whole countrie: For which I know no present remedie, but by taking the sharper account of them in their Offices; vsing all punishment against the slouthfull, that the Law will permit: and[151] euer as they vaike, for any offences committed by them, dispone them neuer heritably againe: preassing, with time, to draw it to the laudable custome of England:[152] which ye may the easilier doe, being King of both, as I hope in God ye shall.

And as to the third and last estate,[153] which is our Burghes (for the small Barrones are but an inferiour part of the Nobilitie and of their estate) they are composed of two sorts of men; Merchants and Craftes-men: either of these sorts being subiect to their owne infirmities.

The Merchants thinke the whole common-weale ordeined for making them vp;[154] and accounting it their lawfull gaine and trade, to enrich themselues vpon the losse of all the rest of the people, they transport from vs things necessarie; bringing backe sometimes vnnecessary things, and at other times nothing at all. They buy for vs the worst wares, and sell them at the dearest prices: and albeit the victuals fall or rise of their prices, according to the aboundance or skantnesse thereof; yet the prices of their wares euer rise, but neuer fall: being as constant in that their euill custome, as if it were a setled Law for them. They are also the speciall cause of the corruption of the coyne, transporting all our owne, and bringing in forraine, vpon what price they please to set on it: For order putting to them, put the good Lawes in execution that are already made anent these abuses; but especially doe three things: Establish honest, diligent, but few Searchers, for many hands make slight worke; and haue an honest and diligent Thesaurer to take count of them: Permit and allure forraine Merchants to trade here:[155] so shall ye haue best and best cheape wares, not buying them at the third hand: And set euery yeere downe a certaine price of all things; considering first, how it is in other countries: and the price being set reasonably downe, if the Merchants will not bring them home on the price, cry forrainers free to bring them.

And because I haue made mention here of the coyne,[156] make your money of fine Gold and Siluer; causing the people be payed with substance, and not abused with number: so shall ye enrich the common-weale, and haue a great treasure laid vp in store, if ye fall in warres or in any straites: For the making it baser, will breed your commoditie; but it is not to bee vsed, but at a great necessitie.

And the Craftes-men thinke,[157] we should be content with their worke, how bad and deare soeuer it be:[158] and if they in any thing be controlled, vp goeth the blew-blanket: But for their part, take example by ENGLAND,[159] how it hath flourished both in wealth and policie, since the strangers Craftes-men came in among them: Therefore[160] not onely permit, but allure strangers to come heere also; taking as strait order for repressing the mutining of ours at them, as was done in ENGLAND, at their first in-bringing there.

But vnto one fault is all the common people of this Kingdome subiect,[161] as well burgh as land; which is, to iudge and speake rashly of their Prince, setting the Common-weale vpon foure props, as wee call it; euer[162] wearying of the present estate, and desirous of nouelties. For remedie whereof (besides the execution of Lawes that are to be vsed against vnreuerent speakers) I know no better meane, then so to rule, as may iustly stop their mouthes from all such idle and vnreuerent speeches; and so to prop the weale of your people, with prouident care for their good gouernment, that iustly, *Momus* himselfe may haue no ground to grudge at: and yet so to temper and mixe your seueritie with mildnes, that as the vniust railers may be restrained with a reuerent awe; so the good and louing Subiects, may not onely liue in suretie and wealth, but be stirred vp and inuited by your benigne courtesies, to open their mouthes in the iust praise of your so well moderated regiment. In respect whereof,[163] and therewith also the more to allure them to a common amitie among themselues, certaine dayes in the yeere would be appointed, for delighting the people with publicke spectacles of all honest games, and exercise of armes: as also for conueening of neighbours, for entertaining friendship and heartlinesse, by honest feasting and merrinesse: For I cannot see what greater superstition can be in making playes and lawfull games in Maie, and good cheere at Christmas, then in eating fish in Lent, and vpon Fridayes, the Papists as well vsing the one as the other: so that alwayes the Sabboths be kept holy, and no vnlawfull pastime be vsed: And as this forme of contenting the peoples mindes, hath beene vsed in all well gouerned Republicks: so will it make you to performe in your gouernment that olde good sentence,

Omne tulit punctum, qui miscuit vtile dulci.[164]

Ye see now (my Sonne) how for the zeale I beare to acquaint you with the plaine and single veritie of all things, I haue not spared to be something Satyricke, in touching well quickly the faults in all the estates of my kingdome: But I protest before God, I doe it with the fatherly loue that I owe to them all; onely hating their vices, whereof there is a good number of honest men free in euery estate.

And because, for the better reformation of all these abuses among your estates, it will be a great helpe vnto you, to be well acquainted with the nature and humours of all your Subiects, and to know particularly the estate of euery part of your dominions; I[165] would therefore counsell you, once in the yeere to visite the principall parts of the countrey,[166] ye shal be in for the time: and because I hope ye shall be King of moe countries then this; once in the three yeeres to visite all your Kingdomes; not lipening to Vice-royes, but hearing your selfe their complaints; and hauing ordinarie Councels and iustice-seates in euerie Kingdome, of their owne countriemen: and the principall matters euer to be decided by your selfe when ye come in those parts.

Ye haue also to consider, that yee must not onely bee carefull to keepe your subiects, from receiuing anie wrong of others within; but[167] also yee must be careful to keepe them from the wrong of any forraine Prince without:[168] sen the sword[169] is giuen you by God not onely to reuenge vpon your owne subiects, the wrongs committed amongst themselues; but further, to reuenge and free them of forraine iniuries done vnto them: And therefore warres vpon iust quarrels are lawful: but aboue all, let not the wrong cause be on your side.

Vse all other Princes, as your brethren, honestly and kindely:[170] Keepe precisely your promise vnto them, although to your hurt: Striue with euerie one of them in courtesie and thankefulnesse: and as with all men,[171] so especially with them, bee plaine and trewthfull; keeping euer that Christian rule, *to doe as yee would be done to*: especially in counting rebellion against any other Prince, a crime against your owne selfe, because of the preparatiue. Supplie not therefore, nor trust not other Princes rebels; but pittie and succour all lawfull Princes in their troubles. But if any of them will not abstaine,[172] notwithstanding what-soeuer your good deserts, to wrong you or your subiects, craue[173] redresse at leasure; heare and doe all reason: and if no offer that is lawfull or honourable, can make him to abstaine, nor repaire his wrong doing; then for last refuge, commit the iustnesse of your cause to God,[174] giuing first honestly vp with him, and in a publicke and honourable forme.

But omitting now to teach you the forme of making warres,[175] because that arte is largely treated of by many, and is better learned by practise then speculation;[176] I will onely set downe to you heere a few precepts therein. Let first the iustnesse of your cause be your greatest strength;[177] and then omitte not to vse all lawfull meanes for backing of the same. Consult therefore with no Necromancier nor false Prophet, vpon the successe of your warres, remembring on king *Saules*[178] miserable end: but keepe your land cleane of all South-sayers, according to the commaund in the Law of God,[179] dilated by *Ieremie*.[180] Neither commit your quarrell to bee tried by a Duell: for beside that generally all Duell appeareth to bee vnlawful, committing the quarrell, as it were, to a lot; whereof there is no warrant in the Scripture, since the abrogating of the olde Lawe: it is specially moste vn-lawfull in the person of a King; who[181] being a publicke person hath no power therefore to dispose of himselfe, in respect, that to his preseruation or fall, the safetie or wracke of the whole common-weale is necessarily coupled, as the body is to the head.

Before ye take on warre, play the wise Kings part described by Christ; fore-seeing how ye may beare it out with all necessarie proui-sion:[182] especially remember,[183] that money is *Neruus belli*.[184] Choose old experimented Captaines, and yong able souldiers. Be extreamely strait and seuere in martiall Discipline,[185] as well for keeping of order, which is as requisite as hardinesse in the warres, and punishing of slouth,[186] which at a time may put the whole armie in hazard;[187] as likewise for repressing of mutinies, which in warres are wonderfull dangerous.[188] And looke to the *Spaniard*, whose great successe in all his warres, hath onely come through straitnesse of Discipline and order: for such errours may be committed in the warres, as cannot be gotten mended againe.

Be in your owne person walkrife, diligent, and painefull;[189] vsing the aduice of such as are skilfullest in the craft, as ye must also doe in all other. Be homely with your souldiers as your companions, for winning their hearts;[190] and extreamly liberall, for then is no time of sparing. Be cold and foreseeing in deuising,[191] constant in your resolutions, and forward and quicke in your executions. Fortifie well your Campe,[192] and assaile not rashly without an aduantage: neither feare not lightly your enemie. Be curious in deuising stratagems,[193] but alwayes honestly: for of any thing they worke greatest effects in the warres, if secrecie be ioyned to inuention. And once or twise in your owne person hazard your selfe fairely;[194] but, hauing acquired so the fame of courage and magnanimitie, make not a daily souldier of your selfe, exposing rashly your person to euery perill: but conserue your selfe thereafter for the weale of your people, for whose sake yee must more care for your selfe, then for your owne.

And as I haue counselled you to be slow in taking on a warre, so[195] aduise I you to be slow in peace-making.[196] Before ye agree, looke that the ground of your warres be satisfied in your peace; and that ye see a good suretie for you and your people:[197] otherwaies a honour-able and iust warre is more tollerable, then a dishonourable and dis-aduantageous peace.

But it is not enough to a good King, by the scepter of good Lawes well execute to gouerne, and by force of armes to protect his people; if he ioyne not therewith his vertuous life in his owne person, and in the person of his Court and company; by good example alluring his Subiects to the loue of vertue, and hatred of vice. And therefore (my Sonne) sith all people are naturally inclined to follow their Princes example[198] (as I shewed you before) let it not be said,[199] that ye command others to keepe the contrary course to that, which in your owne person ye practise, making so your wordes and deedes to fight together: but by the contrary, let your owne life be a law-booke and a mirrour to your people; that therein they may read the practise of their owne Lawes; and therein they may see, by your image, what life they should leade.

And this example in your owne life and person, I likewise diuide in two parts: The first, in the gouernment of your Court and followers, in all godlinesse and vertue: the next, in hauing your owne minde decked and enriched so with all vertuous qualities, that therewith yee may worthily rule your people: For it is not ynough that ye haue and retaine (as prisoners) within your selfe neuer so many good qualities and vertues,[200] except ye employ them, and set them on worke,[201] for the weale of them that are committed to your charge: *Virtutis enim laus omnis in actione consistit.*[202]

First then, as to the gouernment of your Court and followers,[203] King *Dauid* sets downe the best precepts, that any wise and Christian King can practise in that point:[204] For as yee ought to haue a great care for the ruling well of all your Subiects, so ought yee to haue a double care for the ruling well of your owne seruants; since vnto them yee are both a Politicke and Oeconomicke gouernour. And as euery one of the people will delite to follow the example of any of the Courteours, as well in euill as in good;[205] so what crime so horrible can there be committed and ouer-seene in a Courteour, that will not be an exemplare excuse for any other boldly to commit the like? And therfore in two points haue ye to take good heed anent your Court and houshold: first, in choosing them wisely; next, in carefully ruling them whom ye haue chosen.

It is an olde and trew saying, That a kindly Auer will neuer become a good horse: for[206] albeit good education and company be great helpes to Nature, and education be therefore most iustly called *altera natura*,[207] yet is it euill to get out of the flesh,[208] that is bred in the bone, as the olde prouerbe sayth. Be very ware then in making choice of your seruants and companie; —— *Nam*

Turpius eiicitur, quam non admittitur hospes:[209]

and many respects may lawfully let an admission, that will not be sufficient causes of depriuation.

All your seruants and Court must be composed partly of minors,[210] such as young Lords, to be brought vp in your company, or Pages and such like; and partly of men of perfit aage, for seruing you in such roumes, as ought to be filled with men of wisedome and discretion. For the first sort, ye can doe no more, but choose them within aage, that are come of a good and vertuous kinde,[211] *In fide parentum*,[212] as Baptisme is vsed: For though *anima non venit ex traduce*,[213] but is immediatly created by God,[214] and infused from aboue; yet it is most certaine, that vertue or vice will oftentimes, with the heritage, be transferred from the parents to the posteritie,[215] and runne on a blood (as the Prouerbe is) the sickenesse of the minde becomming as kindly to some races, as these sickenesses of the body, that infect in the seede: Especially[216] choose such minors as are come of a trew and honest race, and haue not had the house whereof they are descended, infected with falshood.

And as for the other sort of your companie and seruants, that ought to be of perfit aage; first see that they be of a good fame and without blemish;[217] otherwise, what can the people thinke, but that yee haue chosen a company vnto you, according to your owne humour, and so haue preferred these men, for the loue of their vices and crimes, that ye knew them to be guiltie of? For the people that see you not within, cannot iudge of you,[218] but according to the outward appearance of your actions and companie, which onely is subiect to their sight: And next, see that they be indued with such honest qualities, as are meete for such offices,[219] as ye ordaine them to serue in; that your iudgement may be knowen in imploying euery man according to his giftes: And shortly, follow good king *Dauids* counsell in the choise of your seruants,[220] by setting your eyes vpon the faithfull and vpright of the land to dwell with you.

But here I must not forget to remember, and according to my fatherly authoritie,[221] to charge you to preferre specially to your seruice, so many as haue trewly serued me, and are able for it: the rest, honourably to reward them, preferring their posteritie before others, as kindliest: so shall ye not onely be best serued, (for if the haters of

your parents cannot loue you, as I shewed before, it followeth of
necessitie their louers must loue you) but further, ye shall kyth your
thankefull memorie of your father, and procure the blessing of these
olde seruants, in not missing their olde master in you; which otherwise would be turned in a prayer for me, and a curse for you. Vse
them therefore when God shall call me, as the testimonies of your
affection towards me; trusting and aduancing those farthest, whom I
found faithfullest: which ye must not discerne by their rewards at my
hand (for rewards, as they are called *Bona fortunæ*,[222] so are they
subiect vnto fortune) but according to the trust I gaue them; hauing
oft-times had better heart then hap to the rewarding of sundry; And
on the other part, as I wish you to kyth your constant loue towards
them that I loued, so desire I you to kyth in the same measure, your
constant hatred to them that I hated: I meane, bring not home, nor
restore not such, as ye finde standing banished or fore-faulted by
me. The contrary would kyth in you ouer great a contempt of me,
and lightnesse in your owne nature: for how can they be trew to the
Sonne, that were false to the Father?

But to returne to the purpose anent the choise of your seruants,
yee shall by this wise forme of doing, eschew the inconuenients, that
in my minoritie I fell in, anent the choise of my seruants: For by them
that had the command where I was brought vp, were my seruants put
vnto mee; not choosing them that were meetest to serue me, but
whom they thought meetest to serue their turne about me,[223] as
kythed well in many of them at the first rebellion raised against
mee,[224] which compelled mee to make a great alteration among my
seruants. And yet the example of that corruption made mee to be long
troubled there-after with solliciters, recommending seruants vnto me,
more for seruing in effect, their friends that put them in, then their
master that admitted them. Let my example then teach you to follow
the rules here set downe, choosing your seruants for your owne vse,
and not for the vse of others;[225] And since ye must bee *communis
parens*[226] to all your people, so choose your seruants indifferently out
of all quarters; not respecting other mens appetites, but their owne
qualities: For as ye must command all, so reason would, ye should
be serued out of al, as ye please to make choice.

But specially take good heed to the choice of your seruants, that
ye preferre to the offices of the Crowne and estate:[227] for in other
offices yee haue onely to take heede to your owne weale;[228] but these

concerne likewise the weale of your people, for the which yee must bee answerable to God. Choose then for all these Offices, men of knowen wisedome, honestie, and good conscience;[229] well practised in the points of the craft, that yee ordaine them for, and free of all factions and partialities; but specially free of that filthie vice of Flatterie, the pest of all Princes, and wracke of Republicks: For[230] since in the first part of this Treatise, I fore-warned you to be at warre with your owne inward flatterer φιλαυτία, how much more should ye be at war with outward flatterers, who are nothing so sib to you, as your selfe is; by the selling of such counterfeit wares, onely preassing to ground their greatnesse vpon your ruines? And therefore bee carefull to preferre none, as yee will bee answerable to God but onely for their worthinesse: But[231] specially choose honest, diligent, meane, but responsall men, to bee your receiuers in money matters: meane I say, that ye may when yee please, take a sharpe account of their intromission, without perill of their breeding any trouble to your estate: for this ouersight hath beene the greatest cause of my misthriuing in money matters. Especially,[232] put neuer a forrainer, in any principall office of estate: for that will neuer faile to stirre vp sedition and enuie in the countrey-mens hearts, both against you and him: But[233] (as I saide before) if God prouide you with moe countries then this; choose the borne-men of euery countrey, to bee your chief counsellers therein.

And for conclusion of my aduice anent the choice of your seruants, delight to be serued with men of the noblest blood that may bee had:[234] for besides that their seruice shall breed you great good-will and least enuie, contrarie to that of start-vps; ye shall oft finde vertue follow noble races, as I haue said before speaking of the Nobilitie.

Now, as to the other point, anent your gouerning of your seruants when yee haue chosen them; make your Court[235] and companie to bee a patterne of godlinesse and all honest vertues,[236] to all the rest of the people. Bee a daily watch-man ouer your seruants,[237] that they obey your lawes precisely: For how can your lawes bee kept in the countrey, if they be broken at your eare? Punishing the breach thereof in a Courteour, more seuerely, then in the person of any other of your subiects: and aboue all, suffer none of them (by abusing their credite with you) to oppresse or wrong any of your subiects. Be homely or strange with them,[238] as ye thinke their behauiour deserueth, and their nature may beare with.[239] Thinke a quarrellous

man a pest in your companie. Bee carefull euer to preferre the gen-
tilest natured and trustiest, to the inwardest Offices about you,[240]
especially in your chalmer. Suffer none about you to meddle in any
mens particulars,[241] but like the Turkes Ianisaries, let them know no
father but you, nor particular but yours. And if any wil meddle in
their kinne or friends quarrels, giue them their leaue: for since ye
must be of no surname nor kinne, but equall to all honest men; it
becommeth you not to bee followed with partiall or factious seruants.
Teach obedience to your seruants,[242] and not to thinke themselues
ouer-wise: and, as when any of them deserueth it, ye must not spare
to put them away, so, without a seene cause, change none of them.
Pay them, as all others your subiects, with *præmium*[243] or *poena*[244] as
they deserue, which is the very ground-stone of good gouernement.[245]
Employ euery man as ye thinke him qualified, but vse not one in all
things, lest he waxe proude, and be enuied of his fellowes.[246] Loue
them best, that are plainnest with you, and disguise not the trewth
for all their kinne: suffer none to be euill tongued, nor backbiters of
them they hate: command a hartly and brotherly loue among all them
that serue you.[247] And shortly, maintaine peace in your Court,[248]
bannish enuie, cherish modestie, bannish deboshed insolence, foster
humilitie, and represse pride: setting downe such a comely and honourable order in all the points of your seruice; that when strangers
shall visite your Court, they may with the Queene of *Sheba*, admire
your wisedome in the glorie of your house;[249] and comely order
among your seruants.

But[250] the principall blessing that yee can get of good companie,
will stand in your marrying of a godly and vertuous wife: for shee
must bee nearer vnto you, then any other companie, being *Flesh
of your flesh, and bone of your bone,*[251] as *Adam* saide of *Heuah*.[252]
And because I know not but God may call me, before ye be
readie for Mariage; I will shortly set downe to you heere my
aduice therein.

First of all consider, that Mariage is the greatest earthly felicitie
or miserie, that can come to a man, according as it pleaseth God to
blesse or curse the same. Since then without the blessing of GOD,
yee cannot looke for a happie successe in Mariage, yee must bee
carefull both in your preparation for it,[253] and in the choice and vsage
of your wife, to procure the same. By your preparation, I meane, that
yee must keepe your bodie cleane and vnpolluted, till yee giue it to

your wife, whom-to onely it belongeth. For how can ye iustly craue to bee ioyned with a pure virgine, if your bodie be polluted? why should the one halfe bee cleane, and the other defiled? And although I know, fornication is thought but a light and veniall sinne, by the most part of the world, yet remember well what I said to you in my first Booke anent conscience; and count euery sinne and breach of Gods law, not according as the vaine world esteemeth of it, but as God the Iudge and maker of the lawe accounteth of the same. Heare God commanding by the mouth of *Paul*, to *abstaine from fornication*, declaring that the *fornicator shall not inherite the Kingdome of heauen*:[254] and by the mouth of *Iohn*, reckoning out fornication amongst other grieuous sinnes, that debarre the committers amongst *dogs and swine, from entry in that spirituall and heauenly Ierusalem*.[255] And consider, if a man shall once take vpon him, to count that light, which God calleth heauie; and veniall that, which God calleth grieuous; beginning first to measure any one sinne by the rule of his lust and appetites, and not of his conscience;[256] what shall let him to doe so with the next, that his affections shall stirre him to, the like reason seruing for all: and so to goe forward till he place his whole corrupted affections in Gods roome? And then what shall come of him; but, as a man giuen ouer to his owne filthy affections, shall perish into them? And because wee are all of that nature, that sibbest examples touch vs neerest, consider the difference of successe that God granted in the Mariages of the King my grand-father,[257] and me your owne father:[258] the reward of his incontinencie, (proceeding from his euill education) being the suddaine death at one time of two pleasant yong Princes; and a daughter onely borne to succeed to him, whom hee had neuer the hap, so much as once to see or blesse before his death: leauing a double curse behinde him to the land, both a Woman of sexe, and a new borne babe of aage to reigne ouer them. And as for the blessing God hath bestowed on mee, in granting me both a greater continen-cie, and the fruits following there-upon, your selfe, and sib folkes to you, are (praise be to God) sufficient witnesses: which, I hope the same God of his infinite mercie, shall continue and increase, without repentance to me and my posteritie. Be not ashamed then, to keepe cleane your body, which is the Temple of the holy Spirit,[259] notwith-standing all vaine allurements to the contrary, discerning trewly and wisely of euery vertue and vice, according to the trew qualities therof, and not according to the vaine conceits of men.

As for your choise in Mariage, respect chiefly the three causes, wherefore Mariage was first ordeined by God; and then ioyne three accessories, so farre as they may be obtained, not derogating to the principalles.

The three causes it was ordeined for,[260] are, for staying of lust, for procreation of children, and that man should by his Wife, get a helper like himselfe. Deferre not then to Marie till your aage:[261] for it is ordeined for quenching the lust of your youth: Especially a King must tymouslie Marie for the weale of his people. Neither Marie yee,[262] for any accessory cause or worldly respects, a woman vnable, either through aage, nature, or accident, for procreation of children: for in a King that were a double fault, aswell against his owne weale, as against the weale of his people. Neither also Marie one of knowne euill conditions, or vicious education: for the woman is ordeined to be a helper, and not a hinderer to man.

The three accessories,[263] which as I haue said, ought also to be respected, without derogating to the principall causes,[264] are beautie, riches, and friendship by alliance, which are all blessings of God. For beautie increaseth your loue to your Wife, contenting you the better with her, without caring for others: and riches and great alliance, doe both make her the abler to be a helper vnto you. But if ouer great respect being had to these accessories, the principall causes bee ouer-seene (which is ouer oft practised in the world) as of themselues they are a blessing being well vsed; so the abuse of them will turne them in a curse. For what can all these worldly respects auaile, when a man shall finde himselfe coupled with a diuel, to be one flesh with him, and the halfe marrow in his bed? Then (though too late) shall he finde that beautie without bountie, wealth without wisdome, and great friendship without grace and honestie; are but faire shewes, and the deceitfull masques of infinite miseries.

But haue ye respect, my Sonne, to these three speciall causes in your Mariage, which flow from the first institution thereof, *& cætera omnia adijcientur vobis*.[265] And[266] therefore I would rathest haue you to Marie one that were fully of your owne Religion; her ranke and other qualities being agreeable to your estate. For although that to my great regrate, the number of any Princes of power and account, professing our Religion, bee but very small; and that therefore this aduice seemes to be the more strait and difficile: yet ye haue deeply to weigh, and consider vpon these doubts, how ye and your wife can bee of one flesh, and keepe vnitie betwixt you, being members of two opposite Churches: disagreement in Religion bringeth euer with it, disagreement in maners; and the dissention betwixt your Preachers and hers, wil breed and foster a dissention among your subiects, taking their example from your family; besides the perill of the euill education of your children. Neither pride you that ye wil be able to frame and make her as ye please: that deceiued *Salomon* the wisest King that euer was; the grace of Perseuerance, not being a flowre that groweth in our garden.

Remember also that Mariage is one of the greatest actions that a man doeth in all his time, especially in taking of his first Wife: and if hee Marie first basely beneath his ranke, he will euer be the lesse accounted of thereafter. And[267] lastly, remember to choose your Wife as I aduised you to choose your seruants: that she be of a whole and cleane race, not subiect to the hereditary sicknesses, either of the soule or the body:[268] For if a man wil be careful to breed horses and dogs of good kinds, how much more careful should he be, for the breed of his owne loines?[269] So shal ye in your Mariage haue respect to your conscience, honour, and naturall weale in your successours.

When yee are Maried, keepe inuiolably your promise made to God in your Mariage; which standeth all in doing of one thing, and abstayning from another: to treat her in all things as your wife, and the halfe of your selfe; and to make your body (which then is no more yours, but properly hers) common with none other.[270] I trust I need not to insist here to disswade you from the filthy vice of adulterie: remember onely what solemne promise yee make to God at your Mariage: and since it is onely by the force of that promise that your children succeed to you, which otherwayes they could not doe; æquitie and reason would, ye should keepe your part thereof. God is euer a seuere auenger of all periuries; and it is no oath made in iest,[271] that giueth power to children to succeed to great kingdomes. Haue the King my grand-fathers[272] example before your eyes, who by his adulterie, bred the wracke of his lawfull daughter and heire; in begetting that bastard, who vnnaturally rebelled, and procured the ruine of his owne Souerane and sister. And what good her posteritie hath gotten sensyne, of some of that vnlawfull generation, *Bothuell* his treacherous attempts can beare witnesse. Keepe præcisely then your promise made at Mariage, as ye would wish to be partaker of the blessing therein.

And for your behauiour to your Wife, the Scripture can best giue you counsell therein: Treat her as your owne flesh, command her as her Lord, cherish her as your helper, rule her as your pupill, and please her in all things reasonable; but teach her not to be curious in things that belong her not:[273] Ye are the head, shee is your body; It is your office to command, and hers to obey; but yet with such a sweet harmonie, as shee should be as ready to obey, as ye to command; as willing to follow, as ye to go before; your loue being wholly knit vnto her, and all her affections louingly bent to follow your will.

And to conclude, keepe specially three rules with your Wife: first, suffer her neuer to meddle with the Politicke gouernment of the Commonweale, but holde her at the Oeconomicke rule of the house: and yet all to be subiect to your direction:[274] keepe carefully good and chaste company about her, for women are the frailest sexe; and be neuer both angry at once, but when ye see her in passion, ye should with reason danton yours: for both when yee are setled, ye are meetest to iudge of her errours; and when she is come to her selfe, she may be best made to apprehend her offence, and reuerence your rebuke.

If God send you succession, be carefull for their vertuous education:[275] loue them as ye ought, but let them know as much of it, as the gentlenesse of their nature will deserue; contayning them euer in a reuerent loue and feare of you. And in case it please God to prouide you to all these three Kingdomes,[276] make your eldest sonne *Isaac*, leauing him all your kingdomes; and prouide the rest with priuate possessions: Otherwayes[277] by deuiding your kingdomes, yee shall leaue the seed of diuision and discord among your posteritie; as befell to this Ile, by the diuision and assignement thereof, to the three sonnes of *Brutus, Locrine, Albanact*, and *Camber*.[278] But if God giue you not succession,[279] defraud neuer the nearest by right, whatsoeuer conceit yee haue of the person: For Kingdomes are euer at Gods disposition, and in that case we are but liue-rentars, lying no more in the Kings, nor peoples hands to dispossesse the righteous heire.

And as your company should be a paterne to the rest of the people, so should your person be a lampe and mirrour to your company:[280] giuing light to your seruants to walke in the path of vertue, and representing vnto them such worthie qualities, as they should preasse to imitate.

I need not to trouble you with the particular discourse of the foure Cardinall vertues,[281] it is so troden a path: but[282] I will shortly say vnto you; make one of them, which is Temperance,[283] Queene of all the rest within you. I meane not by the vulgar interpretation of Temperance, which onely consists in *gustu & tactu*,[284] by the moderating of these two senses: but, I meane of that wise moderation, that first commaunding your selfe, shall as a Queene, command all the affections and passions of your minde, and as a Phisician, wisely mixe all your actions according thereto. Therefore, not onely in all your affections and passions, but euen in your most vertuous actions, make euer moderation to be the chiefe ruler: For[285] although holinesse be the first and most requisite qualitie of a Christian, as proceeding from a feeling feare and trew knowledge of God: yet yee remember how in the conclusion of my first booke, I aduised you to moderate al your outward actions flowing there-fra. The like say I now of Iustice, which is the greatest vertue that properly belongeth to a Kings office.

Vse Iustice,[286] but with such moderation, as it turne not in Tyrannie:[287] otherwaies *summum Ius*, is *summa iniuria*.[288] As for example: if a man of a knowen honest life, be inuaded by brigands or theeues for his purse, and in his owne defence slay one of them, they beeing both moe in number, and also knowen to bee deboshed and insolent liuers; where by the contrarie, hee was single alone, beeing a man of sound reputation: yet because they were not at the horne, or there was no eye-witnesse present that could verifie their first inuading of him, shall hee therefore lose his head? And likewise, by the law-burrowes in our lawes, men are prohibited vnder great pecuniall paines, from any wayes inuading or molesting their neighbours person or bounds: if then his horse breake the halter, and pastour in his neighbours medow, shall he pay two or three thousand pounds for the wantonnesse of his horse, or the weaknesse of his halter? Surely no: for lawes are ordained as rules of vertuous and sociall liuing,[289] and not to bee snares to trap your good subiects: and therefore the lawe must be interpreted according to the meaning, and not to the literall sense thereof: *Nam ratio est anima legis*.[290]

And as I said of Iustice, so say I of Clemencie, Magnanimitie, Liberalitie, Constancie, Humilitie, and all other Princely vertues; *Nam in medio stat virtus*.[291] And it is but the craft of the Diuell that falsly coloureth the two vices that are on either side thereof,[292] with the borrowed titles of it, albeit in very deede they haue no affinitie therewith and the two extremities themselues, although they seeme contrarie, yet growing to the height, runne euer both in one: For[293] *in infinitis omnia concurrunt*;[294] and what difference is betwixt extreame tyrannie, delighting to destroy all mankinde; and extreame slackenesse of punishment, permitting euery man to tyrannize ouer his companion? Or what differeth extreame prodigalitie, by wasting of all to possesse nothing; from extreame niggardnesse, by hoarding vp all to enioy nothing; like the Asse that carying victuall on her backe, is like to starue for hunger, and will bee glad of thrissels for her part? And what is betwixt the pride of a glorious *Nebuchadnezzar*, and the preposterous humilitie of one of the proud Puritanes, claiming to their Paritie, and crying, Wee are all but vile wormes, and yet will iudge and giue Law to their King, but will be iudged nor controlled by none? Surely there is more pride vnder such a ones blacke bonnet, then vnder *Alexander* the great his Diademe, as was said of *Diogenes* in the like case.

But aboue all vertues, study to know well your owne craft,[295] which is to rule your people. And when I say this, I bid you know all crafts: For except ye know euery one, how can yee controll euery one, which is your proper office? Therefore besides your education, it is necessarie yee delight in reading, and seeking the knowledge of all lawfull things;[296] but with these two restrictions: first, that yee choose idle houres for it, not interrupting therewith the discharge of your office: and next, that yee studie not for knowledge nakedly,[297] but that your principall ende be, to make you able thereby to vse your office; practising according to your knowledge in all the points of your calling: not like these vaine Astrologians, that studie night and day on the course of the starres,[298] onely that they may, for satisfying their curiositie, know their course. But since all Artes and sciences are linked euery one with other, their greatest principles agreeing in one (which mooued the Poets to faine the nine Muses to be all sisters) studie them, that out of their harmonie, ye may sucke the knowledge of all faculties; and consequently be on the counsell of all crafts, that yee may be able to containe them all in order, as I haue alreadie said: For knowledge and learning is a light burthen, the weight whereof will neuer presse your shoulders.

First of all then,[299] study to be well seene in the Scriptures,[300] as I remembred you in the first booke; as well for the knowledge of your owne saluation, as that ye may be able to containe your Church in their calling, as *Custos vtriusque Tabulæ*.[301] For the ruling them well, is no small point of your office; taking specially heede, that they vague not from their text in the Pulpit: and if euer ye would haue peace in your land, suffer them not to meddle in that place with the estate or policie; but punish seuerely the first that presumeth to it. Doe nothing towards them without a good ground and warrant, but reason not much with them: for I haue ouer-much surfeited them with that, and it is not their fashion to yeeld. And suffer no conuentions nor meetings among Church-men, but by your knowledge and permission.

Next the Scriptures, studie well your owne Lawes:[302] for how can ye discerne by the thing yee know not? But preasse to draw all your Lawes and processes, to be as short and plaine as ye can: assure your selfe the longsomnesse both of rights and processes, breedeth their vnsure loosenesse and obscuritie,[303] the shortest being euer both the surest and plainest forme, and the longsomnesse seruing onely for the enriching of the Aduocates and Clerkes, with the spoile of the whole countrey:[304] And therefore delite to haunt your Session,[305] and spie carefully their proceedings; taking good heede, if any briberie may be tried among them, which cannot ouer seuerely be punished. Spare not to goe there, for gracing that farre any that yee fauour, by your presence to procure them expedition of Iustice; although that should be specially done, for the poore that cannot waite on, or are debarred by mightier parties. But when yee are there, remember the throne is Gods and not yours, that ye sit in, and let no fauour,[306] nor whatsoeuer respects mooue you from the right. Ye sit not there, as I shewe before, for rewarding of friends or seruants, nor for crossing of contemners, but onely for doing of Iustice. Learne also wisely to discerne betwixt Iustice and equitie; and for pitie of the poore, rob not the rich, because he may better spare it, but giue the little man the larger coat if it be his; eschewing the errour of young *Cyrus*[307] therein: For Iustice, by the Law, giueth euery man his owne; and equitie in things arbitrall, giueth euery one that which is meetest for him.

Be an ordinarie sitter in your secret Counsell:[308] that iudicature is onely ordained for matters of estate, and repressing of insolent oppressions. Make that iudgement as compendious and plaine as ye can; and suffer no Aduocates to be heard there with their dilatours, but let euery partie tell his owne tale himselfe:[309] and wearie not to heare the complaints of the oppressed, *aut ne Rex sis*.[310] Remit euery thing to the ordinary iudicature, for eschewing of confusion: but let it be your owne craft, to take a sharpe account of euery man in his office.

And next the Lawes, I would haue you to be well versed in authentick histories,[311] and in the Chronicles of all nations, but specially in our owne histories (*Ne sis peregrinus domi*)[312] the example whereof most neerely concernes you: I meane not of such infamous inuectiues, as *Buchanans* or *Knoxes* Chronicles: and if any of these infamous libels remaine vntill your dayes, vse the Law vpon the keepers thereof: For in that point I would haue you a Pythagorist,[313] to thinke that the very spirits of these archibellouses of rebellion, haue made transition in them that hoardes their bookes, or maintaines their opinions; punishing them, euen as it were their authours risen againe.[314] But by reading of authenticke histories and Chronicles, yee shall learne experience by Theoricke, applying the bypast things to the present estate, *quia nihil nouum sub sole*:[315] such is the continuall volubilitie of things earthly, according to the roundnesse of the world, and reuolution of the heauenly circles: which is expressed by the wheeles in *Ezechiels* visions,[316] and counterfeited by the Poets *in rota Fortunae*.[317] And likewise by the knowledge of histories, yee shall knowe how to behaue your selfe to all Embassadours and strangers; being able to discourse with them vpon the estate of their owne countrey. And among al prophane histories, I must not omit most specially to recommend vnto you, the Commentaries of *Cæsar*; both for the sweete flowing of the stile, as also for the worthinesse of the matter it selfe: For I haue euer beene of that opinion, that of all the Ethnick Emperors, or great Captaines that euer were, he hath farthest excelled, both in his practise, and in his precepts in martiall affaires.

As for the studie of other liberall artes and sciences,[318] I would haue you reasonably versed in them,[319] but not preassing to bee a passe-master in any of them: for that cannot but distract you from the points of your calling, as I shewed you before: and when, by the enemie winning the towne, yee shall bee interrupted in your demonstration, as *Archimedes* was;[320] your people (I thinke) will looke very bluntly vpon it. I graunt it is meete yee haue some entrance, specially in the Mathematickes;[321] for the knowledge of the arte militarie, in situation of Campes, ordering of battels, making Fortifications, placing of batteries, or such like.[322] And let not this your knowledge be dead without fruites, as Saint *Iames* speaketh of Faith:[323] but let it appeare in your daily conuersation, and in all the actions of your life.

Embrace trew magnanimitie,[324] not in beeing vindictiue, which the corrupted iudgements of the world thinke to be trew Magnanimitie;[325] but by the contrarie, in thinking your offendour not worthie of your wrath, empyring ouer your owne passion, and triumphing in the commaunding your selfe to forgiue:[326] husbanding the effects of your courage and wrath, to be rightly employed vpon repelling of iniuries within, by reuenge taking vpon the oppressours; and in reuenging iniuries without, by iust warres vpon forraine enemies. And so, where ye finde a notable iniurie, spare not to giue course to the torrents of your wrath. *The wrath of a King, is like to the roaring of a Lyon.*[327]

Foster trew Humilitie,[328] in bannishing pride, not onely towards God (considering yee differ not in stuffe, but in vse, and that onely by his ordinance, from the basest of your people) but also towards your Parents. And if it fall out that my Wife shall out-liue me,[329] as euer ye thinke to purchase my blessing, honour your mother: set *Beersheba* in a throne on your right hand: offend her for nothing, much lesse wrong her: remember her

Quæ longa decem tulerit fastidia menses;[330]

and that your flesh and blood is made of hers: and beginne not, like the young lordes and lairdes, your first warres vpon your Mother; but preasse earnestly to deserue her blessing. Neither deceiue your selfe with many that say, they care not for their Parents curse, so they deserue it not. O inuert not the order of nature, by iudging your superiours, chiefly in your owne particular! But assure your selfe, the blessing or curse of the Parents, hath almost euer a Propheticke power ioyned with it: and if there were no more, honour your Parents,[331] for the lengthning of your owne dayes, as GOD in his Law promiseth.[332] Honour also them that are *in loco Parentum*[333] vnto you,[334] such as your gouernours, vp-bringers, and Præceptours: be thankefull vnto them and reward them, which is your dewtie and honour.

But on the other part, let not this trew humilitie stay your high indignation to appeare,[335] when any great oppressours shall præsume to come in your presence; then frowne as ye ought: And in-case they vse a colour of Law in oppressing their poore ones, as ouer-many doe; that which ye cannot mend by Law,[336] mend by the withdrawing of your countenance from them: and once in the yeere crosse them, when their erands come in your way, recompencing the oppressour, according to Christs parable of the two debtours.[337]

Keepe trew Constancie,[338] not onely in your kindenesse towards honest men; but being also *inuicti animi*[339] against all aduersities:[340] not with that Stoicke insensible stupiditie, wherewith many in our dayes, preassing to winne honour, in imitating that ancient sect, by their inconstant behauiour in their owne liues, belie their profession.[341] But although ye are not a stocke, not to feele calamities; yet let not the feeling of them, so ouer-rule and doazen your reason, as may stay you from taking and vsing the best resolution for remedie, that can be found out.

Vse trew Liberalitie in rewarding the good,[342] and bestowing frankly for your honour and weale: but with that proportionall discretion, that euery man may be serued according to his measure, wherein respect must be had to his ranke, deserts, and necessitie:[343] And prouide how to haue, but cast not away without cause. In speciall, empaire not by your Liberalitie the ordinarie rents of your crowne; whereby the estate Royall of you, and your successours, must be maintained, *ne exhaurias fontem liberalitatis:*[344] for that would euer be kept *sacrosanctum & extra commercium:*[345] otherwaies, your Liberalitie would decline to Prodigalitie, in helping others with your, and your successours hurt. And aboue all, enrich not your selfe with exactions vpon your subiects;[346] but thinke the riches of your people your best treasure, by the sinnes of offenders, where no præuention can auaile, making iustly your commoditie. And in-case necessitie of warres, or other extraordinaries compell you to lift Subsidies, doe it as rarely as ye can: employing it onely to the vse it was ordained for;[347] and vsing your selfe in that case, as *fidus depositarius*[348] to your people.

And principally, exercise trew Wisedome; in discerning wisely betwixt trew and false reports;[349] First, considering the nature of the person reporter;[350] Next, what entresse he can haue in the weale or euill of him, of whom hee maketh the report;[351] Thirdly, the likely-hood of the purpose it selfe; And last, the nature and by-past life of the dilated person: and where yee finde a tratler, away with him. And although it bee true, that a Prince can neuer without secrecie doe great things, yet it is better ofttimes to try reports, then by credulitie to foster suspicion vpon an honest man. For since suspition is the Tyrants sickenesse,[352] as the fruites of an euill Conscience, *potius in alteram partem peccato*;[353] I meane, in not mistrusting one, whom-to no such vnhonestie was knowne before. But as for such as haue slipped before, former experience may iustly breed præuention by fore-sight.

And to conclude my aduice anent your behauiour in your person; consider that GOD is the authour of all vertue, hauing imprinted in mens mindes by the very light of nature, the loue of all morall vertues;[354] as was seene by the vertuous liues of the old *Romanes*: and preasse then to shine as farre before your people, in all vertue and honestie; as in greatnesse of ranke: that the vse thereof in all your actions, may turne, with time, to a naturall habitude in you; and as by their hearing of your Lawes, so by their sight of your person, both their eyes and their eares, may leade and allure them to the loue of vertue, and hatred of vice.

OF A KINGS BEHAVI-
OVR IN INDIFFERENT
THINGS.
THE THIRD BOOKE.

IT is a trew old saying, That a King is as one set on a stage,[355] whose smallest actions and gestures, all the people gazingly doe behold:[356] and therefore although a King be neuer so præcise in the discharging of his Office, the people, who seeth but the outward part, will euer iudge of the substance, by the circumstances; and according to the outward appearance, if his behauiour bee light or dissolute, will conceiue præ-occupied conceits of the Kings inward intention: which although with time, (the trier of all trewth,) it will euanish, by the euidence of the contrary effects, yet *interim patitur iustus*;[357] and præiudged conceits will,[358] in the meane time, breed contempt, the mother of rebellion and disorder. And[359] besides that, it is certaine, that all the indifferent actions and behauiour of a man, haue a certaine holding and dependance,[360] either vpon vertue or vice, according as they are vsed or ruled: for there is not a middes betwixt them, no more then betwixt their rewards, heauen and hell.

49

Be carefull then, my Sonne, so to frame all your indifferent actions and outward behauiour, as they may serue for the furtherance and forth-setting of your inward vertuous disposition.

The whole indifferent actions of a man, I deuide in two sorts;[361] in his behauiour in things necessary, as food, sleeping, raiment, speaking, writing, and gesture; and in things not necessary, though conuenient and lawfull, as pastimes or exercises, and vsing of company for recreation.

As to the indifferent things necessary,[362] although that of themselues they cannot bee wanted, and so in that case are not indifferent; as likewise in-case they bee not vsed with moderation, declining so to the extremitie, which is vice; yet the qualitie and forme of vsing them, may smell of vertue or vice, and be great furtherers to any of them.

To beginne then at the things necessarie; one of the publickest indifferent actions of a King, and that maniest, especially strangers, will narrowly take heed to; is his maner of refection at his Table, and his behauiour thereat.[363] Therefore, as Kings vse oft to eate publickly, it is meete and honourable that ye also doe so,[364] as well to eschew the opinion that yee loue not to haunt companie, which is one of the markes of a Tyrant; as likewise, that your delight to eate priuatlie, be not thought to be for priuate satisfying of your gluttonie; which ye would be ashamed should bee publicklie seene. Let your Table bee honourably serued; but serue your appetite with few dishes, as yong *Cyrus* did:[365] which both is holesommest, and freest from the vice of delicacie, which is a degree of gluttonie.[366] And vse most to eate of reasonablie-grosse, and common-meates; aswell for making your bodie strong and durable for trauell at all occasions, either in peace or in warre: as that yee may bee the heartlier receiued by your meane Subiects in their houses, when their cheare may suffice you: which otherwayes would be imputed to you for pride and daintinesse, and breed coldnesse and disdaine in them.[367] Let all your food bee simple, without composition or sauces; which are more like medecines then meate. The vsing of them was counted amongst the ancient *Romanes* a filthie vice of delicacie; because they serue onely for pleasing of the taste, and not for satisfying of the necessitie of nature;[368] abhorring *Apicius* their owne citizen, for his vice of delicacie and monsterous gluttonie.[369] Like as both the *Grecians* and *Romanes* had in detestation the very name of *Philoxenus*,[370] for his filthie wish of a Crane-craig. And therefore was that sentence vsed amongst them, against these artificiall false appetites,[371] *optimum condimentum fames.*[372] But beware with vsing excesse of meat and drinke; and chiefly, beware of drunkennesse, which is a beastlie vice,[373] namely in a King: but specially beware with it, because it is one of those vices that increaseth with aage. In the forme of your meate-eating, bee neither vnciuill, like a grosse Cynicke; nor affectatlie mignarde, like a daintie dame; but eate in a manlie, round, and honest fashion.[374] It is no wayes comely to dispatch affaires, or to be pensiue at meate: but keepe then an open and cheerefull countenance, causing to reade pleasant histories vnto you, that profite may be mixed with pleasure: and when ye are not disposed, entertaine pleasant, quicke, but honest discourses.

And because meat prouoketh sleeping,[375] be also moderate in your sleepe;[376] for it goeth much by vse: and remember that if your whole life were deuided in foure parts, three of them would be found to be consumed on meat, drinke, sleepe, and vnnecessarie occupations.

But albeit ordinarie times would commonly bee kept in meate and sleepe;[377] yet vse your selfe some-times so, that any time in the foure and twentie houres may bee alike to you for any of them;[378] that thereby your diet may be accommodate to your affaires, and not your affaires to your diet: not therefore vsing your selfe to ouer great softnesse and delicacie in your sleepe, more then in your meate; and specially in-case yee haue adoe with the warres.

Let not your Chalmer be throng and common in the time of your rest,[379] aswell for comelinesse as for eschewing of carrying reports out of the same. Let them that haue the credite to serue in your Chalmer, be trustie and secret;[380] for a King will haue need to vse secrecie in many things:[381] but yet behaue your selfe so in your greatest secrets, as yee neede not bee ashamed, suppose they were all proclaimed at the mercate crosse:[382] But specially see that those of your Chalmer be of a sound fame, and without blemish.

Take no heede to any of your dreames,[383] for all prophecies, visions, and propheticke dreames are accomplished and ceased in Christ: And therefore take no heede to freets either in dreames, or any other things; for that errour proceedeth of ignorance, and is vnworthy of a Christian, who should be assured, *Omnia esse pura puris,*[384] as *Paul* sayth; all dayes and meates being alike to Christians.

Next followeth to speake of raiment,[385] the on-putting whereof is the ordinarie action that followeth next to sleepe.[386] Be also moderate in your raiment, neither ouer superfluous, like a deboshed waster; nor yet ouer base, like a miserable wretch; not artificially trimmed and decked, like a Courtizane, nor yet ouer sluggishly clothed, like a countrey clowne; not ouer lightly like a Candie souldier or a vaine young Courtier; nor yet ouer grauely, like a Minister: but[387] in your garments be proper, cleanely, comely and honest, wearing your clothes in a carelesse, yet comely forme: keeping in them a midde forme, *inter Togatos & Paludatos*,[388] betwixt the grauitie of the one and lightnesse of the other: thereby to signifie, that by your calling yee are mixed of both the professions;[389] *Togatus*,[390] as a Iudge making and pronouncing the Law; *Paludatus*,[391] by the power of the sword: as your office is likewise mixed, betwixt the Ecclesiasticall and ciuill estate: For a King is not *mere laicus*,[392] as both the Papists and Anabaptists would haue him, to the which error also the Puritanes incline ouer farre. But to returne to the purpose of garments, they ought to be vsed according to their first institution by God, which was for three causes: first to hide our nakednesse and shame; next and consequently, to make vs more comely; and thirdly, to preserue vs from the iniuries of heate and colde. If to hide our nakednesse and shamefull parts, then these naturall parts ordained to be hid, should not be represented by any vndecent formes in the cloathes: and if they should helpe our comelinesse, they should not then by their painted preened fashion, serue for baites to filthie lecherie, as false haire and fairding does amongst vnchast women: and if they should preserue vs from the iniuries of heat and colde, men should not, like senselesse stones, contemne God, in lightlying the seasons, glorying to conquere honour on heate and colde. And although it be praise-worthy and necessarie in a Prince, to be *patiens algoris & æstus*,[393] when he shall haue adoe with warres vpon the fields; yet I thinke it meeter that ye goe both cloathed and armed, then naked to the battell, except you would make you light for away-running: and yet for cowards, *metus addit alas.*[394] And shortly, in your cloathes keepe a proportion, aswell with the seasons of the yeere, as of your aage: in the fashions of them being carelesse, vsing them according to the common forme of the time,[395] some-times richlier, some-times meanlier cloathed, as occasion serueth, without keeping any precise rule therein:[396] For if your mind be found occupied vpon them, it wil be thought idle otherwaies, and ye shall bee accounted in the number of one of these *compti iuuenes*;[397] which wil make your spirit and iudgment to be lesse thought of. But specially eschew to be effeminate in your cloathes, in perfuming, preening, or such like: and faile neuer in time of warres to bee galliardest and brauest, both in cloathes and countenance. And make not a foole of yourselfe in disguising or wearing long haire or nailes, which are but excrements of nature, and bewray such misusers of them, to bee either of a vindictiue, or a vaine light naturall. Especially, make no vowes in such vaine and outward things, as concerne either meate or cloathes.

Let your selfe and all your Court weare no ordinarie armour with your cloathes, but such as is knightly and honourable;[398] I meane rapier-swordes, and daggers: For tuilyesome weapons in the Court, betokens confusion in the countrey. And therefore bannish not onely from your Court, all traiterous offensiue weapons, forbidden by the Lawes, as guns and such like (whereof I spake alreadie) but also all traiterous defensiue armes, as secrets, plate-sleeues, and such like vnseene armour: For, besides that the wearers thereof, may be pre-supposed to haue a secret euill intention, they want both the vses that defensiue armour is ordained for; which is, to be able to holde out violence, and by their outward glaunsing in their enemies eyes, to strike a terrour in their hearts: Where by the contrary, they can serue for neither, being not onely vnable to resist, but dangerous for shots, and giuing no outward showe against the enemie; beeing onely ordained, for betraying vnder trust, whereof honest men should be ashamed to beare the outward badge, not resembling the thing they are not. And for answere against these arguments, I know none but the olde Scots fashion; which if it be wrong, is no more to be allowed for ancientnesse, then the olde Masse is, which also our forefathers vsed.

The next thing that yee haue to take heed to, is your speaking and language;[399] whereunto I ioyne your gesture,[400] since action is one of the chiefest qualities, that is required in an oratour: for as the tongue speaketh to the eares, so doeth the gesture speake to the eyes of the auditour.[401] In both your speaking and your gesture, vse a naturall and plaine forme, not fairded with artifice:[402] for (as the French-men say) *Rien contre-faict fin*:[403] but eschew all affectate formes in both.

In your language be plaine,[404] honest, naturall, comely, cleane, short, and sententious, eschewing both the extremities, aswell in not vsing any rusticall corrupt leide, as booke-language, and pen and inke-horne termes: and least of all mignard and effoeminate tearmes. But let the greatest part of your eloquence consist in a naturall, cleare, and sensible forme of the deliuerie of your minde, builded euer vpon certaine and good grounds;[405] tempering it with grauitie, quickenesse, or merinesse, according to the subiect, and occasion of the time; not taunting in Theologie, nor alleadging and prophaning the Scripture in drinking purposes, as ouer many doe.

Vse also the like forme in your gesture;[406] neither looking sillily, like a stupide pedant; nor vnsetledly, with an vncouth morgue, like a new-come-ouer Cavalier: but let your behauiour be naturall, graue, and according to the fashion of the countrey. Be not ouer-sparing in your courtesies,[407] for that will be imputed to inciuilitie and arrogancie: nor yet ouer prodigall in iowking or nodding at euery step: for that forme of being popular, becommeth better aspiring *Absalons*, then lawfull Kings:[408] framing euer your gesture according to your present actions:[409] looking grauely and with a maiestie when yee sit in iudgement, or giue audience to Embassadours, homely, when ye are in priuate with your owne seruants: merily, when ye are at any pastime or merrie discourse; and let your countenance smell of courage and magnanimitie when ye are at the warres. And remember (I say ouer againe) to be plaine and sensible in your language:[410] for besides that it is the tongues office, to be the messenger of the mind, it may be thought a point of imbecillitie of spirit in a King, to speake obscurely, much more vntrewly; as if he stood in awe of any in vttering his thoughts.[411]

Remember also, to[412] put a difference betwixt your forme of language in reasoning,[413] and your pronouncing of sentences, or declaratour of your wil in iudgement, or any other waies in the points of your office: For in the former case, yee must reason pleasantly and patiently, not like a king, but like a priuate man and a scholer; otherwaies, your impatience of contradiction will be interpreted to be for lacke of reason on your part. Where in the points of your office, ye should ripely aduise indeede, before yee giue foorth your sentence: but fra it be giuen foorth, the suffering of any contradiction diminisheth the maiestie of your authoritie,[414] and maketh the processes endlesse.[415] The like forme would also bee obserued by all your inferiour Iudges and Magistrates.

Now as to your writing, which is nothing else, but a forme of en-registrate speech;[416] vse a plaine, short, but stately stile, both in your Proclamations and missiues, especially to forraine Princes. And if your engine spur you to write any workes, either in verse or in prose, I cannot but allow you to practise it: but take no longsome workes in hand, for distracting you from your calling.

Flatter not your selfe in your labours,[417] but before they bee set foorth, let them first bee priuily censured by some of the best skilled men in that craft, that in these workes yee meddle with. And because your writes will remaine as true pictures of your minde, to all posterities; let them bee free of all vncomelinesse and vn-honestie: and according to *Horace* his counsell

———*Nonumque premantur in annum.*[418]

I meane both your verse and your prose; letting first that furie and heate, wherewith they were written, coole at leasure; and then as an vncouth iudge and censour, reuising them ouer againe, before they bee published,

———*quia nescit vox missa reuerti*[419]

If yee would write worthily, choose subiects worthie of you, that bee not full of vanitie, but of vertue; eschewing obscuritie, and delighting euer to bee plaine and sensible. And if yee write in verse, remember that it is not the principall part of a Poeme to rime right, and flowe well with manie pretie wordes: but the chiefe commendation of a Poeme is, that when the verse shall bee shaken sundrie in prose,[420] it shall bee found so rich in quicke inuentions, and poeticke flowers, and in faire and pertinent comparisons; as it shall retaine the lustre of a Poeme, although in prose. And I would also aduise you to write in your owne language: for there is nothing left to be saide in Greeke and Latine alreadie; and ynew of poore schollers would match you in these languages; and besides that, it best becommeth a King to purifie and make famous his owne tongue; wherein he may goe before all his subiects; as it setteth him well to doe in all honest and lawfull things.

And amongst all vnnecessarie things that are lawfull and expedient, I thinke exercises of the bodie[421] most commendable to be vsed by a young Prince, in such honest games or pastimes,[422] as may further abilitie and maintaine health: For albeit I graunt it to be most requisite for a King to exercise his engine, which surely with idlenesse will ruste and become blunt; yet certainely bodily exercises and games are very commendable; as[423] well for bannishing of idlenesse (the mother of all vice) as for making his bodie able and durable for trauell, which is very necessarie for a King. But from this count I debarre all rough and violent exercises, as the footeball; meeter for laming, then making able the vsers thereof: as likewise such tumbling trickes as only serue for Comoedians and Balladines, to win their bread with. But[424] the exercises that I would haue you to vse (although but moderately, not making a craft of them) are running, leaping, wrastling, fencing, dancing, and playing at the caitch or tennise, archerie, palle maillé, and such like other faire and pleasant field-games. And[425] the honourablest and most commendable games that yee can vse, are on horsebacke: for it becommeth a Prince best of any man, to be a faire and good horse-man. Vse therefore to ride and danton great and couragious horses; that I may say of you, as *Philip*[426] said of great *Alexander* his sonne, Μακεδονία οὐ σε χωρεῖ.[427] And specially vse such games on horse-backe, as may teach you to handle your armes thereon; such as the tilt, the ring, and low-riding for handling of your sword.

I cannot omit heere the hunting, namely with running hounds;[428] which is the most honourable and noblest sorte thereof: for it is a theeuish forme of hunting to shoote with gunnes and bowes; and greyhound hunting is not so martiall a game: But because I would not be thought a partiall praiser of this sport, I remit you to *Xeno-phon*,[429] an olde and famous writer, who had no minde of flattering you or me in this purpose: and who also setteth downe a faire pat-terne, for the education of a yong king, vnder the supposed name of *Cyrus*.[430]

As for hawking I condemne it not,[431] but I must praise it more sparingly, because it neither resembleth the warres so neere as hunt-ing doeth, in making a man hardie, and skilfully ridden in all grounds, and is more vncertaine and subiect to mischances; and (which is worst of all) is there-through an extreme stirrer vp of passions: But in vsing either of these games, obserue that moderation,[432] that ye slip not therewith the houres appointed for your affaires, which ye ought euer precisely to keepe; remembring that these games are but ordained for you, in enabling you for your office, for the which ye are ordained.

And as for sitting house-pastimes,[433] wherewith men by driuing time, spurre a free and fast ynough running horse (as the prouerbe is) although they are not profitable for the exercise either of minde or body,[434] yet can I not vtterly condemne them; since they may at times supply the roome, which being emptie, would be patent to pernicious idlenesse, *quia nihil potest esse vacuum*.[435] I will not therefore agree with the curiositie of some learned men in our aage,[436] in forbidding cardes, dice, and other such like games of hazard;[437] although otherwayes surely I reuerence them as notable and godly men: For they are deceiued therein, in founding their argument vpon a mistaken ground, which is, that the playing at such games, is a kind of casting of lot, and therefore vnlawfull; wherein they deceiue themselues: For the casting of lot was vsed for triall of the trewth in any obscure thing, that otherwayes could not be gotten cleared; and therefore was a sort of prophecie: where by the contrary, no man goeth to any of these playes, to cleare any obscure trewth, but onely to gage so much of his owne money, as hee pleaseth, vpon the hazard of the running of the cardes or dice, aswell as he would doe vpon the speede of a horse or a dog, or any such like gaigeour: And so, if they be vnlawfull, all gaigeours vpon vncertainties must likewayes be condemned: Not that thereby I take the defence of vaine carders and dicers, that waste their moyen, and their time (whereof fewe consider the pretiousnesse) vpon prodigall and continuall playing:[438] no, I would rather allow it to be discharged, where such corruption cannot be eschewed. But only I cannot condemne you at some times, when ye haue no other thinge adoe (as a good King will be seldome) and are wearie of reading, or euill disposed in your person, and when it is foule and stormie weather; then, I say, may ye lawfully play at the cardes or tables: For as to dicing, I thinke it becommeth best deboshed souldiers to play at, on the head of their drums, being onely ruled by hazard, and subiect to knauish cogging. And as for the chesse, I thinke it ouer fond, because it is ouer-wise and Philosophicke a folly: For where all such light playes, are ordained to free mens heades for a time, from the fashious thoughts on their affaires; it by the contrarie filleth and troubleth mens heades, with as many fashious toyes of the play, as before it was filled with thoughts on his affaires.

But in your playing, I would haue you to keepe three rules:[439] first, or ye play, consider yee doe it onely for your recreation, and resolue to hazard the losse of all that ye play; and next, for that cause play no more then yee care to cast among Pages: and last, play alwaies faire play precisely, that ye come not in vse of tricking and lying in ieast: otherwise, if yee cannot keepe these rules, my counsell is that yee allutterly abstaine from these playes: For neither a madde passion for losse, nor falshood vsed for desire of gaine, can be called a play.

Now, it is not onely lawfull, but necessarie, that yee haue companie meete for euery thing yee take on hand,[440] aswell in your games and exercises, as in your graue and earnest affaires: But learne to distinguish time according to the occasion,[441] choosing your companie accordingly. Conferre not with hunters at your counsell, nor in your counsell affaires: nor dispatch not affaires at hunting or other games. And haue the like respect to the seasons of your aage, vsing your sortes of recreation and companie therefore, agreeing thereunto: For it becommeth best, as kindliest, euery aage to smell of their owne qualitie,[442] insolence and vnlawful things beeing alwaies eschewed: and not that a colt should draw the plough, and an olde horse run away with the harrowes. But take heede specially, that your companie for recreation, be chosen of honest persons, not defamed or vicious, mixing filthie talke with merrinesse,

Corrumpunt bonos mores colloquia praua.[443]

And chiefly abstaine from haunting before your mariage, the idle companie of dames, which are nothing else, but *irritamenta libidinis.*[444] Bee warre likewaies to abuse your selfe, in making your sporters your counsellers: and delight not to keepe ordinarily in your companie, Comoedians or Balladines: for[445] the Tyrans delighted most in them, glorying to bee both authors and actors of Comoedies and Tragedies themselues: Wherupon the answere that the poet *Philoxenus* disdainefully gaue to the Tyran of *Syracuse* there-anent, is now come in a prouerbe,[446] *reduc me in latomias.*[447] And all the ruse that *Nero* made of himselfe when he died, was *Qualis artifex pereo?*[448] meaning of his skill in menstrally, and playing of Tragoedies: as indeede his whole life and death, was all but one Tragoedie.

Delight not also to bee in your owne person a player vpon instruments; especially on such as commonly men winne their liuing with: nor yet to be fine of any mechanicke craft: *Leur esprit s'en fuit au bout des doigts,*[449] saith *Du Bartas:*[450] whose workes, as they are all most worthie to bee read by any Prince, or other good Christian; so would I especially wish you to bee well versed in them. But spare not sometimes by merie company, to be free from importunitie; for ye should be euer mooued with reason, which is the onely qualitie whereby men differ from beasts; and not with importunitie: For[451] the which cause (as also for augmenting your Maiestie) ye shall not be so facile of accesse-giuing at all times, as I haue beene; and yet not altogether retired or locked vp,[452] like the Kings of *Persia*; appointing also certaine houres for publicke audience.

And since my trust is, that God hath ordained you for moe Kingdomes then this (as I haue oft alreadie said) preasse by the outward behauiour as well of your owne person, as of your court, in all indifferent things, to allure piece and piece,[453] the rest of your kingdomes, to follow the fashions of that kingdome of yours, that yee finde most ciuill, easiest to be ruled, and most obedient to the Lawes: for these outward and indifferent things will serue greatly for allurements to the people, to embrace and follow vertue. But beware of thrawing or constraining them thereto; letting it bee brought on with time, and at leisure; specially by so mixing through alliance and daily conuersation, the inhabitants of euery kingdom with other, as may with time make them to grow and welde all in one: Which may easily be done betwixt these two nations, being both but one Ile of *Britaine*, and alreadie ioyned in vnitie of Religion and language. So that euen as in the times of our ancestours,[454] the long warres and many bloodie battels betwixt these two countreys, bred a naturall and hereditarie hatred in euery of them, against the other: the vniting and welding of them hereafter in one, by all sort of friendship, commerce, and alliance, will by the contrary produce and maintaine a naturall and inseparable vnitie of loue amongst them. As we haue already (praise be to God) a great experience of the good beginning hereof,[455] and of the quenching of the olde hate in the hearts of both the people; procured by the meanes of this long and happy amitie, betweene the Queene my dearest sister and me; which during the whole time of both our Reignes, hath euer beene inuiolably obserued.

And for conclusion of this my whole Treatise,[456] remember my Sonne, by your trew and constant depending vpon God, to looke for a blessing to all your actions in your office: by the outward vsing thereof, to testifie the inward vprightnesse of your heart; and by your behauiour in all indifferent things, to set foorth the viue image of your vertuous disposition; and in respect of the greatnesse and weight of your burthen, to be patient in hearing, keeping your heart free from præoccupation, ripe in concluding, and constant in your resolution:[457] For better it is to bide at your resolution, although there were some defect in it,[458] then by daily changing, to effectuate nothing: taking the paterne thereof from the microcosme of your owne body; wherein ye haue two eyes, signifying great foresight and prouidence, with a narrow looking in all things; and also two eares, signifying patient hearing, and that of both the parties: but ye haue but one tongue, for pronouncing a plaine, sensible, and vniforme sentence; and but one head, and one heart, for keeping a constant & vniforme resolution, according to your apprehension: hauing two hands and two feete, with many fingers and toes for quicke execution, in employing all instruments meet for effectuating your deliberations.

But forget not to digest euer your passion, before ye determine vpon anything, since *Ira furor breuis est*[459] vttering onely your anger according to the Apostles rule, *Irascimini, sed ne peccetis:*[460] taking pleasure, not only to reward, but to aduance the good, which is a chiefe point of a Kings glory (but make none ouer-great, but[461] according as the power of the countrey may beare) and punishing the euill; but euery man according to his owne offence: not[462] punishing nor blaming the father for the sonne, nor the brother for the brother; much lesse generally to hate a whole race for the fault of one: for *noxa caput sequitur.*[463]

And aboue all, let the measure of your loue to euery one, be according to the measure of his vertue; letting your fauour to be no longer tyed to any, then the continuance of his vertuous disposition shall deserue: not admitting the excuse vpon a iust reuenge, to procure ouersight to an iniurie: For the first iniurie is committed against the partie; but the parties reuenging thereof at his owne hand, is a wrong committed against you, in vsurping your office, whom-to onely the sword belongeth, for reuenging of all the iniuries committed against any of your people.

Thus hoping in the goodnes of God, that your naturall inclination shall haue a happy sympathie with these præcepts, making the wise-mans schole-master, which is the example of others, to bee your teacher, according to that old verse, *Foelix quem faciunt aliena pericula cautum*;[464]

eschewing so the ouer-late repentance by your owne experience, which is the schoole-master of fooles; I wil for end of all, require you my Sonne, as euer ye thinke to deserue my fatherly blessing, to keepe continually before the eyes of your minde, the greatnesse of your charge: making[465] the faithfull and due discharge thereof, the principal butt ye shoot at in all your actions: counting it euer the principall, and all your other actions but as accessories, to be emploied as middesses for the furthering of that principall. And being content to let others excell in other things, let it be your chiefest earthly glory, to excell in your owne craft: according to the worthy counsel and charge of *Anchises* to his posteritie, in that sublime and heroicall Poet, wherein also my diction is included;

> *Excudent*[466] *alij spirantia mollius æra,*
> *Credo equidem, & viuos ducent de marmore vultus,*
> *Orabunt causas melius, coelique meatus*
> *Describent radio, & surgentia sydera dicent.*
> *Tu, regere imperio populos, Romane, memento*
> *(Hæ tibi erunt artes) pacique imponere morem,*
> 'Parcere subiectis, & debellare superbos.[467]

THE[468] TREW[469] LAW OF FREE MONARCHIES:
OR
THE RECIPROCK AND
MVTVALL DVETIE BETWIXT
A FREE KING, AND HIS
naturall Subiects.

AN ADVERTISEMENT
TO THE READER.

Accept, I pray you (my deare countreymen) as thankefully this Pamphlet that I offer vnto you, as louingly it is written for your weale. I would be loath both to be faschious, and fectlesse: And therefore, if it be not sententious,[470] at least it is short. It may be yee misse many things that yee looke for in it: But for excuse thereof, consider rightly that I onely lay downe herein the trew grounds, to teach you the right-way, without wasting time vpon refuting the aduersaries. And yet I trust, if ye will take narrow tent, ye shall finde most of their great gunnes payed home againe, either with contrary conclusions, or tacite obiections, suppose in a dairned forme, and indirectly: For my intention is to instruct, and not irritat, if I may eschew it. The profite I would wish you to make of it, is, as well so to frame all your actions according to these grounds, as may confirme you in the course of honest and obedient Subiects to your King in all times comming, as also, when ye shall fall in purpose with any that shall praise or excuse the by-past rebellions that brake foorth either in this countrey, or in any other, ye shall herewith bee armed against their Sirene songs, laying their particular examples to the square of these grounds. Whereby yee shall soundly keepe the course of righteous Judgement, decerning wisely of euery action onely according to the qualitie thereof, and not according to your pre-iudged conceits of the committers: So shall ye, by reaping profit to your selues, turne my paine into pleasure. But least the whole Pamphlet runne out at the gaping mouth of this Preface, if it were any more enlarged; I end, with committing you to God, and me to your charitable censures.

C. Φιλοπατρις[471]

THE TREW[472] LAW OF
FREE MONARCHIES:
OR
The Reciprock and mutuall duetie betwixt a free King and his naturall Subiects.

AS there is not a thing so necessarie to be knowne by the people of any land, next the knowledge of their God, as the right knowledge of their alleageance, according to the forme of gouernement established among them, especially in a *Monarchie* (which forme of gouernment, as resembling the Diuinitie, approcheth nearest to perfection, as all the learned and wise men from the beginning haue agreed vpon; Vnitie being the perfection of all things,) So hath the ignorance, and (which is worse) the seduced opinion of the multitude blinded by them, who thinke themselues able to teach and instruct the ignorants, procured the wracke and ouerthrow of sundry flourishing Common-wealths; and heaped heauy calamities, threatning vtter destruction vpon others. And the smiling successe, that vnlawfull rebellions haue oftentimes had against Princes in aages past (such hath bene the misery, and iniquitie of the time) hath by way of practise strengthened many in their errour: albeit there cannot be a more deceiueable argument; then to iudge ay the iustnesse of the cause by the euent thereof; as hereafter shalbe proued more at length. And among others, no Commonwealth, that euer hath bene since the beginning, hath had greater need of the trew knowledge of this ground, then this our so long disordered, and distracted Common-wealth hath: the misknowledge hereof being the onely spring, from whence haue flowed so many endlesse calamities, miseries, and confusions, as is better felt by many, then the cause thereof well knowne, and deepely considered. The naturall zeale therefore, that I beare to this my natiue countrie, with the great pittie I haue to see the so-long disturbance thereof for lacke of the trew knowledge of this ground (as I haue said before) hath compelled me at last to breake silence, to discharge my conscience to you my deare country men herein, that knowing the ground from whence these your many endlesse troubles haue proceeded, as well as ye haue already too-long tasted the bitter fruites thereof, ye may by knowledge, and eschewing of the cause escape, and diuert the lamentable effects that euer necessarily follow thereupon. I haue chosen then onely to set downe in this short Treatise, the trew grounds of the mutuall duetie, and alleageance betwixt a free and absolute *Monarche*, and his people; not to trouble your patience with answering the contrary propositions, which some haue not bene ashamed to set downe in writ, to the poysoning of infinite number of simple soules, and their owne perpetuall, and well deserued infamie: For by answering them, I could not haue eschewed whiles to pick, and byte wel saltly their persons; which would rather haue bred contentiousnesse among the readers (as they had liked or misliked) then sound instruction of the trewth: Which I protest to him that is the searcher of all hearts, is the onely marke that I shoot at herein.

First then, I will set downe the trew grounds, whereupon I am to build, out of the Scriptures, since *Monarchie* is the trew paterne of Diuinitie, as I haue already said: next, from the fundamental Lawes of our owne Kingdome, which nearest must concerne vs: thirdly, from the law of Nature, by diuers similitudes drawne out of the same: and will conclude syne by answering the most waighty and appearing incommodities that can be obiected.

The Princes duetie to his Subiects is so clearely set downe in many places of the Scriptures, and so openly confessed by all the good Princes, according to their oath in their Coronation, as not needing to be long therein, I shall as shortly as I can runne through it.

Kings are called Gods[473] by the propheticall King *Dauid*, because they sit vpon GOD his Throne in the earth, and haue the count of their administration to giue vnto him. Their office is, *To minister Iustice and Iudgement to the people*,[474] as the same *Dauid* saith: *To aduance the good, and punish the euill*,[475] as he likewise saith: *To establish good Lawes to his people, and procure obedience to the same* as diuers good Kings of *Iudah* did:[476] *To procure the peace of the people*, as the same *Dauid* saith:[477] *To decide all controuersies that can arise among them*,[478] as *Salomon* did: *To be the Minister of God for the weale of them that doe well, and as the minister of God, to take vengeance vpon them that doe euill*,[479] as S. *Paul* saith. And finally, *As a good Pastour, to goe out and in before his people*[480] as is said in the first of *Samuel*: *That through the Princes prosperitie, the peoples peace may be procured*,[481] as *Ieremie* saith.

And therefore in the Coronation of our owne Kings, as well as of euery Christian *Monarche*, they giue their Oath, first to maintaine the Religion presently professed within their countrie, according to their lawes, whereby it is established, and to punish all those that should presse to alter, or disturbe the profession thereof; And next to maintaine all the lowable and good Lawes made by their predecessours: to see them put in execution, and the breakers and violaters thereof, to be punished, according to the tenour of the same: And lastly, to maintaine the whole countrey, and euery state therein, in all their ancient Priuiledges and Liberties, as well against all forreine enemies, as among themselues: And shortly to procure the weale and flourishing of his people, not onely in maintaining and putting to execution the olde lowable lawes of the countrey, and by establishing of new (as necessitie and euill maners will require) but by all other meanes possible to fore-see and preuent all dangers, that are likely to fall vpon them, and to maintaine concord, wealth, and ciuilitie among them, as a louing Father, and careful watchman, caring for them more then for himselfe, knowing himselfe to be ordained for them, and they not for him; and therefore countable to that great God, who placed him as his lieutenant ouer them, vpon the perill of his soule to procure the weale of both soules and bodies, as farre as in him lieth, of all them that are committed to his charge. And this oath in the Coronation is the clearest, ciuill, and fundamentall Law, whereby the Kings office is properly defined.

By the Law of Nature the King becomes a naturall Father to all his Lieges at his Coronation: And as the Father of his fatherly duty is bound to care for the nourishing, education, and vertuous gouernment of his children; euen so is the king bound to care for all his subiects. As all the toile and paine that the father can take for his children, will be thought light and well bestowed by him, so that the effect thereof redound to their profite and weale; so ought the Prince to doe towards his people. As the kindly father ought to foresee all inconuenients and dangers that may arise towards his children, and though with the hazard of his owne person presse to preuent the same; so ought the King towards his people. As the fathers wrath and correction vpon any of his children that offendeth, ought to be by a fatherly chastisement seasoned with pitie, as long as there is any hope of amendment in them; so ought the King towards any of his Lieges that offend in that measure. And shortly, as the Fathers chiefe ioy ought to be in procuring his childrens welfare, reioycing at their weale, sorrowing and pitying at their euill, to hazard for their safetie, trauell for their rest, wake for their sleepe; and in a word, to thinke that his earthly felicitie and life standeth and liueth more in them, nor in himselfe; so ought a good Prince thinke of his people.

As to the other branch of this mutuall and reciprock band, is the duety and alleageance that the Lieges owe to their King: the ground whereof, I take out of the words of *Samuel*, dited by Gods Spirit, when God had giuen him commandement to heare the peoples voice in choosing and annointing them a King. And because that place of Scripture being well vnderstood, is so pertinent for our purpose, I haue insert herein the very words of the Text.

> 9 *NOw therefore hearken to their voice: howbeit yet testifie vnto them, and shew them the maner of the King, that shall raigne ouer them.*
>
> 10 *So* Samuel *tolde all the wordes of the Lord vnto the people that asked a King of him.*
>
> 11 *And he said, This shall be the maner of the King that shall raigne ouer you: he will take your sonnes, and appoint them to his Charets, and to be his horsemen, and some shall runne before his Charet.*
>
> 12 *Also, hee will make them his captaines ouer thousands, and captaines ouer fifties and to eare his ground, and to reape his haruest, and to make instruments of warre and the things that serue for his charets:*
>
> 13 *Hee will also take your daughters, and make them Apothicaries, and Cookes, and Bakers.*
>
> 14 *And hee will take your fields, and your vineyards, and your best Oliue trees, and giue them to his seruants.*
>
> 15 *And he will take the tenth of your seed, and of your Vineyards, and giue it to his Eunuches, and to his seruants.*
>
> 16 *And he will take your men-seruants, and your maid-seruants, and the chiefe of your yong men, and your asses, and put them to his worke.*
>
> 17 *He wil take the tenth of your sheepe: and ye shall be his seruants.*
>
> 18 *And ye shall cry out at that day, because of your King, whom ye haue chosen you: and the Lord God will not heare you at that day.*
>
> 19 *But the people would not heare the voice of* Samuel, *but did say: Nay, but there shalbe a King ouer vs.*
>
> 20 *And we also will be like all other Nations, and our King shall iudge vs, and goe out before vs, and fight our battels.*

That these words, and discourses of *Samuel* were dited by Gods Spirit, it needs no further probation, but that it is a place of Scripture;

since the whole Scripture is dited by that inspiration, as *Paul* saith: which ground no good Christian will, or dare denie. Whereupon it must necessarily follow, that these speeches proceeded not from any ambition in *Samuel*, as one loath to quite the reines that he so long had ruled, and therefore desirous, by making odious the gouernment of a King, to disswade the people from their farther importunate crauing of one: For, as the text proueth it plainly, he then conueened them to giue them a resolute grant of their demand, as God by his owne mouth commanded him, saying,

Hearken to the voice of the people.

And to presse to disswade them from that, which he then came to grant vnto them, were a thing very impertinent in a wise man; much more in the Prophet of the most high God. And likewise, it well appeared in all the course of his life after, that his so long refusing of their sute before came not of any ambition in him: which he well proued in praying, & as it were importuning God for the weale of *Saul*. Yea, after God had declared his reprobation vnto him, yet he desisted not, while God himselfe was wrath at his praying, and discharged his fathers suit in that errand. And that these words of *Samuel* were not vttered as a prophecie of *Saul* their first Kings defection, it well appeareth, as well because we heare no mention made in the Scripture of any his tyrannie and oppression, (which, if it had beene, would not haue been left vnpainted out therein, as well as his other faults were, as in a trew mirrour of all the Kings behauiours, whom it describeth) as likewise in respect that *Saul* was chosen by God for his vertue, and meet qualities to gouerne his people: whereas his defection sprung after-hand from the corruption of his owne nature, & not through any default in God, whom they that thinke so, would make as a step-father to his people, in making wilfully a choise of the vnmeetest for gouerning them, since the election of that King lay absolutely and immediatly in Gods hand. But by the contrary it is plaine, and euident, that this speech of *Samuel* to the people, was to prepare their hearts before the hand to the due obedience of that King, which God was to giue vnto them; and therefore opened vp vnto them, what might be the intollerable qualities that might fall in some of their kings, thereby preparing them to patience, not to resist to Gods ordinance: but as he would haue said; Since God hath granted your importunate suit in giuing you a king, as yee haue else committed an errour in shaking off Gods yoke, and ouer-hastie seeking of a King; so beware yee fall not into the next, in casting off also rashly that yoke, which God at your earnest suite hath laid vpon you, how hard that euer it seeme to be: For as ye could not haue obtained one without the permission and ordinance of God, so may yee no more, fro hee be once set ouer you, shake him off without the same warrant. And therefore in time arme your selues with patience and humilitie, since he that hath the only power to make him, hath the onely power to vnmake him; and ye onely to obey, bearing with these straits that I now foreshew you, as with the finger of God, which lieth not in you to take off.

And will ye consider the very wordes of the text in order, as they are set downe, it shall plainely declare the obedience that the people owe to their King in all respects.

First, God commandeth *Samuel* to doe two things: the one, to grant the people their suit in giuing them a king; the other, to fore-warne them, what some kings will doe vnto them, that they may not thereafter in their grudging and murmuring say, when they shal feele the snares here fore-spoken; We would neuer haue had a king of God, in case when we craued him, hee had let vs know how wee would haue beene vsed by him, as now we finde but ouer-late. And this is meant by these words:

Now therefore hearken vnto their voice: howbeit yet testifie vnto them, and shew them the maner of the King that shall rule ouer them.

And next, *Samuel* in execution of this commandement of God, hee likewise doeth two things.

First, hee declares vnto them, what points of iustice and equitie their king will breake in his behauiour vnto them: And next he putteth them out of hope, that wearie as they will, they shall not haue leaue to shake off that yoke, which God through their importunitie hath laide vpon them. The points of equitie that the King shall breake vnto them, are expressed in these words:

11 *He will take your sonnes, and appoint them to his Charets, and to be his horsemen, and some shall run before his Charet.*
12 *Also he will make them his captaines ouer thousands, and cap-taines ouer fifties, and to eare his ground, and to reape his haruest, and to make instruments of warre, and the things that serue for his charets.*

13 *He will also take your daughters, and make them Apothecaries, and Cookes, and Bakers.*

The points of Iustice, that hee shall breake vnto them, are expressed in these wordes:

14 *Hee will take your fields, and your vineyards, and your best Oliue trees, and giue them to his seruants.*

15 *And he will take the tenth of your seede, and of your vineyards, and giue it to his Eunuches and to his seruants: and also the tenth of your sheepe.*

As if he would say; The best and noblest of your blood shall be compelled in slauish and seruile offices to serue him: And not content of his owne patrimonie, will make vp a rent to his owne vse out of your best lands, vineyards, orchards, and store of cattell: So as inuerting the Law of nature, and office of a King, your persons and the persons of your posteritie, together with your lands, and all that ye possesse shal serue his priuate vse, and inordinate appetite.

And as vnto the next point (which is his fore-warning them, that, weary as they will, they shall not haue leaue to shake off the yoke, which God thorow their importunity hath laid vpon them) it is expressed in these words:

18 *And yee shall crie out at that day, because of your King whom yee haue chosen you: and the Lord will not heare you at that day.*

As he would say; When ye shall finde these things in proofe that now I fore-warne you of, although you shall grudge and murmure, yet it shal not be lawful to you to cast it off, in respect it is not only the ordinance of God, but also your selues haue chosen him vnto you, thereby renouncing for euer all priuiledges, by your willing consent out of your hands, whereby in any time hereafter ye would claime, and call backe vnto your selues againe that power, which God shall not permit you to doe. And for further taking away of all excuse, and retraction of this their contract, after their consent to vnder-lie this yoke with all the burthens that hee hath declared vnto them, he craues their answere, and consent to his proposition: which appeareth by their answere, as it is expressed in these words:

19 *Nay, but there shall be a King ouer vs.*

20 *And we also will be like all other nations: and our king shall iudge vs, and goe out before vs and fight our battels.*

As if they would haue said; All your speeches and hard conditions shall not skarre vs, but we will take the good and euill of it vpon vs, and we will be content to beare whatsoeuer burthen it shal please our King to lay vpon vs, aswell as other nations doe. And for the good we will get of him in fighting our battels, we will more patiently beare any burthen that shall please him to lay on vs.

Now then, since the erection of this Kingdome and Monarchie among the Iewes, and the law thereof may, and ought to bee a paterne to all Christian and well founded Monarchies, as beeing founded by God himselfe, who by his Oracle, and out of his owne mouth gaue the law thereof: what liberty can broiling spirits, and rebellious minds claime iustly to against any Christian Monarchie; since they can claime to no greater libertie on their part, nor the people of God might haue done, and no greater tyranny was euer executed by any Prince or tyrant, whom they can obiect, nor was here fore-warned to the people of God, (and yet all rebellion countermanded vnto them) if tyrannizing ouer mens persons, sonnes, daughters and seruants; redacting noble houses, and men, and women of noble blood, to slauish and seruile offices; and extortion, and spoile of their lands and goods to the princes owne priuate vse and commoditie, and of his courteours, and seruants, may be called a tyrannie?

And that this proposition grounded vpon the Scripture, may the more clearely appeare to be trew by the practise oft prooued in the same booke, we neuer reade, that euer the Prophets perswaded the people to rebell against the Prince, how wicked soeuer he was.

When *Samuel* by Gods command pronounced to the same king *Saul*,[482] that his kingdome was rent from him, and giuen to another (which in effect was a degrading of him) yet his next action following that, was peaceably to turne home, and with floods of teares to pray to God to haue some compassion vpon him.

And *Dauid*, notwithstanding hee was inaugurate in that same degraded Kings roome, not onely (when he was cruelly persecuted, for no offence; but good seruice done vnto him) would not presume, hauing him in his power, skantly, but with great reuerence, to touch the garment of the annoynted of the Lord, and in his words blessed him:[483] but likewise, when one came to him vanting himselfe vntrewly to haue slaine *Saul*, hee, without forme of proces, or triall of his guilt, caused onely for guiltinesse of his tongue, put him to sodaine death.[484]

And although there was neuer a more monstrous persecutor, and tyrant nor *Achab* was: yet all the rebellion, that *Elias* euer raised against him, was to flie to the wildernes: where for fault of sustentation, he was fed with the Corbies. And I thinke no man will doubt but *Samuel*, *Dauid*, and *Elias*, had as great power to perswade the people, if they had like to haue employed their credite to vproares & rebellions against these wicked kings, as any of our seditious preachers in these daies of whatsoeuer religion, either in this countrey or in France, had, that busied themselues most to stir vp rebellion vnder cloake of religion. This farre the only loue of veritie, I protest, without hatred at their persons, haue mooued me to be somewhat satyricke.

And if any will leane to the extraordinarie examples of degrading or killing of kings in the Scriptures, thereby to cloake the peoples rebellion, as by the deed of *Iehu*, and such like extraordinaries: I answere, besides that they want the like warrant that they had, if extraordinarie examples of the Scripture shall bee drawne in daily practise; murther vnder traist as in the persons of *Ahud*, and *Iael*; theft, as in the persons of the *Israelites* comming out of *Egypt*; lying to their parents to the hurt of their brother, as in the person of *Iacob*, shall all be counted as lawfull and allowable vertues, as rebellion against Princes. And to conclude, the practise through the whole Scripture prooueth the peoples obedience giuen to that sentence in the law of God:

> *Thou shalt not rayle vpon the Iudges, neither speake euill of the ruler of thy people.*[485]

To end then the ground of my proposition taken out of the Scripture, let two speciall, and notable examples, one vnder the law, another vnder the Euangel, conclude this part of my alleageance. Vnder the lawe, *Ieremie*[486] threatneth the people of God with vtter destruction for rebellion to *Nabuchadnezar* the king of Babel: who although he was an idolatrous persecuter, a forraine King, a Tyrant, and vsurper of their liberties; yet in respect they had once receiued and acknowledged him for their king, he not only commandeth them to obey him, but euen to pray for his prosperitie, adioyning the reason to it; because in his prosperitie stood their peace.[487]

And vnder the Euangel, that king, whom *Paul* bids the *Romanes obey* and serue *for conscience sake*,[488] was *Nero* that bloody tyrant, an infamie to his aage, and a monster to the world, being also an idolatrous persecuter, as the King of *Babel* was. If then Idolatrie and defection from God, tyranny ouer their people, and persecution of the Saints, for their profession sake, hindred not the Spirit of God to command his people vnder all highest paine to giue them all due and heartie obedience for conscience sake, giuing to *Cæsar* that which was *Cæsars*, and to God that which was Gods, as Christ saith; and that this practise throughout the booke of God agreeth with this lawe, which he made in the erection of that Monarchie (as is at length before deduced) what shamelesse presumption is it to any Christian people now adayes to claime to that vnlawfull libertie, which God refused to his owne peculiar and chosen people? Shortly then to take vp in two or three sentences, grounded vpon all these arguments, out of the lawe of God, the duetie, and alleageance of the people to their lawfull king, their obedience, I say, ought to be to him, as to Gods Lieutenant in earth, obeying his commands in all things, except directly against God, as the commands of Gods Minister, acknowledging him a Iudge set by GOD ouer them, hauing power to iudge them, but to be iudged onely by GOD, whom to onely hee must giue count of his iudgement; fearing him as their Iudge, louing him as their father; praying for him as their protectour; for his continuance, if he be good; for his amendement, if he be wicked; following and obeying his lawfull commands, eschewing and flying his fury in his vnlawfull, without resistance, but by sobbes and teares to God, according to that sentence vsed in the primitiue Church in the time of the persecution.

Preces, & Lachrymæ sunt arma Ecclesiæ.[489]

Now, as for the describing the alleageance, that the lieges owe to their natiue King, out of the fundamentall and ciuill Lawe, especially of this countrey, as I promised, the ground must first be set downe of the first maner of establishing the Lawes and forme of gouernement among vs; that the ground being first right laide, we may thereafter build rightly thereupon. Although it be trew (according to the affirmation of those that pryde themselues to be the scourges of Tyrants) that in the first beginning of Kings rising among Gentiles, in the time of the first aage, diuers commonwealths and societies of men choosed out one among themselues, who for his vertues and valour, being more eminent then the rest, was chosen out by them, and set vp in that roome, to maintaine the weakest in their right, to throw downe oppressours, and to foster and continue the societie among men; which could not otherwise, but by vertue of that vnitie be wel done: yet these examples are nothing pertinent to vs; because our Kingdome and diuers other Monarchies are not in that case, but had their beginning in a farre contrary fashion.

For as our Chronicles beare witnesse, this Ile, and especially our part of it, being scantly inhabited, but by very few, and they as barbarous and scant of ciuilitie, as number, there comes our first King *Fergus*, with a great number with him, out of *Ireland*, which was long inhabited before vs, and making himselfe master of the countrey, by his owne friendship, and force, as well of the *Ireland-men* that came with him, as of the countrey-men that willingly fell to him, hee made himselfe King and Lord, as well of the whole landes, as of the whole inhabitants within the same. Thereafter he and his successours, a long while after their being Kinges, made and established their lawes from time to time, and as the occasion required. So the trewth is directly contrarie in our state to the false affirmation of such seditious writers, as would perswade vs, that the Lawes and state of our countrey were established before the admitting of a king: where by the contrarie ye see it plainely prooued, that a wise king comming in among barbares, first established the estate and forme of gouernement, and thereafter made lawes by himselfe, and his successours according thereto.

The kings therefore in *Scotland* were before any estates or rankes of men within the same, before any Parliaments were holden, or lawes made: and by them was the land distributed (which at the first was whole theirs) states erected and decerned, and formes of gouernement deuised and established: And so it followes of necessitie, that the kings were the authors and makers of the Lawes, and not the Lawes of the kings. And to prooue this my assertion more clearly, it is euident by the rolles of our Chancellery (which containe our eldest and fundamentall Lawes) that the King is *Dominus omnium bonorum*,[490] and *Dominus directus totius Dominij*,[491] the whole subiects being but his vassals, and from him holding all their lands as their ouer-lord, who according to good seruices done vnto him, chaungeth their holdings from tacke to few, from ward to blanch, erecteth new Baronies, and vniteth olde, without aduice or authoritie of either Parliament or any other subalterin iudiciall seate: So as if wrong might bee admitted in play (albeit I grant wrong should be wrong in all persons) the King might haue a better colour for his pleasure, without further reason, to take the land from his lieges, as ouer-lord of the whole, and doe with it as pleaseth him, since all that they hold is of him, then, as foolish writers say, the people might vnmake the king, and put an other in his roome: But either of them as vnlawful, and against the ordinance of God, ought to be alike odious to be thought, much lesse put in practise.

And according to these fundamentall Lawes already alledged, we daily see that in the Parliament (which is nothing else but the head Court of the king and his vassals) the lawes are but craued by his subjects, and onely made by him at their rogation, and with their aduice: For albeit the king make daily statutes and ordinances, enioyning such paines thereto as hee thinkes meet, without any aduice of Parliament or estates; yet it lies in the power of no Parliament, to make any kinde of Lawe or Statute, without his Scepter be to it, for giuing it the force of a Law: And although diuers changes haue beene in other countries of the blood Royall, and kingly house, the kingdome being reft by conquest from one to another, as in our neighbour countrey in *England*, (which was neuer in ours) yet the same ground of the kings right ouer all the land, and subiects thereof remaineth alike in all other free Monarchies, as well as in this: For when the Bastard of *Normandie* came into *England*, and made himselfe king, was it not by force, and with a mighty army? Where he gaue the Law, and tooke none, changed the Lawes, inuerted the order of gouernement, set downe the strangers his followers in many of the old possessours roomes, as at this day well appeareth a great part of the Gentlemen in *England*, beeing come of the *Norman* blood, and their old Lawes, which to this day they are ruled by, are written in his language, and not in theirs: And yet his successours haue with great happinesse enioyed the Crowne to this day; Whereof the like was also done by all them that conquested them before.

And for conclusion of this point, that the king is ouer-lord ouer the whole lands, it is likewise daily proued by the Law of our hoordes, of want of Heires, and of Bastardies: For if a hoord be found vnder the earth, because it is no more in the keeping or vse of any person, it of the law pertains to the king. If a person, inheritour of any lands or goods, dye without any sort of heires, all his landes and goods returne to the king. And if a bastard die vnrehabled without heires of his bodie (which rehabling onely lyes in the kings hands) all that hee hath likewise returnes to the king. And as ye see it manifest, that the King is ouer-Lord of the whole land: so is he Master ouer euery person that inhabiteth the same, hauing power ouer the life and death of euery one of them: For although a iust Prince will not take the life of any of his subiects without a cleare law; yet the same lawes whereby he taketh them, are made by himselfe, or his predecessours; and so the power flowes alwaies from him selfe; as by daily experience we see, good and iust Princes will from time to time make new laws and statutes, adioyning the penalties to the breakers thereof, which before the law was made, had beene no crime to the subiect to haue committed. Not that I deny the old definition of a King, and of a law; which makes the king to bee a speaking law, and the Law a dumbe king: for certainely a king that gouernes not by his lawe, can neither be countable to God for his administration, nor haue a happy and established raigne: For albeit it be trew that I haue at length prooued, that the King is aboue the law, as both the author and giuer of strength thereto; yet a good king will not onely delight to rule his subiects by the lawe, but euen will conforme himselfe in his owne actions thervnto,[492] alwaies keeping that ground, that the health of the common-wealth be his chiefe lawe: And where he sees the lawe doubtsome or rigorous, hee may interpret or mitigate the same, lest otherwise *Summum ius* bee *summa iniuria:*[493] And therefore generall lawes, made publikely in Parliament, may vpon knowen respects to the King by his authoritie bee mitigated, and suspended vpon causes onely knowen to him.

As likewise, although I haue said, a good king will frame all his actions to be according to the Law; yet is hee not bound thereto but of his good will, and for good example-giuing to his subiects: For as in the law of abstaining from eating of flesh in *Lenton*, the king will, for examples sake, make his owne house to obserue the Law; yet no man will thinke he needs to take a licence to eate flesh. And although by our Lawes, the bearing and wearing of hag-buts, and pistolets be forbidden, yet no man can find any fault in the King, for causing his traine vse them in any raide vpon the Borderers, or other malefactours or rebellious subiects. So as I haue alreadie said, a good King, although hee be aboue the Law, will subiect and frame his actions thereto, for examples sake to his subiects, and of his owne free-will, but not as subiect or bound thereto.

Since I haue so clearely prooued then out of the fundamentall lawes and practise of this country, what right & power a king hath ouer his land and subiects, it is easie to be vnderstood, what allegeance & obedience his lieges owe vnto him; I meane alwaies of such free Monarchies as our king is, and not of electiue kings, and much lesse of such sort of gouernors, as the dukes of *Venice* are, whose Aristocratick and limited gouernment, is nothing like to free Monarchies; although the malice of some writers hath not beene ashamed to mis-know any difference to be betwixt them. And if it be not lawfull to any particular Lordes tenants or vassals, vpon whatsoeuer pretext, to controll and displace their Master, and ouer-lord (as is clearer nor the Sunne by all Lawes of the world) how much lesse may the subiects and vassals of the great ouer-lord the KING controll or displace him? And since in all inferiour iudgements in the land, the people may not vpon any respects displace their Magistrates, although but subaltern: for the people of a borough, cannot displace their Prouost before the time of their election: nor in Ecclesiasticall policie the flocke can vpon any pretence displace the Pastor, nor iudge of him: yea euen the poore Schoolemaster cannot be displaced by his schollers: If these, I say (whereof some are but inferiour, subaltern, and temporall Magistrates, and none of them equall in any sort to the dignitie of a King) cannot be displaced for any occasion or pretext by them that are ruled by them: how much lesse is it lawfull vpon any pretext to controll or displace the great Prouost, and great Schoole-master of the whole land: except by inuerting the order of all Law and reason, the commanded may be made to command their commander, the iudged to iudge their Iudge, and they that are gouerned, to gouerne their time about their Lord and gouernour.

And the agreement of the Law of nature in this our ground with the Lawes and constitutions of God, and man, already alledged, will by two similitudes easily appeare. The King towards his people is rightly compared to a father of children, and to a head of a body composed of diuers members: For as fathers, the good Princes, and Magistrates of the people of God acknowledged themselues to their subiects. And for all other well ruled Common-wealths, the stile of *Pater patriae*[494] was euer, and is commonly vsed to Kings. And the proper office of a King towards his Subiects, agrees very wel with the office of the head towards the body, and all members thereof: For from the head, being the seate of Iudgement, proceedeth the care and foresight of guiding, and preuenting all euill that may come to the body or any part thereof. The head cares for the body, so doeth the King for his people. As the discourse and direction flowes from the head, and the execution according thereunto belongs to the rest of the members, euery one according to their office: so is it betwixt a wise Prince, and his people. As the iudgement comming from the head may not onely imploy the members, euery one in their owne office as long as they are able for it; but likewise in case any of them be affected with any infirmitie must care and prouide for their remedy, in-case it be curable, and if otherwise, gar cut them off for feare of infecting of the rest: euen so is it betwixt the Prince, and his people. And as there is euer hope of curing any diseased member by the direction of the head, as long as it is whole; but by the contrary, if it be troubled, all the members are partakers of that paine, so is it betwixt the Prince and his people.

And now first for the fathers part (whose naturall loue to his children I described in the first part of this my discourse, speaking of the dutie that Kings owe to their Subiects) consider, I pray you what duetie his children owe to him, & whether vpon any pretext whatsoeuer, it wil not be thought monstrous and vnnaturall to his sons, to rise vp against him, to control him at their appetite, and when they thinke good to sley him, or cut him off, and adopt to themselues any other they please in his roome: Or can any pretence of wickednes or rigor on his part be a iust excuse for his children to put hand into him? And although wee see by the course of nature, that loue vseth to descend more then to ascend, in case it were trew, that the father hated and wronged the children neuer so much, will any man, endued with the least sponke of reason, thinke it lawfull for them to meet him with the line? Yea, suppose the father were furiously following his sonnes with a drawen sword, is it lawfull for them to turne and strike againe, or make any resistance but by flight? I thinke surely, if there were no more but the example of bruit beasts & vnreasonable creatures, it may serue well enough to qualifie and proue this my argument. We reade often the pietie that the Storkes haue to their olde and decayed parents: And generally wee know, that there are many sorts of beasts and fowles, that with violence and many bloody strokes will beat and banish their yong ones from them, how soone they perceiue them to be able to fend themselues; but wee neuer read or heard of any resistance on their part, except among the vipers; which prooues such persons, as ought to be reasonable creatures, and yet vnnaturally follow this example, to be endued with their viperous nature.

And for the similitude of the head and the body, it may very well fall out that the head will be forced to garre cut off some rotten member (as I haue already said) to keepe the rest of the body in integritie: but what state the body can be in, if the head, for any infirmitie that can fall to it, be cut off, I leaue it to the readers iudgement.

So as (to conclude this part) if the children may vpon any pretext that can be imagined, lawfully rise vp against their Father, cut him off, & choose any other whom they please in his roome; and if the body for the weale of it, may for any infirmitie that can be in the head, strike it off, then I cannot deny that the people may rebell, controll, and displace, or cut off their king at their owne pleasure, and vpon respects moouing them. And whether these similitudes represent better the office of a King, or the offices of Masters or Deacons of crafts, or Doctors in Physicke (which iolly comparisons are vsed by such writers as maintaine the contrary proposition) I leaue it also to the readers discretion.

And in case any doubts might arise in any part of this treatise, I wil (according to my promise) with the solution of foure principall and most weightie doubts, that the aduersaries may obiect, conclude this discourse. And first it is casten vp by diuers, that employ their pennes vpon Apologies for rebellions and treasons, that euery man is borne to carry such a naturall zeale and duety to his commonwealth, as to his mother; that seeing it so rent and deadly wounded, as whiles it will be by wicked and tyrannous Kings, good Citizens will be forced, for the naturall zeale and duety they owe to their owne natiue countrey, to put their hand to worke for freeing their common-wealth from such a pest.

Whereunto I giue two answeres: First, it is a sure Axiome in *Theologie*, that euill should not be done, that good may come of it: The wickednesse therefore of the King can neuer make them that are ordained to be iudged by him, to become his Iudges. And if it be not lawfull to a priuate man to reuenge his priuate iniury vpon his priuate aduersary (since God hath onely giuen the sword to the Magistrate) how much lesse is it lawfull to the people, or any part of them (who all are but priuate men, the authoritie being alwayes with the Magistrate, as I haue already proued) to take vpon them the vse of the sword, whom to it belongs not, against the publicke Magistrate, whom to onely it belongeth.

Next, in place of relieuing the common-wealth out of distresse (which is their onely excuse and colour) they shall heape double distresse and desolation vpon it; and so their rebellion shall procure the contrary effects that they pretend it for: For a king cannot be imagined to be so vnruly and tyrannous, but the common-wealth will be kept in better order, notwithstanding thereof, by him, then it can be by his way-taking. For first, all sudden mutations are perillous in common-wealths, hope being thereby giuen to all bare men to set vp themselues, and flie with other mens feathers, the reines being loosed to all the insolencies that disordered people can commit by hope of impunitie, because of the loosenesse of all things.

And next, it is certaine that a king can neuer be so monstrously vicious, but hee will generally fauour iustice, and maintaine some order, except in the particulars, wherein his inordinate lustes and passions cary him away; where by the contrary, no King being, nothing is vnlawfull to none: And so the olde opinion of the Philosophers prooues trew, That better it is to liue in a Common-wealth, where nothing is lawfull, then where all things are lawfull to all men; the Common-wealth at that time resembling an vndanted young horse that hath casten his rider: For as the diuine Poet Dv Bartas sayth, *Better it were to suffer some disorder in the estate, and some spots in the Common wealth, then in pretending to reforme, vtterly to ouerthrow the Republicke.*[495]

The second obiection they ground vpon the curse that hangs ouer the common-wealth, where a wicked king reigneth: and, say they, there cannot be a more acceptable deed in the sight of God, nor more dutiful to their common-weale, then to free the countrey of such a curse, and vindicate to them their libertie, which is naturall to all creatures to craue.

Whereunto for answere, I grant indeed, that a wicked king is sent by God for a curse to his people, and a plague for their sinnes: but that it is lawfull to them to shake off that curse at their owne hand, which God hath laid on them, that I deny, and may so do iustly. Will any deny that the king of *Babel* was a curse to the people of God, as was plainly fore-spoken and threatned vnto them in the prophecie of their captiuitie? And what was *Nero* to the Christian Church in his time? And yet *Ieremy* and *Paul* (as yee haue else heard) commanded them not onely to obey them, but heartily to pray for their welfare.

It is certaine then (as I haue already by the Law of God sufficiently proued) that patience, earnest prayers to God, and amendment of their liues, are the onely lawful meanes to moue God to relieue them of that heauie curse. As for vindicating to themselues their owne libertie, what lawfull power haue they to reuoke to themselues againe those priuiledges, which by their owne consent before were so fully put out of their hands? for if a Prince cannot iustly bring backe againe to himself the priuiledges once bestowed by him or his predecessors vpon any state or ranke of his subiects; how much lesse may the subiects reaue out of the princes hand that superioritie, which he and his Predecessors haue so long brooked ouer them?

But the vnhappy iniquitie of the time, which hath oft times giuen ouer good successe to their treasonable attempts, furnisheth them the ground of their third obiection: For, say they, the fortunate successe that God hath so oft giuen to such enterprises, prooueth plainely by the practise, that God fauoured the iustnesse of their quarrell.

To the which I answere, that it is trew indeed, that all the successe of battels, as well as other worldly things, lyeth onely in Gods hand: And therefore it is that in the Scripture he takes to himselfe the style of God of Hosts. But vpon that generall to conclude, that hee euer giues victory to the iust quarrell, would prooue the *Philistims*, and diuers other neighbour enemies of the people of God to haue oft times had the iust quarrel against the people of God, in respect of the many victories they obtained against them. And by that same argument they had also iust quarrell against the Arke of God: For they wan it in the field, and kept it long prisoner in their countrey. As likewise by all good Writers, as well Theologues, as other, the Duels and singular combats are disallowed; which are onely made vpon pretence, that GOD will kith thereby the iustice of the quarrell: For wee must consider that the innocent partie is not innocent before God: And therefore God will make oft times them that haue the wrong side reuenge iustly his quarrell; and when he hath done, cast his scourge in the fire; as he oft times did to his owne people, stirring vp and strengthening their enemies, while they were humbled in his sight, and then deliuered them in their hands. So God, as the great Iudge may iustly punish his Deputie, and for his rebellion against him, stir vp his rebels to meet him with the like: And when it is done, the part of the instrument is no better then the diuels part is in tempting and torturing such as God committeth to him as his hangman to doe: Therefore, as I said in the beginning, it is oft times a very deceiueable argument, to iudge of the cause by the euent.

And the last obiection is grounded vpon the mutuall paction and adstipulation (as they call it) betwixt the King and his people, at the time of his coronation: For there, say they, there is a mutuall paction, and contract bound vp, and sworne betwixt the king, and the people: Whereupon it followeth, that if the one part of the contract or the Indent bee broken vpon the Kings side, the people are no longer bound to keepe their part of it, but are thereby freed of their oath: For (say they) a contract betwixt two parties, of all Law frees the one partie, if the other breake vnto him.

As to this contract alledged made at the coronation of a King, although I deny any such contract to bee made then, especially containing such a clause irritant as they alledge; yet I confesse, that a king at his coronation, or at the entry to his kingdome, willingly promiseth to his people, to discharge honorably and trewly the office giuen him by God ouer them: But presuming that thereafter he breake his promise vnto them neuer so inexcusable; the question is, who should bee iudge of the breake, giuing vnto them, this contract were made vnto them neuer so sicker, according to their alleageance. I thinke no man that hath but the smallest entrance into the ciuill Law, will doubt that of all Law, either ciuil or municipal of any nation, a contract cannot be thought broken by the one partie, and so the other likewise to be freed therefro, except that first a lawfull triall and cognition be had by the ordinary Iudge of the breakers thereof: Or else euery man may be both party and Iudge in his owne cause; which is absurd once to be thought. Now in this contract (I say) betwixt the king and his people, God is doubtles the only Iudge, both because to him onely the king must make count of his administration (as is oft said before) as likewise by the oath in the coronation, God is made iudge and reuenger of the breakers: For in his presence, as only iudge of oaths, all oaths ought to be made. Then since God is the onely Iudge betwixt the two parties contractors, the cognition and reuenge must onely appertaine to him: It followes therefore of necessitie, that God must first giue sentence vpon the King that breaketh, before the people can thinke themselues freed of their oath. What iustice then is it, that the partie shall be both iudge and partie, vsurping vpon himselfe the office of God, may by this argument easily appeare: And shall it lie in the hands of headlesse multitude, when they please to weary off subiection, to cast off the yoake of gouernement that God hath laid vpon them, to iudge and punish him, whom-by they should be iudged and punished; and in that case, wherein by their violence they kythe themselues to be most passionate parties, to vse the office of an vngracious Iudge or Arbiter? Nay, to speake trewly of that case, as it stands betwixt the king and his people, none of them ought to iudge of the others breake: For considering rightly the two parties at the time of their mutuall promise, the king is the one party, and the whole people in one body are the other party. And therfore since it is certaine, that a king, in case so it should fal out, that his people in one body had rebelled against him, hee should not in that case, as thinking himselfe free of his promise and oath, become an vtter enemy, and practise the wreake of his whole people and natiue country: although he ought iustly to punish the principall authours and bellowes of that vniuersall rebellion: how much lesse then ought the people (that are alwaies subiect vnto him, and naked of all authoritie on their part) presse to iudge and ouer-throw him? otherwise the people, as the one partie contracters, shall no sooner challenge the king as breaker, but hee assoone shall iudge them as breakers: so as the victors making the tyners the traitors (as our prouerbe is) the partie shall aye become both iudge and partie in his owne particular, as I haue alreadie said.

And it is here likewise to be noted, that the duty and alleageance, which the people sweareth to their prince, is not only bound to them-selues, but likewise to their lawfull heires and posterity, the lineall succession of crowns being begun among the people of God, and happily continued in diuers christian common-wealths: So as no obiection either of heresie, or whatsoeuer priuate statute or law may free the people from their oath-giuing to their king, and his succes-sion, established by the old fundamentall lawes of the kingdome: For, as hee is their heritable ouer-lord, and so by birth, not by any right in the coronation, commeth to his crowne; it is a like vnlawful (the crowne euer standing full) to displace him that succeedeth thereto, as to eiect the former: For at the very moment of the expiring of the king reigning, the nearest and lawful heire entreth in his place: And so to refuse him, or intrude another, is not to holde out vncomming in, but to expell and put out their righteous King. And I trust at this time whole *France* acknowledgeth the superstitious rebellion of the liguers, who vpon pretence of heresie, by force of armes held so long out, to the great desolation of their whole countrey, their natiue and righteous king from possessing of his owne crowne and naturall kingdome.

Not that by all this former discourse of mine, and Apologie for kings, I meane that whatsoeuer errors and intollerable abominations a souereigne prince commit, hee ought to escape all punishment, as if thereby the world were only ordained for kings, & they without controlment to turne it vpside down at their pleasure: but by the contrary, by remitting them to God (who is their onely ordinary Iudge) I remit them to the sorest and sharpest schoolemaster that can be deuised for them: for the further a king is preferred by God aboue all other ranks & degrees of men, and the higher that his seat is aboue theirs, the greater is his obligation to his maker. And therfore in case he forget himselfe (his vnthankfulnes being in the same measure of height) the sadder and sharper will his correction be; and according to the greatnes of the height he is in, the weight of his fall wil recompense the same: for the further that any person is obliged to God, his offence becomes and growes so much the greater, then it would be in any other. *Ioues* thunder-claps light oftner and sorer vpon the high & stately oakes, then on the low and supple willow trees: and the highest bench is sliddriest to sit vpon. Neither is it euer heard that any king forgets himselfe towards God, or in his vocation; but God with the greatnesse of the plague reuengeth the greatnes of his ingratitude: Neither thinke I by the force and argument of this my discourse so to perswade the people, that none will hereafter be raised vp, and rebell against wicked Princes. But remitting to the iustice and prouidence of God to stirre vp such scourges as pleaseth him, for punishment of wicked kings (who made the very vermine and filthy dust of the earth to bridle the insolencie of proud *Pharaoh*) my onely purpose and intention in this treatise is to perswade, as farre as lieth in me, by these sure and infallible grounds, all such good Christian readers, as beare not onely the naked name of a Christian, but kith the fruites thereof in their daily forme of life, to keepe their hearts and hands free from such monstrous and vnnaturall rebellions, whensoeuer the wickednesse of a Prince shall procure the same at Gods hands: that, when it shall please God to cast such scourges of princes, and instruments of his fury in the fire, ye may stand vp with cleane handes, and vnspotted consciences, hauing prooued your selues in all your actions trew Christians toward

God, and dutifull subiects towards your King, hauing remitted the iudgement and punishment of all his wrongs to him, whom to onely of right it appertaineth.

But crauing at God, and hoping that God shall continue his blessing with vs, in not sending such fearefull desolation, I heartily wish our kings behauiour so to be, and continue among vs, as our God in earth, and louing Father, endued with such properties as I described a King in the first part of this Treatise. And that ye (my deare countreymen, and charitable readers) may presse by all meanes to procure the prosperitie and welfare of your King; that as hee must on the one part thinke all his earthly felicitie and happinesse grounded vpon your weale, caring more for himselfe for your sake then for his owne, thinking himselfe onely ordained for your weale; such holy and happy emulation may arise betwixt him and you, as his care for your quietnes, and your care for his honour and preseruation, may in all your actions daily striue together, that the Land may thinke themselues blessed with such a King, and the king may thinke himselfe most happy in ruling ouer so louing and obedient subiects.

FINIS.

Triplici[496] nodo, triplex cuneus.[497]
OR
AN APOLOGIE FOR
THE OATH OF
ALLEGIANCE.
AGAINST THE TWO BREVES
OF POPE PAVLVS QVINTVS, AND THE
late Letter of Cardinall BELLARMINE to G.
BLACKWEL the Arch-priest.

*Tunc omnes populi clamauerunt & dixerunt, Magna est Veritas, &
præualet.*[498] ESDR. 3.[499]

WHat a monstrous, rare, nay neuer heard-of Treacherous attempt,
was plotted within these few yeeres here in England, for the destruction of Mee, my Bed-fellow, and our posteritie, the whole house of
Parliament, and a great number of good Subiects of all sorts and
degrees;[500] is so famous already through the whole world by the
infamie thereof, as it is needlesse to bee repeated or published any
more; the horrour of the sinne it selfe doeth so lowdly proclaime it.
For if those crying[501] sinnes, (whereof mention is made in the
Scripture) haue that epithet giuen them for their publique infamie,
and for procuring as it were with a lowd cry from heauen a iust
vengeance and recompense, and yet those sinnes are both old and
too common, neither the world, nor any one Countrey being euer at
any time cleane voyd of them: If those sinnes (I say) are said in the
Scripture to cry so lowd; What then must this sinne doe, plotted
without cause, infinite in crueltie, and singular from all examples?
What proceeded hereupon is likewise notorious to the whole world;
our Iustice onely taking hold vpon the offenders, and that in as honourable and publique a forme of Triall, as euer was vsed in this
Kingdome.

2. For although the onely reason they gaue for plotting so heinous
an attempt, was the zeale they caried to the Romish Religion; yet
were neuer any other of that profession the worse vsed for that cause,

as by our gracious Proclamation immediatly after the discouery of the said fact doeth plainly appeare:[502] onely at the next sitting downe againe of the Parliament, there were Lawes made, setting downe some such orders as were thought fit for preuenting the like mischiefe in time to come. Amongst which a forme of OATH was framed to be taken by my Subiects, whereby they should make a cleare profession of their resolution, faithfully to persist in their obedience vnto mee, according to their naturall allegiance; To the end that I might hereby make a separation, not onely betweene all my good Subiects in generall, and vnfaithfull Traitors, that intended to withdraw themselues from my obedience; But specially to make a separation betweene so many of my Subiects, who although they were otherwise Popishly affected, yet retained in their hearts the print of their naturall duetie to their Soueraigne; and those who being caried away with the like fanaticall zeale that the Powder-Traitors were, could not conteine themselues within the bounds of their naturall Allegiance, but thought diuersitie of religion a safe pretext for all kinde of treasons, and rebellions against their Soueraigne. Which godly and wise intent, God did blesse with successe accordingly: For very many of my Subiects that were Popishly affected, aswell Priests, as Layicks, did freely take the same Oath: whereby they both gaue me occasion to thinke the better of their fidelitie, and likewise freed themselues of that heauie slander, that although they were fellow professors of one Religion with the powder-Traitors, yet were they not ioyned with them in treasonable courses against their Soueraigne; whereby all quietly minded Papists were put out of despaire, and I gaue a good proofe that I intended no persecution against them for conscience cause, but onely desired to be secured of them for ciuill obedience, which for conscience cause they were bound to performe.

3. But the diuel could not haue deuised a more malicious tricke for interrupting this so calme and clement a course, then fell out by the sending hither, and publishing a *Breue* of the Popes, countermanding all them of his profession to take this Oath; Thereby sowing new seeds of ielousie betweene me and my Popish Subiects, by stirring them vp to disobey that lawfull commandement of their Soueraigne, which was ordeined to bee taken of them as a pledge of their fidelitie; And so by their refusall of so iust a charge, to giue mee so great and iust a ground for punishment of them, without touching any matter of conscience: throwing themselues needlesly

into one of these desperate straits; either with the losse of their liues and goods to renounce their Allegiance to their naturall Soueraigne; or else to procure the condemnation of their soules by renouncing the Catholicke faith, as he alleadgeth.

4. And on the other part, although disparitie of Religion (the Pope being head of the contrary part) can permit no intelligence nor intercourse of messengers betweene mee and the Pope: yet there being no denounced warre betweene vs, he hath by this action broken the rules of common ciuilitie and iustice betweene Christian Princes, in thus condemning me vnheard, both by accounting me a persecutor, which cannot be but implied by exhorting the Papists to endure Martyrdome; as likewise by so straitly commanding all those of his profession in England, to refuse the taking of this Oath; thereby refusing to professe their naturall obedience to me their Soueraigne. For if he thinke himselfe my lawfull Iudge, wherefore hath he condemned me vnheard? And, if he haue nothing to doe with me and my gouernment (as indeed he hath not) why doeth he *mittere falcem in alienam messem*,[503] to meddle betweene me and my Subiects, especially in matters that meerely and onely concerne ciuill obedience? And yet could *Pius Quintus* in his greatest fury and auowed quarrell against the late Queene, doe no more iniurie vnto her; then hee hath in this case offered vnto mee, without so much as a pretended or an alleadged cause. For what difference there is, betweene the commanding Subiects to rebell, and loosing them from their Oath of Allegiance as *Pius Quintus* did; and the commanding of Subiects not to obey in making profession of their Oath of their dutifull Allegiance, as this Pope hath now done: no man can easily discerne.

5. But to draw neere vnto his *Breue*, wherein certainely hee hath taken more paines then he needed, by setting downe in the said *Breue* the whole body of the Oath at length; whereas the onely naming of the Title thereof might as well haue serued, for any answere hee hath made thereunto (making *Vna litura*,[504] that is, the flat and generall condemnation of the whole Oath to serue for all his refutation.) Therein hauing as well in this respect as in the former, dealt both vndiscreetly with me, and iniuriously with his owne Catholickes. With mee; in not refuting particularly what speciall words he quarrelled in that Oath; which if hee had done, it might haue beene that for the fatherly care I haue not to put any of my Subiects to a needlesse extremitie, I might haue beene contented in some sort to haue

reformed or interpreted those wordes. With his owne Catholickes: for either if I had so done, they had beene thereby fully eased in that businesse; or at least if I would not haue condescended to haue altered any thing in the saide Oath, yet would thereby some appearance or shadow of excuse haue beene left vnto them for refusing the same: not as seeming thereby to swarue from their Obedience and Allegiance vnto mee, but onely beeing stayed from taking the same vpon the scrupulous tendernesse of their consciences, in regard of those particular words which the Pope had noted and condemned therein.

And now let vs heare the words of his thunder.

POPE PAVLUS THE FIFT,
to the ENGLISH Catholickes.

WElbeloued[505] Sonnes, Salutation and Apostolicall Benediction. *The tribulations and calamities, which yee haue continually sustained for the keeping of the Catholike Faith, haue alwayes afflicted vs with great griefe of minde. But for as much as we vnderstand that at this time all things are more grieuous, our affliction hereby is wonderfully increased. For mee haue heard how you are compelled, by most grieuous punishments set before you, to goe to the Churches of Heretikes, to frequent their assemblies, to be present at their Sermons. Truely wee doe vndoubtedly beleeue, that they which with so great constancie and fortitude, haue hitherto indured most cruell persecutions and almost infinite miseries, that they may walke without spot in the Law of the Lord; will neuer suffer themselues to be defiled with the communion of those that haue forsaken the diuine Law. Yet notwithstanding, being compelled by the zeale of our Pastorall Office, and by our Fatherly care which we doe continually take for the saluation of your soules, we are inforced to admonish and desire you, that by no meanes you come vnto the Churches of the Heretickes, or heare their Sermons, or communicate with them in their Rites, lest you incurre the wrath of God: For these things may ye not doe without indamaging the worship of God, and your owne saluation. As likewise you cannot, without most euident and grieuous wronging of Gods Honour, bind your selues by the Oath, which in like maner we haue heard with very great griefe of our heart is administred vnto you, of the tenor vnder-written. viz.*

I[506] A.B. doe trewly and sincerely acknowledge, professe, testifie and declare in my conscience before God and the world, That our Soueraigne Lord King IAMES, is lawfull King[507] of this Realme, and of all other his Maiesties Dominions and Coun-

88

treyes: And that the *Pope* neither of himselfe, nor by any authority of the Church or Sea of *Rome*, or by any other meanes with any other, hath any power or authoritie to depose the King, or to dispose[508] any of his Maiesties Kingdomes or Dominions, or to authorize any forreigne Prince to inuade or annoy him or his Countreys, or to discharge any of his Subiects of their Allegiance and obedience to his Maiestie, or to giue Licence or leaue to any of them to beare Armes, raise tumults, or to offer any violence or hurt to his Maiesties Royall Person, State or Gouernment, or to any of his Maiesties subiects within his Maiesties Dominions. Also I doe sweare from my heart, that, notwithstanding any declaration or sentence of Excommunication, or depriuation made or granted, or to be made or granted, by the *Pope* or his successors, or by any Authoritie deriued, or pretended to be deriued from him or his Sea, against the said King, his heires or successors, or any absolution of the said subiects from their obedience; I will beare faith and trew Allegiance to his Maiestie, his heires and successors, and him and them will defend to the vttermost of my power, against all conspiracies and attempts whatsoeuer, which shalbe made against his or their Persons, their Crowne and dignitie, by reason or colour of any such sentence, or declaration, or otherwise, and will doe my best endeuour to disclose and make knowne vnto his Maiestie, his heires and suc-cessors, all Treasons and traiterous conspiracies, which I shall know or heare of, to be against him or any of them. And I doe further sweare, That I doe from my heart abhorre, detest and abiure as impious and Hereticall, this damnable doctrine and position, That Princes which be excommunicated or depriued by the *Pope*, may be deposed or murthered by their Subiects or any other whatsoeuer. And I doe beleeue, and in conscience am resolued, that neither the *Pope* nor any person whatsoeuer, hath power to absolue me of this Oath, or any part therof; which I acknowledge by good and full authoritie to bee lawfully ministred vnto mee, and doe renounce all Pardons and Dispensations to the contrarie. And all these things I doe plainely and sincerely acknowledge and sweare, according to these expresse words by mee spoken, and according to the plaine and common sense and vnderstanding of the same words, without any Equiuocation, or mentall euasion, or secret reseruation whatsoeuer. And I do make this Recognition and acknowledgment heartily, willingly, and trewly, vpon the trew faith of a Christian. So helpe me GOD.

Which things since they are thus; it must euidently appeare vnto you by the words themselues, That such an Oath cannot be taken without hurting of the Catholike Faith and the saluation of your soules; seeing it conteines many things which are flat contrary to Faith and saluation. Wherefore wee doe admonish you, that you doe vtterly abstaine from taking this and the like Oathes: which thing wee doe the more earnestly require of you, because wee haue experience of the constancie of your faith, which is tried like gold in the fire of perpetuall tribulation. Wee doe well know, that you will cheerfully vnder-goe all kinde of cruell torments whatsoeuer, yea and constantly endure death it selfe, rather then you will in any thing offend the Maiestie of GOD. *And this our confidence is confirmed by those things, which are dayly reported vnto vs, of the singular vertue, valour, and fortitude which in these last times doeth no lesse shine in your* Martyrs, *then it did in the first beginning of the Church. Stand therefore, your loynes being girt about with veritie, and hauing on the brest-plate of righteousnesse, taking the shield of Faith, be ye strong in the Lord, and in the power of his might; And let nothing hinder you. Hee which will crowne you, and doeth in Heauen behold your conflicts, will finish the good worke which hee hath begun in you. You know how hee hath promised his disciples, that hee will neuer leaue them Orphanes: for hee is faithfull which hath promised. Hold fast therefore his correction, that is, being rooted and grounded in Charitie, whatsoeuer ye doe, whatsoeuer ye indeuour, doe it with one accord, in simplicitie of heart, in meekenesse of Spirit, without murmuring or doubting. For by this doe all men know that we are the disciples of* CHRIST, *if we haue loue one to another. Which charitie, as it is very greatly to be desired of all faithfull Christians; So certainely is it altogether necessary for you, most blessed sonnes. For by this your charitie, the power of the diuel is weakened, who doeth so much assaile you, since that power of his is especially vpheld by the contentions and disagreement of our sonnes. Wee exhort you therefore by the bowels of our Lord* IESVS CHRIST, *by whose loue we are taken out of the iawes of eternall death; That aboue all things, you would haue mutuall charitie among you. Surely Pope* Clement *the eight of happy memory, hath giuen you most profitable precepts of practising brotherly charitie one to another, in his Letters in forme of a* Breue, *to our welbeloued sonne* M. George *Arch-priest of the Kingdome of England, dated the 5. day of the moneth of October* 1602. *Put them therefore diligently in practise, and be not hindered by any difficultie or doubtfulnesse. We command you that ye doe exactly obserue the words of those letters, and that yee take and vnderstand them simply as they sound, and as they lie; all power to interpret them otherwise, being taken away. In the meane while, we will neuer cease to pray to the Father of Mercies, that he would with pitie behold your afflictions* and *your paines; And that he would keepe and defend you with his continuall protection: whom wee doe gently greet with our Apostolicall Benediction.* Dated at Rome *at* S. Marke, *vnder the Signet of the Fisherman, the tenth of the Calends of October,*[509] 1606. *the second yeere of our* Popedome.

THE ANSWERE TO
THE FIRST *BREVE.*

FIrst, the *Pope* expresseth herein his sorrow, for that persecution which the Catholiques sustaine for the faiths sake. Wherein, besides the maine vntrewth whereby I am so iniuriously vsed, I must euer auow and maintaine, as the trewth is according to mine owne knowledge, that the late Queene of famous memory, neuer punished any Papist for Religion, but that their owne punishment was euer extorted out of her hands against her will, by their owne misbehauiour, which both the time and circumstances of her actions will manifestly make proofe of. For before *Pius Quintus* his excommunication giuing her ouer for a prey, and setting her Subiects at libertie to rebell, it is well knowne she neuer medled with the blood or hard punishment of any Catholique, nor made any rigorous Lawes against them. And since that time, who list to compare with an indifferent eye, the manifold intended inuasions against her whole Kingdome, the forreine practises, the internall publike rebellions, the priuate plots and machinations, poysonings, murthers, and all sorts of deuises, *& quid non?*[510] daily set abroach; and all these wares continually fostered and fomented from *Rome*; together with the continuall corrupting of her Subiects, as well by temporall bribes, as by faire and specious promises of eternall felicitie; and nothing but booke vpon booke publikely set foorth by her fugitiues, for approbation of so holy designes: who list, I say, with an indifferent eye, to looke on the one part, vpon those infinite and intollerable temptations, and on the other part vpon the iust, yet moderate punishment of a part of these hainous offendors; shall easily see that that blessed defunct LADIE was as free from persecution, as they shall free these hellish Instruments from the honour of martyrdome.

5.[511] But now hauing sacrificed (if I may so say) to the *Manes*[512] of my late Predecessour, I may next with Saint PAVL iustly vindicate mine owne fame, from those innumerable calumnies spread against me, in testifying the trewth of my behauiour toward the Papists: wherein I may trewly affirme, That whatsoeuer was her iust and mercifull Gouernement ouer the Papists in her time, my Gouernement ouer them since hath so farre exceeded hers, in Mercie and Clemencie, as not onely the Papists themselues grewe to that height of pride, in confidence of my mildnesse, as they did directly expect, and assuredly promise to themselues libertie of Conscience, and equalitie with other of my Subiects in all things; but euen a number of the best and faithfullest[513] of my sayde Subiects, were cast in great feare and amazement of my course and proceedings, euer prognosticating and iustly suspecting that sowre fruite to come of it, which shewed it selfe clearely in the Powder-Treason. How many did I honour with Knighthood, of knowen and open Recusants? How indifferently did I giue audience, and accesse to both sides, bestowing equally all fauours and honours on both professions? How free and continuall accesse, had all rankes and degrees of Papists in my Court and company? And aboue all, how frankely and freely did I free Recusants of their ordinarie paiments? Besides, it is euident what strait order was giuen out of my owne mouth to the Iudges, to spare the execution of all Priests, (notwithstanding their conuiction,) ioyning thereunto a gracious Proclamation, whereby all Priests, that were at libertie, and not taken, might goe out of the countrey by such a day:[514] my generall Pardon hauing beene extended to all conuicted Priestes in prison: whereupon they were set at libertie as good Subiects: and all Priests that were taken after, sent ouer and set at libertie there. But time and paper will faile me to make enumeration of all the benefits and fauours that I bestowed in generall and particular vpon Papists: in recounting whereof, euery scrape of my penne would serue but for a blot of the Popes ingratitude and iniustice, in meating me with so hard a measure for the same. So as I thinke I haue sufficiently, or at least with good reason wiped the *teares*[515] from the Popes eyes, for complaining vpon such persecution, who if hee had beene but politickely wise, although hee had had no respect to Iustice and Veritie, would haue in this complaint of his, made a difference betweene my present time, and the time of the late Queene: And so by his commending of my moderation, in regard of former times, might haue had hope to haue mooued me to haue continued in the same clement course: For it is a trew saying, that alledged kindnesse vpon noble mindes, doeth euer worke much. And for the maine vntrewth of any persecution in my time, it can neuer bee prooued, that any were, or are put to death since I came to the Crowne for cause of Conscience; except that now this discharge giuen by the Pope to all Catholiques to take their Oath of Allegiance to me, be the cause of the due punishment of many: which if it fall out to be, let the blood light vpon the Popes head, who is the onely cause thereof.

As for the next point contained in his *Breue* concerning his discharge of all Papists to come to our Church, or frequent our rites and ceremonies, I am not to meddle at this time with that matter, because my errand now onely is to publish to the world the Iniurie and Iniustice done vnto me, in discharging my subiects to make profession of their obedience vnto mee. Now[516] as to the point where the Oath is quarrelled, it is set downe in fewe, but very weighty wordes; to wit, *That it ought to be cleare vnto all Catholiques, that this Oath cannot bee taken with safetie of the Catholique Faith, and of their soules health, since it containeth many things that are plainely and directly contrarie to their faith and saluation.* To this, the old saying fathered vpon the Philosopher, may very fitly bee applied, *Multa dicit, sed pauca probat;*[517] nay indeed, *Nihil omnino probat:*[518] For how the profession of the naturall Allegiance of Subiects to their Prince can be directly opposite to the faith and saluation of soules, is so farre beyond my simple reading in Diuinitie, as I must thinke it a strange and new Assertion, to proceede out of the mouth of that pretended generall Pastor of all Christian soules. I reade indeede and not in one, or two, or three places of Scripture, that Subiects are bound to obey their Princes for conscience sake, whether they were good or wicked Princes. So said the people to *Ioshua,*[519] *As wee obeyed Moses in all things, so will wee obey thee.* So the Prophet[520] commanded the people to obey the King of Babel, saying, *Put your neckes vnder the yoke of the King of Babel, and serue him and his people, that yee may liue.* So were the children of Israel, vnto *Pharaoh,*[521] desiring him to let them goe: so to *Cyrus,*[522] obtaining leaue of him to returne to build the Temple: and in a word, the Apostle willed all men *to*[523] *bee subiect to the higher powers for conscience sake.* Agreeable to the Scriptures did the Fathers teach. *Augustine*[524] speaking of *Iulian,* saith, *Iulian was an vnbeleeuing Emperour: was hee not an Apostata, an Oppressour, and an Idolater? Christian Souldiers serued that vnbeleeuing Emperour: when they came to the cause of* CHRIST, *they would acknowledge no Lord, but him that is in heauen. When hee would haue them to worship Idoles and to sacrifice, they preferred* GOD *before him: But when he said, Goe forth to fight, inuade such a nation, they presently obeyed. They distinguished their eternall Lord from their temporall, and yet were they subiect euen vnto their temporall Lord, for his sake that was their eternall Lord and Master.* Tertullian[525] sayth, *A Christian is enemie to no man, much lesse to the Prince, whom hee knoweth to bee appointed of God; and so of necessitie must loue, reuerence and honour him, and wish him safe with the whole Romane Empire, so long as the world shall last: for so long shall it endure. Wee honour therefore the Emperour in such sort, as is lawfull for vs, and expedient for him, as a man, the next vnto God, and obtaining from God whatsoeuer hee hath, and onely inferiour vnto God. This the Emperour himselfe would: for so is hee greater then all, while hee is inferiour onely to the trew God.* Iustine[526] Martyr; *Wee onely adore the Lord, and in all other things cheerefully performe seruice to you, professing that you are Emperours and Princes of men.* Ambrose;[527] *I may lament, weepe, and sigh: My teares are my weapons against their armes, souldiers, and the* Gothes *also: such are the weapons of a Priest: Otherwise neither ought I, neither can I resist.* Optatus;[528] *Ouer the Emperour, there is none but onely God, that made the Emperour.* And *Gregory*[529] writing to *Mauritius* about a certaine Law, that a Souldier should not be receiued into a Monasterie, *nondum expleta militia,*[530] *The Almightie God,* sayth hee, *holdes him guiltie, that is not vpright to the most excellent Emperour in all things that hee doeth or speaketh.* And then calling himselfe the vnworthy seruant of his Godlinesse, goeth on in the whole Epistle to shewe the iniustice of that Lawe, as hee pretendeth: and in the end concludes his Epistle with these wordes; *I being subiect to your command, haue caused the same Law to be sent through diuers parts of your Dominions: and because the Law it selfe doeth not agree to the Law of the Almightie God, I haue signified the same by my Letters to your most excellent Lordship: so that on both parts I haue payed what I ought; because I haue yeelded obedience to the Emperour, and haue not holden my peace, in what I thought for God.* Now how great a contrarietie there is, betwixt this ancient Popes action in obeying an Emperour by the publication of his Decree, which in his owne conscience hee thought vnlawfull, and this present Popes prohibition to a Kings Subiects from obedience vnto him in things most lawfull and meere temporall; I remit it to the Readers indifferencie. And answerably to the Fathers, spake the Councels in their Decrees. As the Councell of *Arles,*[531] submitting the whole

Councell to the Emperour in these wordes; *These things wee haue decreed to be presented to our Lord the Emperour, beseeching his Clemencie, that if wee haue done lesse then wee ought, it may be supplyed by his wisedome: if any thing otherwise then reason requireth, it may be corrected by his iudgement: if any thing be found fault with by vs with reason, it may be perfected by his aide with* GODS *fauourable assistance*.

But why should I speak of *Charles* the great, to whome not one Councell, but six seuerall Councels, *Frankeford, Arles, Tours, Chalons, Ments* and *Rhemes* did wholy submit themselues? and not rather speake of all the generall Councels, that of *Nice, Constantinople, Ephesus, Chalcedon,* and the foure other commonly so reputed, which did submit themselues to the Emperours wisedome and piety in all things? Insomuch as that of *Ephesus* repeated it foure seuerall times, *That they were summoned by the Emperours Oracle, becke, charge and commaund, and betooke themselues to his Godlinesse; beseeching*[532] *him, that the Decrees made against* Nestorius *and his followers, might by his power haue their full force and validitie,* as appeareth manifestly in the Epistle of the generall Councell of *Ephesus* written *ad Augustos.* I also reade that Christ said, *His kingdome*[533] *was not of this world,* bidding, *Giue to Cesar*[534] *what was Cesars, and to God what was Gods.* And I euer held it for an infallible Maxime in Diuinitie, That temporall obedience to a temporall Magistrate, did nothing repugne to matters of faith or saluation of soules: But that euer temporall obedience was against faith and saluation of soules, as in this *Breue* is alledged, was neuer before heard nor read of in the Christian Church. And therefore I would haue wished the *Pope,* before hee had set downe this commandement to all Papists here, That, since in him is the power by the infallibility[535] of his spirit, to make new Articles of Faith when euer it shall please him; he had first set it downe for an Article of Faith, before he had commanded all Catholikes to beleeue and obey it. I will then conclude the answere to this point in a *Dilemma.*

Either[536] it is lawfull to obey the Soueraigne in temporall things, or not.

If[537] it be lawfull (as I neuer heard nor read it doubted of) then why is the *Pope* so vniust, and so cruell towards his owne Catholikes, as to command them to disobey their Soueraignes lawfull commandement?

If[538] it be vnlawfull, why hath hee neither expressed any one cause or reason thereof, nor yet will giue them leaue (nay rather hee should command and perswade them in plaine termes) not to liue vnder a King whom vnto they ought no obedience? And[539] as for the vehement exhortation vnto them to perseuere in constancie, and to suffer Martyrdome and all tribulation for this cause; it requireth no other answere then onely this, That if the ground be good whereupon hee hath commaunded them to stand, then exhortation to constancie is necessarie: but if the ground be vniust and naught (as indeed it is, and I haue in part already proued) then this exhortation of his can worke no other effect, then to make him guilty of the blood of so many of his sheepe, whom hee doeth thus wilfully cast away; not onely to the needlesse losse of their liues, and ruine of their families, but euen to the laying on of a perpetuall slander vpon all Papists; as if no zealous Papist could be a trew subiect to his Prince; and that the profession of that Religion, and the Temporall obedience to the Ciuill Magistrate, were two things repugnant and incompatible in themselues. But euill information, and vntrew reports[540] (which being caried so farre as betweene this and *Rome*, cannot but increase by the way) might haue abused the *Pope*, and made him dispatch this *Breue* so rashly: For that great Citie, Queene of the World, and as themselues confesse, mystically[541] *Babylon*, cannot but be so full of all sorts of Intelligencies. Besides, all complainers (as the Catholikes here are) be naturally giuen to exaggerate their owne griefes, and multiply thereupon: So that it is no wonder, that euen a iust Iudge sitting there, should vpon wrong information, giue an vnrighteous sentence; as some of their owne partie doe not sticke to confesse, That *Pius Quintus* was too rashly caried vpon wrong information, to pronounce his thunder of Excommunication vpon the late Queene. And it may be, the like excuse shall hereafter be made for the two *Breues*, which *Clemens*[542] *Octauus* sent to ENGLAND immediatly before her death, for debarring me of the Crowne, or any other that either would professe, or any wayes tolerate the professours of our Religion; contrary to his manifold vowes and protestations, *simul & eodem tempore*,[543] and as it were, deliuered *vno & eodem spiritu*,[544] to diuers of my ministers abroad, professing such kindnesse, and shewing such forwardnesse to aduance me to this Crowne. Nay, the most part of Catholikes here,[545] finding this *Breue* when it came to their handes to bee so farre against Diuinitie, Policie, or naturall sense, were firmely perswaded that it was but a counterfeit Libell, deuised in hatred of the Pope; or at the farthest, a thing hastily done vpon wrong information, as was before said. Of which opinion were not onely the simpler sort of Papists, but euen some amongst them of best account, both for learning and experience; whereof the Archpriest himselfe was one: But for soluing of this obiection, the Pope himselfe hath taken new paines by sending foorth a second *Breue*, onely for giuing faith and confirmation to the former; That whereas before, his sinne might haue beene thought to haue proceeded from rashnesse and mis-information, he will now wilfully and willingly double the same; whereof the Copy followeth.

TO OVR BELOVED SONNES
the English Catholikes, *Paulus P. P. V*^{tus}

BEloued[546] sonnes, Salutation and Apostolicall Benediction. *It is reported vnto vs, that there are found certaine amongst you, who when as we haue sufficiently declared by our Letters, dated the last yeere on the tenth of the Calends of October in the forme of a* Breue, *that yee cannot with safe Conscience take the Oath, which was then required of you; and when as wee haue further straitly commanded you, that by no meanes yee should take it: yet there are some, I say, among you, which dare now affirme, that such Letters concerning the forbidding of the Oath, were not written of our owne accord, or of our owne proper will, but rather for the respect and at the instigation of other men. And for that cause the same men doe goe about to perswade you, that our commands in the said Letters are not to be regarded. Surely this newes did trouble vs; and that so much the more, because hauing had experience of your obedience (most dearely beloued sonnes) who to the end ye might obey this holy Sea, haue godlily and valiantly contemned your riches, wealth, honour, libertie, yea and life it selfe; wee should neuer haue suspected that the trewth of our Apostolike Letters could once be called into question among you, that by this pretence ye might exempt your selues from our Commandements. But we doe herein perceiue the subtiltie and craft of the enemie of mans saluation, and we doe attribute this your backwardnesse rather to him, then to your owne will. And for this cause, wee haue thought good to write the second time vnto you, and to signifie vnto you againe, That our Apostolike Letters dated the last yeere on the tenth of the Calends of October, concerning the prohibition of the Oath, were written not only vpon our proper motion, and of our certaine knowledge, but also after long and weightie deliberation vsed concerning all those things, which are contained in them; and that for that cause ye are bound fully to obserue them, reiecting all interpretation perswading to the contrary. And this is our meere, pure, and perfect will, being alwayes carefull of your saluation, and alwayes minding those things, which are most profitable vnto you. And we doe pray without ceasing, that hee that hath appointed our lowlinesse to the keeping of the flocke of Christ, would inlighten our thoughts and our counsels: whom we doe also continually desire, that he would increase in you (our beloued Sonnes) faith, constancie, and mutuall charitie and peace one to another. All whom, we doe most louingly blesse with all charitable affection.*

Dated at Rome *at Saint* Markes *vnder the Signet of the* Fisherman, *the x. of the Calends of September,*[547] 1607, *the third yeere of our* Popedome.

THE ANSWERE TO THE
second BREVE.

NOw for this *Breue*, I may iustly reflect his owne phrase vpon him, in tearming it to be *The craft of the Deuill*. For if the Deuill had studied a thousand yeeres, for to finde out a mischiefe for our Catholikes heere, hee hath found it in this: that now when many Catholikes haue taken their Oath, and some Priests also; yea, the Arch-priest himselfe, without compunction or sticking, they shall not now onely be bound to refuse the profession of their naturall Allegiance to their Soueraigne, which might yet haue beene some way coloured vpon diuers scruples conceiued vpon the words of the Oath; but they must now renounce and forsweare their profession of obedience alreadie sworne, and so must as it were at the third instance forsweare their former two Oathes, first closely sworne, by their birth in their naturall Allegiance; and next, clearely confirmed by this Oath, which doeth nothing but expresse the same: so as no man can now holde the faith, or procure the saluation of his soule in ENGLAND that must not abiure and renounce his borne and sworne Allegiance to his naturall Soueraigne.

And yet it is not sufficient to ratifie the last yeeres *Breue*, by a new one come forth this yeere; but (that not only euery yeere, but euery moneth may produce a new monster) the great and famous Writer of the Controuersies, the late vn-Iesuited Cardinall *Bellarmine*, must adde his talent to this good worke, by blowing the bellowes of sedition, and sharpening the spurre to rebellion, by sending such a Letter of his to the Arch-priest here, as it is a wonder how passion, and an ambitious desire of maintaining that Monarchie, should charme the wits of so famously learned a man.

The Copy whereof here followeth.

TO THE VERY REVEREND

Mr. *GEORGE BLACKWELL*, ARCH-PRIEST

of the ENGLISH: ROBERT BELLARMINE

Cardinall of the holy Church of *Rome*, Greeting.

REuerend Sir, and brother in CHRIST; *It is almost fourtie yeeres since we did see one the other: but yet I haue neuer bene vnmindfull of our ancient acquaintance, neither haue I ceased, seeing I could doe you no other good, to commend your labouring most painfully in the Lords Vineyard, in my prayers to God. And I doubt not, but that I haue liued all this while in your memory, and haue had some place in your prayers at the Lords Altar. So therefore euen vnto this time we haue abidden, as* S. Iohn *speaketh, in the mutuall loue one of the other, not by word or letter, but in deed and trewth. But a late message which was brought vnto vs within these few dayes, of your bonds and imprisonment, hath inforced mee to breake off this silence; which message, although it seemed heauie in regard of the losse which that Church hath receiued, by their being thus depriued of the comfort of your pastorall function amongst them, yet withall it seemed ioyous, because you drew neere vnto the glory of* Martyrdome, *then the which gift of God there is none more happy; That you, who haue fedde your flocke so many yeeres with the word and doctrine, should now feed it more gloriously by the example of your patience. But another heauie tidings did not a little disquiet and almost take away this ioy, which immediatly followed, of the aduersaries assault, and peraduenture of the slip and fall of your constancie in refusing an vnlawfull Oath. Neither trewly (most deare brother) could that Oath therefore bee lawfull, because it was offered in sort tempered and modified: for you know that those kinde of modifications are nothing else, but sleights and subtilties of Satan, that the Catholique faith touching the Primacie of the Sea Apostolike, might either secretly or openly be shot at; for the which faith so many worthy Martyrs euen in that very* England *it selfe, haue resisted vnto blood. For most certaine it is, that in whatsoeuer words the Oath is conceiued by,*[548] *the aduersaries of the faith in that Kingdome, it tends to this end, that the Authoritie of the head of the Church in* England, *may bee transferred from the successour of* S. Peter, *to the successour of King* Henry *the eight: For that which is pretended of the danger of the Kings life, if the high Priest should haue the same*

99

power in England, *which hee hath in all other Christian Kingdomes, it is altogether idle, as all that haue any vnderstanding, may easily perceiue. For it was neuer heard of from the Churches infancie vntill this day, that euer any* Pope *did command, that any Prince, though an Heretike, though an Ethnike, though a persecutour, should be murdered; or did approue of the fact, when it was done by any other. And why, I pray you, doeth onely the King of* England *feare that, which none of all other the Princes in Christendome either doeth feare, or euer did feare?*

But, as I said, these vaine pretexts are but the traps and stratagemes of Satan: Of which kinde I could produce not a fewe out of ancient Stories, if I went about to write a Booke and not an Epistle. One onely for example sake, I will call to your memory. S. Gregorius Nazianzenus *in his first Oration against* Iulian *the Emperour, reporteth, That hee, the more easily to beguile the simple Christians, did insert the Images of the false gods into the pictures of the Emperour, which the Romanes did vse to bow downe vnto with a ciuill kinde of reuerence: so that no man could doe reuerence to the Emperours picture, but withall hee must adore the Images of the false gods; whereupon it came to passe that many were deceiued. And if there were any that found out the Emperours craft, and refused to worship his picture, those were most grieuously punished, as men that had contemned the Emperour in his Image. Some such like thing, me thinkes, I see in the Oath that is offered to you; which is so craftily composed, that no man can detest Treason against the King, and make profession of his Ciuill subiection, but he must bee constrained perfidiously to denie the Primacie of the Apostolicke Sea. But the seruants of Christ, and especially the chiefe Priests of the Lord, ought to bee so farre from taking an vnlawfull Oath, where they may indamage the Faith, that they ought to beware that they giue not the least suspicion of dissimulation that they haue taken it, least they might seeme to haue left any example of preuarication to faithfull people. Which thing that worthy* Eleazar *did most notably performe, who would neither eate swines flesh, nor so much as faine to haue eaten it, although hee sawe the great torments that did hang ouer his head; least, as himselfe speaketh in the second Booke of* the Machabees, *many young men might bee brought through that simulation, to preuaricate with the Lawe. Neither did* Basil *the Great by his example, which is more fit for our purpose, cary himselfe lesse worthily toward* Valens *the Emperour. For as* Theodoret *writeth in his Historie, when the Deputy of that hereticall Emperour did perswade Saint* Basil, *that hee would not resist the Emperour for a little subtiltie of a few points of doctrine; that most holy and prudent man made answere,* That it was not to be indured, that the least syllable of Gods word should bee corrupted, but rather all kind of torment was to be embraced, for the maintenance of the Trewth thereof. *Now I suppose, that there wants not amongst you, who say that they are but subtilties of Opinions that are contained in the Oath that is offered to the Catholikes, and that you are not to striue against the Kings Authoritie for such a little matter. But there are not wanting also amongst you holy men like vnto* Basil *the Great, which will openly auow, that the very least syllable of Gods diuine Trewth is not to bee corrupted, though many torments were to bee endured, and death it selfe set before you: Amongst whom it is meete, that you should bee one, or rather the Standard bearer, and Generall to the rest. And whatsoeuer hath been the cause, that your Constancie hath quailed, whether it bee the suddainenesse of your apprehension, or the bitternesse of your persecution, or the imbecilitie of your old aage: yet wee trust in the goodnesse of God, and in your owne long continued vertue, that it will come to passe, that as you seeme in some part to haue imitated the fall of* Peter *and* Marcellinus, *so you shall happily imitate their valour in recouering your strength, and maintaining the Trewth: For if you will diligently weigh the whole matter with your selfe, trewly you shall see, it is no small matter that is called in question by this Oath, but one of the principall heads of our Faith, and foundations of Catholique Religion. For heare what your Apostle* Saint Gregorie *the Great hath written in his* 24.[549] *Epistle of his* II. *Booke.* Let not the reuerence due to the Apostolique Sea, be troubled by any mans presumption; for then the state of the members doeth remaine entire, when the Head of the Faith is not bruised by any iniurie: *Therefore by* Saint Gregories *testimonie, when they are busie about disturbing or diminishing, or taking away of the Primacie of the Apostolique Sea; then are they busie about cutting off the very head of the faith, and dissoluing of the state of the whole body, and of all the members. Which selfe same thing* S. Leo *doth confirme in his third Sermon of his Assumption to the Popedom, when he saith,* Our Lord had a special care of *Peter,* & praied properly for *Peters* faith, as though the state of others were more stable, when their Princes mind was not to be ouercome. *Whereupon himselfe in his Epistle to the bishops of the prouince of Vienna, doth not doubt to affirme,* that he is not partaker of the diuine Mysterie, that dare depart from the solidity of *Peter*; *who also saith,* That who[550] thinketh the Primacy to be denied to that Sea, he can in no sort lessen the authority of it; but by being puft vp with the spirit of his owne pride, doth cast himselfe headlong into hel. *These and many other of this kind, I am very sure are most familiar to you: who besides many other books, haue diligently read ouer the visible Monarchy of your owne* Sanders, *a most diligent writer, and one who hath worthily deserued of the Church of* England. *Neither can you be ignorant, that these most holy and learned men,* Iohn *bishop of* Rochester, *and* Tho. Moore, *within our memory, for this one most weighty head of doctrine, led the way to* Martyrdome *to many others, to the exceeding glory of the English nation. But I would put you in remembrance that you should take heart, and considering the weightines of the cause, not to trust too much to your owne iudgement, neither be wise aboue that is meet to be wise: and if peraduenture your fall haue proceeded not vpon want of consideration, but through humane infirmity, & for feare of punishment and imprisonment, yet do not preferre a temporall liberty to the liberty of the glory of the Sonnes of God: neither for escaping a light & momentarie tribulation, lose an eternal weight of glory, which tribulation it selfe doeth worke in you. You haue fought a good fight a long time, you haue wel-neere finished your course; so many yeeres haue you kept the faith: do not therefore lose the reward of such labors; do not depriue your selfe of that crowne of righteousnes, which so long agone is prepared for you; Do not make the faces of so many yours both brethren and children ashamed. Vpon you at this time are fixed the eyes of all the Church: yea also, you are made a spectacle to the world, to Angels, to men; Do not so carry your selfe in this your last act, that you leaue nothing but laments to your friends, and ioy to your enemies. But rather on the contrary, which we assuredly hope, and for which we continually powre forth prayers to God, display gloriously the banner of faith, and make to reioyce the Church, which you haue made heauy; so shall you not onely merite pardon at Gods hands, but a Crowne. Farewell. Quite you like a man, and let your heart be strengthened. From Rome the* 28. *day of September,*[551] 1607.

Your very Reuerendships brother and seruant in Christ,
Robert Bellarmine Cardinall.

THE ANSWERE TO THE CARDINALS LETTER.

ANd now that I am to enter into the field against him by refuting his Letter, I must first vse this protestation; That no desire of vaine-glory by matching with so learned a man, maketh me to vndertake this taske; but onely the care and conscience I haue, that such smooth *Circes* charmes and guilded pilles, as full of exterior eloquence, as of inward vntrewths, may not haue that publike passage through the world without an answere: whereby my reputation might vniustly be darkened, by such cloudie and foggie mists of vntrewths and false imputations, the hearts of vnstayed and simple men be misse-led, and the trewth it selfe smothered.

But before I come to the particular answere of this Letter, I must here desire the world to wonder with me, at the committing of so grosse an errour by so learned a man:[552] as that he should haue pained himselfe to haue set downe so elaborate a Letter, for the refutation of a quite mistaken question: For it appeareth, that our English Fugitiues, of whose inward societie with him he so greatly vaunteth, haue so fast hammered in his head the Oath of Supremacie, which hath euer bene so great a scarre vnto them, as he thinking by his Letter to haue refuted the last Oath, hath in place thereof onely paied the Oath of Supremacie, which was most in his head; as a man that being earnestly caried in his thoughts vpon another matter, then he is presently in doing, will often name the matter or person he is thinking of, in place of the other thing he hath at that time in hand.

For as the Oath of Supremacie was deuised for putting a difference betweene Papists, and them of our profession:[553] so was this Oath, which hee would seeme to impugne, ordained for making a difference betweene the ciuilly obedient Papists, and the peruerse disciples of the Powder-Treason. Yet doeth all his Letter runne vpon an Inuectiue against the compulsion of Catholiques to deny the authoritie of *S. Peters* successors, and in place thereof to acknowledge the Successors of King *Henry the eight:* For in K. *Henry the eights* time, was the Oath of Supremacie first made: By him were *Thomas Moore* and *Roffensis* put to death, partly for refusing of it: From his time till now, haue all the Princes of this land professing this Religion, successiuely in effect maintained the same: and in that Oath onely is contained the Kings absolute power, to be Iudge ouer all persons, aswell Ciuill as Ecclesiastical, excluding al forraigne powers and Potentates to be Iudges within his dominions; whereas this last made Oath containeth no such matter, onely medling with the ciuill obedience of Subiects to their Soueraigne, in meere temporall causes.

And that it may the better appeare, that whereas by name hee seemeth to condemne the last Oath; yet indeed his whole Letter runneth vpon nothing, but vpon the condemnation of the Oath of Supremacie: I haue here thought good to set downe the said Oath, leauing it then to the discretion of euery indifferent reader to iudge, whether he doth not in substance onely answere to the Oath of Supremacie, but that hee giues the child a wrong name.

> I *A.B. doe vtterly testifie and declare in my conscience, that the Kings Highnesse is the onely Supreame Gouernour of this Realme, and all other his Highnesse Dominions and Countries, aswell in all Spirituall, or Ecclesiasticall things or causes, as Temporall: And that no forraine Prince, Person, Prelate, State or Potentate, hath or ought to haue any Iurisdiction, Power, Superioritie, Preeminence or Authoritie Ecclesiasticall or Spirituall within this Realme. And therefore I doe vtterly renounce and forsake all forraine Iurisdictions, Powers, Superiorities and Authorities; and doe promise that from hencefoorth I shall beare faith and trew Allegiance to the Kings Highnesse, his Heires and lawfull Successours: and to my power shall assist and defend all Iurisdictions, Priuiledges, Preeminences and Authorities granted or belonging to the Kings Highnesse, his Heires and Successours, or vnited and annexed to the Imperiall Crowne of the Realme: So helpe me God; and by the Contents of this booke.*[554]

And that the iniustice, as well as the error of his grosse mistaking in this point, may yet be more clearely discouered; I haue also thought good to insert here immediatly after the Oath of Supremacie, the contrary conclusions to all the points and Articles, whereof this other late Oath doeth consist: whereby it may appeare, what vnreasonable and rebellious points hee would driue my Subiects vnto, by refusing the whole body of that Oath, as it is conceiued: For he that shall refuse to take this Oath, must of necessitie hold all, or some of these propositions following.

That[555] I King IAMES, am not lawfull King of this Kingdome, and of all other my Dominions.

That[556] the *Pope* by his owne authoritie may depose me: If not by his owne authoritie, yet by some other authoritie of the Church, or of the Sea of *Rome*: If not by some other authoritie of the Church and Sea of *Rome*, yet by other meanes with others helpe, he may depose me.

That[557] the *Pope* may dispose of my Kingdomes and Dominions.

That[558] the *Pope* may giue authoritie to some forreine Prince to inuade my Dominions.

That[559] the *Pope* may discharge my Subiects of their Allegiance and Obedience to me.

That[560] the *Pope* may giue licence to one, or more of my Subiects to beare armes against me.

That[561] the *Pope* may giue leaue to my Subiects to offer violence to my Person, or to my gouernement, or to some of my Subiects.

That[562] if the *Pope* shall by Sentence excommunicate or depose mee, my Subiects are not to beare Faith and Allegiance to me.

If[563] the *Pope* shall by Sentence excommunicate or depose me, my Subiects are not bound to defend with all their power my Person and Crowne.

If[564] the *Pope* shall giue out any Sentence of Excommunication or Depriuation against me, my Subiects by reason of that Sentence, are not bound to reueale all Conspiracies and Treasons against mee, which shall come to their hearing and knowledge.

That[565] it is not hereticall and detestable to hold, that Princes being excommunicated by the *Pope*, may be either deposed or killed by their Subiects, or any other.

That[566] the *Pope* hath power to absolue my Subiects from this Oath, or from some part thereof.

That[567] this Oath is not administred to my Subiects, by a full and lawfull authoritie.

That[568] this Oath is to be taken with Equiuocation, mentall euasion, or secret reseruation; and not with the heart and good will, sincerely in the trew faith of a Christian man.

These are the trew and naturall branches of the body of this Oath. The affirmatiue of all which negatiues, doe neither concerne in any case the *Popes* Supremacie in Spirituall causes: nor yet were euer concluded, and defined by any complete generall Councell[569] to belong to the *Popes* authoritie; and their owne schoole Doctors are at irreconciliable[570] oddes and iarres about them.

And that the world may yet farther see ours and the whole States setting downe of this Oath, did not proceed from any new inuention of our owne, but as it is warranted by the word of GOD: so[571] doeth it take the example from an Oath of Allegiance decreed a thousand yeeres agone, which a famous Councell then, together with diuers other Councels, were so farre from condemning (as the *Pope* now hath done this Oath) as I haue thought good to set downe their owne wordes here in that purpose: whereby it may appear that I craue nothing now of my Subiects in this Oath, which was not expresly and carefully commaunded then, by the Councels to be obeyed without exception of persons. Nay not in the very particular point of *Equiuocation*, which I in this Oath was so carefull to haue eschewed:[572] but you shall here see the said Councels in their Decrees, as carefull to prouide for the eschewing of the same; so as almost euery point of that action, & this of ours shalbe found to haue relation & agreeance one with the other, saue onely in this, that those old Councels were careful and strait in commanding the taking of the same: whereas[573] by the contrary, he that now vanteth himselfe to be head of al Councels, is as careful & strait in the prohibition of all men from the taking of this Oath of Allegiance.

The words of the Councell be these:

Heare our Sentence.

Whosoeuer of vs,[574] *or of all the people thorowout all Spaine, shall goe about by any meanes of conspiracie or practise, to violate the Oath of his fidelitie, which he hath taken for the preseruation of his Countrey, or of the Kings life; or who shall attempt to put violent handes vpon the King; or to depriue him of his kingly power; or that by tyrannicall presumption would vsurpe the Soueraigntie of the Kingdome: Let him bee accursed in the sight of God the Father, and of his Angels; and let him bee made and declared a stranger from the Catholique Church, which hee hath prophaned by his periurie; and an aliant from the companie of all Christian people, together with all the complices of his impietie; because it behooueth all those that bee guiltie of the like offence, to vnder-lie the like punishment.* Which sentence is three seuerall times together, and almost in the same wordes, repeated in the same Canon. After this, *the Synode desired, That this Sentence of theirs now this third time rehearsed, might bee confirmed by the voyce and consent of all that were present. Then the whole Clergie and people answered, Whosoeuer shall cary himselfe presumptuously against this your definitiue sentence, let them be Anathema maranatha, that is, let them bee vtterly destroyed at the Lords comming, and let them and their complices haue their portion with Iudas Iscarioth. Amen.*

And in the fifth Councell,[575] there it is decreed, That this Acte touching the Oath of Allegiance, shall bee repeated in euery Councell of the Bishops of *Spaine.* The Decree is in these wordes: *In consideration that the mindes of men are easily inclined to euill and forgetfulnesse, therefore this most holy Synode hath ordained; and doeth enact, That in euery Councell of the Bishops of* Spaine, *the Decree of the generall Councell*[576] *which was made for the safetie of our Princes, shall bee with an audible voyce proclaimed and pronounced, after the conclusion of all other things in the Synode: That so it beeing often sounded into their eares, at least by continuall remembrance, the mindes of wicked men beeing terrified, might bee reformed, which by obliuion and facilitie [to euill] are brought to preuaricate.*

And in the sixt Councell,[577] *Wee doe protest before God, and all the orders of Angels, in the presence of the Prophets and Apostles, and all the companie of Martyrs, and before all the Catholique Church, and assemblies of the Christians; That no man shall goe about to seeke the destruction of the King: No man shall touch the life of the Prince: No man shall depriue him of the Kingdome: No man by any tyrannical presumption shall vsurpe to himselfe the Soueraigntie of the Kingdome: No man by any Machination shall in his aduersitie associate to himselfe any packe of Conspirators against him: And that if any of vs shall be presumptuous by rashnesse in any of these cases, let him be stricken with the anatheme of God, and reputed as condemned in eternall iudgement without any hope of recouery.*

And in the tenth Councell[578] (to omit diuers others held also at *Toledo*) it is said: *That if any religious man, euen from the Bishop to the lowest Order of the Church-men or Monkes, shall bee found to haue violated the generall Oathes made for the preseruation of the Kings Person, or of the Nation and Countrey with a prophane minde; foorthwith let him bee depriued of all dignitie, and excluded from all place and Honour.* The occasion of the Decrees made for this Oath, was, That the Christians were suspected for want of fidelitie to their Kings; and did either equiuocate in taking their Oath, or make no conscience to keepe it, when they had giuen it; as may appeare by sundry speeches in the Councell,[579] saying, *There is a generall report, that there is that perfidiousnesse in the mindes of many people of diuers Nations, that they make no conscience to keepe the Oath and fidelitie that they haue sworne vnto their Kings: but doe dissemble a profession of fidelitie in their mouthes, when they hold an impious perfidiousnesse in their mindes.* And againe,[580] *They sweare to their Kings, and yet doe they preuaricate in the fidelitie which they haue promised: Neither doe they feare the Volume of Gods iudgement, by the which the curse of God is brought vpon them, with great threatning of punishments, which doe sweare lyingly in the Name of God.* To the like effect spake they in the Councill of *Aquisgran:*[581] *If any of the Bishops, or other Church-man of inferiour degree, hereafter thorow feare or couetousnesse, or any other perswasion, shall make defection from our Lord the Orthodoxe Emperour* Lodowicke, *or shall violate the Oath of fidelitie made vnto him, or shall with their peruerse intention adhere to his enemies; let him by this Canonicall and Synodall sentence bee depriued of whatsoeuer place hee is possessed of.*

And now to come to a particular answere of his Letter. First, as concerning the sweet memory hee hath of his old acquaintance with the Arch-priest; it may indeed be pleasing for him to recount: but sure I am, his acquaintance with him and the rest of his societie, our Fugitiues (whereof he also vanteth himselfe in his Preface to the Reader in his Booke of Controuersies) hath prooued sowre to vs and our State: For some of such Priests and Iesuits, as were the greatest Traitors and fomenters of the greatest conspiracies against the late Queene, gaue vp Father *Rob: Bellarmine*[582] for one of their greatest authorities and oracles: And therfore I do not enuy the great honour he can winne, by his vaunt of his inward familiarity with an other Princes traitors & fugitiues; whom vnto if he teach no better maners then hitherto he hath done, I thinke his fellowship are litle beholding vnto him.

And for desiring him to remember him in his prayers at the Altar of the Lord: if the Arch-Priests prayers prooue no more profitable to his soule, then *Bellarmines* counsell is like to proue profitable, both to the soule and bodie of *Blackwell* (if he would follow it) the authour of this Letter might very well be without his prayers.

Now the first messenger that I can finde which brought ioyfull newes of the Arch-Priest to *Bellarmine*, was hee that brought the newes of the Arch-Priests taking, and first appearance of Martyrdome. A great signe surely of the Cardinals mortification, that hee was so reioyced to heare of the apprehension, imprisonment and appearance of putting to death of so old and deare a friend of his. But yet apparantly he should first haue beene sure, that hee was onely to bee punished for cause of Religion, before hee had so triumphed vpon the expectation of his Martyrdome. For first, by what rule of charitie[583] was it lawfull for him to iudge mee a persecutour, before proofe had beene made of it by the said Arch-Priests condemnation and death? What could hee know, that the said Arch-Priest was not taken vpon suspicion of his guiltinesse in the Powder-Treason? What certaine information had hee then receiued vpon the particulars, whereupon hee was to bee accused? And last of all, by what inspiration could he foretell whereupon hee was to bee accused? For at that time there was yet nothing layed to his charge. And if charitie should not bee suspicious, what warrant had hee absolutely to condemne mee of vsing persecution and tyrannie, which could not bee but implyed vpon mee, if *Blackwel* was to bee a Martyr? But surely it may iustly be sayd of *Bellarmine* in this case, that our Sauiour CHRIST saith of all worldly and carnall men, who thinke it enough to loue their friends,[584] and hate their enemies; the limits of the Cardinals charitie extending no farther, then to them of his owne profession. For what euer hee added in superfluous charitie to *Blackwel*, in reioycing in the speculation of his future Martyrdome; hee detracted as much vniustly and vncharitably from me, in accounting of me thereby as of a bloody Persecutour. And whereas this ioy of his was interrupted by the next messenger, that brought the newes of the saide Arch-Priest his failing in his constancie, by taking of this Oath; he needed neuer to haue beene troubled, either with his former ioy or his second sorrow, both beeing alike falsly grounded. For as it was neuer my intention to lay any thing vnto the said Arch-Priests charge, as I haue neuer done to any for cause of conscience; so was *Blackwels* constancie neuer brangled by taking of this Oath; It beeing a thing which he euer thought lawfull before his apprehension, and whereunto hee perswaded all Catholiques to giue obedience; like as after his apprehension, hee neuer made doubt nor[585] stop in it; but at the first offering it vnto him, did freely take it, as a thing most lawfull; neither meanes of threatening, or flatterie being euer vsed vnto him, as himselfe can yet beare witnesse.

And as for the temperature and modification of this Oath, except that a reasonable and lawfull matter is there set downe in reasonable and temperate wordes, agreeing thereunto; I know not what he can meane, by quarelling it for that fault: For no temperatnesse nor modifications in words therein, can iustly be called the Deuils craft; when the thing it selfe is so plaine, and so plainely interpreted to all them that take it; as the onely troublesome thing in it all, bee the wordes vsed in the end thereof, for eschewing *Æquiuocation* and *Mentall reseruation*. Which new Catholike doctrine, may farre iustlier bee called the Deuils craft, then any plaine and temperate wordes, in so plaine and cleare a matter. But what shall we say of these strange countrey clownes, whom of with the *Satyre* we may iustly complaine, that they blow both hote & cold out of one mouth? For *Luther* and all our bold and free-speaking Writers are mightily railed vpon by them, as hote-brained fellowes, and speakers by the Deuils instinct: and now if we speake moderately and temperately of them, it must be tearmed the Deuils craft: And therefore wee may iustly complaine with CHRIST, that when we mourne,[586] they wil not lament: and when we pipe, they wil not dance. But neither *Iohn Baptist* his seueritie, nor CHRIST his meekenesse and lenitie can please them, who build but to their owne Monarchie vpon the ground of their owne Traditions; and not to C<small>HRIST</small> vpon the ground of his word and infallible trewth.

But what can bee meant by alleadging, that the craft of the Deuill herein, is onely vsed for subuersion of the Catholique Faith, and euersion of Saint *Peters* Primacie; had neede bee commented anew by *Bellarmine* himselfe: For in all this Letter of his; neuer one word is vsed, to prooue that by any part of this Oath the Primacie of Saint *Peter* is any way medled with, except Master *Bellarmine* his bare alleadging; which without proouing it by more cleare demonstration, can neuer satisfie the conscience of any reasonable man. For (for ought that I know) heauen and earth are no farther asunder, then the profession of a temporall obedience to a temporall King, is different from any thing belonging to the Catholique Faith, or Supremacie of Saint *Peter*: For as for the Catholique Faith;[587] can there be one word found in all that Oath tending or sounding to matter of Religion? Doeth he that taketh it, promise there to beleeue, or not to beleeue any article of Religion? Or doeth hee so much as name a trew or false Church there? And as for Saint *Peters* Primacie; I know no Apostles name that is therein named, except the name of I<small>AMES</small>, it being my Christen name: though it please him not to deigne to name me in all the Letter; albeit, the contents thereof concerne mee in the highest degree. Neither is there any mention at all made therein, either *disertis verbis*,[588] or by any other indirect meanes, either of the Hierarchie of the Church, of Saint *Peters* succession, of the Sea Apostolike, or of any such matter: but that the Author of our Letter doeth brauely make mention of Saint *Peters* succession, bringing it in comparison with the succession of *Henry* the eight. Of which vnapt and vnmannerly similitude, I wonder he should not be much ashamed: For as to King *Henries* Successour (which hee meaneth by mee) as I, I say, neuer did, nor will presume to create any Article of Faith, or to bee Iudge thereof; but to submit my exemplarie obedience vnto them, in as great humilitie as the meanest of the land: so if the Pope could bee as well able to prooue his either Personall or Doctrinall Succession from Saint *Peter*, as I am able to prooue my lineall descent from the Kings of *England* and *Scotland*; there had neuer beene so long adoe, nor so much sturre kept about this question in Christendome; neither had Master[589] *Bellarmine* himselfe needed to haue bestowed so many sheetes of paper *De summo Pontifice*, in his great bookes of Controuersies: And when all is done, to conclude with a morall certitude, and a *pie credendum*;[590] bringing in the Popes,[591] that are parties in this cause, to be his witnesses: and yet their historicall narration must bee no article of Faith. And I am without vanterie sure, that I doe farre more neerely imitate the worthie actions of my Predecessours, then the *Popes* in our aage can be well proued to be *similes Petro*,[592] especially in cursing of Kings, and setting free their Subiects from their Allegiance vnto them.

But now wee come to his strongest argument, which is, That he would alledge vpon mee a Panicke terrour, as if I were possessed with a needlesse feare: *For*, saith the Cardinall,[593] *from the beginning of the Churches first infancie, euen to this day, where was it euer heard, that euer a* Pope *either commaunded to bee killed, or allowed the slaughter of any Prince whatsoeuer, whether hee were an Hereticke, an Ethnicke, or Persecutour?* But first, wherefore doeth he here wilfully, and of purpose omit the rest of the points mentioned in that Oath, for deposing, degrading, stirring vp of armes, or rebelling against them, which are as well mentioned in that Oath, as the killing of them? as beeing all of one consequence against a King, no Subiect beeing so scrupulous, as that hee will attempt the one, and leaue the other vnperformed if hee can. And yet surely I cannot blame him for passing it ouer, since he could not otherwise haue eschewed the direct belying of himselfe in tearmes, which hee now doeth but in substance and effect: For as[594] for the *Popes* deposing and degrading of Kings, hee maketh so braue vaunts and bragges of it in his former bookes, as he could neuer with ciuill honestie haue denied it here.

But to returne to the *Popes* allowing of killing of Kings, I know not with what face hee can set so stout a deniall vpon it against his owne knowledge. How many Emperours did the *Pope* raise warre against in their owne bowels? Who as they were ouercome in battaile, were subiect to haue beene killed therein, which I hope the *Pope* could not but haue allowed, when he was so farre inraged at *Henry*[595] the fifth for giuing buriall to his fathers dead corpes, after the *Pope*[596] had stirred him vp to rebell against his father, and procured his ruine. But leauing these olde Histories to *Bellarmines* owne bookes, that doe most authentically cite them, as I haue already said, let vs turne our eyes vpon our owne time, and therein remember what a Panegyricke Oration[597] was made by the *Pope*, in praise and approbation of the Frier and his fact, that murthered king *Henry* the third of *France*, who was so farre from either being Hereticke, Ethnicke, or Persecutor in their account, that the said *Popes* owne wordes in that Oration are, *That a trew Friar hath killed a counterfeit Frier.*[598] And besides that vehement Oration and congratulation for that fact, how neere it scaped, that the said Frier was not canonized for that glorious act, is better knowen to *Bellarmine* and his followers, then to vs here.

But sure I am, if some Cardinals had not beene more wise and circumspect in that errand, then the *Pope* himselfe was, the *Popes* owne Kalender of his Saints would haue sufficiently proued *Bellarmin* a lier in this case. And to draw yet neerer vnto our selues; how many practises and attempts were made against the late Queenes life, which were directly enioyned to those Traitours by their Confessors, and plainly authorized by the *Popes* allowance? For verification whereof, there needs no more proofe, then that neuer *Pope* either then or since, called any Church-man in question for medling in any of those treasonable conspiracies: nay, the Cardinals owne S. *Sanderus* mentioned in his Letter, could well verifie this trewth, if hee were aliue; and who will looke his bookes, will finde them filled with no other doctrine then this. And what difference there is betweene the killing, or allowing the slaughter of Kings, and the stirring vp and approbation of practises to kill them; I remit to *Bellarmines* owne iudgement. It may then very clearely appeare, how strangely this Authors passion hath made him forget himselfe, by implicating himselfe in so strong a contradiction against his owne knowledge and conscience, against the witnesse of his former bookes, and against the practise of our owne times. But who can wonder at this contradiction of himselfe in this point, when his owne great Volumes are so filled with contradictions? which when either he, or any other shall euer bee able to reconcile, I will then beleeue that hee may easily reconcile this impudent strong deniall of his in his Letter, of any *Popes* medling against Kings, with his owne former bookes, as I haue already said.

And that I may not seeme to imitate him in affirming boldly that which I no wayes prooue; I will therefore send the Reader to looke for witnesses of his contradictions, in such places here mentioned in his owne booke. In his bookes of Iustification,[599] there he affirmeth, *That for the vncertaintie of our owne proper righteousnesse, and for auoiding of vaine-glory, it is most sure and safe, to repose our whole confidence in the alone mercy and goodnesse of God;* Which[600] proposition of his, is directly contrary to the discourse, and current of all his fiue bookes *de Iustificatione,* wherein the same is contained.

God doeth not encline a man to euill, either naturally[601] *or morally.*
Presently after, hee affirmeth the contrary, *That God doeth not encline to euill naturally, but morally.*[602]
All the Fathers teach constantly, *That Bishops*[603] *doe succeed the Apostles, and Priests the seuentie disciples.*
Elsewhere he affirmeth the contrary, That *Bishops*[604] *doe not properly succeede the Apostles.*
That Iudas did not beleeue.[605]
Contrary, *That Iudas*[606] *was iust and certainly good.*
The keeping of the Law[607] *according to the substance of the worke, doeth require that the Commandement be so kept, that sinne be not committed, and the man be not guiltie for hauing not kept the Commandement.*
Contrary, *It*[608] *is to be knowen, that it is not all one, to doe a good morall worke, and to keepe the Commandement according to the substance of the worke: For the Commandement may be kept according to the substance of the worke, euen with sinne; as if one should restore to his friend the thing committed to him of trust, to the end that theeues might afterward take it from him.*
Peter[609] *did not loose that faith, whereby the heart beleeueth vnto iustification.*
Contrary, Peters[610] *sinne was deadly.*
Antichrist[611] *shall be a Magician, and after the maner of other Magicians shall secretly worship the diuel.*
Contrary,[612] *He shall not admit of idolatrie: he shall hate idoles, and reedifie the Temple.*
By the wordes of Consecration[613] *the trew and solemne oblation is made.*
Contrary, *The sacrifice doeth not consist in the words: but in the oblation*[614] *of the thing it selfe.*
That[615] *the end of the world cannot be knowne.*
Contrary,[616] *After the death of* Antichrist, *there shall be but fiue and fourtie dayes till the end of the world.*
That[617] *the tenne Kings shall burne the scarlet Whore, that is,* Rome.
Contrary,[618] Antichrist *shall hate* Rome, *and fight against it, and burne it.*
The[619] *name of vniuersall Bishop may be vnderstood two wayes; one way, that he which is said to be vniuersall Bishop, may bee thought to be the onely Bishop of all Christian Cities; so that all others are not indeed Bishops, but onely Vicars to him, who is called vniuersall Bishop: in which sense, the* Pope *is not vniuersall Bishop.*

Contrary, *All ordinary iurisdiction*[620] *of Bishops doeth descend imme-diatly from the Pope; and is in him, and from him is deriued to others.* Which few places I haue onely selected amongst many the like, that the discreet and iudicious Reader may discerne *ex vngue Leonem:*[621] For when euer he is pressed with a weighty obiection, hee neuer careth, nor remembreth how his solution and answere to that, may make him gainesay his owne doctrine in some other places, so it serue him for a shift to put off the present storme withall.

But now to returne to our matter againe: *Since Popes,* sayeth hee, *haue neuer at any time medled against Kings, wherefore, I pray you, should onely the King of* ENGLAND *be afraid of that, whereof neuer Christian King is, or was afraid?* Was neuer Christian Emperour or King afraid of the *Popes?* How then were these miserable Emperours tost and turmoiled, and in the end vtterly ruined by the *Popes:* for proofe whereof I haue already cited *Bellarmines* owne bookes? Was not the Emperour[622] afraid, who waited[623] barefooted in the frost and snow three dayes at the *Popes* gate, before he could get entrie? Was not the Emperour[624] also afraid, who[625] was driuen to lie agroofe on his belly, and suffer another *Pope* to tread vpon his necke? And was not another Emperour[626] afraid, who[627] was constrained in like maner to endure a third *Pope* to beat off from his head the Imperiall Crowne with his foot? Was not *Philip*[628] afraid, being made Emperour against *Pope Innocentius* the thirds good liking, when he brake out into these words, *Either the Pope shall take the Crowne from* Philip, *or* Philip *shall take the Miter from the Pope?* whereupon the *Pope* stirred vp *Ottho* against him, who caused him to be slaine; and presently went to *Rome,* and was crowned Emperour by the *Pope,* though afterward the *Pope* deposed[629] him too. Was not the Emperour *Fredericke*[630] afraid, when *Innocentius* the fourth excommunicated him, depriued him of his crowne, absolued Princes of their Oath of fidelitie to him, and in *Apulia* corrupted one to giue him poison? whereof the Emperour recouering, hee hired his bastard sonne *Manfredus* to poison him; whereof he died. What did *Alexander*[631] the third write to the *Soldan?* That if he would liue quietly, hee should by some slight murther the emperour;[632] and to that end sent him the Emperours picture. And did not *Alexander*[633] the sixt take of the Turke *Baiazetes* two hundred thousand crownes to kill his brother *Gemen;* or as some call him, *Sisimus,* whom he helde captiue at *Rome?* Did hee not accept of the conditions to poyson the man, and had his pay? Was not our *Henry*[634] the second afraid after the slaughter of *Thomas Becket*; that besides his going bare-footed in Pilgrimage, was whipped vp and down the Chapter-house like a schoole-boy, and glad to escape so to? Had not this French King his great grandfather King *Iohn* reason to be afraid, when the *Pope*[635] gaue away his kingdome of *Nauarre* to the King of *Spaine*, whereof he yet possesseth the best halfe? Had not this King, his Successour reason to be afraid, when he was forced to begge so submissiuely the relaxation of his Excommunication, as he was content likewise to suffer his Ambassadour to be whipped at *Rome* for penance? And had not the late Queene reason to looke to her selfe, when she was excommunicated by *Pius Quintus*, her Subiects loosed from their fidelitie and Allegiance toward her, her Kingdome of *Ireland* giuen to the King of *Spaine*, and that famous fugitiue diuine, honoured with the like degree of a redde Hat as *Bellarmine* is, was not ashamed to publish in Print an Apologie[636] for *Stanleys* treason, maintaining, that by reason of her excommunication and heresie, it was not onely lawfull for any of her Subiects, but euen they were bound in conscience to depriue her of any strength, which lay in their power to doe? And whether it were armies, townes, or fortresses of hers which they had in their hands, they were obliged to put them in the King of *Spaine* her enemies hands, shee no more being the right owner of any thing? But albeit it be trew, that wise men are mooued by the examples of others dangers to vse prouidence and caution, according to the olde Prouerbe, *Tum tua res agitur, paries cum proximus ardet*:[637] yet was I much neerlier summoned to vse this caution, by the practise of it in mine owne person.

First, by the sending foorth of these Bulles whereof I made mention already, for debarring me from entrie vnto this Crowne, and Kingdome. And next after my entrie, and full possession thereof, by the horrible Powder-treason, which should haue bereft both me and mine, both of crowne and life. And howsoeuer the Pope will seeme to cleare himselfe of any allowance of the said Powder-treason; yet can it not be denied, that his principall ministers here, and his chiefe *Mancipia*[638] the Iesuites, were the plaine practisers thereof: for which the principall of them[639] hath died confessing it, and others[640] haue fled the Countrey for the crime; yea, some of them gone into *Italy*: and yet neither these that fled out of this Countrey for it, nor yet *Baldwine*, who though he then remained in the Low-countreys, was of counsell in it, were euer called to account for it by the Pope; much lesse punished for medling in so scandalous and enormous businesse. And now what needs so great wonder and exclamation, that *the only King of* England *feareth*: And *what other Christian King doeth, or euer did feare but hee?* As if by the force of his rhetoricke he could make me and my good Subiects to mistrust our senses, deny the Sunne to shine at midday, and not with the serpent to stop our eares to his charming, but to the plaine and visible veritie it selfe. And yet for all this wonder, he can neuer prooue mee to be troubled with such a Panicke terrour. Haue I euer importuned the Pope with any request for my securitie? Or haue I either troubled other Christian Princes my friends and allies, to intreat for me at the Popes hand? Or yet haue I begged from them any aide or assistance for my farther securi-tie? No. All this wondred-at feare of mine, stretcheth no further, then wisely to make distinction betweene the sheepe and goats in my owne pasture. For since, what euer the Popes part hath beene in the Powder-treason; yet certaine it is, that all these caitife monsters did to their death maintaine, that onely zeale of Religion mooued them to that horrible attempt: yea, some of them at their death, would not craue pardon at God or King for their offence; exhorting other of their followers to the like constancie. Had not wee then, and our Parliament great reason, by this Oath to set a marke of distinction betweene good Subiects, and bad? Yea, betweene Papists, though peraduenture zealous in their religion, yet otherwise ciuilly honest and good Subiects, and such terrible firebrands of hell, as would maintaine the like maximes, which these Powder-men did? Nay, could there be a more gracious part in a King, suppose I say it, towards Subiects of a contrary Religion, then by making them to take this Oath, to publish their honest fidelitie in temporal things to me their Soueraigne, and thereby to wipe off that imputation and great slander which was laide vpon the whole professours of that Religion, by the furious enterprise of these Powder-men?

And whereas for illustration of this strong argument of his, hee hath brought in for a similitude the historie of *Iulian*[641] the *Apostata* his dealing with the Christians, when as he straited them either to commit idolatrie, or to come within the compasse of treason: I would wish the authour to remember, that although a similitude may be permitted *claudicare vno pede*;[642] yet this was a very ill chosen similit-ude,[643] which is lame both of feete and hands, and euery member of the body: For I shall in fewe wordes prooue, that it agreeth in no

one point saue one, with our purpose, which is, that *Iulian* was an
Emperour, and I a King. First, *Iulian* was an *Apostata*, one that had
renounced the whole Christian faith, which he had once professed,
and became an Ethnike againe, or rather an Atheist: whereas I am a
Christian, who neuer changed that Religion, that I dranke in with
my milke: nor euer, I thanke GOD, was ashamed of my profession.
Iulian dealt against Christians onely for the profession of CHRISTES
cause: I deale in this cause with my Subiects, onely to make a distinction betweene trew Subiects, and false-hearted traitours. *Iulians* end
was the ouerthrow of the Christians: my onely end is, to maintaine
Christianitie in a peaceable gouernement. *Iulians* drift was to make
them commit Idolatrie: my purpose is, to cause my Subiects to make
open profession of their naturall Allegiance, and ciuill Obedience.
Iulians meanes whereby he went about it, was by craft, and insnaring
them before they were aware: my course in this is plaine, cleare, and
voyd of all obscuritie; neuer refusing leaue to any that are required
to take this Oath, to study it at leisure, and giuing them all the
interpretation of it they can craue. But the greatest dissimilitude of
all, is in this: that *Iulian* pressed them to commit idolatrie to Idoles
and Images: but as well I, as all the Subiects of my profession are so
farre from guilt in this point, as wee are counted heretiques by you,
because we will not commit idolatrie. So as in the maine point of
all, is the greatest contrarietie. For, *Iulian* persecuted the Christians
because they would not commit idolatrie; and ye count me a persecutour, because I will not admit idolatrie: So as to conclude this point,
this old sentence may well be applied to *Bellarmine*, in vsing so vnapt
a similitude,

Perdere quos vult Iupiter, hos dementat.[644]

And therefore his vncharitable conclusion doeth not rightly follow:
That it seemeth vnto him, that some such thing should be subtilly or fraudu-
lently included in this Oath: as if no man can detest Treason against
the King, or professe ciuill subiection, except hee renounce the Primacie of the Apostolique Sea. But how he hath suckt this apprehension
out at his fingers ends, I cannot imagine: for sure I am, as I haue oft
said, hee neuer goeth about to prooue it: and to answere an improb-
able imagination, is to fight against a vanishing shadow. It cannot he
denied indeed, that many seruants of CHRIST, as well Priests, as
others, haue endured constantly all sorts of torments, and death, for

the profession of CHRIST: and therefore to all such his examples, as hee bringeth in for verifying the same, I need not to giue him any other answere, saue onely to remember him, that he playeth the part of a sophister in all these his examples of the constancie of Martyrs; euer taking *Controuersum pro confesso*,[645] as if this our case were of the same nature.

But yet that the Reader may the better discouer, not onely how vnaptly his similitudes are applied, but likewise how dishonestly hee vseth himselfe in all his citations: I haue thought good to set downe the very places themselues cited by him, together with a short deduction of the trew state of those particular cases: whereby, how little these examples can touch our case; nay, by the contrary, how rightly their trew sense may bee vsed, as our owne weapons to be throwen backe vpon him that alledgeth them, shall easily appeare. And first, for *Eleazar*:[646] If the Arch-priest his ground of refusing the Oath, were as good as *Eleazars* was, to forbeare to eate the swines flesh, it might not vnfitly be applied by the Cardinal to this purpose: For as *Eleazar* was a principall Scribe, so is he a principall Priest: As *Eleazars* example[647] had a great force in it, to animate the yonger Scribes to keepe the Lawe, or in his colourable eating it, to haue taught them to dissemble: so hath the Arch-priests, either to make the inferiour Priests to take the Oath, or to refuse it: but the ground failing, the building cannot stand: For what example is there in all the Scripture, in which disobedience to the Oath of the King, or want of Allegiance is allowed? If the Cardinall would remember, that when the Church maketh a Lawe (suppose to forbid flesh on certaine dayes) he that refuseth to obey it, incurreth the iust censure of the Church: If a man then ought to die rather then to breake the least of Gods Ceremoniall Lawes, and to pine and starue his body, rather then to violate the Church his positiue Law: will he not giue leaue to a man to redeeme his soule from sinne, and to keepe his body from punishment, by keeping a Kings politike Law, and by giuing good example in his Person, raise vp a good opinion in me of like Allegiance in the inferiours[648] of his order? This application, as I take it, would haue better fitted this example.

But let mee remember the Cardinall of another Oath[649] inioyned by a King to his people, whereby he indangered his owne life, and hazarded the safetie of the whole armie, when hee made the people sweare in the morning, not to taste of any meate vntill night: which

Oath he exacted so strictly, that his eldest sonne, and heire apparant, *Ionathan*, for breaking of it, by tasting a little hony of the top of his rodde, though he heard not when the King gaue that Oath, had well-nigh died for it. And shall an Oath giuen vpon so vrgent an occasion as this was, for the apparant safetie of me and my posteritie, forbidding my people to drinke so deeply in the bitter cup of Antichristian fornications, but that they may keepe so much hony in their hearts, as may argue them still espoused to me their Soueraigne in the maine knot of trew Allegiance; shall this Law, I say, by him bee condemned to hell for a *stratageme of Sathan?* I say no more, but Gods lot in that[650] Oath of *Sauls*, and *Bellarmines* verdict vpon this Oath of ours, seeme not to be cast out of one lap.

Now to this example of *Basill*,[651] which is (as he sayth) so fit for his purpose: First, I must obserue,[652] that if the Cardinall would leaue a common and ordinarie tricke of his in all his Citations, which is to take what makes for him, and leaue out what makes against him; and cite the Authours sense, as well as his Sentence, we should not be so much troubled with answering the Ancients which he alledgeth. To instance it in this very place: if he had continued his allegation one line further, hee should haue found this place out of *Theodoret*, of more force to haue mooued *Blackwell* to take the Oath, then to haue disswaded him from it: For in the very next words it followeth, *Imperatoris quidem amicitiam magni se pendere, cum pietate; qua remota, perniciosam esse dicere.*[653] But that it may appeare, whether of vs haue greatest right to this place, I will in few words shew the Authours drift.

The Emperour *Valens* being an Arrian, at the perswasion of his wife, when he had depriued all the Churches of their Pastours, came to *Cæsarea*, where S. *Basil*[654] was then Bishop, who, as the historie reporteth, was accounted the *Light of the world*. Before hee came, hee sent his deputie[655] to worke it, that S. *Basil* should hold fellowship with *Eudoxius* (which *Eudoxius*[656] was bishop of *Constantinople*, and the principall of the Arrian faction) or if he would not, that hee should put him to banishment. Now when the Emperours Deputie came to *Cæsarea*, he sent for *Basil*, intreated him honourably, spake pleasingly vnto him, desired he would giue way to the time, neither that he would hazard the good of so many Churches *tenui exquisitione dogmatis*:[657] promised him the Emperours fauour, and himselfe to be mediatour for his good. But S. *Basill* answered, *These intising speeches were fit to bee vsed to children, that vse to gape after such things: but for them that were throughly instructed in Gods word, they could neuer suffer any syllable thereof to be corrupted: Nay, if need required, they would for the maintenance thereof refuse no kind of death. Indeed the loue of the Emperour ought to bee greatly esteemed with pietie; but pietie taken away, it was pernicious.*

This is the trewth of the historie. Now compare the case of *Basill* with the Arch-priests: *Basill* was sollicited to become an Arrian: the Arch-priest not once touched for any article of faith. *Basill* would haue obeyed the Emperour, but that the word of GOD forbade him: this man is willed to obey, because the word of GOD commandeth him. *Basill* highly esteemed the Emperours fauour, if it might haue stood with pietie: the Arch-priest is exhorted to reiect it, though it stand with trew godlinesse in deed, to embrace it. But that he may lay load vpon the Arch-priest, it is not sufficient to exhort him to courage and constancie by *Eleazars*[658] and *Basils* examples; but he must be vtterly cast downe with the comparing his fall to *S. Peters*,[659] and *Marcellinus*:[660] which two mens cases were the most fearefull, considering their persons and places, that are to be found, or read of, either in all the bookes of diuine Scripture, or the volumes of Ecclesiasticall histories; the one denying the onely trew GOD, the other our Lord and Sauiour IESVS CHRIST; the one sacrificing to Idoles, with the prophane heathen: the other forswearing his Lord and Master, with the hard-hearted *Iewes*. Vnlesse the Cardinall would driue the Arch-priest to some horrour of conscience, and pit of despaire, I know not what he can meane by this comparison: For sure I am, all that are not intoxicated with their cup, cannot but wonder to heare of an Oath of Allegiance to a naturall Soueraigne, to be likened to an *Apostats* denying of God, and forswearing of his Sauiour.

But to let passe the *Disdiapason* of the cases (as his ill-fauoured coupling S. *Peter* the head of their Church, with an apostate Pope) I marueile hee would remember this example of *Marcellinus*,[661] since his brother Cardinall *Baronius*, and the late Edition of the Councels by *Binnius*[662] seeme to call the credit of the whole historie into question, saying, *That it might plainely be refuted, and that it is probably to be shewed, that the story is but obreptitious,*[663] but that he would not swarue from the common receiued opinion.

And if a man might haue leaue to coniecture; so would his Cardin-alship too, if it were not for one or two sentences in that Councell[664] of *Sinuessa*, which serued for his purpose; namely, that *Prima sedes a nemine iudicatur:*[665] And, *Iudica causam tuam: nostra sententia non condemnaberis.*[666] But to what purpose a great Councell (as he termes it) of three hundred Bishops and others, should meete together, who before they met, knew they could doe nothing; when they were there, did nothing, but like Cuckowes, sing ouer and ouer the same song: that, *Prima sedes a nemine iudicatur,*[667] and so after three dayes sitting (a long time indeed for a great and graue Councell) brake so bluntly vp: and yet, that there should be seuentie two witnesses brought against him, and that they should subscribe his excommunication, and that at his owne mouth hee tooke the *Anathema maranatha*: how these vntoward contradictions shall be made to agree, I must send the Cardinall to *Venice*, to *Padre Paulo,*[668] who in his Apologie[669] against the Cardinals oppositions,[670] hath handled them very learnedly.

But from one Pope, let vs passe to another:[671] (for, what a principall article of Faith and Religion this Oath is, I haue alreadie sufficiently proued.) Why hee called S. *Gregory*[672] our Apostle, I know not, vnlesse perhaps it be, for that hee sent *Augustine*[673] the Monke and others with him into England, to conuert vs to the faith of Christ, wherein I wish the *Popes* his successours would follow his patterne: For albeit hee sent them by diuine reuelation (as hee said) into Eng-land vnto King *Ethelbert*; yet when they came, they exercised no part of their function, but by the Kings leaue and permission. So did King *Lucius*[674] send to *Eleutherius* his predecessour, and hee sent him diuers Bishops, who were all placed by the Kings authoritie. These conuerted men to the faith, and taught them to obey the King. And if the *Popes* in these dayes would but insist in these steppes of their fore-fathers; then would they not entertaine Princes fugitiues abroad, nor send them home, not onely without my leaue, but directly against the Lawes, with plots of treason and doctrine of rebellion, to draw Subiects from their obedience to me their naturall King: nor be so cruell to their owne *Mancipia,*[675] as returning them with these wares, put either a State in iealousie of them; or them in hazard of their owne liues. Now to our Apostle (since the Cardinall will haue him so called) I perswade my selfe I should doe a good seruice to the

Church in this my labour, if I could but reape this one fruit of it, to moue the Cardinall to deale faithfully with the Fathers, & neuer to alledge their opinions against their own purpose: For, this letter of *Gregorius* was written to *Iohn* Bishop of *Palermo*[676] in *Sicily*, to whom he granted *vsum pallij*,[677] to be worne in such times, and in such order as the Priests in the Ile of *Sicily*, and his predecessors were wont to vse: and withall giueth him a caueat, *That the reuerence to the Apostolike Sea, be not disturbed by the presumption of any: for then the state of the members doeth remaine sound, when the head of the Faith is not bruised by any iniury, and the authoritie of the Canons alwayes remaine safe and sound.*

Now let vs examine the words. The Epistle was written to a Bishop, especially to grant him the vse of the Pall; a ceremonie and matter indifferent. As it appeareth, the Bishop of *Rome* tooke it well at his hands, that he would not presume to take it vpon him without leaue from the Apostolike Sea, giuing him that admonition which followeth in the wordes alledged out of him: which doctrine we are so farre from impugning, that we altogether approoue and allow of the same, that whatsoeuer ceremony for order is thought meet by the Christian Magistrate, and the Church, the same ought inuiolably to be kept: and where the head and gouernour in matters of that nature are not obeyed, the members of that Church must needs run to hellish confusion: But that *Gregory* by that terme, *caput fidei*,[678] held himselfe the head of our faith, and the head of all religion, cannot stand with the course of his doctrine and writings: For first, when an other would haue had this stile to be called *Vniuersalis Episcopus*,[679] hee said, *I*[680] *doe confidently auouch, that whosoeuer called himselfe or desireth to be called Vniuersall Bishop, in this aduancing of himselfe, is the fore-runner of the Antichrist*: which notwithstanding was a stile farre inferiour to that of *Caput fidei*. And when it was offered to himselfe the wordes of S. *Gregory* be these, refusing that Title: *None*[681] *of my predecessours* [Bishops of Rome,] *euer consented to vse this prophane name* [of vniuersall Bishop.] *None of my predecessours euer tooke vpon him this name of singularitie, neither consented to vse it, Wee the Bishops of* Rome *doe not seeke, nor yet accept this glorious title offered vnto vs.* And now, I pray you, would he that refused to be called Vniuersall Bishop, be stiled *Caput fidei*, vnlesse it were in that sense, as I haue expressed? which sense if he will not admit, giue me leaue to say that of *Gregorie*, which himselfe sayeth of *Lyra*,[682] *Minus caute locutus est*:[683] or which he elsewhere sayth of *Chrysostome, Locutus*[684] *est per excessum.*[685] To redeeme therefore our Apostle out of his hands, and to let him remaine ours, and not his in this case; it is very trew that he sayth in that sense he spake it. When yee goe about to disturbe, diminish, or take away the authoritie or supremacie of the Church, which resteth on the head of the King, within his dominions, ye cut off the head and chiefe gouernour thereof, and disturbe the state and members of the whole body. And for a conclusion of this point, I pray him to think, that we are so well perswaded of the good minde of our Apostle S. *Gregory* to vs, that wee desire no other thing to be suggested to the Pope and his Cardinals, then our Apostle S. *Gregory* desired *Sabinian*[686] to suggest vnto the Emperour and the State in his time. His words be these: *One thing there is, of which I would haue you shortly to suggest to your most noble Lord and Master: That if I his seruant would haue had my hand in slaying of the Lombards, at this day the Nation of the Lombards had neither had King, nor Dukes, nor Earles, and had beene diuided asunder in vtter confusion: but because I feare God, I dread to haue my hand in the blood of any man.*

And thus hauing answered to S. *Gregory*, I come to another Pope, his Apostle, S. *Leo.*[687] And that hee may see, I haue not in the former citations, quarelled him like a Sophister for contention sake, but for finding out of the trewth, I doe grant, that the authorities out of *Leo*,[688] are rightly alledged all three, the wordes trewly set downe, together with his trew intent and purpose: but withall, let me tell him, and I appeale vnto his owne conscience, whether I speake not trewly, that what *Tullie* said to *Hortensius*,[689] when he did immoderately praise eloquence, that hee would haue lift her vp to Heauen, that himselfe might haue gone vp with her; So his S. *Leo* lift vp S. *Peter* with praises to the skie, that he being his heire,[690] might haue gone vp with him: For his S. *Leo* was a great Oratour, who by the power of his eloquence redeemed *Rome* from fire, when both *Attilas*[691] and *Gensericus* would haue burnt it.

Some fruites of this rhetoricke hee bestowed vpon S. *Peter*, saying, *The Lord did*[692] *take Peter into the fellowship of the indiuisible vnitie:* which wordes being coupled to the sentence alledged by the Cardinall (*that he hath no part in the diuine Mysterie, that dare depart from the soliditie of Peter*) should haue giuen him, I thinke, such a skarre, as hee should neuer haue dared to haue taken any aduantage by the wordes immediatly preceding, for the benefite of the Church of *Rome*, and the head thereof; since those which immediatly follow, are so much derogatorie to the diuine Maiestie. And againe, *My writings*[693] *be strengthened by the authoritie and merit of my Lord, most blessed S. Peter. We beseech*[694] *you to keepe the things decreed by vs through the inspiration of God, and the Apostle most blessed S. Peter. If any*[695] *thing be well done, or decreed by vs; If any thing be obtained of Gods mercy by daily prayers, it is to be ascribed to* S. Peters *workes and merits, whose power doeth liue, and authoritie excell in his owne Sea. Hee was*[696] *so plentifully watered of the very fountaine of all graces, that whereas he receiued many things alone, yet nothing passeth ouer to any other, but hee was partaker of it.* And in a word, hee was so desirous to extoll Saint Peter, that a messenger from him was *an embassage*[697] *from* Saint Peter: *any*[698] *thing done in his presence, was in* S. Peters *presence.* Neither did he vse all this Rhetoricke without purpose: for at that time the Patriarch of *Constantinople* contended with him for Primacie. And in the Councell of *Chalcedon*,[699] the Bishops, sixe hundred and more, gaue equall authoritie to the Patriarch of that Sea, and would not admit any Priuiledge to the Sea of *Rome* aboue him; but went against him. And yet he that gaue so much to *Peter*, tooke nothing from *Caesar*; but gaue him both his Titles and due, giuing the power of calling a Councell to the Emperour; as it may appeare by these one or two places following of many. *If it may please your godlinesse*[700] *to vouchsafe at our supplication to condiscend, that you will command a Councell of Bishops to be holden within Italy.* And writing vnto the Bishop of Constantinople: *Because the most clement Emperour*,[701] *carefull of the peace of the Church, will haue a Councell to be holden; albeit it euidently appeare, the matter to be handled doeth in no case stand in neede of a Councell.* And againe, *Albeit my*[702] *occasions will not permit me to be present vpon the day of the Councell of Bishops, which your godlinesse hath appointed.* So as by this it may well appeare, that hee that gaue so much to *Peter*, gaue also to *Cæsar* his due and prerogatiue. But yet he playeth not faire play in this, that euen in all these his wrong applied arguments and examples, hee produceth no other witnesses, but the parties themselues; bringing euer the *Popes* sentences for approbation of their owne authoritie.

Now indeed for one word of his in the middest of his examples, I cannot but greatly commend him; that is, that Martyrs ought to endure all sorts of tortures and death, before they suffer one syllable to be corrupted of the Law of God. Which lesson, if hee and all the rest of his owne profession would apply to themselues, then would not the Sacrament be administred *sub vna specie*,[703] directly contrary to Christs institution, the practise of the Apostles and of the whole Primitive Church for many hundred yeeres: then would not the priuate Masses be in place of the Lordes Supper: then would not the words of the Canon[704] of the Masse be opposed to the words of S. *Paul* and S. *Luke*, as our Aduersarie himselfe confesseth, and cannot reconcile them: nor then would not so many hundreths other traditions of men be set vp in their Church, not onely as equall, but euen preferred to the word of God. But sure in this point I feare I haue mistaken him: for I thinke hee doeth not meane by his *Diuina Dogmata*,[705] the word of the God of heauen, but onely the Canons and Lawes of his *Dominus Deus Papa*:[706] otherwise all his Primacie of the Apostolike Sea would not be so much sticken vpon, hauing so slender ground ⸬ ⸜ne word of God.

And for the great feare he hath, that the suddennes of the apprehension, the bitternesse of the persecution, the weaknesse of his aage, and other such infirmities might haue been the cause of the Arch-priests fall; in this, I haue already sufficiently answered him; hauing declared, as the trewth is, and as the said *Blackwell* himselfe will yet testifie, that he tooke this Oath freely of himselfe, without any inducement thereunto, either *Precibus* or *Minis*.[707]

But amongst all his citations, hee must not forget holy *Sanderus*[708] and his *visibilis Monarchia*, whose person and actions I did alreadie a little touch. And surely who will with vnpartiall eyes reade his bookes, they may well thinke, that hee hath deserued well of his English Romane-Church; but they can neuer thinke, but that hee deserued very ill of his English Soueraigne and State: Witnesse his owne books; whereout I haue made choice to set downe heere these fewe sentences following, as flowers pickt out of so worthy a garland. *Elizabeth*[709] *Queene of* ENGLAND, *doeth exercise the Priestly acte of teaching and preaching the Gospel in* ENGLAND, *with no lesse authority then Christ himselfe, or* Moses *euer did. The supremacie of a woman*[710] *in Church matters is from no other, then from the Deuill.* And of all Kings[711] in generall thus he speaketh, *The King*[712] *that will not inthrall himselfe to the Popes authoritie, he ought not to be tolerated; but his Subiects ought to giue all diligence, that another may be chosen in his place assoone as may be. A King that is an Heretike,*[713] *ought to be remooued from the Kingdome that hee holdeth ouer Christians; and the Bishops ought to endeauour to set vp another, assoone as possibly they can. Wee doe constantly affirme,*[714] *that all Christian Kings are so farre vnder Bishops and Priests in all matters appertaining to faith, that if they shall continue in a fault against Christian Religion, after one or two admonitions, obstinately, for that cause they may and ought to be deposed by the Bishops from their temporall authoritie they holde ouer Christians. Bishops*[715] *are set ouer temporall kingdomes, if those kingdomes doe submit themselues to the faith of Christ. We doe iustly affirme,*[716] *that all Secular power, whether Regall, or any other, is of men. The anoynting*[717] *which is powred vpon the head of the King by the Priest, doeth declare that hee is inferiour to the Priest. It is altogether against the will of Christ,*[718] *that Christian kings should haue supremacie in the Church.*

And whereas for the crowne and conclusion of all his examples, he reckoneth his two English Martyrs,[719] *Moore* and *Roffensis*, who died for that one most weightie head of doctrine, as he alledgeth, refusing the Oath of Supremacie; I must tell him, that he hath not been well informed in some materiall points, which doe very neerely concerne his two said Martyrs: For it is cleare and apparantly to be prooued by diuers Records, that they were both of them committed to the Tower about a yeere before either of them was called in question vpon their liues, for the *Popes* Supremacie; And that partly for their backwardnesse in the point of the establishment of the Kings succession, whereunto the whole Realme had subscribed, and partly for that one of them, to wit, *Fisher*, had had his hand in the matter of the holy maide[720] of *Kent*; hee being for his concealment of that false prophets abuse, found guiltie of misprision of Treason. And as these were the principall causes of their imprisonment (the King resting secure of his Supremacie, as the Realme stood then affected, but especially troubled for setling the Crowne vpon the issue of his second mariage) so was it easily to be conceiued, that being thereupon discontented, their humors were thereby made apt to draw them by degrees, to further opposition against the King and his authoritie, as indeede it fell out: For in the time of their being in prison, the Kings lawfull authoritie in cases Ecclesiasticall being published and promulged, as well by a generall decree of the Clergie in their Synode, as by an Acte of Parliament made thereupon; they behaued themselues so peeuishly therein, as the olde coales of the Kings anger being thereby raked vp of new, they were againe brought in question; as well for this one most weighty head of doctrine of the *Pope* his supremacy, as for the matter of the Kings mariage and succession, as by the confession of one of themselues, euen *Thomas Moore*, is euident: For being condemned, he vsed these words at the barre before the Lords, *Non ignoro cur me morti adiudicaueritis; videlicet ob id, quod nunquam voluerim assentiri in negotio matrimonii Regis.*[721] That is, *I am not ignorant why you haue adiudged mee to death: to wit, for that I would neuer consent in the businesse of the new mariage of the King.* By which his owne confession it is plaine, that this great martyr himselfe tooke the cause of his owne death, to be onely for his being refractary to the King in this said matter of Marriage and Succession; which is but a very fleshly cause of Martyrdome, as I conceiue.

And as for *Roffensis* his fellow Martyr (who could haue bene content to haue taken the Oath of the Kings Supremacie, with a certaine modification, which *Moore* refused) as his imprisonment was neither onely, nor principally for the cause of Supremacie, so died hee but a halting and a singular Martyr or witnesse for that most weighty head of doctrine; the whole Church of *England* going at that time, in one current and streame as it were against him in that Argument, diuers of them being of farre greater reputation for learning and sound iudgement, then euer he was. So as in this point we may well arme our selues with the Cardinals owne reason, where he giueth amongst other notes of the trew Church, *Vniuersalitie* for one, wee hauing the generall and Catholique conclusion of the whole Church of *England*, on our side in this case, as appeareth by their booke set out by the whole Conuocation of *England*, called, *The Institution of a Christian man*;[722] the same matter being likewise very learnedly handled by diuers particular learned men of our Church, as by *Steuen Gardiner* in his booke *De vera obedientia*, with a Preface of Bishop *Boners* adioyning to it, *De summo & absoluto Regis Imperio*, published by M. *Bekinsaw*, *De vera differentia Regiæ Potestatis & Ecclesiasticæ*, Bishop *Tonstals* Sermon, Bishop *Longlands* Sermon, the letter of *Tonstall* to Cardinall *Poole*, and diuers other both in English and Latine. And if the bitternesse of *Fishers* discontentment had not bene fed with his dayly ambitious expectation of the Cardinals hat, which came so neere as *Calis* before he lost his head to fill it with, I haue great reason to doubt, if he would haue constantly perseuered in induring his Martyrdome for that one most waighty head of doctrine.

And surely these two Captaines and ringleaders to Martyrdome were but ill followed by the rest of their countreymen: for I can neuer reade of any after them, being of any great accompt, and that not many, that euer sealed that weighty head of doctrine with their blood in *England*. So as the trew causes of their first falling in trouble (whereof I haue already made mention) being rightly considered vpon the one part, and vpon the other the scant number of witnesses, that with their blood sealed it (a point so greatly accompted of by our Cardinal) there can but smal glory redound thereby to our English nation, these onely two, *Enoch* and *Elias*, seruing for witnesses against our Antichristian doctrine.

And I am sure the Supremacie of Kings may,[723] & wil euer be better maintained by the word of God (which must euer be the trew rule to discerne all waighty heads of doctrine by) to be the trew and proper office of Christian Kings in their owne dominions, then he will be euer able to maintaine his annihilating Kings, and their authorities, together with his base and vnreuerend speaches of them, wherewith both his former great Volumes, and his late Bookes against *Venice* are filled. In the old Testament, Kings were directly Gouernours[724] over the Church within their Dominions, purged[725] their corruptions; reformed their abuses, brought the Arke[726] to her resting place, the King dancing[727] before it; built[728] the Temple; dedicated[729] the same, assisting in their owne persons to the sanctification thereof; made[730] the Booke of the Law new-found, to bee read to the people; renewed[731] the Couenant betweene God and his people; bruised[732] the brasen serpent in pieces, which was set vp by the expresse commandement of God, and was a figure of Christ; destroyed all[733] Idoles, and false gods; made a[734] publike reformation, by a Commission of Secular men and Priests mixed for that purpose; deposed the[735] high Priest, and set vp another in his place: and generally, ordered euery thing belonging to the Church-gouernment, their Titles and Prerogatiues giuen them by God, agreeing to these their actions. They are called *the Sonnes*[736] *of the most High*, nay, *Gods themselues*;[737] *The Lords*[738] *anoynted, Sitting in*[739] *Gods throne; His seruants*;[740] *The Angels of*[741] *God; According to his hearts*[742] *desire; The light of*[743] *Israel; The nursing*[744] *fathers of the Church*, with innumerable such stiles of honour, wherwith the old Testament is filled; whereof our aduersary can pretend no ignorance. And as to the new Testament, *Euery soule* is commaunded *to be subiect vnto them, euen for conscience*[745] *sake*. All men must[746] be prayed for; *but especially Kings, and those that are in Authoritie, that vnder them we may leade a godly, peaceable, and an honest life.*

The Magistrate[747] *is the minister of God, to doe vengeance on him that doeth euill, and reward him that doeth well. Ye must obey all higher powers, but especially*[748] *Princes, and those that are supereminent. Giue euery man his due, feare to*[749] *whom feare belongeth, and honour to whome honour. Giue vnto*[750] *Cæsar what is Cæsars, and to God what is Gods. Regnum*[751] *meum non est huius mundi.*[752] *Quis*[753] *me constituit Iudicem super vos?*[754] *Reges*[755] *gentium dominantur eorum, vos autem non sic.*[756] If these examples, sentences, titles, and prerogatiues, and innumerable other in the Olde and New Testament doe not warrant Christian Kings, within their owne dominions, to gouerne their Church, as well as the rest of their people, in being *Custodes vtriusque Tabulæ,*[757] not by making new Articles of Faith, (which is the Popes office as I said before) but by commanding obedience to be giuen to the word of God, by reforming the religion according to his prescribed will, by assisting the spirituall power with the temporall sword, by reforming of corruptions, by procuring due obedience to the Church, by iudging, and cutting off all friuolous questions and schismes, as *Constantine*[758] did; and finally, by making *decorum* to be obserued in euery thing, and establishing orders to bee obserued in all indifferent things for that purpose, which is the onely intent of our Oath of Supremacie: If this Office of a King, I say, doe not agree with the power giuen him by Gods word, let any indifferent man voyd of passion, iudge. But how these honourable offices, styles, and prerogatiues giuen by God to Kings in the Old and New Testament, as I haue now cited, can agree with the braue styles and titles that *Bellarmine* giueth them, I can hardly conceiue.

That[759] *Kings are rather slaues then Lords.*

That[760] *they are not onely subiects to Popes, to Bishops, to Priests, but euen to Deacons.*

That[761] *an Emperour must content himselfe to drinke, not onely after a Bishop, but after a Bishops Chaplen.*

That[762] *Kings haue not their Authoritie nor Office immediatly from God, nor his Law, but onely from the Law of Nations.*

That[763] *Popes haue degraded many Emperours, but neuer Emperour degraded the Pope; nay, euen Bishops,*[764] *that are but the Popes vassals, may depose Kings, and abrogate their lawes.*

That[765] *Church-men are so farre aboue Kings, as the soule is aboue the body.*

That[766] *Kings may be deposed by their people, for diuers respects.*

But[767] *Popes can by no meanes be deposed: for no flesh hath power to iudge of them.*

That[768] *obedience due to the Pope, is for conscience sake.*

But[769] *the obedience due to Kings, is onely for certaine respects of order and policie.*

That[770] *these very Church-men that are borne, and inhabite in Soueraigne Princes countreys, are notwithstanding not their Subiects, and cannot bee iudged by them, although they may iudge them.*

And,[771] that *the obedience that Church-men giue to Princes, euen in the meanest and meere temporall things, is not by way of any necessarie subiection, but onely out of discretion, and for obseruation of good order and custome.*

These contrarieties betweene the Booke of God, and *Bellarmines* bookes, haue I heere set in opposition each to other, *Vt ex contrariis iuxta se positis, veritas magis elucescere possit.*[772] And thus farre I dare boldly affirme, that whosoeuer will indifferently weigh these irreconciliable[773] contradictions here set downe, will easily confesse, that CHRIST is no more contrarie to Belial, light to darknesse, and heauen to hell, then *Bellarmines* estimation of Kings, is to Gods.

Now as to the conclusion of his letter, which is onely filled with strong and pithie exhortations, to perswade and confirme *Blackwell* to the patient and constant induring of martyrdome, I haue nothing to answere, saue by way of regrate; that so many good sentences drawen out of the Scripture, so well and so handsomely packed vp together, should be so ill and vntrewly applied: But an euill cause is neuer the better for so good a cloake; and an ill matter neuer amended by good wordes: And therefore I may iustly turne ouer that craft of the diuell vpon himselfe, in vsing so holy-like an exhortation to so euill a purpose. Onely I could haue wished him, that hee had a little better obserued his *decorum* herein, in not letting slippe two or three prophane words amongst so many godly mortified Scripture sentences. For in all the Scripture, especially in the New Testament, I neuer read of *Pontifex Maximus.*[774] And the Pope must be content in that style to succeed according to the Law and institution of *Numa Pompilius,*[775] and not to S. *Peter,* who neuer heard nor dreamed of such an Office.

And for his *Caput fidei,*[776] which I remembred before, the Apostles (I am sure) neuer gaue that style to any, but to CHRIST: So as these styles, whereof some were neuer found in Scripture, and some were neuer applyed but the CHRIST in that sense, as hee applieth it, had beene better to haue beene left out of so holy and mortified a letter.

To conclude then this present Discourse, I heartily wish all indifferent readers of the *Breues* and Letter, not to iudge by the speciousnesse of the wordes, but by the weight of the matter; not looking to that which is strongly alledged, but iudiciously to consider what is iustly prooued: And for all my owne good and naturall Subiects, that their hearts may remaine established in the trewth; that these forraine inticements may not seduce them from their natall and naturall duetie; and that all, aswell strangers, as naturall subiects, to whose eyes this Discourse shall come, may wisely and vnpartially iudge of the Veritie, as it is nakedly here set downe, for clearing these mists and cloudes of calumnies, which were iniustly heaped vpon me; for which end onely I heartily pray the courteous Reader to be perswaded, that I tooke occasion to publish this Discourse.

A SPEACH, AS IT WAS[777] DELIVERED IN THE VPPER HOVSE OF THE PARLIAMENT TO THE LORDS SPIRITVALL AND Temporall, and to the Knights, Citizens and Burgesses there assembled, *ON MVNDAY THE XIX.* DAY OF MARCH 1603. BEING THE FIRST DAY OF THE first Parliament.

IT did no sooner please God to lighten his hand, and relent the violence of his deuouring Angel against the poore people of this Citie,[778] but as soone did I resolue to call this Parliament, and that for three chiefe and principall reasons: The first whereof is, (and which of it selfe, although there were no more, is not onely a sufficient, but a most full and necessary ground and reason for conuening of this Assembly) This first reason I say is, That you who are here presently assembled to represent the Body of this whole Kingdome, and of all sorts of people within the same, may with your owne eares heare, and that I out of mine owne mouth may deliuer vnto you the assurance of my due thankefulnes for your so ioyfull and generall applause to the declaring and receiuing of mee in this Seate (which GOD by my Birthright and lineall descent had in the fulnesse of time prouided for me) and that, immediatly after it pleased God to call your late Soueraigne of famous memory, full of dayes, but fuller of immortall trophes of Honour, out of this transitorie life. Not that I am able to expresse by wordes, or vtter by eloquence the viue Image of mine inward thankfulnes, but onely that out of mine owne mouth you may rest assured to expect that measure of thankefulnes at my hands, which is according to the infinitenes of your deserts, and to my inclination and abilitie for requitall of the same. Shall I euer? nay, can I euer be able, or rather so vnable in memorie, as to forget your vnexpected readinesse and alacritie, your euer memorable resolution, and your most wonderfull coniunction and harmonie of your hearts in declaring and embracing mee as your vndoubted and lawfull King and Gouernour? Or shall it euer bee blotted out of my minde, how at my first entrie into this Kingdome, the people of all sorts rid and ran, nay rather flew to meet mee? their eyes flaming nothing but sparkles of affection, their mouthes and tongues vttering nothing but sounds of ioy, their hands, feete, and all the rest of their members in their gestures discouering a passionate longing, and earnestnesse to meete and embrace their new Soueraigne. *Quid ergo retribuam?*[779] Shall I allow in my selfe, that which I could neuer beare with in another? No I must plainely and freely confesse here in all your audiences, that I did euer naturally so farre mislike a tongue to smoothe, and diligent in paying their creditors with lip payment and verball thankes, as I euer suspected that sort of people meant not to pay their debtors in more substantiall sort of coyne. And therefore for expressing of my thankefulnesse, I must resort vnto the other two reasons of my conuening of this Parliament, by them in action to vtter my thankefulnesse: Both the said reasons hauing but one ground, which is the deedes, whereby all the dayes of my life, I am by Gods grace to expresse my said thankfulnesse towards you, but diuided in this, That in the first of these two, mine actions of thankes, are so inseparably conioyned with my Person, as they are in a maner become indiuidually annexed to the same: In the other reason, mine actions are such, as I may either doe them, or leaue them vndone, although by Gods grace I hope neuer to be weary of the doing of them.

As to the first: It is the blessings which God hath in my Person bestowed vpon you all, wherein I protest, I doe more glorie at the same for your weale, then for any particular respect of mine owne reputation, or aduantage therein.

The[780] first then of these blessings, which God hath ioyntly with my Person sent vnto you, is outward Peace: that is, peace abroad with all forreine neighbours: for I thanke God I may iustly say, that neuer since I was a King, I either receiued wrong of any other Christian Prince or State, or did wrong to any: I haue euer, I praise God, yet kept Peace and amitie with all, which hath bene so farre tyed to my person, as at my comming here you are witnesses I found the State embarqued in a great and tedious warre, and onely by mine arriuall here, and by the Peace in my Person, is now amitie kept, where warre was before,[781] which is no smal blessing to a Christian Common-wealth: for by Peace abroad with their neighbours the Townes flourish, the Merchants become rich, the Trade doeth encrease, and the people of all sorts of the Land enioy free libertie to exercise themselues in their seuerall vocations without perill or disturbance. Not that I thinke this outward Peace so vnseparably tyed to my Person, as I dare assuredly promise to my selfe and to you, the certaine continuance thereof: but thus farre I can very well assure you, and in the word of a King promise vnto you. That I shall neuer giue the first occasion of the breach thereof, neither shall I euer be moued for any particular or priuate passion of mind to interrupt your publique Peace, except I be forced thereunto, either for reparation of the honour of the Kingdom, or else by necessitie for the weale and preseruation of the same: In which case, a secure and honourable warre must be preferred to an vnsecure and dishonourable Peace: yet doe I hope by my experience of the by-past blessings of Peace, which God hath so long euer since my Birth bestowed vpon mee, that hee wil not be weary to continue the same, nor repent him of his grace towards me, transferring that sentence of King *Dauids* vpon his by-past victories of warre, to mine of Peace, That, *that God who preserued me from the deuouring iawes of the Beare and of the Lion, and deliuered them into my hands, shall also now grant me victory ouer that vncircumcised Philistine.*[782]

But[783] although outward Peace be a great blessing; yet is it as farre inferiour to peace within, as Ciuill warres are more cruell and vnnaturall then warres abroad. And therefore the second great blessing that GOD hath with my Person sent vnto you, is Peace within, and that in a double forme. First, by my descent lineally out of the loynes of *Henry* the seuenth, is reunited and confirmed in mee the Vnion of the two Princely Roses of the two Houses of LANCASTER and YORKE, whereof that King of happy memorie was the first Vniter, as he was also the first ground-layer of the other Peace.[784] The lamentable and miserable euents by the Ciuill and bloody dissention betwixt these two Houses was so great and so late, as it need not be renewed vnto your memories: which, as it was first setled and vnited in him, so is it now reunited and confirmed in me, being iustly and lineally descended, not onely of that happie coniunction, but of both the Branches thereof many times before. But the Vnion of these two princely Houses, is nothing comparable to the Vnion of two ancient and famous Kingdomes, which is the other inward Peace annexed to my Person.

And here I must craue your patiences for a little space, to giue me leaue to discourse more particularly of the benefits that doe arise of that Vnion which is made in my blood, being a matter that most properly belongeth to me to speake of, as the head wherein that great Body is vnited. And first, if we were to looke no higher then to naturall and Physicall reasons, we may easily be perswaded of the great benefits that by that Vnion do redound to the whole Island: for if twentie thousand men be a strong Armie, is not the double thereof, fourtie thousand, a double the stronger Armie? If a Baron enricheth himselfe with double as many lands as hee had before, is he not double the greater? Nature teacheth vs, that Mountaines are made of Motes, and that at the first, Kingdomes being diuided, and euery particular Towne or little Countie, as Tyrants or Vsurpers could obtaine the possession, a Segniorie apart, many of these little King-domes are now in processe of time, by the ordinance of God, ioyned into great Monarchies, whereby they are become powerfull within themselues to defend themselues from all outward inuasions, and their head and gouernour thereby enabled to redeeme them from forreine assaults, and punish priuate transgressions within. Do we not yet remember, that this Kingdome was diuided into seuen little Kingdomes, besides Wales? And is it not now the stronger by their vnion? And hath not the vnion of Wales to England added a greater strength thereto? Which though it was a great Principalitie, was noth-ing comparable in greatnesse and power to the ancient and famous Kingdome of Scotland. But what should we sticke vpon any naturall appearance, when it is manifest that God by his Almightie prouidence hath preordained it so to be? Hath not God first vnited these two Kingdomes both in Language, Religion, and similitude of maners? Yea, hath hee not made vs all in one Island, compassed with one Sea, and of it selfe by nature so indiuisible, as almost those that were borderers themselues on the late Borders, cannot distinguish, nor know, or discerne their owne limits? These two Countries being sep-arated neither by Sea, nor great Riuer, Mountaine, nor other strength of nature, but onely by little small brookes, or demolished little walles, so as rather they were diuided in apprehension, then in effect; And now in the end and fulnesse of time vnited, the right and title of both in my Person, alike lineally descended of both the Crownes, whereby

it is now become like a little World within it selfe, being intrenched
and fortified round about with a naturall, and yet admirable strong
pond or ditch, whereby all the former feares of this Nation are now
quite cut off: The other part of the Island being euer before now not
onely the place of landing to all strangers, that was to make inuasion
here, but likewise moued by the enemies of this State by vntimely
incursions, to make inforced diuersion from their Conquests, for
defending themselues at home, and keeping sure their backe-doore,
as then it was called, which was the greatest hinderance and let that
euer my Predecessors of this Nation gat in disturbing them from
their many famous and glorious conquests abroad: What God hath
conioyned then, let no man separate. I am the Husband, and all the
whole Isle is my lawfull Wife; I am the Head, and it is my Body; I
am the Shepherd, and it is my flocke: I hope therefore no man will
be so vnreasonable as to thinke that I that am a Christian King vnder
the Gospel, should be a Polygamist and husband to two wiues; that
I being the Head, should haue a diuided and monstrous Body; or
that being the Shepheard to so faire a Flocke (whose fold hath no
wall to hedge it but the foure Seas) should haue my Flocke parted
in two. But as I am assured, that no honest Subiect of whatsoeuer
degree within my whole dominions, is lesse glad of this ioyfull Vnion
then I am; So may the friuolous obiection of any that would bee
hinderers of this worke, which God hath in my Person already established, bee easily answered, which can be none, except such as are
either blinded with Ignorance, or els transported with Malice, being
vnable to liue in a well gouerned Commonwealth, and onely
delighting to fish in troubled waters. For if they would stand vpon
their reputation and priuiledges of any of the Kingdomes, I pray you
was not both the Kingdomes Monarchies from the beginning, and
consequently could euer the Body bee counted without the Head,
which was euer vnseparably ioyned thereunto? So that as Honour
and Priuiledges of any of the Kingdomes could not be diuided from
their Soueraigne, So are they now confounded & ioyned in my
Person, who am equall and alike kindly Head to you both. When this
Kingdome of *England* was diuided into so many little Kingdoms as I
told you before; one of them behooued to eate vp another, till they
were all vnited in one. And yet can *Wiltshire* or *Deuonshire*, which
were of the *West Saxons*, although their Kingdome was of longest
durance, and did by Conquest ouercome diuers of the rest of the

little Kingdomes, make claime to Prioritie of Place or Honour before *Sussex, Essex,* or other Shires which were conquered by them? And haue we not the like experience in the Kingdome of *France,* being composed of diuers Dutchies, and one after another conquered by the sword? For euen as little brookes lose their names by their running and fall into great Riuers, and the very name and memorie of the great Riuers swallowed vp in the Ocean: so by the coniunction of diuers little Kingdomes in one, are all these priuate differences and questions swallowed vp. And since the successe was happie of the *Saxons* Kingdomes being conquered by the speare of *Bellona*;[785] How much greater reason haue wee to expect a happie issue of this greater Vnion, which is only fastened and bound vp by the wedding Ring of *Astrea*?[786] And as God hath made *Scotland* the one halfe of this Isle to enioy my Birth, and the first and most vnperfect halfe of my life, and you heere to enioy the perfect and the last halfe thereof; so can I not thinke that any would be so iniurious to me, no not in their thoughts and wishes, as to cut asunder the one halfe of me from the other. But in this matter I haue farre enough insisted, resting assured that in your hearts and mindes you all applaud this my discourse.

Now[787] although these blessings before rehearsed of Inward and Outward peace, be great: yet seeing that in all good things, a great part of their goodnesse and estimation is lost, if they haue not apparance of perpetuity or long continuance; so hath it pleased Almighty God to accompany my person also with that fauour, hauing healthful and hopefull Issue of my body, whereof some are here present, for continuance and propagation of that vndoubted right which is in my Person; vnder whom I doubt not but it will please God to prosper and continue for many yeeres this Vnion, and all other blessings of Inward and outward Peace, which I haue brought with me.

Bvt[788] neither Peace outward, nor Peace inward, nor any other blessings that can follow thereupon, nor appearance of the perpetuitie thereof, by propagation in the posteritie, is but a weake pillar and a rotten reed to leane vnto, if God doe not strengthen and by the staffe of his blessing make them durable: For in vaine doeth the Watchman watch the Citie, if the Lord be not the prinicipall defence thereof: In vaine doeth the builder build the house, if God giue not the success:[789] And in vaine (as *Paul* saith) doeth *Paul* plant and *Apollo* water, if God giue not the increase:[790] For all worldly blessings are but like swift passing shadowes, fading flowers, or chaffe blowen before the wind, if by the profession of trew Religion, and works according thereunto, God be not moued to maintaine and settle the Thrones of Princes. And although that since mine entry into this Kingdome, I haue both by meeting with diuers of the Ecclesiastical Estate, and likewise by diuers Proclamations clearely declared my minde in points of Religion, yet doe I not thinke it amisse in this so solemne an Audience, I should now take occasion to discouer somewhat of the secrets of my heart in that matter: For I shall neuer (with Gods grace) bee ashamed to make publike profession thereof at all occasions, lest God should bee ashamed to professe and allow mee before men and Angels, especially lest that at this time men might presume further vpon the misknowledge of my meaning to trouble this Parliament of ours then were conuenient. At my first comming, although I found but one Religion, and that which by my selfe is professed, publikely allowed, and by the Law maintained: Yet found I another sort of Religion, besides a priuate Sect, lurking within the bowels of this Nation. The first is the trew Religion, which by me is professed, and by the Law is established: The second is the falsly called Catholikes, but trewly Papists: The third, which I call a sect rather then Religion, is the *Puritanes* and *Nouelists*, who doe not so farre differ from vs in points of Religion, as in their confused forme of Policie and Paritie, being euer discontented with the present gouernment, & impatient to suffer any superiority, which maketh their sect vnable to be suffred in any wel gouerned Commonwealth. But as for my course toward them, I remit it to my Proclamations made vpon that Subiect. And now for the Papists, I must put a difference betwixt mine owne priuate profession of mine owne saluation, and my politike gouernment of the Realme for the weale and quietnes thereof. As for mine owne profession, you haue me your Head now amongst you of the same Religion that the body is of. As I am no stranger to you in blood, no more am I a stranger to you in Faith, or in the matters concerning the house of God. And although this my profession be according to mine education, wherein (I thanke God) I sucked the milke of Gods trewth, with the milke of my Nurse: yet do I here protest vnto you, that I would neuer for such a conceit of constancy or other preiudicate opinion, haue so firmly kept my first profession, if I had not found it agreeable to all reason, and to the rule of my Conscience. But I was neuer violent nor vnreasonable in my profession: I acknowledge the Romane Church to be our Mother Church, although defiled with some infirmities and corruptions, as the Iewes were when they crucified Christ: And as I am none enemie to the life of a sicke man, because I would haue his bodie purged of ill humours; no more am I enemie to their Church, because I would haue them reforme their errors, not wishing the downethrowing of the Temple, but that it might be purged and cleansed from corruption: otherwise how can they wish vs to enter, if their house be not first made cleane? But as I would be loather to dispense in the least point of mine owne Conscience for any worldly respect, then the foolishest Precisian of them all; so would I bee as sory to straight the politique Gouernement of the bodies and mindes of all my Subiectes to my priuate opinions: Nay, my minde was euer so free from persecution, or thralling of my Subiects in matters of Conscience, as I hope that those of that profession within this Kingdome haue a proofe since my comming, that I was so farre from encreasing their burdens with *Rehoboam*, as I haue so much as either time, occasion, or law could permit, lightened them. And euen now at this time haue I bene carefull to reuise and consider deepely vpon the Lawes made against them, that some ouerture may be proponed to the present Parliament for clearing these Lawes by reason (which is the soule of the Law) in case they haue bene in times past further, or more rigorously extended by Iudges, then the meaning of the Law was, or might tend to the hurt aswell of the innocent as of guiltie persons. And as to the persons of my Subiects which are of that profession, I must diuide them into two rankes, Clerickes and Layickes; for the part of the Layicks, certainely I euer thought them farre more excusable then the other sort, because that sort of Religion containeth such an ignorant, doubtfull, and implicit kinde of faith in the Layickes grounded vpon their Church, as except they doe generally beleeue whatsoeuer their Teachers please to affirme, they cannot be thought guilty of these particular points of heresies and corruptions, which their Teachers doe so wilfully professe. And againe I must subdiuide the same Layickes into two rankes, that is, either quiet and well minded men, peaceable Subiects, who either being old, haue retayned their first drunken in liquor vpon a certaine shamefastnesse to be thought curious or changeable: Or being young men, through euill education haue neuer bene nursed or brought vp, but vpon such venim in place of wholesome nutriment. And that sort of people I would be sorry to punish their bodies for the errour of their minds, the reformation whereof must onely come of God and the trew Spirit. But the other ranke of Layicks, who either through Curiositie, affectation of Noueltie, or discontentment in their priuat humours, haue changed their coates, onely to be factious stirrers of Sedition, and Perturbers of the common wealth, their backwardnesse in their Religion giueth a ground to me the Magistrate, to take the better heed to their proceeding, and to correct their obstinacie. But for the part of the Clerickes, I must directly say and affirme, that as long as they maintaine one speciall point of their doctrine, and another point of their practise, they are no way sufferable to remaine in this Kingdome. Their point of doctrine is that arrogant and ambitious Supremacie of their Head the Pope, whereby he not onely claimes to bee Spirituall head of all Christians, but also to haue an Imperiall ciuill power ouer all Kings and Emperors, dethroning and decrowning Princes with his foot as pleaseth him, and dispensing and disposing of all Kingdomes and Empires at his appetite. The other point which they obserue in continuall practise, is the assassinates and murthers of Kings, thinking it no sinne, but rather a matter of saluation, to doe all actions of rebellion and hostilitie against their naturall Soueraigne Lord, if he be once cursed, his subiects discharged of their fidelitie, and his Kingdome giuen a prey by that three crowned Monarch, or rather Monster their Head. And in this point, I haue no occasion to speak further here, sauing that I could wish from my heart, that it would please God to make me one of the members of such a generall Christian vnion in Religion, as laying wilfulnesse aside on both hands, wee might meete in the middest, which is the Center and perfection of all things. For if they would leaue, and be ashamed of such new and grosse Corruptions of theirs, as themselues cannot maintaine, nor denie to bee worthy of reformation, I would for mine owne part be content to meete them in the mid-way, so that all nouelties might be renounced on either side. For as my faith is the Trew, Ancient, Catholike and Apostolike faith, grounded vpon the Scriptures and expresse word of God: so will I euer yeeld all reuerence to antiquitie in the points of Ecclesiasticall pollicy; and by that meanes shall I euer with Gods grace keepe my selfe from either being an hereticke in Faith, or schismatick in matters of Pollicie. But of one thing would I haue the Papists of this Land to bee admonished, That they presume not so much vpon my

Lenitie (because I would be loath to be thought a Persecuter) as thereupon to thinke it lawfull for them dayly to encrease their number and strength in this Kingdome, whereby if not in my time, at least in the time of my posteritie, they might be in hope to erect their Religion againe. No, let them assure themselues, that as I am a friend to their persons if they be good subiects: so am I a vowed enemie, and doe denounce mortall warre to their errors: And that as I would be sory to bee driuen by their ill behauiour from the protection and conseruation of their bodies and liues; So will I neuer cease as farre as I can, to tread downe their errors and wrong opinions. For I could not permit the encrease and growing of their Religion, without first betraying of my selfe, and mine owne conscience: Secondly, this whole Isle, aswell the part I am come from, as the part I remaine in, in betraying their Liberties, and reducing them to the former slauish yoke, which both had casten off, before I came amongst them: And thirdly, the libertie of the Crowne in my posteritie, which I should leaue againe vnder a new slauery, hauing found it left free to me by my Predecessors. And therefore would I wish all good Subiects that are deceiued with that corruption, first if they find any beginning of instinction in themselues of knowledge and loue to the Trewth, to foster the same by all lawfull meanes, and to beware of quenching the spirit that worketh within them; And if they can find as yet no motion tending that way, to be studious to reade and conferre with learned men, and to vse all such meanes as may further their Resolution, assuring themselues, that as long as they are disconformable in Religion from vs, they cannot bee but halfe my Subiects, bee able to doe but halfe seruice, and I to want the best halfe of them, which is their soules. And here haue I occasion to speake to you my Lords the Bishops: For as you, my Lord of Durham,[791] said very learnedly to day in your Sermon, Correction without instruction, is but a Tyrannie: So ought you, and all the Clergie vnder you, to be more carefull, vigilant, and diligent then you haue bene, to winne Soules to God, aswell by your exemplary life, as doctrine. And since you see how carefull they are, sparing neither labour, paines, nor extreme perill of their persons to diuert, (the Deuill is so busie a Bishop) yee should bee the more carefull and wakefull in your charges. Follow the rule prescribed you by S. *Paul, Bee carefull to exhort and to instruct in season, and out of season:*[792] and where you haue beene any way sluggish before, now waken your selues vp againe with a new dili-

gence in this point, remitting the successe to God, who calling them
either at the second, third, tenth or twelfth houre, as they are alike
welcome to him, so shall they bee to mee his Lieutenant here.

The[793] third reason of my conuening of you at this time, which
conteineth such actions of my thankefulnesse toward you, as I may
either doe, or leaue vndone, yet shall with Gods grace euer presse
to performe all the dayes of my life: It consists in these two points;
In making of Lawes at certaine times, which is onely at such times
as this in Parliament; or in the carefull execution thereof at all other
times. As for the making of them, I will thus farre faithfully promise
vnto you, That I will euer preferre the weale of the body, and of the
whole Common-wealth, in making of good Lawes and constitutions,
to any particular or priuate ends of mine, thinking euer the wealth
and weale of the Common-wealth to bee my greatest weale and
worldly felicitie: A point wherein a lawfull King doeth directly differ
from a Tyrant. But at this time I am onely thus farre to forewarne
you in that point, That you beware to seeke the making of too many
Lawes, for two especiall reasons: First, because *In corruptissima
Republica plurimæ leges*;[794] and the execution of good Lawes is farre
more profitable in a Common-wealth, then to burden mens memories
with the making of too many of them. And next, because the making
of too many Lawes in one Parliament, will bring in confusion, for
lacke of leisure wisely to deliberate before you conclude: For the
Bishop said well to day, That to Deliberation would a large time be
giuen, but to Execution a greater promptnesse was required. As for
the execution of good Lawes, it hath bene very wisely and honourably
foreseene and ordered by my predecessours in this Kingdome, in
planting such a number of Iudges, and all sorts of Magistrates in
conuenient places for the execution of the same: And therefore must
I now turne mee to you that are Iudges and Magistrates vnder mee,
as mine Eyes and Eares in this case. I can say none otherwise to you,
then as *Ezekias* the good King of *Iuda* said to their Iudges, *Remember
that the Thrones that you sit on are Gods, and neither yours nor mine*:
And that as you must be answerable to mee, so must both you and
I be answerable to GOD, for the due execution of our Offices. That
place is no place for you to vtter your affections in, you must not
there hate your foe nor loue your friend, feare the offence of the
greater partie or pity the miserie of the meaner; yee must be blinde
and not see distinctions of persons, handlesse, not to receiue bribes;

but keepe that iust temper and mid-course in all your proceedings, that like a iust ballance ye may neither sway to the right nor left hand. Three principall qualities are required in you; Knowledge, Courage, and Sinceritie: that you may discerne with knowledge, execute with courage, and doe both in vpright sinceritie. And as for my part. I doe vow and protest here in the presence of God, and of this honourable Audience, I neuer shall be wearie, nor omit no occasion, wherein I may shew my carefulnesse of the execution of good Lawes. And as I wish you that are Iudges not to be weary in your Office in doing of it; so shall I neuer be wearie, with Gods grace, to take account of you, which is properly my calling.

And thus hauing tolde you the three causes of my conuening of this Parliament, all three tending onely to vtter my thankefulnesse, but in diuers formes, the first by word, the other two by action; I doe confesse that when I haue done and performed all that in this Speech I haue promised, *Inutilis seruus sum:*[795] Inutile, because the meaning of the word *Inutilis* in that place of Scripture is vnderstood, that in doing all that seruice which wee can to God, it is but our due, and wee doe nothing to God but that which wee are bound to doe. And in like maner, when I haue done all that I can for you, I doe nothing but that which I am bound to doe, and am accomptable to God vpon the contrary: For I doe acknowledge, that the speciall and greatest point of difference that is betwixt a rightfull King and an vsurping Tyrant is in this; That whereas the proude and ambitious Tyrant doeth thinke his Kingdome and people are onely ordeined for satisfaction of his desires and vnreasonable appetites; The righteous and iust King doeth by the contrary acknowledge himselfe to bee ordeined for the procuring of the wealth and prosperitie of his people, and that his greatest and principall worldly felicitie must consist in their prosperitie. If you bee rich I cannot bee poore, if you bee happy I cannot but bee fortunate, and I protest that your welfare shall euer be my greatest care and contentment: And that I am a Seruant it is most trew, that as I am Head and Gouernour of all the people in my Dominion who are my naturall vassals and Subiects, considering them in numbers and distinct Rankes; So if wee will take the whole People as one body and Masse, then as the Head is ordeined for the body and not the Body for the Head; so must a righteous King know himselfe to bee ordeined for his people, and not his people for him: For although a King and people be *Relata*;[796] yet can hee be no King if he want people and Subiects. But there be many people in the world that lacke a Head, wherefore I will neuer bee ashamed to confesse it my principall Honour to bee the great Seruant of the Common-wealth, and euer thinke the prosperitie thereof to be my greatest felicitie, as I haue already said.

But as it was the whole Body of this Kingdome, with an vniforme assent and harmonie, as I tolde you in the beginning of my Speech, which did so farre oblige mee in good will and thankefulnesse of requitall by their alacritie and readinesse in declaring and receiuing mee to that place which God had prouided for mee, and not any particular persons: (for then it had not bene the body) So is my thankefulnesse due to the whole State. For euen as in matter of faults, *Quod a multis peccatur, impune peccatur:*[797] Euen so in the matter of vertuous and good deedes, what is done by the willing consent and harmonie of the whole body, no particular person can iustly claime thankes as proper to him for the same. And therefore I must heere make a little Apologie for my selfe, in that I could not satisfie the particular humours of euery person, that looked for some aduancement or reward at my hand since my entrie into this Kingdome. Three kinde of things were craued of mee: Aduancement to honour, Preferment to place of Credit about my Person, and Reward in matters of land or profit. If I had bestowed Honour vpon all, no man could haue beene aduanced to Honour: for the degrees of Honour doe consist in preferring some aboue their fellowes. If euery man had the like accesse to my Priuy or Bed-chamber, then no man could haue it, because it cannot containe all. And if I had bestowed Lands and Rewards vpon euery man, the fountaine of my liberalitie would be so exhausted and dried, as I would lacke meanes to bee liberall to any man. And yet was I not so sparing, but I may without vaunting affirme that I haue enlarged my fauour in all the three degrees, towards as many and more then euer King of *England* did in so short a space: No, I rather craue your pardon that I haue beene so bountifull: for if the meanes of the Crowne bee wasted, I behoued then to haue recourse to you my Subiects, and bee burdensome to you, which I would bee lothest to bee of any King aliue. For as it is trew, that as I haue already said, it was a whole Body which did deserue so well at my hand, and not euery particular person of the people: yet were there some who by reason of their Office, credit with the people or otherwise, tooke occasion both before, and at the time of my comming amongst you, to giue proofe of their loue and affection towards me. Not that I am any way in doubt, that if other of my Subiects had beene in their places, and had had the like occasion, but they would haue vttered the like good effects, (so generall and so great were the loue and affection of you all towards mee:) But yet this hauing beene performed by some speciall persons, I could not without vnthankfulnesse but requite them accordingly. And therefore had I iust occasion to aduance some in Honour, some to places of seruice about mee, and by rewarding to enable some who had deserued well of mee, and were not otherwise able to maintaine the rankes I thought them capable of, and others who although they had not particularly deserued before, yet I found them capable and worthy of place of preferment and credit, and not able to sustaine those places for which I thought them fit, without my helpe. Two especiall causes moued mee to be so open handed: whereof the one was reasonable and honourable; but the other I will not bee ashamed to confesse vnto you, proceeded of mine owne infirmitie. That which was iust and honourable, was: That being so farre beholding to the body of the whole State, I thought I could not refuse to let runne some small brookes out of the fountaine of my thankefulnesse to the whole, for refreshing of particular persons that were members of that multitude. The other which proceeded out of mine owne infirmitie, was the multitude and importunitie of Sutors. But although reason come by infusion in a maner, yet experience groweth with time and labour: And therefore doe I not doubt, but experience in time comming will both teach the particular Subiects of this Kingdome, not to be so importune and vndiscreete in crauing: And mee not to be so easily and lightly mooued, in granting that which may be harmefull to my Estate, and consequently to the whole Kingome.

And thus hauing at length declared vnto you my minde in all the points, for the which I called this Parliament: My conclusion shall onely now be to excuse my selfe, in case you haue not found such Eloquence in my Speech, as peraduenture you might haue looked for at my hands. I might, if I list, alledge the great weight of my Affaires and my continuall businesse and distraction, that I could neuer haue leasure to thinke vpon what I was to speake, before I came to the place where I was to speake: And I might also alledge that my first sight of this so famous and Honourable an Assembly, might likewise breede some impediment. But leauing these excuses,

I will plainely and freely in my maner tell you the trew cause of it, which is; That it becommeth a King, in my opinion, to vse no other Eloquence then plainnesse and sinceritie. By plainenesse I meane, that his Speeches should be so cleare and voyd of all ambiguitie, that they may not be throwne, nor rent asunder in contrary sences like the old Oracles of the Pagan gods. And by sinceritie, I vnderstand that vprightnesse and honestie which ought to be in a Kings whole Speeches and actions: That as farre as a King is in Honour erected aboue any of his Subiects, so farre should he striue in sinceritie to be aboue them all, and that his tongue should be euer the trew Messenger of his heart: and this sort of Eloquence may you euer assuredly looke for at my hands.

A SPEACH IN THE[798] PARLIAMENT HOVSE, AS NEERE THE VERY WORDS As COVLD BE GATHERED at the instant.

My Lords Spirituall and Temporall, and you the Knights and Burgesses of this Parliament, It was farre from my thoughts till very lately
before my comming to this place, that this Subiect should haue bene
ministred vnto mee, whereupon I am now to speake. But now it so
falleth out, That whereas in the preceding Session of this Parliament,
the principall occasion of my Speach was, to thanke and congratulate
all you of this House, and in you, all the whole Common-wealth (as
being the representatiue body of the State) for your so willing, and
louing receiuing and embracing of mee in that place, which God and
Nature by descent of blood, had in his owne time prouided for me:
So now my Subiect is, to speake of a farre greater Thankesgiuing
then before I gaue to you, being to a farre greater person, which is
to God, for the great and miraculous Deliuery he hath at this time
granted to me, and to you all, and consequently to the whole body
of this Estate.

I must therefore begin with this old and most approued Sentence
of Diuinitie, *Misericordia Dei supra omnia opera eius.*[799] For Almightie
God did not furnish so great matter to his glory by the Creation of
this great World, as he did by the Redemption of the same. Neither
did his generation of the little world in our old & first Adam, so
much set forth the praises of God in his Iustice and Mercy, as did
our Regeneration in the last & second Adam.

And now I must craue a little pardon of you, That since Kings are
in the word of God it selfe called Gods, as being his Lieutenants
and Vice-gerents on earth, and so adorned and furnished with some
sparkles of the Diuinitie; to compare some of the workes of God the

great KING, towards the whole and generall world, to some of his workes towards mee, and this little world of my Dominions, compassed and seuered by the Sea from the rest of the earth. For as GOD for the iust punishment of the first great sinnes in the originall world, when the sonnes of GOD went in to the daughters of men, and the cup of their iniquities of all sorts was filled, and heaped vp to the full, did by a generall deluge and ouerflowing of waters, baptize the world to a generall destruction, and not to a generall purgation (onely excepted NOAH and his family, who did repent and beleeue the threatnings of GODS iudgement:) So now when the world shall waxe old as a garment, and that all the impieties and sinnes that can be deuised against both the first and second Table, haue and shall bee committed to the full measure; GOD is to punish the world the second time by fire, to the generall destruction and not purgation thereof. Although as was done in the former to NOAH and his family by the waters; So shall all we that beleeue be likewise purged, and not destroyed by the fire. In the like sort, I say, I may iustly compare these two great and fearefull *Domes-dayes*,[800] wherewith GOD threatned to destroy mee and all you of this little world that haue interest in me. For although I confesse, as all mankinde, so chiefly Kings, as being in the higher places like the high Trees, or stayest Mountaines, and steepest Rockes, are most subiect to the dayly tempests of innumerable dangers; and I amongst all other Kings haue euer bene subiect vnto them, not onely euer since my birth, but euen as I may iustly say, before my birth: and while I was yet in my mothers belly: yet haue I bene exposed to two more speciall and greater dangers then all the rest.

The first of them, in the Kingdome where I was borne, and passed the first part of my life: And the last of them here, which is the greatest. In the former I should haue bene baptized in blood, and in my destruction not onely the Kingdom wherein I then was, but ye also by your future interest, should haue tasted of my ruine: Yet it pleased GOD to deliuer mee, as it were from the very brinke of death, from the point of the dagger, and so to purge me by my thankefull acknowledgement of so great a benefite. But in this, which did so lately fall out, and which was a destruction prepared not for me alone, but for you all that are here present, and wherein no ranke, aage, nor sexe should haue bene spared; This was not a crying sinne of blood, as the former, but it may well be called a roaring, nay a thundring sinne of fire and brimstone, from the which GOD hath so miraculously deliuered vs all. What I can speake of this, I know not: Nay rather, what can I not speake of it? And therefore I must for horror say with the Poet, *Vox faucibus hæret.*[801]

In[802] this great and horrible attempt, whereof the like was neuer either heard or read, I obserue three wonderfull, or rather miraculous euents.

First,[803] in the crueltie of the Plot it selfe, wherein cannot be enough admired the horrible and fearefull crueltie of their deuice, which was not onely for the destruction of my Person, nor of my Wife and posteritie onely, but of the whole body of the State in generall; wherein should neither haue bene spared, or distinction made of yong nor of old, of great nor of small, of man nor of woman: The whole Nobilitie, the whole reuerend Clergie, Bishops, and most part of the good Preachers, the most part of the Knights and Gentrie; yea, and if that any in this Societie were fauourers of their profession, they should all haue gone one way: The whole Iudges of the land, with the most of the Lawyers, and the whole Clerkes: And as the wretch himselfe which is in the Tower,[804] doeth confesse, it was purposely deuised by them, and concluded to be done in this house; That where the cruell Lawes (as they say) were made against their Religion, both place and persons should all be destroyed and blowne vp at once. And[805] then consider therewithall the cruel fourme of that practise: for by three different sorts in generall may mankinde be put to death.

The[806] first, by other men, and reasonable creatures, which is least cruell: for then both defence of men against men may be expected, and likewise who knoweth what pitie God may stirre vp in the hearts of the Actors at the very instant? besides the many wayes and meanes, whereby men may escape in such a present furie.

And[807] the second way more cruell then that, is by *Animal* and vnreasonable creatures: for as they haue lesse pitie then men, so is it a greater horror and more vnnaturall for men to deale with them: But yet with them both resistance may auaile, and also some pitie may be had, as was in the Lions, in whose denne *Daniel* was throwne; or that thankefull Lion, that had the Romane in his mercie.

But[808] the third, which is most cruell and vnmercifull of all, is the destruction by insensible and inanimate things, and amongst them all, the most cruell are the two Elements of Water and Fire; and of those two, the fire most raging and mercilesse.

Secondly,[809] how wonderfull it is when you shall thinke vpon the small, or rather no ground, whereupon the practisers were entised to inuent this Tragedie. For if these Conspirators had onely bene bankrupt persons, or discontented vpon occasion of any disgraces done vnto them; this might haue seemed to haue bene but a worke of reuenge. But for my owne part, as I scarcely euer knew any of them, so cannot they alledge so much as a pretended cause of griefe: And the wretch himselfe in hands doeth confesse, That there was no cause moouing him or them, but meerely and only Religion. And specially that christian men, at least so called, Englishmen, borne within the Countrey, and one of the specials of them my sworne Seruant in an Honourable place,[810] should practise the destruction of their King, his Posterity, their Countrey and all: Wherein their following obstinacie is so ioyned to their former malice, as the fellow himselfe that is in hand, cannot be moued to discouer any signes or notes of repentance, except onely that he doeth not yet stand to auow, that he repents for not being able to performe his intent.

Thirdly,[811] the discouery hereof is not a little wonderfull, which would bee thought the more miraculous by you all, if you were aswell acquainted with my naturall disposition, as those are who be neere about me: For as I euer did hold Suspition to be the sicknes of a Tyrant, so was I so farre vpon the other extremity, as I rather contemned all aduertisements, or apprehensions of practises. And yet now at this time was I so farre contrary to my selfe, as when the Letter was shewed to me by my Secretary, wherein a generall obscure aduertisement was giuen of some dangerous blow at this time, I did vpon the instant interpret and apprehend some darke phrases therein, contrary to the ordinary Grammer construction of them, (and in an other sort then I am sure any Diuine, or Lawyer in any Vniuersitie would haue taken them) to be meant by this horrible forme of blowing vs vp all by Powder; And thereupon ordered that search to be made, whereby the matter was discouered, and the man apprehended: whereas if I had apprehended or interpreted it to any other sort of danger, no worldly prouision or preuention could haue made vs escape our vtter destruction.

And in that also was there a wonderfull prouidence of God, that when the party himselfe was taken, he was but new come out of his house from working, hauing his Fireworke for kindling ready in his pocket, wherewith as he confesseth, if he had bene taken but immediatly before when he was in the House, he was resolued to haue blowen vp himselfe with his Takers.

One thing for mine owne part haue I cause to thanke GOD in, That if GOD for our sinnes had suffered their wicked intents to haue preuailed, it should neuer haue bene spoken nor written in aages succeeding, that I had died ingloriously in an Ale-house, a Stews, or such vile place, but mine end should haue bene with the most Honourable and best company, and in that most Honourable and fittest place for a King to be in, for doing the turnes most proper to his Office. And the more haue We all cause to thanke and magnifie GOD for this his mercifull Deliuery; And specially I for my part, that he hath giuen me yet once leaue, whatsoeuer should come of me hereafter, to assemble you in this Honourable place; And here in this place, where our generall destruction should haue bene, to magnifie and praise him for Our generall deliuery: That I may iustly now say of mine Enemies and yours, as *Dauid* doeth often say in the Psalme, *Inciderunt in foueam quam fecerunt.*[812] And since *Scipio* an Ethnick, led onely by the light of Nature, That day when he was accused by the *Tribunes* of the people of *Rome* for mispending and wasting in his *Punick* warres the Cities Treasure, even vpon the sudden brake out with that diuersion of them from that matter, calling them to remembrance how that day, was the day of the yeere, wherein God had giuen them so great a victory against *Hannibal*, and therefore it was fitter for them all, leauing other matters, to runne to the Temple to praise God for that so great deliuery, which the people did all follow with one applause: How much more cause haue we that are Christians to bestow this time in this place for Thankes-giuing to God for his great Mercy, though we had had no other errant of assembling here at this time? wherein if I haue spoken more like a Diuine then would seeme to belong to this place, the matter it selfe must plead for mine excuse: For being here commen to thanke God for a diuine worke of his Mercy, how can I speake of this deliuerance of vs from so hellish a practise, so well as in language of Diuinitie, which is the direct opposite to so damnable an intention? And therefore may I iustly end this purpose, as I did begin it with this Sentence, *The Mercie of God is aboue all his workes.*

It resteth now that I should shortly informe you what is to bee done hereafter vpon the occasion of this horrible and strange accident. As for your part that are my faithfull and louing Subiects of all degrees,

I know that your hearts are so burnt vp with zeale in this errant, and your tongues so ready to vtter your duetifull affections, and your hands and feete so bent to concurre in the execution thereof, (for which as I neede not to spurre you, so can I not but praise you for the same:) As it may very well be possible that the zeale of your hearts shall make some of you in your speaches rashly to blame such as may bee innocent of this attempt; But vpon the other part I wish you to consider, That I would be sorie that any being innocent of this practise, either domesticall or forraine, should receiue blame or harme for the same. For although it cannot be denied, That it was the onely blinde superstition of their errors in Religion, that led them to this desperate deuice; yet doth it not follow, That all professing that *Romish* religion were guiltie of the same. For as it is trew, That no other sect of heretiques, not excepting *Turke*, *Iew*, nor *Pagan*, no not euen those of *Calicute*, who adore the deuill, did euer maintaine by the grounds of their religion, That it was lawfull, or rather merit-orious (as the *Romish* Catholickes call it) to murther Princes or people for quarrell of Religion. And although particular men of all profes-sions of Religion haue beene some Theeues, some Murtherers, some Traitors, yet euer when they came to their end and iust punishment, they confessed their fault to bee in their nature, and not in their profession, (These *Romish* Catholicks only excepted:) Yet it is trew on the other side, that many honest men blinded peraduenture with some opinions of Popery, as if they be not sound in the questions of the *Reall presence*, or in the number of the Sacraments, or some such Schoole-question: yet doe they either not know, or at least not beleeue all the trew grounds of Popery, which is in deed *The mysterie of iniquitie*. And therefore doe we iustly confesse, that many Papists, especially our forefathers, laying their onely trust vpon CHRIST and his Merits at their last breath, may be, and often times are saued; detesting in that point, and thinking the crueltie of Puritanes worthy of fire, that will admit no saluation to any Papist. I therefore thus doe conclude this point, That as vpon the one part many honest men, seduced with some errors of Popery, may yet remaine good and faithfull Subiects: So vpon the other part, none of those that trewly know and beleeue the whole grounds, and Schoole conclusions of their doctrine, can euer proue either good Christians, or faithfull Subiects. And for the part of forraine Princes and States, I may so much the more acquite them, and their Ministers of their knowledge and consent to any such villanie, as I may iustly say, that in that point I better know all Christian Kings by my selfe, That no King nor Prince of Honour will euer abase himselfe so much, as to thinke a good thought of so base and dishonourable a Treachery, wishing you therefore, that as God hath giuen me an happie Peace and Amitie, with all other Christian Princes my neighbours (as was euen now very grauely told you by my L. Chancellor) that so you will reuerently iudge and speake of them in this case. And for my part I would wish with those ancient Philosophers, that there were a Christall window in my brest, wherein all my people might see the secretest thoughts of my heart, for then might you all see no alteration in my minde for this accident, further then in these two points. The first, Caution and warinesse in gouernment, to discouer and search out the mysteries of this wickednesse as farre as may be: The other, after due triall, Seueritie of punishment vpon those that shall bee found guilty of so detestable and vnheard of villanie. And now in this matter if I haue troubled your eares with an abrupt speach, vndigested in any good methode or order; you haue to consider that an abrupt, and vnaduised speach doeth best become in the relation of so abrupt and vnorderly an accident.

And although I haue ordained the proroguing of this Parliament vntil after Christmas vpon two necessary respects: whereof the first is, that neither I nor my Councell can haue leisure at this time both to take order for the Apprehension and triall of these Conspiratours, and also to wait vpon the dayly affaires of the Parliament, as the Councell must doe: And the other reason is, the necessitie at this time of diuers of your presences in your Shires that haue Charges and Commandements there. For as these wretches thought to haue blowen vp in a maner the whole world of this Island, euery man being now commen vp here, either for publike causes of Parliament, or else for their owne priuate causes in Law, or otherwise: So these Rebels that now wander through the Countrey, could neuer haue gotten so fit a time of safetie in their passage, or whatsoeuer vnlawfull Actions, as now when the Countrey by the foresaid occasions is in a maner left desolate, and waste vnto them. Besides that, it may be that I shall desire you at your next Session, to take vpon you the Iudgement of this Crime: For as so extraordinary a Fact deserues extraordinary Iudgement, So can there not I thinke (following euen their owne Rule) be a fitter Iudgement for them, then that they should be measured with the same measure wherewith they thought to measure vs: And that the same place and persons, whom they thought to destroy, should be the iust auengers of their so vnnaturall a Parricide: Yet not knowing that I will haue occasion to meete with you my selfe in this place at the beginning of the next Session of this Parliament, (because if it had not been for deliuering of the Articles agreed vpon by the Commissioners of the Vnion, which was thought most conuenient to be done in my presence, where both Head and Members of the Parliament were met together, my presence had not otherwise been requisite here at this time:) I haue therefore thought good for conclusion of this Meeting, to discourse to you somewhat anent the trew nature and definition of a Parliament, which I will remit to your memories till your next sitting downe, that you may then make vse of it as occasion shall bee ministred.

For albeit it be trew, that at the first Session of my first Parliament, which was not long after mine Entrie into this Kingdome, It could not become me to informe you of any thing belonging to Law or State heere: (for all knowledge must either bee infused or acquired, and seeing the former sort thereof is now with Prophecie ceased in the world, it could not be possible for me at my first Entry here, before Experience had taught it me, to be able to vnderstand the particular mysteries of this State:) yet now that I haue reigned almost three yeeres amongst you, and haue beene carefull to obserue those things that belong to the office of a King, albeit that Time be but a short time for experience in others, yet in a King may it be thought a reasonable long time, especially in me, who, although I be but in a maner a new King heere, yet haue bene long acquainted with the office of a King in such another Kingdome, as doeth neerest of all others agree with the Lawes and customes of this State. Remitting to your consideration to iudge of that which hath beene concluded by the Commissioners of the Vnion, wherein I am at this time to signifie vnto you, That as I can beare witnesse to the foresaid Commissioners, that they haue not agreed nor concluded therein any thing, wherein they haue not foreseen as well the weale and commodity of the one Countrey, as of the other; So can they all beare mee record, that I was so farre from pressing them to agree to any thing, which might bring with it any preiudice to this people; as by the contrary I did euer admonish them, neuer to conclude vpon any such Vnion, as might cary hurt or grudge with it to either of the said

Nations: for the leauing of any such thing, could not but be the greatest hinderance that might be to such an Action, which God by the lawes of Nature had prouided to be in his owne time, and hath now in effect perfected in my Person, to which purpose my Lord Chancellour hath better spoken, then I am able to relate.

And as to the nature of this high Court of Parliament, It is nothing else but the Kings great Councell, which the King doeth assemble either vpon occasion of interpreting, or abrogating old Lawes, or making of new, according as ill maners shall deserue, or for the publike punishment of notorious euill doers, or the praise and reward of the vertuous and well deseruers; wherein these foure things are to be considered.

First,[813] whereof this Court is composed.
Secondly,[814] what matters are proper for it.
Thirdly,[815] to what end it is ordeined.
And[816] fourthly, what are the meanes and wayes whereby this end should bee brought to passe.

As for the thing it selfe, It is composed of a Head and a Body: The Head is the King, the Body are the members of the Parliament. This Body againe is subdiuided into two parts; The Vpper and Lower House: The Vpper compounded partly of Nobility, Temporall men, who are heritable Councellors to the high Court of Parliament by the honour of their Creation and Lands: And partly of Bishops, Spirituall men, who are likewise by the vertue of their place and dignitie Councellours, Life Renters, or *Ad vitam*[817] of this Court. The other House is composed of Knights for the Shire; and Gentry, and Burgesses for the Townes. But because the number would be infinite for all the Gentlemen and Burgesses to bee present at euery Parliament, Therefore a certaine number is selected and chosen out of that great Body, seruing onely for that Parliament, where their persons are the representation of that Body.

Now the matters whereof they are to treate ought therefore to be generall, and rather of such matters as cannot well bee performed without the assembling of that generall Body, and no more of these generals neither, then necessity shall require: for as *in Corruptissima Republica sunt plurimæ leges*:[818] So doeth the life and strength of the Law consist not in heaping vp infinite and confused numbers of Lawes, but in the right interpretation and good execution of good and wholesome Lawes. If this be so then, neither is this a place on the one side for euery rash and harebrained fellow to propone new Lawes of his owne inuention: nay rather I could wish these busie heads to remember that Law of the Lacedemonians, That whosoeuer came to propone a new Law to the people, behooued publikely to present himselfe with a rope about his necke, that in case the Law were not allowed, he should be hanged therwith. So warie should men be of proponing Nouelties, but most of all not to propone any bitter or seditious Laws, which can produce nothing but grudges and discontentment betweene the Prince and his people: Nor yet is it on the other side a conuenient place for priuate men vnder the colour of general Lawes, to propone nothing but their owne particular gaine, either to the hurt of their priuate neighbours, or to the hurt of the whole State in generall, which many times vnder faire and pleasing Titles, are smoothly passed ouer, and so by stealth procure without consideration, that the priuate meaning of them tendeth to nothing but either to the wrecke of a particular partie, or else vnder colour of publike benefite to pill the poore people and serue as it were for a generall Impost vpon them for filling the purses of some priuate persons.

And as to the end for which the Parliament is ordeined, being only for the aduancement of Gods glory, and the establishment and wealth of the King and his people: It is no place then for particular men to vtter there their priuate conceipts, nor for satisfaction of their curiosities, and least of all to make shew of their eloquence by tyning the time with long studied and eloquent Orations: No, the reuerence of God, their King, and their Countrey being well setled in their hearts, will make them ashamed of such toyes, and remember that they are there as sworne Councellours to their King, to giue their best aduise for the furtherance of his Seruice, and the florishing Weale of his Estate.

And lastly, if you will rightly consider the meanes and wayes how to bring all your labours to a good end, you must remember, That you are heere assembled by your lawfull King to giue him your best aduises, in the matters proposed by him vnto you, being of that nature, which I haue already told, wherein you are grauely to deliberate, and vpon your consciences plainely to determine how farre those things propounded doe agree with the weale, both of your King and of your Countrey, whose weales cannot be separated. And as for my selfe, the world shall euer beare mee witnesse, That I neuer shall propone any thing vnto you, which shall not as well tend to the weale publike, as to any benefite for me: So shall I neuer oppone my selfe to that, which may tend to the good of the Common-wealth, for the which I am ordeined, as I haue often said. And as you are to giue your aduise in such things as shall by your King be proposed: So is it on your part your dueties to propone any thing that you can after mature deliberation iudge to be needefull, either for these ends already spoken of, or otherwise for the discouery of any latent euill in the Kingdome, which peraduenture may not haue commen to the Kings eare. If this then ought to bee your graue maner of proceeding in this place, Men should bee ashamed to make shew of the quicknesse of their wits here, either in taunting, scoffing, or detracting the Prince or State in any point, or yet in breaking iests vpon their fellowes, for which the Ordinaries or Ale-houses are fitter places, then this Honourable and high Court of Parliament.

In conclusion then since you are to breake up, for the reasons I haue already told you, I wish such of you as haue any charges in your Countreys, to hasten you home for the repressing of the insolencies of these Rebels, and apprehension of their persons, wherin as I heartily pray to the Almightie for your prosperous successe: So doe I not doubt, but we shall shortly heare the good newes of the same; And that you shall haue an happie returne, and meeting here to all our comforts.

Here the Lord Chancellor spake touching the proroguing of the Parliament:
And hauing done, his Maiestie rose againe, and said,

Since it pleased God to graunt mee two such notable Deliueries vpon one day of the weeke, which was Tuesday, and likewise one day of the Moneth, which was the fifth; Thereby to teach mee, That as it was the same deuill that still persecuted mee; So it was one and the same GOD that still mightily deliuered mee: I thought it therefore not amisse, That the one and twentieth day of Ianuary, which fell to be vpon Tuesday, should bee the day of the meeting of this next Session of Parliament, hoping and assuring my selfe, that the same GOD, who hath now granted me and you all so notable and gracious a deliuerie, shall prosper all our affaires at that next Session, and bring them to an happie conclusion. And now I consider GOD hath well prouided it, that the ending of this Parliament hath bene so long continued: For as for my owne part, I neuer had any other intention, but onely to seeke so farre my weale, and prosperitie, as might coniunctly stand with the flourishing State of the whole Common-wealth, as I haue often told you; So on the other part I confesse, if I had bene in your places at the beginning of this Parliament, (which was so soone after mine entry into this Kingdome, wherein ye could not possibly haue so perfect a knowledge of mine inclination, as experience since hath taught you,) I could not but haue suspected, and mis-interpreted diuers things, In the trying whereof, now I hope, by your experience of my behauiour and forme of gouernment, you are well ynough cleared, and resolued.

A SPEACH TO BOTH[819] THE HOVSES OF PARLIAMENT, DELIVERED IN THE GREAT CHAMBER AT WHITE-HALL, *THE LAST DAY OF March* 1607.

MY Lords of the higher House, and you Knights and Burgesses of the Lower house, All men at the beginning of a Feast bring foorth good Wine first, and after, worse. This was the saying of the Gouernour of the Feast at *Cana* in *Galile*, where CHRIST wrought his first miracle by changing water into Wine. But in this case now whereof I am to speake vnto you, I must follow that Gouernours rule, and not CHRISTS example, in giuing you the worst and sowrest Wine last. For all the time of this long Session of the Parliament you haue bene so fed and cloy'd, (specially you of the Lower house) with such banquets, and choise of delicate speeches, and your eares so seasoned with the sweetnesse of long precogitate Orations; as this my Speach now in the breaking vp of this Assembly, cannot but appeare vnto your taste as the worst Wine proposed in the end of the Banquet, since I am onely to deliuer now vnto you matter without curious forme, substance without ceremonie, trewth in all sinceritie. Yet considering the Person that speaketh, the parties to whom I speake, the matter whereof I meane to speake; it fits better to vtter matter, rather then wordes, in regard of the greatnesse of my place who am to speake to you, the grauitie of you the Auditorie, which is the high Court of Parliament; the weight of the matter, which concernes the securitie and establishment of this whole Empire, and litle world. Studied Orations and much eloquence vpon little matter is fit for the Vniuersities, where not the Subiect which is spoken of, but the triall of his wit that speaketh, is most commendable: but on the contrary, in all great Councels of Parliaments, fewest wordes with most matter doeth become best, where the dispatch of the great errands in hand,

and not the praise of the person is most to bee looked vnto: like the garment of a chaste woman, who is onely set forth by her naturall beautie, which is properly her owne: other deckings are but ensignes of an harlot that flies with borrowed feathers. And besides the conueniencie, I am forced hereunto by necessitie, my place calling me to action, and not leauing me to the libertie of contemplation, hauing alwayes my thoughts busied with the publique care of you all, where euery one of you hauing but himselfe, and his owne priuate to thinke of, are at more leisure to make studied speeches. And therefore the matter which I deliuer you confusedly as in a sacke, I leaue it to you when you are in your chambers, and haue better leysure then I can haue, to ranke them in order, euery one in their owne place.

Thus much by way of Preface. But I proceed to the matter: Whereof I might say with *S. Paul*, I could speake in as many tongues as you all, but I had rather speake three wordes to edification, then talke all day without vnderstanding.[820] In vaine (saith the *Psalmist*) doeth the builder build the house, or the watchman watch the Citie, vnlesse the Lord giue his blessing thereunto.[821] And in the New Testament *S. Paul* saith, That hee may plant, *Apollo* may water, but it is GOD onely that must giue the increase.[822] This I speake, because of the long time which hath bene spent about the Treatie of the Vnion. For my selfe, I protest vnto you all, When I first propounded the Vnion, I then thought there could haue bene no more question of it, then of your declaration and acknowledgement of my right vnto this Crowne, and that as two Twinnes, they would haue growne vp together. The errour was my mistaking; I knew mine owne ende, but not others feares: But now finding many crossings, long disputations, strange questions, and nothing done; I must needs thinke it proceeds either of mistaking of the errand, or else from some iealousie of me the Propounder, that you so adde delay vnto delay, searching out as it were the very bowels of Curiositie, and conclude nothing. Neither can I condemne you for being yet in some iealousie of my intention in this matter, hauing not yet had so great experience of my behauiour and inclination in these few yeeres past, as you may peraduenture haue in a longer time hereafter, and not hauing occasion to consult dayly with my selfe, and heare mine owne opinion in all those particulars which are debated among you.

But here I pray you now mistake mee not at the first, when as I seeme to finde fault with your delayes and curiositie, as if I would haue you to resolue in an houres time, that which will take a moneths aduisement: for you all know, that *Rex est lex loquens*;[823] And you haue oft heard mee say, That the Kings will and intention being the speaking Law, ought to bee *Luce clarius*;[824] and I hope you of the Lower house haue the proofe of this my clearenesse by a Bil sent you downe from the Vpper house within these few dayes, or rather few houres:[825] wherein may very well appeare vnto you the care I haue to put my Subiects in good securitie of their possessions for all posterities to come. And therefore that you may clearely vnderstand my meaning in that point, I doe freely confesse, you had reason to aduise at leasure vpon so great a cause: for great matters doe euer require great deliberation before they be well concluded. *Deliberandum est diu quod statuendum est semel.*[826] Consultations must proceed *lento pede*,[827] but the execution of a sentence vpon the resolution would be speedie. If you will goe on, it matters not though you goe with leaden feet, so you make still some progresse, and that there be no let or needlesse delay, and doe not *Nodum in scirpo quærere.*[828] I am euer for the *Medium* in euery thing. Betweene foolish rashnesse and extreame length, there is a middle way. Search all that is reasonable, but omit that which is idle, curious and vnnecessary; otherwise there can neuer be a resolution or end in any good worke.

And now from the generall I wil descend to particulars, and wil onely for the ease of your memories diuide the matter that I am to speake of, into foure heads, by opening vnto you, First, what I craue: Secondly, in what maner I desire it: Thirdly, what commodities will ensue to both the Kingdomes by it: Fourthly, what the supposed inconueniencie may be that giues impediments thereunto.

For the first, what I craue, I protest before GOD who knowes my heart, and to you my people before whom it were a shame to lie, that I claime nothing but with acknowledgement of my Bond to you; that as yee owe to me subiection and obedience: So my Soueraigntie obligeth mee to yeeld to you loue, gouernment and protection: Neither did I euer wish happinesse to my selfe, which was not conioyned with the happinesse of my people. I desire a perfect Vnion of Lawes and persons, and such a Naturalizing as may make one body of both Kingdomes vnder mee your King. That I and my posteritie (if it so please God) may rule ouer you to the worlds ende; Such an Vnion as was of the Scots and Pictes in Scotland, and of the Heptarchie here in England. And for Scotland I auow such an Vnion, as if you had got it by Conquest, but such a Conquest as may be cemented by loue, the onely sure bond of subiection or friendship: that as there is ouer both but *vnus Rex*,[829] so there may be in both but *vnus Grex & vna Lex*;[830] For no more possible is it for one King to gouerne two Countreys *Contiguous*, the one a great, the other a lesse, a richer and a poorer, the greater drawing like an Adamant the lesser to the Commodities thereof, then for one head to gouerne two bodies, or one man to be husband of two wiues, whereof Christ himselfe said, *Ab initio non fuit sic.*[831]

But in the generall Vnion you must obserue two things: for I will discouer my thoughts plainly vnto you; I study clearenes, not eloquence, And therefore with the olde Philosophers, I would heartily wish my brest were a transparent glasse for you all to see through, that you might looke into my heart, and then would you be satisfied of my meaning. For when I speake of a perfect Vnion, I meane not confusion of all things: you must not take from Scotland those particular Priuiledges that may stand as well with this Vnion, as in England many particular customes in particular Shires, (as the Customes of Kent, and the Royalties of the Countie Palatine of Chester) do with the Common Law of the Kingdome: for euery particular Shire almost, and much more euery Countie, haue some particular customes that are as it were naturally most fit for that people. But I meane of such a generall Vnion of Lawes as may reduce the whole Iland, that as they liue already vnder one Monarch, so they may all bee gouerned by one Law: For I must needs confesse by that little experience I haue had since my comming hither, and I thinke I am able to prooue it, that the grounds of the Common Law of England, are the best of any Law in the world, either Çiuill or Municipall, and the fittest for this people. But as euery Law would be cleare and full, so the obscuritie in some points of this our written Law, and want of fulnesse in others, the variation of Cases and mens curiositie, breeding euery day new questions, hath enforced the Iudges to iudge in many Cases here, by Cases and presidents, wherein I hope Lawyers themselues will not denie but that there must be a great vncertaintie, and I am sure all the rest of you that are Gentlemen of other professions were long agoe wearie of it, if you could haue had it amended: For where there is varietie and vncertaintie, although a iust Iudge may do rightly, yet an ill Iudge may take aduantage to doe wrong; and then are all honest men that succeede him, tied in a maner to his vniust and partiall conclusions. Wherefore, leaue not the Law to the pleasure of the Iudge, but let your Lawes be looked into: for I desire not the abolishing of the Lawes, but onely the clearing and the sweeping off the rust of them, and that by Parliament our Lawes might be cleared and made knowen to all the Subiects. Yea rather it were lesse hurt, that all the approued Cases were set downe and allowed by Parliament for standing Lawes in all time to come: For although some of them peraduenture may bee vniust as set downe by corrupt Iudges; yet better it is to haue a certaine Law with some spots in it, nor liue vnder such an vncertaine and arbitrarie Law, since as the prouerbe is, It is lesse harme to suffer an inconuenience then a mischiefe. And now may you haue faire occasion of amending and polishing your Lawes, when Scotland is to bee vnited with you vnder them: for who can blame Scotland to say, If you will take away our owne Lawes, I pray you giue vs a better and cleerer in place thereof.

But this is not possible to bee done without a fit preparation. Hee that buildeth a Ship, must first prouide the timber; and as Christ himselfe said, No man will build an house, but he will first prouide the materials: nor a wise King will not make warre against another, without he first make prouision of money: and all great workes must haue their preparation: and that was my end in causing the Instrument of the Vnion to be made. Vnion is a mariage: would he not bee thought absurd that for furthering of a mariage betweene two friends of his, would make his first motion to haue the two parties be laid in bedde together, and performe the other turnes of mariage? must there not precede the mutuall sight and acquaintance of the parties one with another, the conditions of the contract, the Ioincture to be talked of and agreed vpon by their friends, and such other things as in order ought to goe before the ending of such a worke? The vnion is an eternall agreement and reconciliation of many long bloody warres that haue beene betweene these two ancient Kingdomes. Is it the readiest way to agree a priuate quarell betweene two, to bring them at the first to shake hands, and as it were kisse other, and lie vnder one roofe or rather in one bedde together, before that first the ground of their quarell be communed vpon, their mindes mitigated, their affections prepared, and all other circumstances first vsed, that ought to be vsed to proceed to such a finall agreement? Euery honest man desireth a perfect Vnion, but they that say so, and admit no preparation thereto, haue *mel in ore, fel in corde.*[832] If after your so long talke of Vnion in all this long Session of Parliament, yee rise without agreeing vpon any particular; what will the neighbour Princes iudge, whose eyes are all fixed vpon the conclusion of this Action, but that the King is refused in his desire, whereby the Nation should bee taxed, and the King disgraced? And what an ill preparation is it for the mindes of Scotland toward the Vnion, when they shall heare that ill is spoken of their whole Nation, but nothing is done nor aduanced in the matter of the Vnion it selfe? But this I am glad was but the fault of one,[833] and one is no number: yet haue your neighbours of Scotland this aduantage of you, that none of them haue spoken ill of you (nor shall as long as I am King) in Parliament, or any such publique place of Iudicature. Consider therefore well, if the mindes of Scotland had not neede to be well prepared to perswade their mutuall consent, seeing you here haue all the great aduantage by the Vnion. Is not here the personall residence of the King, his whole Court and family? Is not here the seate of Iustice, and the fountaine of Gouernment? must they not be subiected to the Lawes of England, and so with time become but as Cumberland and Northumberland, and those other remote and Northerne Shires? you are to be the husband, they the wife: you conquerours, they as conquered, though not by the sword, but by the sweet and sure bond of loue. Besides that, they as other Northerne Countreys will be seldome seene and saluted by their King, and that as it were but in a posting or hunting iourney.

How little cause then they may haue of such a change of so ancient a Monarchie into the case of priuate Shires, iudge rightly herein. And that you may be the more vpright Iudges, suppose your selues the Patients of whom such sentence should be giuen. But what preparation is it which I craue? onely such as by the entrance may shew something is done, yet more is intended. There is a conceipt intertained, and a double iealousie possesseth many, wherein I am misiudged.

First, that this Vnion will be the *Crisis* to the ouerthrow of England, and setting vp of Scotland: England will then bee ouerwhelmed by the swarming of the Scots, who if the Vnion were effected, would raigne and rule all.

The second is, my profuse liberalitie to the Scottish men more then the English, and that with this Vnion all things shalbe giuen to them, and you turned out of all: To you shall bee left the sweat and labour, to them shall bee giuen the fruite and sweet; and that my forbearance is but till this Vnion may be gained. How agreeable this is to the trewth, Iudge you; And that not by my wordes, but by my Actions. Doe I craue the Vnion without exceptions? doe I not offer to binde my selfe and to reserue to you, as in the Instrument, all places of Iudicature? doe I intend any thing which standeth not with the equall good of both Nations? I could then haue done it, and not spoken of it: For all men of vnderstanding must agree, that I might dispose without assent of Parliament, Offices of Iudicature, and others, both Ecclesiasticall and Temporall: But herein I did voluntarily offer by my Letters from Royston to the Commissioners, to bind my Prerogatiue.

Some thinke that I will draw the Scottish Nation hither, talking idlely of transporting of Trees out of a barren ground into a better, and of leane cattell out of bad pasture into a more fertile soile. Can any man displant you, vnlesse you will? or can any man thinke that Scotland is so strong to pull you out of your houses? or doe you not thinke I know England hath more people, Scotland more wast ground? So that there is roumth in Scotland rather to plant your idle people that swarme in London streets, and other Townes, and disburden you of them, then to bring more vnto you; And in cases of Iustice, if I bee partiall to either side, let my owne mouth condemne me, as vnworthy to be your King.

I appeale to your selues, if in fauour or Iustice I haue beene partiall: Nay, my intention was euer, you should then haue most cause to praise my discretion, when you saw I had most power. If hitherto I haue done nothing to your preiudice, much lesse meane I hereafter. If when I might haue done it without any breach of promise; Thinke so of mee, that much lesse I will doe it, when a Law is to restraine me. I owe no more to the Scottish men then to the English. I was borne there, and sworne here, and now raigne ouer both. Such particular persons of the Scottish Nation, as might claime any extraordinary merit at my handes, I haue already reasonably rewarded, and I can assure you that there is none left, whom for I meane extraordinary to straine my selfe further, then in such ordinary benefit as I may equally bestow without mine owne great hurt, vpon any Subiect of either Nation; In which case no Kings handes can euer be fully closed. To both I owe Iustice and protection, which with Gods grace I shall euer equally ballance.

For my Liberalitie, I haue told you of it heretofore: my three first yeeres were to me as a Christmas, I could not then be miserable: should I haue bene ouersparing to them? they might haue thought *Ioseph* had forgotten his brethren, or that the King had beene drunke with his new Kingdome. But Suites goe not now so cheape as they were wont, neither are there so many fees taken in the Hamper and Pettibagge for the great Seale as hath beene. And if I did respect the English when I came first, of whom I was receiued with ioy, and came as in a hunting iourney, what might the Scottish haue iustly said, if I had not in some measure dealt bountifully with them that so long had serued me, so farre aduentured themselues with me, and beene so faithfull to mee. I haue giuen you now foure yeeres proofe since my comming, and what I might haue done more to haue raised the Scottish nation you all know, and the longer I liue, the lesse cause haue I to be acquainted with them, and so the lesse hope of extraordinary fauour towards them: For since my comming from them I doe not alreadie know the one halfe of them by face, most of the youth being now risen vp to bee men, who were but children when I was there, and more are borne since my comming thence.

Now for my lands and reuenues of my Crowne which you may thinke I haue diminished, They are not yet so farre diminished, but that I thinke no prince of Christendome hath fairer possessions to his Crowne then yet I haue: and in token of my care to preserue the same to my posteritie for euer, the intaile of my lands to the Crowne hath beene long agoe offered vnto you: and that it is not yet done, is not my fault as you know. My Treasurer here knoweth my care, and hath already in part declared it, and if I did not hope to treble my Reuenue more then I haue empaired it, I should neuer rest quietly in my bed. But notwithstanding my comming to the Crowne, with that extraordinarie applause which you all know, and that I had two Nations to bee the obiects of my liberalitie, which neuer any Prince had here before; will you compare my gifts out of mine inheritance with some Princes here that had onely this Nation to respect, and whose whole time of reigne was litle longer then mine hath bene already? It will be found that their gifts haue farre surpassed mine, albeit as I haue already said, they had nothing so great cause of vsing their liberalitie.

For the maner of the Vnion presently desired,[834] It standeth in 3. parts: The first, taking away of hostile Lawes: for since there can bee now no Warres betwixt you, is it not reason hostile Lawes should cease? For, *deficiente causa deficit effectus.*[835] The King of England now cannot haue warres with the King of Scotland, therefore this failes of it selfe. The second is communitie of Commerce. I am no stranger vnto you: for you all know I came from the loynes of your ancient Kings. They of Scotland be my Subiects as you are. But how can I bee naturall Liege Lord to you both, and you strangers one to the other? Shall they which be of one alleagance with you, be no better respected of you, nor freer amongst you, then Frenchmen and Spaniards? Since I am Soueraigne ouer both, you as Subiects to one King, it must needes follow that you conuerse and haue Commerce together. There is a rumour of some ill dealings that should be vsed by the Commissioners, Merchants of Scotland. They be heere in England, and shall remaine till your next meeting, and abide triall, to prooue themselues either honest men or knaues.

For[836] the third point, of Naturalization, All you agree that they are no Aliens, and yet will not allow them to bee naturall. What kinde of prerogatiue will you make? But for the *Post nati*, your owne Lawyers and Iudges at my first comming to this Crowne, informed me, there was a difference betweene the *Ante* and the *Post nati* of each Kingdome, which caused mee to publish a Proclamation, that the *Post nati* were Naturalized (*Ipso facto*) by my Accession to this Crowne.[837] I doe not denie but Iudges may erre as men, and therefore I doe not presse you here to sweare to all their reasons. I onely vrge at this time the conueniencie for both Kingdomes, neither pressing you to iudge nor to be iudged. But remember also it is as possible and likely your owne Lawyers may erre as the Iudges: Therefore as I wish you to proceede herein so farre as may tend to the weale of both Nations; So would I haue you on the other part to beware to disgrace either my Proclamations or the Iudges, who when the Parliament is done, haue power to trie your lands and liues, for so you may disgrace both your King and your Lawes. For the doing of any acte that may procure lesse reuerence to the Iudges, cannot but breede a loosenesse in the Gouernement, and a disgrace to the whole Nation. The reason that most mooues mee for ought I haue yet heard, that there cannot but bee a difference betweene the *Ante nati* and the *Post nati*, and that in the fauour of the last, is that they must bee neerer vnto you being borne vnder the present Gouernement and common Allegiance: but in point of conueniencie, there is no question but the *Post nati* are more to bee respected: For if you would haue a perfect and perpetuall Vnion, that cannot be in the *Ante nati*, who are but few in comparison of those that shall be in all aages succeeding, and cannot liue long. But in the *Post nati* shall the Vnion be continued and liue euer aage after aage, which wanting a difference cannot but leaue a perpetuall marke of separation in the worke of the Vnion: as also that argument of iealousie will be so farre remooued in the case of the *Post nati* which are to reape the benefit in all succeeding aages, as by the contrary there will then rise *Pharaos* which neuer knew *Ioseph*. The Kings my Successours, who beeing borne and bred heere, can neuer haue more occasion of acquaintance with the Scottish Nation in generall, then any other English King that was before my time. Bee not therefore abused with the flattering speeches of such as would haue the *Ante nati* preferred, alleadging their merit in my Seruice, and such other reasons which indeede are but Sophismes: For, my rewarding out of my Liberalitie of any particular men, hath nothing adoe with the generall acte of the Vnion, which must not regard the deserts of priuate persons, but the generall weale and conioyning of the Nations. Besides that, the actuall Naturalizing, which is the onely point that is in your handes, is already graunted to by your selues to the most part of such particular persons as can haue any vse of it heere: and if any other well deseruing men were to sue for it hereafter, I doubt not but there would neuer bee question mooued among you for the granting of it. And therefore it is most euident, that such discourses haue *mel in ore, fel in corde*,[838] as I said before; carying an outward appearance of loue to the Vnion, but indeed a contrary resolution in their hearts. And as for limitations and restrictions, such as shall by me be agreed vpon to be reasonable and necessary after you haue fully debated vpon them, you may assure your selues I will with indifferencie grant what is requisite without partiall respect of Scotland. I am, as I haue often said, borne and sworne King ouer both Kingdomes; onely this farre let me entreat you, in debating the point at your next meeting, That yee be as ready to resolue doubts as to mooue them, and to be satisfied when doubts are cleered.

And[839] as for Commodities that come by the Vnion of these King-domes, they are great and euident; Peace, Plentie, Loue, free Inter-course and common Societie of two great Nations. All forreigne Kings that haue sent their Ambassadours to congratulate with me since my comming, haue saluted me as Monarch of the whole Isle, and with much more respect of my greatnesse, then if I were King alone of one of these Realmes: and with what comfort doe your selues behold Irish, Scottish, Welsh, and English, diuers in Nation, yet all walking as Subiects and seruants within my Court, and all liuing vnder the allegiance of your King, besides the honour and lustre that the encrease of gallant men in the Court of diuers Nations carries in the eyes of all strangers that repaire hither? Those confining places which were the Borders of the two Kingdomes, where heretofore much blood was shed, and many of your ancestours lost their liues; yea, that lay waste and desolate, and were habitations but for runna-gates, are now become the Nauell or Vmbilick of both Kingdomes, planted and peopled with Ciuilitie and riches: their Churches begin to bee planted, their doores stand now open, they feare neither rob-bing nor spoiling: and where there was nothing before heard nor seene in those parts but bloodshed, oppressions, complaints and out-cries, they now liue euery man peaceably vnder his owne figgetree, and all their former cryes and complaints turned onely into prayers to God for their King, vnder whom they enjoy such ease and happy quietnesse. The Marches beyond and on this side Twede, are as fruitfull and as peaceable as most parts of England: If after all this there shall be a Scissure, what inconuenience will follow, iudge you.

And as for the inconueniences that are feared on Englands part, It is alleadged, that the Scots are a populous Nation, they shall be harboured in our nests, they shall be planted and flourish in our good Soile, they shall eate our commons bare, and make vs leane: These are foolish and idle surmises. That which you possesse, they are not to enioy; by Law they cannot, nor by my partialitie they shall not: for set apart conscience and honour, (which if I should set apart indeede, I had rather wish my selfe to bee set apart and out of all being) can any man conclude either out of common reason or good policie, that I will preferre those which perhaps I shall neuer see, or but by poste for a moneth, before those with whom I must alwayes dwell? Can they conquer or ouercome you with swarmes of people, as the Goths and the Vandals did *Italy*? Surely the world knowes they are nothing so populous as you are: and although they haue had the honour and good fortune neuer to be conquered, yet were they euer but vpon the defensiue part, and may in a part thanke their hilles and inaccessible passages that preserued them from an vtter ouerthrow at the handes of all that pretended to conquer them. Or are they so very poore and miserable in their owne habitations, that necessitie should force them all to make incursions among you?

And for my part, when I haue two Nations vnder my gouernment, can you imagine I will respect the lesser, and neglect the greater? would I not thinke it a lesse euill and hazard to mee that the plague were at Northampton or Barwicke, then at London, so neere Westminster, the Seat of my habitation, and of my wife and children? will not a man bee more carefull to quench the fire taken in his neerest neighbours house, then if a whole Towne were a fire farre from him? You know that I am carefull to preserue the woods and game through all England, nay, through all the Isle: yet none of you doubts, but that I would be more offended with any disorder in the Forrest of Waltham, for stealing of a Stagge there, which lieth as it were vnder my nose, and in a maner ioyneth with my garden, then with cutting of timber, or stealing of a Deare in any Forest of the North parts of Yorkeshire or the Bishopricke.[840] Thinke you that I will preferre them that be absent, lesse powerfull, and farther off to doe me good or hurt, before you, with whom my security and liuing must be, and where I desire to plant my posterity? If I might by any such fauours raise my selfe to a greatnesse, it might bee probable: All I cannot draw, and to lose a whole state here to please a few there, were madnesse. I neede speake no more of this with protestations. Speake but of wit, it is not likely: and to doubt of my intention in this, were more then deuilish.

For mine owne part, I offer more then I receiue, and conueniencie I preferre before law, in this point. For, three parts, wherein I might hurt this Nation, by partiality to the Scots, you know doe absolutely lie in my hands and power: for either in disposition of rents, or whatsoeuer benefit, or in the preferring of them to any dignitie or office, ciuill or Ecclesiasticall, or in calling them to the Parliament, it doeth all fully and onely lie within the compasse of my Prerogatiue, which are the parts wherein the Scottish men can receiue either benefite or preferment by the Vnion, and wherein for the care I haue of this people, I am content to binde my selfe with some reasonable restrictions.

As for the fourth part, the Naturalizing, which onely lieth in your hands; It is the point wherein they receiue least benefit of any: for in that they can obteine nothing, but what they buy by their purse, or acquire by the selfe same meanes that you doe. And as for the point of naturalizing, which is the point thought so fit, and so precisely belonging to Parliament; not to speake of the Common law, wherein as yet I can professe no great knowledge, but in the Ciuill law wherein I am a little better versed, and which in the point of Coniunction of Nations should beare a great sway, it being the Law of Nations; I will mainteine two principles in it, which no learned and graue Ciuilian will deny, as being clearely to be proued, both out of the text it selfe in many places, and also out of the best approued Doctours and interpreters of that law; The one, that it is a speciall point of the Kings owne Prerogatiue, to make Aliens Citizens, and *donare Ciuitate*;[841] The other, that in any case wherein the Law is thought not to be cleare (as some of your selues doe doubt, that in this case of the *post nati*, the Law of England doth not clearely determine) then in such a question wherein no positiue Law is resolute, *Rex est Iudex*,[842] for he is *Lex loquens*,[843] and is to supply the Law, where the Law wants, and if many famous histories be to be beleeued, they giue the example for mainteining of this Law in the persons of the Kings of England and France especially, whose speciall Prerogatiue they alleadge it to be. But this I speake onely as knowing what belongeth to a King, although in this case I presse no further then that which may agree with your loues, and stand with the weale and conueniencie of both Nations.

And whereas some may thinke this Vnion will bring preiudice to some Townes and Corporations within England; It may bee, a Merchant or two of Bristow, or Yarmouth, may haue an hundred pounds lesse in his packe: But if the Empire gaine, and become the greater, it is no matter: You see one Corporation is euer against another, and no priuate Companie can be set vp, but with some losse to another.

For[844] the supposed inconueniences rising from Scotland, they are three. First, that there is an euill affection in the Scottish Nation to the Vnion. Next, the Vnion is incompatible betweene two such Nations. Thirdly, that the gaine is smal or none. If this be so, to what end do we talke of an Vnion? For proofe of the first point, there is alleadged an auersenesse in the Scottish Nation expressed in the Instrument, both in the preface and body of their Acte; in the preface, where they declare, That they will remaine an absolute and free Monarchie; And in the body of the Acte, where they make an exception of the ancient fundamentall Lawes of that Kingdome. And first for the generall of their auersenes, All the maine current in your Lower-house ranne this whole Session of Parliament with that opinion, That Scotland was so greedy of this Vnion, and apprehended that they should receiue so much benefit by it, as they cared not for the strictnesse of any conditions, so they might attaine to the substance: And yet you now say, they are backwards and auerse from the Vnion. This is a direct contradiction *in adiecto*:[845] For how can they both be beggers and backwards, in one and the selfe same thing, at the same time?

But for answere to the particulars, It is an old Schoole point, *Eius est explicare, cuius est condere.*[846] You cannot interpret their Lawes, nor they yours; I that made them with their assent, can best expound them.

And first I confesse, that the English Parliaments are so long, and the Scottish so short, that a meane betweene them would doe well: For the shortnesse of their continuing together, was the cause of their hastie mistaking, by setting these wordes of exception of fundamentall Lawes in the body of the Acte, which they onely did in pressing to imitate word by word the English Instrument, wherein the same wordes be conteined in your Preface. And as to their meaning and interpretation of that word, I will not onely deliuer it vnto you out of mine owne conceipt, but as it was deliuered vnto mee by the best Lawyers of Scotland, both Counsellours and other Lawyers, who were at the making thereof in Scotland, and were Commissioners here for performance of the same.

Their meaning in the word of Fundamentall Lawes, you shall perceiue more fully hereafter, when I handle the obiection of the difference of Lawes: For they intend thereby onely those Lawes whereby confusion is auoyded, and their Kings descent mainteined, and the heritage of the succession and Monarchie, which hath bene a Kingdome, to which I am in descent, three hundreth yeeres before CHRIST: Not meaning it as you doe, of their Common Law, for they haue none, but that which is called Ivs REGIS: and their desire of continuing a free Monarchie, was onely meant, That all such particular Priuiledges (whereof I spake before) should not bee so confounded, as for want either of Magistrate, Law, or Order, they might fall in such a confusion, as to become like a naked Prouince, without Law or libertie vnder this Kingdome. I hope you meane not I should set Garrisons ouer them, as the Spaniards doe ouer Sicily and

Naples, or gouerne them by Commissioners, which are seldome found succeedingly all wise and honest men.

This I must say for Scotland, and I may trewly vaunt it; Here I sit and gouerne it with my Pen, I write and it is done, and by a Clearke of the Councell I gouerne Scotland now, which others could not doe by the sword. And for their auersenesse in their heart against the Vnion, It is trew indeede, I protest they did neuer craue this Vnion of me, nor sought it either in priuate, or the State by letters, nor euer once did any of that Nation presse mee forward or wish mee to accelerate that businesse. But on the other part, they offered alwayes to obey mee when it should come to them, and all honest men that desire my greatnesse haue beene thus minded, for the personall reuerence and regard they beare vnto my Person, and any of my reasonable and iust desires.

I know there are many *Piggots*[847] amongst them, I meane a number of seditious and discontented particular persons, as must be in all Common-wealths, that where they dare, may peraduenture talke lewdly enough: but no Scottish man euer spake dishonourably of England in Parliament. For here must I note vnto you the difference of the two Parliaments in these two Kingdomes, for there they must not speake without the Chauncellours leaue, and if any man doe propound or vtter any seditious or vncomely speeches, he is straight interrupted and silenced by the Chauncellors authoritie: where as here, the libertie for any man to speake what hee list, and as long as he list, was the onely cause he was not interrupted.

It hath bin obiected that there is a great Antipathy of the Lawes and Customes of these two Nations. It is much mistaken: for Scotland hath no Common Law as here, but the Law they haue is of three sorts.

All the Lawe of Scotland for Tenures, Wards and Liueries, Seigniories and Lands, are drawen out of the Chauncerie of England, and for matters of equitie and in many things else, differs from you but in certaine termes: *Iames* the first, bred here in England, brought the Lawes thither in a written hand. The second is Statute Lawes, which be their Acts of Parliament, wherein they haue power as you, to make and alter[848] Lawes: and those may be looked into by you, for I hope you shall be no more strangers to that Nation. And the principall worke of this Vnion will be, to reconcile the Statute Lawes of both Kingdomes. The third is the Ciuill Law: *Iames* the fift brought it out of France by establishing the Session there, according to the forme of the Court of Parliament of Fraunce, which he had seene in the time of his being there: who occupie there the place of Ciuill Iudges in all matters of Plee or controuersie, yet not to gouerne absolutely by the Ciuill Law as in Fraunce. For if a man plead that the Law of the Nation is otherwise, it is a barre to the Ciuill, and a good Chauncellor or President, will oftentimes repell and put to silence an Argument that the Lawyers bring out of the Ciuill Law, where they haue a cleare solution in their owne Law. So as the Ciuill Law in Scotland is admitted in no other cases, but to supply such cases wherein the Municipall Law is defectiue. Then may you see it is not so hard a matter as is thought, to reduce that Countrey to bee vnited with you vnder this Law, which neither are subiect to the Ciuill Lawe, nor yet haue any olde Common Law of their owne, but such as in effect is borrowed from yours. And for their Statute Lawes in Parliament, you may alter and change them as oft as occasion shall require, as you doe here. It hath likewise beene obiected as an other impediment, that in the Parliament of Scotland the King hath not a negatiue voice, but must passe all the Lawes agreed on by the Lords and Commons. Of this I can best resolue you: for I am the eldest Parliament man in Scotland, and haue sit in more Parliaments then any of my Predecessors. I can assure you, that the forme of Parliament there, is nothing inclined to popularitie. About a twentie dayes or such a time before the Parliament, Proclamation is made throughout the Kingdome, to deliuer in to the Kings Clearke of Register (whom you heere call the Master of the Rolles) all Bills to be exhibited that Session before a certaine day. Then are they brought vnto the King, and perused and considered by him, and onely such as I allowe of are put into the Chancellors handes to bee propounded to the Parliament, and none others: And if any man in Parliament speake of any other matter then is in this forme first allowed by mee, The Chancellor tells him there is no such Bill allowed by the King.

Besides, when they haue passed them for lawes, they are presented vnto me, and I with my Scepter put into my hand by the Chancellor, must say, *I ratifie and approue all things done in this present Parliament.* And if there bee any thing that I dislike, they rase it out before. If this may bee called a negatiue voyce, then I haue one I am sure in that Parliament.

The last impediment is the French liberties: which is thought so great, as except the Scots farsake Fraunce, England cannot bee vnited to them. If the Scottish Nation would bee so vnwilling to leaue them as is said, it would not lye in their hands: For the League was neuer made betweene the people, as is mistaken, but betwixt the *Princes* onely and their Crownes. The beginning was by a Message from a King of Fraunce, *Charlemaine* I take it (but I cannot certainely remember) vnto a King of Scotland, for a League defensiue and offensiue betweene vs and them against England, Fraunce being at that time in Warres with England.

The like at that time was then desired by England against Fraunce, who also sent their Ambassadours to Scotland. At the first, the Disputation was long maintained in fauour of England, that they being our neerest Neighbours ioyned in one continent, and a strong and powerfull Nation, it was more fitte for the weale and securitie of the State of Scotland, to be in League and Amitie with them, then with a Countrey, though neuer so strong, yet diuided by Sea from vs: especially England lying betwixt vs and them, where we might be sure of a suddaine mischiefe, but behooued to abide the hazard of wind and weather, and other accidents that might hinder our reliefe.

But after, when the contrary part of the Argument was maintained: wherein allegation was made, that England euer sought to conquer Scotland, and therefore in regarde of their pretended interest in the Kingdoome, would neuer keepe any sound Amitie with them longer, then they saw their aduantage; whereas France lying more remote and clayming no interest in the Kingdome, would therefore bee found a more constant and faithfull friend: It was vnhappily concluded in fauour of the last partie, through which occasion Scotland gate many mischiefes after: And it is by the very tenour thereof ordered, to bee renewed and confirmed from King to King successiuely, which accordingly was euer performed by the mediation of their Ambassadours, and therefore meerely personall, and so was it renewed in the Queene my mothers time, onely betweene the two Kings, and not by assent of Parliament or conuention of the three Estates, which it could neuer haue wanted if it had beene a League betweene the people. And in my time when it came to be ratified, because it appeared to be in *odium tertii*,[849] it was by me left vnrenewed or confirmed as a thing incompatible to my Person, in consideration of my Title to this Crowne. Some Priuiledges indeede in the Merchants fauour for point of Commerce, were renewed and confirmed in my time: wherein for my part of it, there was scarce three Counsellours more then my Secretarie, to whose place it belonged, that medled in that matter.

It is trew, that it behooued to be enterteined, as they call it, in the Court of Parliament of *Paris*: but that onely serues for publication, and not to giue it Authoritie: That Parliament (as you know) being but a Iudiciall Seate of Iudges and Lawyers, and nothing agreeing with the definition or office of our Parliaments in this Isle. And therefore that any fruites or Priuiledges possessed by the League with Fraunce is able now to remaine in Scotland, is impossible: For ye may be sure, that the French King stayes onely vpon the sight of the ending of this Vnion, to cut it off himselfe. Otherwise when this great worke were at an end, I would be forced for the generall care I owe to all my Subiects, to craue of France like Priuiledges to them all as Scotland alreadie enioyes, seeing the personall friendship remaines as great betweene vs as betweene our Progenitors; and all my Subiects must be alike deare vnto me: which either hee will neuer grant, and so all will fall to the ground; or else it will turne to the benefite of the whole Island: and so the Scottish Priuiledges cannot hold longer then my League with France lasteth.

And for another Argument to prooue that this league is only betweene the Kings, and not betweene the people: They which haue Pensions, or are priuie Intelligence giuers in France without my leaue, are in no better case by the Law of Scotland, then if they were Pensioners to Spaine.

As for the Scottish Guard in France, the beginning thereof was, when an Earle of *Boghan* was sent in aide of the French with tenne thousand men, and there being made Constable, and hauing obtained a victorie, was murthered with the most of the Scottish Armie. In recompense whereof, and for a future securitie to the Scottish Nation, the Scottish Guard was ordeined to haue the priuiledge and prerogatiue before all other Guards in guarding the Kings person.

And as for the last point of this subdiuision concerning the gaine that England may make by this Vnion, I thinke no wise nor honest man will aske any such question. For who is so ignorant, that doeth not know the gaine will bee great? Doe you not gaine by the Vnion of Wales? And is not Scotland greater then Wales? Shall not your

Dominions bee encreased of Landes, Seas, and persons added to your greatnesse? And are not your Landes and Seas adioyning? For who can set downe the limits of the Borders, but as a Mathematicall line or *Idæa?* Then will that backe doore bee shut, and those portes of *Ianus* be for euer closed: you shall haue them that were your enemies to molest you, a sure backe to defend you: their bodies shall bee your aides, and they must bee partners in all your quarrels: Two snow-balls put together, make one the greater: Two houses ioyned, make one the larger: two Castle walles made in one, makes one as thicke and strong as both. And doe you not see in the Low countreys how auaileable the English and the Scottish are being ioyned together? This is a point so plaine, as no man that hath wit or honestie, but must acknowledge it feelingly.

And where it is obiected that the Scottishmen are not tyed to the seruice of the King in the warres aboue forty dayes; It is an ignorant mistaking. For the trewth is, That in respect the Kings of Scotland did not so abound in Treasure and money to take vp an Armie vnder pay, as the Kings of England did; Therefore was the Scottish Army wont to be raysed onely by Proclamation, vpon the penaltie of their breach of alleageance; So as they were all forced to come to the Warre like Snailes who carry their house about with them; Euery Nobleman and Gentleman bringing with him their Tents, money, prouision for their house, victuals of all sorts, and all other necessaries, the King supplying them of nothing; Necessitie thereupon enforcing a warning to be giuen by the Proclamation of the space of their attendance, without which they could not make their prouision accordingly, especially as long as they were within the bounds of Scotland, where it was not lawfull for them to helpe themselues by the spoile or wasting of the Countrey. But neither is there any Law Prescribing precisely such a certaine number of dayes, nor yet is it without the limits of the Kings power to keepe them together, as many more dayes as hee list, to renew his Proclamations from time to time some reasonable number of dayes, before the expiring of the former, they being euer bound to serue and waite vpon him, though it were an hundreth yeere if need were.

Now to conclude, I am glad of this occasion, that I might *Liberare animam meam*;[850] You are now to recede: when you meete againe, remember I pray you, the trewth and sincerity of my meaning, which in seeking Vnion, is onely to aduance the greatnesse of your Empire seated here in England; And yet with such caution I wish it, as may stand with the weale of both States. What is now desired, hath oft before bene sought when it could not bee obteined: To refuse it now then, were double iniquitie. Strengthen your owne felicitie, *London* must bee the Seate of your King, and Scotland ioyned to this kingdome by a Golden conquest, but cymented with loue, (as I said before) which within will make you strong against all Ciuill and intestine Rebellion, as without wee will bee compassed and guarded with our walles of brasse. Iudge mee charitably, since in this I seeke your equall good, that so both of you might bee made fearefull to your Enemies, powerfull in your selues, and auaileable to your friendes. Studie therefore hereafter to make a good Conclusion, auoyd all delayes, cut off all vaine questions, that your King may haue his lawfull desire, and be not disgraced in his iust endes. And for your securitie in such reasonable points of restrictions, whereunto I am to agree, yee need neuer doubt of my inclination: For I will not say any thing which I will not promise, nor promise any thing which I will not sweare; What I sweare I will signe, and what I signe, I shall with GODS grace euer performe.

A SPEACH TO THE[851] LORDS AND COMMONS OF THE PARLIAMENT AT *WHITE-HALL, ON WEDNESDAY THE* XXI. OF MARCH.

ANNO 1609

WE being now in the middest of this season appointed for penitence and prayer, it hath so fallen out, that these two last dayes haue bene spent in a farre other sort of exercise, I meane in Eucharisticke Sacrifice, and gratulation of thankes, presented vnto mee by both the parts of this body of Parliament: and therefore to make vp the number of three, (which is the number of Trinitie, and perfection) I haue thought good to make this the third Day, to be spent in this exercise.[852]

As ye made mee a faire Present indeed in presenting your thankes and louing dueties vnto mee: So haue I now called you here, to recompence you againe with a great and a rare Present, which is a faire and a Christall Mirror; Not such a Mirror wherein you may see your owne faces, or shadowes; but such a Mirror, or Christall, as through the transparantnesse thereof, you may see the heart of your King. The Philosophers wish, That euery mans breast were a Christall, where-through his heart might be seene, is vulgarly knowne, and I touched it in one of my former Speaches vnto you: But though that were impossible in the generall, yet will I now performe this for my part, That as it is a trew Axiome in Diuinitie, That *Cor Regis* is *in manu Domini*,[853] So wil I now set *Cor Regis in oculis populi*.[854] I know that I can say nothing at this time, whereof some of you that are here, haue not at one time or other, heard me say the like already: Yet as corporall food nourisheth and mainteineth the body, so doeth *Reminiscentia*[855] nourish and mainteine memory.

I Will reduce to three generall and maine grounds, the principall things that haue bene agitated in this Parliament, and whereof I will now speake.

First, the Arrand for which you were called by me; And that was, for supporting of my state, and necessities.

The second is, that which the people are to mooue vnto the King: To represent vnto him such things, whereby the Subiects are vexed, or wherein the state of the Common wealth is to be redressed: And that is the thing which you call grieuances.

The third ground that hath bene handled amongst you, and not onely in talke amongst you in the Parliament, but euen in many other peoples mouthes, aswell within, as without the Parliament, is of a higher nature then any of the former (though it be but an Incident?) and the reason is, because it concernes a higher point; And this is a doubt, which hath bene in the heads of some, of my Intention in two things.

First, whether I was resolued in the generall, to continue still my gouernment according to the ancient forme of this State, and the Lawes of this Kingdome: Or if I had an intention not to limit my selfe within those bounds, but to alter the same when I thought conuenient, by the absolute power of a King.

The other branch is anent the Common Law, which some had a conceit I disliked, and (in respect that I was borne where another forme of Law was established) that I would haue wished the Ciuill Law to haue bene put in place of the Common Law for gouernment of this people. And the complaint made amongst you of a booke written by doctour *Cowell*, was a part of the occasion of this incident: But as touching my censure of that booke, I made it already to bee deliuered vnto you by the Treasurer here sitting, which he did out of my owne directions and notes; and what he said in my name, that had he directly from me: But what hee spake of himselfe therein without my direction, I shal alwayes make good; for you may be sure I will be loth to make so honest a man a lyer, or deceiue your expectations: alwayes within very few dayes my Edict shall come forth anent that matter, which shall fully discouer my meaning.

There was neuer any reason to mooue men to thinke, that I could like of such grounds: For there are two qualities principally, or rather priuations that make Kings subiect to flatterie; *Credulitie* and *Ignorance*; and I hope none of them can bee iustly obiected to mee: For if *Alexander* the great, for all his learning, had bene wise in that point to haue considered the state of his owne naturall body and disposition, hee would neuer haue thought himselfe a god. And now to the matter. As it is a Christian duety in euery man, *Reddere rationem fidei,*[856] and not to be ashamed to giue an account of his profession before men, and Angels, as oft as occasion shall require: So did I euer hold it a necessitie of honour in a iust and wise King, though not to giue an account to his people of his actions, yet clearely to deliuer his heart and intention vnto them vpon euery occasion. But I must inuert my order, and begin first with that incident which was last in my diuision (though highest of nature) and so goe backward.

The State of MONARCHIE is the supremest thing vpon earth: For Kings are not onely GODS Lieutenants vpon earth, and sit vpon GODS throne, but euen by GOD himselfe they are called Gods. There bee three principall similitudes that illustrate the state of MONARCHIE: One taken out of the word of GOD; and the two other out of the grounds of Policie and Philosophie. In the Scriptures Kings are called Gods, and so their power after a certaine relation compared to the Diuine power. Kings are also compared to Fathers of families: for a King is trewly *Parens patriae,*[857] the politique father of his people. And lastly, Kings are compared to the head of this Microcosme of the body of man.

Kings are iustly called Gods, for that they exercise a manner or resemblance of Diuine power vpon earth: For if you wil consider the Attributes to God, you shall see how they agree in the person of a King. God hath power to create, or destroy, make, or vnmake at his pleasure, to giue life, or send death, to iudge all, and to bee iudged nor accomptable to none: To raise low things, and to make high things low at his pleasure, and to God are both soule and body due. And the like power haue Kings: they make and vnmake their subiects: they haue power of raising, and casting downe: of life, and of death: Iudges ouer all their subiects and in all causes, and yet accomptable to none but God onely. They haue power to exalt low things, and abase high things, and make of their subiects like men at the Chesse; A pawne to take a Bishop or a Knight, and to cry vp, or downe any of their subiects, as they do their money. And to the King is due both the affection of the soule, and the seruice of the body of his subiects: And therefore that reuerend Bishop here amongst you, though I heare that by diuers he was mistaken or not wel vnder-stood,[858] yet did he preach both learnedly and trewly annent this point concerning the power of a King: For what he spake of a Kings power in *Abstracto,*[859] is most trew in Diuinitie: For to Emperors, or Kings that are Monarches, their Subiects bodies & goods are due for their defence and maintenance. But if I had bene in his place, I would only haue added two words, which would haue cleared all: For after I had told as a Diuine, what was due by the Subiects to their Kings in generall, I would then haue concluded as an Englishman, shewing this people, That as in generall all Subiects were bound to relieue their King; So to exhort them, that as wee liued in a setled state of a Kingdome which was gouerned by his owne fundamentall Lawes and Orders, that according thereunto, they were now (being assembled for this purpose in Parliament) to consider how to helpe such a King as now they had; And that according to the ancient forme, and order established in this Kingdome: putting so, a difference betweene the generall power of a King in Diuinity, and the setled and established State of this Crowne, and Kingdome. And I am sure that the Bishop meant to haue done the same, if hee had not bene straited by time, which in respect of the greatnesse of the presence preaching before me, and such an Auditory, he durst not presume vpon.

As for the Father of a familie, they had of olde vnder the Law of Nature *Patriam potestatem*,[860] which was *Potestatem vitae & necis*,[861] ouer their children or familie, (I meane such Fathers of families as were the lineall heires of those families whereof Kings did originally come:) For Kings had their first originall from them, who planted and spread themselues in *Colonies* through the world. Now a Father may dispose of his Inheritance to his children, at his pleasure: yea, euen disinherite the eldest vpon iust occasions, and preferre the youngest, according to his liking: make them beggers, or rich at his pleasure; restraine, or banish out of his presence, as hee findes them giue cause of offence, or restore them in fauour againe with the penitent sinner: So may the King deale with his Subiects.

And lastly, as for the head of the naturall body, the head hath the power of directing all the members of the body to that vse which the iudgement in the head thinkes most conuenient. It may apply sharpe cures, or cut off corrupt members, let blood in what proportion it thinkes fit, and as the body may spare, but yet is all this power ordeined by God *Ad aedificationem, non ad destructionem*.[862] For although God haue power aswell of destruction, as of creation or maintenance; yet will it not agree with the wisedome of God, to exercise his power in the destruction of nature, and ouerturning the whole frame of things, since his creatures were made, that his glory might thereby be the better expressed: So were hee a foolish father that would disinherite or destroy his children without a cause, or leaue off the carefull education of them; And it were an idle head that would in place of phisicke so poyson or phlebotomize the body as might breede a dangerous distemper or destruction thereof.

But now in these our times we are to distinguish betweene the state of Kings in their first originall, and betweene the state of setled Kings and Monarches, that doe at this time gouerne in ciuill Kingdomes: For euen as God, during the time of the olde Testament, spake by Oracles, and wrought by Miracles; yet how soone it pleased him to setle a *Church* which was bought, and redeemed by the blood of his onely Sonne *Christ*, then was there a cessation of both; Hee euer after gouerning his people and Church within the limits of his reueiled will. So in the first originall of Kings, whereof some had their beginning by Conquest, and some by election of the people, their wills at that time serued for Law; Yet how soone Kingdomes began to be setled in ciuilitie and policie, then did Kings set downe their minds by Lawes, which are properly made by the King onely; but at the rogation of the people, the Kings grant being obteined thereunto. And so the King became to be *Lex loquens*,[863] after a sort, binding himselfe by a double oath to the obseruation of the fundamentall Lawes of his kingdome: *Tacitly*, as by being a King, and so bound to protect aswell the people, as the Lawes of his Kingdome; And *Expresly*, by his oath at his Coronation: So as euery iust King in a setled Kingdome is bound to obserue that paction made to his people by his Lawes, in framing his gouernment agreeable thereunto, according to that paction which God made with *Noe* after the deluge, *Hereafter Seed-time, and Haruest, Cold and Heate, Summer and Winter, and Day and Night shall not cease, so long as the earth remaines.*[864] And therefore a King gouerning in a setled Kingdome, leaues to be a King, and degenerates into a Tyrant, assoone as he leaues off to rule according to his Lawes. In which case the Kings conscience may speake vnto him, as the poore widow said to Philip of Macedon; Either gouerne according to your Law, *Aut ne Rex sis.*[865] And though no Christian man ought to allow any rebellion of people against their Prince, yet doeth God neuer leaue Kings vnpunished when they transgresse these limits: For in that same Psalme where God saith to Kings, *Vos Dij estis*,[866] hee immediatly thereafter concludes, *But ye shall die like men.*[867] The higher wee are placed, the greater shall our fall be. *Vt casus sic dolor:*[868] the taller the trees be, the more in danger of the winde; and the tempest beats sorest vpon the highest mountaines. Therefore all Kings that are not tyrants, or periured, will be glad to bound themselues within the limits of their Lawes; and they that perswade them the contrary, are vipers, and pests, both against them and the Commonwealth. For it is a great difference betweene a Kings gouernment in a setled State, and what Kings in their originall power might doe in *Indiuiduo vago.*[869] As for my part, I thanke God, I haue euer giuen good proofe, that I neuer had intention to the contrary: And I am sure to goe to my graue with that reputation and comfort, that neuer King was in all his time more carefull to haue his Lawes duely obserued, and himselfe to gouerne thereafter, then I.

I conclude then this point touching the power of Kings, with this Axiome of Diuinitie, That as to dispute what God may doe, is Blasphemie; but *quid vult Deus,*[870] that Diuines may lawfully, and doe ordinarily dispute and discusse; for to dispute *A Posse ad Esse*[871] is both against Logicke and Diuinitie: So is it sedition in Subiects, to dispute what a King may do in the height of his power: But iust Kings wil euer be willing to declare what they wil do, if they wil not incurre the curse of God. I wil not be content that my power be disputed vpon: but I shall euer be willing to make the reason appeare of all my doings, and rule my actions according to my Lawes.

The other branch of this incident is concerning the Common Law, being conceiued by some, that I contemned it, and preferred the Ciuil Law thereunto. As I haue already said, Kings Actions (euen in the secretest places) are as the actions of those that are set vpon the Stages, or on the tops of houses: and I hope neuer to speake that in priuate, which I shall not auow in publique, and Print it if need be (as I said in my BASILICON DORON.) For it is trew, that within these few dayes I spake freely my minde touching the Common Law in my Priuie Chamber, at the time of my dinner, which is come to all your eares; and the same was likewise related vnto you by my Treasurer; and now I will againe repeate and confirme the same my selfe vnto you. First, as a King, I haue least cause of any man to dislike the Common Law: For no Law can bee more fauourable and aduantagious for a King, and extendeth further his Prerogatiue, then it doeth: And for a King of England to despise the Common Law, it is to neglect his owne Crowne. It is trew, that I doe greatly esteeme the Ciuill Law, the profession thereof seruing more for generall learning, and being most necessary for matters of Treatie with all forreine Nations: And I thinke that if it should bee taken away, it would make an entrie to Barbarisme in this Kingdome, and would blemish the honour of England: For it is in a maner LEX GENTIVM, and maintaineth Intercourse with all forreine Nations: but I onely allow it to haue course here, according to those limits of Iurisdiction, which the Common Law it selfe doeth allow it: And therefore though it bee not fit for the generall gouernment of the people here; it doeth not follow, it should be extinct, no more, then because the Latine tongue is not the Mother or Radicall Language of any Nation in the world at this time, that therefore the English tongue should onely now be learned in this Kingdome, which were to bring in Barbarisme. My meaning therefore is not to preferre the Ciuill Law before the Common Law; but onely that it should not be extinguished, and yet so bounded, (I meane to such Courts and Causes) as haue beene in ancient vse; As the Ecclesiasticall Courts, Court of Admiraltie, Court of Requests, and such like, reseruing euer to the Common Law to meddle with the fundamentall Lawes of this Kingdome, either concerning the Kings Prerogatiue, or the possessions of Subiects, in any questions, either betweene the King, and any of them, or amongst themselues, in the points of *Meum & tuum*.[872] For it is trew, that there is no Kingdome in the world, not onely Scotland, but not France, nor Spaine, nor any other Kingdome gouerned meerely by the Ciuill Law, but euery one of them hath their owne municipall Lawes agreeable to their Customes, as this Kingdome hath the Common Law: Nay, I am so farre from disallowing the Common Law, as I protest, that if it were in my hand to chuse a new Law for this Kingdome, I would not onely preferre it before any other Nationall Law, but euen before the very Iudiciall Law of *Moyses*: and yet I speake no blasphemie in preferring it for conueniencie to this Kingdome, and at this time, to the very Law of God: For God gouerned his selected people by these three Lawes, *Ceremoniall, Morall,* and *Iudiciall*: The *Iudiciall*, being onely fit for a certaine people, and a certaine time, which could not serue for the general of all other people and times. As for example, If the Law of hanging for Theft, were turned here to restitution of treble or quadruple, as it was in the Law of *Moyses*, what would become of all the middle

Shires, and all the Irishrie and Highlanders? But the maine point is, That if the fundamentall Lawes of any Kingdome should be altered, who should discerne what is *Meum & tuum*,[873] or how should a King gouerne? It would be like the *Gregorian* Calender, which destroyes the old, and yet doeth this new trouble all the debts and Accompts of Traffiques and Merchandizes: Nay by that accompt I can neuer tell mine owne aage; for now is my Birth-day remooued by the space of ten dayes neerer me then it was before the change. But vpon the other part, though I haue in one point preferred our Common Law, concerning our vse to the very Law of GOD; yet in another respect I must say, both our Law and all Lawes else are farre inferiour to that Iudiciall Law of GOD, for no booke nor Law is perfect nor free from corruption, except onely the booke and Law of GOD. And therefore I could wish some three things specially to be purged & cleared in the Common Law; but alwayes by the aduise of Parliament: For the King with his Parliament here are absolute, (as I vnderstand) in making or forming of any sort of Lawes.

First I could wish that it were written in our vulgar Language: for now it is in an old, mixt, and corrupt Language, onely vnderstood by Lawyers: whereas euery Subiect ought to vnderstand the Law vnder which he liues: For since it is our plea against the Papists, that the language in GODS Seruice ought not to be in an vnknowne tongue, according to the rule in the law of *Moyses*, That the Law should be written in the fringes of the Priests garment, and should be publikely read in the eares of all the people: so mee thinkes ought our Law to be made as plaine as can be to the people, that the excuse of ignorance may be taken from them, for conforming themselues thereunto.

Next, our Common Law hath not a setled Text in all Cases, being chiefly grounded either vpon old Customes, or else vpon the Reports and Cases of Iudges, which ye call *Responsa Prudentum*.[874] The like whereof is in all other Lawes: for they are much ruled by Presidents (saue onely in *Denmarke* and *Norway*, where the letter of the Law resolues all doubts without any trouble to the Iudge,) But though it be trew, that no Text of Law can be so certaine, wherein the circumstances will not make a variation in the Case, (for in this aage, mens wits increase so much by ciuilitie, that the circumstances of euery particular case varies so much from the generall Text of Law, as in the Ciuill Law it selfe, there are therefore so many Doctors that comment vpon the Text, & neuer a one almost agrees with another;

Otherwise there needed no Iudges, but the bare letter of the Law.) Yet could I wish that some more certaintie were set downe in this case by Parliament: for since the very Reports themselues are not alwayes so binding, but that diuers times Iudges doe disclaime them, and recede from the iudgment of their predecessors; it were good, that vpon a mature deliberation, the exposition of the Law were set downe by Acte of Parliament, and such reports therein confirmed, as were thought fit to serue for Law in all times hereafter, and so the people should not depend vpon the bare opinions of Iudges, and vncertaine Reports.

And lastly, there be in the Common Law diuers contrary Reports, and Presidents: and this corruption doeth likewise concerne the Statutes and Acts of Parliament, in respect there are diuers crosse and cuffing Statutes, and some so penned, as they may be taken in diuers, yea contrary sences. And therefore would I wish both those Statutes and Reports, aswell in the Parliament as Common Law, to be once maturely reuiewed, and reconciled; And that not onely all contrarieties should be scraped out of our Bookes, but euen that such penall Statutes as were made, but for the vse of the time (from breach whereof no man can be free) which doe not now agree with the condition of this our time, might likewise be left out of our bookes, which vnder a tyrannous or auaritious King could not be endured. And this reformation might (me thinkes) bee made a worthy worke, and well deserues a Parliament to be set of purpose for it.

I know now that being vpon this point of the Common Law, you looke to heare my opinion concerning *Prohibitions*; and I am not ignorant that I haue bene thought to be an enemie to all *Prohibitions*, and an vtter stayer of them: But I will shortly now informe you what hath bene my course in proceeding therein. It is trew that in respect of diuers honorable Courts, and Iurisdictions planted in this Kingdome, I haue often wished that euery Court had his owne trew limit, and iurisdiction clearely set downe, and certainly knowne; which if it be exceeded by any of them, or that any of them encroch one vpon another, then I grant that a *Prohibition* in that case is to goe out of the *Kings Bench*, but chiefliest out of the *Chancery*; for other Benches I am not yet so well resolued of their Iurisdiction in that point. And for my part, I was neuer against *Prohibitions* of this nature, nor the trew vse of them, which is indeed to keepe euery Riuer within his owne banks and channels. But when I saw the swelling and ouerflowing of *Prohibitions* in a farre greater abundance then euer before, euery Court striuing to bring in most moulture to their owne Mill, by multitudes of Causes, which is a disease very naturall to all Courts and Iurisdictions in the world; Then dealt I with this Cause, and that at two seuerall times, once in the middest of Winter, and againe in the middest of the next following Summer; At euery of which times I spent three whole daies in that labour. And then after a large hearing, I told them as *Christ* said concerning Mariage, *Ab initio non fuit sic*.[875] For as God conteins the Sea within his owne bounds and marches (as it is in the *Psalmes,*) So is it my office to make euery Court conteine himselfe within his own limits; And therfore I gaue admonitions to both sides: To the other Courts, that they should be carefull hereafter euery of them, to conteine themselues within the bounds of their owne Iurisdictions; and to the Courts of Common Law, that they should not bee so forward, and prodigall in multiplying their *Prohibitions*. Two cautions I willed them to obserue in graunting their *Prohibitions*: First, that they should be graunted in a right and lawfull forme: And next, that they should not grant them, but vpon a iust and reasonable cause. As to the forme, it was, That none should be graunted by any one particular Iudge, or in time of Vacation, or in any other place, but openly in Court. And to this the Iudges themselues gaue their willing assent. And as to the Cause, That they should not be granted vpon euery sleight surmise, or information of the partie, but always that a due and graue examination should first precede. Otherwise if *Prohibitions* should rashly, and headily be granted, then no man is the more secure of his owne, though hee hath gotten a Sentence with him: For as good haue no Law, or Sentence, as to haue no execution thereof. A poore Minister with much labour and expense, hauing exhausted his poore meanes, and being forced to forbeare his studie, and to become *non resident* from his flocke, obtaines a *Sentence*, and then when hee lookes to enioy the fruits thereof, he is defrauded of all by a *Prohibition*, according to the parable of Christ, That night when hee thinkes himselfe most happy, shall his soule be taken from him:[876] And so is he tortured like *Tantalus*, who when he hath the Apple at his mouth, and that he is gaping and opening his mouth to receiue it, then must it be pulled from him by a *Prohibition*, and he not suffered to taste thereof. So as to conclude this point, I put a difference betweene the trew vse of *Prohibitions*, and the superabounding abuse thereof: for as a thing which is good, ought not therefore bee abused; so ought not the lawfull vse of a good thing be forborne, because of the abuse thereof.

Now the second generall ground whereof I am to speake, concernes the matter of *Grieuances*: There are two speciall causes of the peoples presenting *Grieuances* to their King in time of Parliament. First, for that the King cannot at other times be so well informed of all the *Grieuances* of his people, as in time of Parliament, which is the representatiue body of the whole Realme. Secondly, the Parliament is the highest Court of Iustice, and therefore the fittest place where diuers natures of *Grieuances* may haue their proper remedie, by the establishment of good and wholsome Lawes. But though my Speech was before directed to the whole Body of Parliament; yet in this case I must addresse my Speech in speciall to you of the Lower House.

I am now then to recommend vnto your considerations the matter and manner of your handling and presenting of *Grieuances*. As for the manner, though I will not denie, but that yee, representing the Body of the people, may as it were both *opportune* and *inopportune*[877] (I meane either in Parliament as a Body, or out of Parliament as priuate men) present your *Grieuances* vnto mee; yet would I haue you to vse this caution in your behauiour in this point: which is, that your *Grieuances* be not as it were greedily sought out by you, or taken vp in the streetes (as one said) thereby to shew a willingnesse that you would haue a shew made, that there are many abuses in the gouernment, and many causes of complaint: but that according to your first institution, ye should only meddle with such *Grieuances* as your selues doe know had neede of reformation, or had informations thereof in your countreys for which you serue, and not so to multiply them, as might make it noised amongst the people, that all things in the gouernment were amisse and out of frame: For euen at the beginning of this very Session of Parliament, the generall name of *Grieuances* being mentioned among you, such a conceipt came in the heads of many, that you had a desire to multiply and make a great muster of them, as euery one exhibited what his particular spleene stirred him vnto. Indeed there fell out an accident vpon this occasion, for which I haue reason to thanke you of the Lower house, I meane for your fire work, wherein I confesse you did Honour to me, and right to your selues: For hauing one afternoone found many *Grieuances* closely presented in papers, and so all thrust vp in a sacke together, (rather like *Pasquils*, then any lawfull Complaints) farre against your owne

Orders, and diuers of them proceeding from grudging and murmuring spirits; you, vpon the hearing read two or three of the first lines of diuers of them, were not content with a publique consent to condemne them, and to discharge any further reading of them, but you also made a publique bonefire of them. In this, I say, you shewed your care and ielousie of my Honour, and I sent you thankes for it by the Chancellour of the Exchequer, a member of your owne House, who by your appointment, that same night acquainted me with your proceedings; And by him also I promised at that time, that you should heare more of my thankes for the same at the first occasion; And now I tell you it my selfe, that you may know how kindely I take your duetifull behauiour in this case. But since this was a good effect of an euill cause, I must not omit also to admonish you vpon the other part, to take a course amongst your selues, to preuent the like accident in all times hereafter: otherwise the Lower house may become a place for *Pasquils*, and at another time such *Grieuances* may be cast in amongst you, as may conteine Treason or scandal against Me, or my Posterity. Therfore in this case, looke ouer your ancient Orders, & follow them, and suffer not hereafter any petitions or *Grieuances* to be deliuered obscurely or in the darke, but openly and auowedly in your Publique house, and there to be presented to the Speaker. And as to the matter of your *Grieuances*, I wish you here now to vnderstand me rightly. And because I see many writing and noting, I will craue your pardons, to holde you a little longer by speaking the more distinctly, for feare of mistaking.

First then, I am not to finde fault that you informe your selues of the particular iust *Grieuances* of the people; Nay, I must tell you, ye can neither be iust nor faithfull to me, or to your Countreys that trust and imploy you, if you doe it not: For true Plaints proceede not from the persons imployed, but from the Body represented, which is the people. And it may very well bee, that many Directions and Commissions iustly giuen forth by me, may be abused in the Execution thereof, vpon the people: and yet I neuer to receiue information, except it come by your meanes, at such a time as this is; (as in the case of *Stephen Procter*).[878] But I would wish you to be carefull to auoide three things in the matter of *Grieuances*.

First, that you doe not meddle with the maine points of Gouernment; that is my craft: *tractent fabrilia fabri*;[879] to meddle with that, were to lesson me: I am now an old King; for six and thirtie yeeres haue I gouerned in *Scotland* personally, and now haue I accomplished my apprenticeship of seuen yeeres heere; and seuen yeeres is a great time for a Kings experience in Gouernment: Therefore there would not bee too many *Phormios* to teach *Hannibal*: I must not be taught my Office.

Secondly, I would not haue you meddle with such ancient Rights of mine, as I haue receiued from my Predecessors, possessing them, *More Maiorum*:[880] such things I would bee sorie should bee accounted for *Grieuances*. All nouelties are dangerous as well in a politique as in a naturall Body: And therefore I would be loth to be quarrelled in my ancient Rights and possessions: for that were to iudge mee vnworthy of that which my Predecessors had, and left me.

And lastly, I pray you beware to exhibit for *Grieuance* any thing that is established by a setled Law, and whereunto (as you haue already had a proofe) you know I will neuer giue a plausible answere: For it is an vndutifull part in Subiects to presse their King, wherein they know beforehand he will refuse them. Now, if any Law or Statute be not conuenient, let it be amended by Parliament, but in the meane time terme it not a *Grieuance*: for to be grieued with the Law, is to be grieued with the King, who is sworne to bee the Patron and mainteiner thereof. But as all men are flesh, and may erre in the execution of Lawes; So may ye iustly make a *Grieuance* of any abuse of the Law, distinguishing wisely betweene the faults of the person, and the thing it selfe. As for example, Complaints may be made vnto you of the high Commissioners:[881] If so be, trie the abuse, and spare not to complaine vpon it, but say not there shall be no Commission; For that were to abridge the power that is in me: and I will plainely tell you, That something I haue with my selfe resolued annent that point, which I meane euer to keepe, except I see other great cause: which is, That in regard the high Commission is of so high a nature, from which there is no appellation to any other Court, I haue thought good to restraine it onely to the two Archbishops, where before it was common amongst a great part of the Bishops in England. This Law I haue set to my selfe, and therefore you may be assured, that I will neuer finde fault with any man, nor thinke him the more Puritane, that will complaine to me out of Parliament, aswell as in Parliament, of any error in execution thereof, so that hee prooue it; Otherwise it were but a calumnie. Onely I would bee loath that any man should grieue at the Commission it selfe, as I haue already said. Yee haue heard (I am sure) of the paines I tooke both in the causes of the Admiralty, and of the Prohibitions: If any man therefore will bring me any iust complaints vpon any matters of so high a nature as this is, yee may assure your selues that I will not spare my labour in hearing it. In faith you neuer had a more painefull King, or that will be readier in his person to determine causes that are fit for his hearing. And when euer any of you shall make experience of me in this point, ye may be sure neuer to want accesse, nor ye shall neuer come wrong to me, in, or out of Parliament.

And now to conclude this purpose of *Grieuances*, I haue one generall *grieuance* to commend vnto you, and that in the behalfe of the Countreys from whence ye come. And this is, to pray you to beware that your *Grieuances* sauour not of particular mens thoughts, but of the generall griefes rising out of the mindes of the people, and not out of the humor of the propounder. And therefore I would wish you to take heede carefully, and consider of the partie that propounds the *grieuance*: for ye may (if ye list) easily discerne whether it bee his owne passion, or the peoples griefe, that makes him to speake: for many a man will in your house propound a *Grieuance* out of his owne humour, because (peraduenture) he accounts highly of that matter: and yet the countrey that imployes him, may perhaps either be of a contrary minde, or (at least) little care for it. As for example, I assure you, I can very well smell betweene a Petition that mooues from a generall *Grieuance*, or such a one as comes from the spleene of some particular person, either against Ecclesiasticall gouernment in generall, or the person of any one Noble man, or Commissioner in particular.

And now the third point remaines to bee spoken of; which is the cause of my calling of this Parliament. And in this I haue done but as I vse to doe in all my life, which is to leaue mine owne errand hindmost.

It may bee you did wonder that I did not speake vnto you publikely at the beginning of this Session of Parliament, to tell you the cause of your calling, as I did (if I bee rightly remembred) in euery Session before. But the trewth is, that because I call you at this time for my particular Errand, I thought it fitter to bee opened vnto you by my Treasurer, who is my publike and most principall Officer in matters of that nature, then that I should doe it my selfe: for I confesse I am lesse naturally eloquent, and haue greater cause to distrust mine elocution in matters of this nature, then in any other thing. I haue made my Treasurer already to giue you a very cleere and trew accompt both of my hauing, and expenses: A fauour I confesse, that Kings doe seldome bestow vpon their Subiects, in making them so particularly acquainted with their state. If I had not more then cause, you may be sure I would be loth to trouble you: But what he hath affirmed in this, vpon the honour of a Gentleman, (whom you neuer had cause to distrust for his honestie,) that doe I now confirme and auow to be trew in the word and honour of a King; And therein you are bound to beleeue me. Duetie I may iustly claime of you as my Subiects; and one of the branches of duetie which Subiects owe to their Soueraigne, is Supply: but in what quantitie, and at what time, that must come of your loues. I am not now therefore to dispute of a Kings power, but to tell you what I may iustly craue, and expect with your good wills. I was euer against all extremes; and in this case I will likewise wish you to auoyd them on both sides. For if you faile in the one, I might haue great cause to blame you as Parliament men, being called by me for my Errands: And if you fall into the other extreme, by supply of my necessities without respectiue care to auoyd oppression or partialitie in the Leuie, both I and the Countrey will haue cause to blame you.

When I thinke vpon the composition of this body of Parliament, I doe well consider that the Vpper house is composed of the Seculer Nobilitie, who are hereditary Lords of Parliament; and of Bishops, that are liue Renter Barons of the same: And therefore what is giuen by the Vpper house, is giuen onely from the trew body of that House, and out of their owne purposes that doe giue it; whereas the Lower house is but the representatiue body of the Commons, and so what you giue, you giue it aswell for others, as for your selues: and therefore you haue the more reason to eschew both the extreames. On the one part, ye may the more easily be liberall, since it comes not all from your selues; and yet vpon the other part, if yee giue more then is fit for good and louing Subiects to yeeld vpon such necessary occasions, yee abuse the King, and hurt the people; And such a gift I will neuer accept: For in such a case you might deceiue a King, in giuing your flattering consent to that which you know might moue the people generally to grudge and murmure at it, and so should the King find himselfe deceiued in his *Calcule*, and the people likewise grieued in their hearts; the loue and possession of which (I protest)

I did, and euer will accompt the greatest earthly securitie (next the fauour of GOD) to any wise or iust King. For though it was vainely saide by one of your House, That yee had need to beware, that by giuing mee too much, your throats were not in danger of cutting at your comming home: yet may ye assure your selues, that I will euer bee lothe to presse you to doe that which may wrong the people, and make you iustly to beare the blame thereof. But that yee may the better bee acquainted with my inclination, I will appeale to a number of my Priuie Councell here present, if that before the calling of this Parliament, and when I found that the necessitie of my estate required so great a supply, they found me more desirous to obtaine that which I was forced to seeke, then carefull that the people might yeeld me a supply in so great a measure as my necessities required, without their too great losse. And you all that are Parliament men, and here present of both Houses can beare me witnesse, if euer I burthened or imployed any of you for any particular Subsidies, or summes by name, further then my laying open the particular necessities of my state, or yet if euer I spake to any Priuie Councellour, or any of my learned Councell, to labour voyces for me to this end; I euer detested the hunting for *Emendicata Suffragia*.[882] A King that will rule and gouerne iustly, must haue regard to Conscience, Honour and Iudgement, in all his great Actions, (as your selfe M. Speaker remembred the other day.) And therefore ye may assure your selues, That I euer limit all my great Actions within that compasse. But as vpon the one side, I doe not desire you should yeeld to that extreame, in giuing me more then (as I said formerly) vpon such necessary occasions are fit for good and louing Subiects to yeeld; For that were to giue me a purse with a knife: So on the other side, I hope you will not make vaine pretences of wants, out of causelesse apprehensions, or idle excuses, neither cloake your owne humours (when your selues are vnwilling) by alledging the pouertie of the people. For although I will be no lesse iust, as a King, to such persons, then any other: (For my Iustice with Gods grace, shalbe alike open to all) yet ye must thinke I haue no reason to thanke them, or gratifie them with any suits or matters of grace, when their errand shall come in my way; And yet no man can say, that euer I quarrelled any man for refusing mee a Subsidie, if hee did it in a moderate fashion, and with good reasons. For him that denies a good Law, I will not spare to

quarrell: But for graunting or denying money, it is but an effect of
loue: And therefore for the point of my necessities, I onely desire
that I be not refused in that which of duety I ought to haue: For I
know if it were propounded in the generall amongst you, whether
the Kings wants ought to be relieued or not, there is not one of you,
that would make question of it. And though in a sort this may seeme
to be my particular; yet it can not bee diuided from the generall good
of the Common wealth; For the King that is *Parens Patriae*,[883] telles
you of his wants. Nay, *Patria ipsa*[884] by him speakes vnto you. For if
the King want, the State wants, and therefore the strengthening of
the King is the preseruation and the standing of the State; And woe
be to him that diuides the weale of the King from the weale of the
Kingdome. And as that King is miserable (how rich soeuer he bee)
that raines ouer a poore people, (for the hearts and riches of the
people, are the Kings greatest treasure,) So is that Kingdome not
able to subsist, how rich and potent soeuer the people be, if their
King wants meanes to maintaine[885] his State: for the meanes of your
King are the sinewes of the kingdome both in warre and peace: for
in peace I must minister iustice vnto you, and in warre I must defend
you by Armes: but neither of these can I do without sufficient meanes,
which must come from your Aide and Supply. I confesse it is farre
against my nature to be burthensome to my people: for it cannot but
grieue me to craue of others, that was borne to be begged of. It is
trew, I craue more then euer King of England did; but I haue farre
greater and iuster cause and reason to craue, then euer King of
England had. And though my Treasurer hath at length declared the
reasons vnto you of my necessities, and of a large supply that he
craued for the same, wherein he omitted no arguments that can be
vsed for that purpose; yet will I my selfe now shortly remember you
some of the weightiest reasons that come in my head, to proue the
equitie of my demaund.

First, ye all know, that by the accession of more Crownes, which
in my Person I haue brought vnto you, my charge must be the greater
in all reason: For the greater your King be, both in his dominion and
number of Subiects, he cannot but be forced thereby to be at the
more charge, and it is the more your honour, so to haue it.

Next, that posteritie and issue which it hath pleased God to send
me for your vse, cannot but bring necessarily with it a greater propor-

tion of charge. You all know that the late Queene of famous memory (notwithstanding her orbitie) had much giuen vnto her, and more then euer any of her predecessors had before her.

Thirdly, the time of creation of my Sonne doeth now draw neere,[886] which I chuse for the greater honour to bee done in this time of Parliament. As for him I say no more; the sight of himselfe here speakes for him.

Fourthly, it is trew I haue spent much; but yet if I had spared any of those things, which caused a great part of my expense, I should haue dishonored the kingdome, my selfe, and the late Queene. Should I haue spared the funerall of the late Queene? or the solemnitie of mine and my wiues entrie into this Kingdome, in some honourable sort? or should I haue spared our entrie into *London*, or our Coronation? And when most of the Monarches, and great Princes in Christendome sent their Ambassadours to congratulate my comming hither, and some of them came in person, was I not bound, both for my owne honour, and the honour of the Kingdome, to giue them good entertainement? But in case it might be obiected by some, that it is onely vpon occasions of warre, that Kings obtaine great Supplies from their Subiects: notwithstanding my interne Peace, I am yet in a kinde of warre, which if it bee without, the more is your safetie: For (as the Treasurer tolde you at large) I am now forced both in respects of State, and my promise, and for the generall cause of Religion, to send a Supply of forces to *Cleues*,[887] and how long that occasion may last, or what greater supply the necessitie of that Errand may draw mee vnto, no man can yet tell. Besides that, although I haue put downe that forme of warlike keeping of *Barwicke*; yet are all those commaunders my pensioners that were the late Queenes souldiers. And I hope I sustaine a prettie Seminarie of Souldiers in my Forts within this Kingdome, besides the two cautionary Townes in the Low-countreys, *Flushing* and *Brill*.[888] And as for *Ireland*, yee all know how vncertaine my charges are euer there, that people being so easily stirred, partly through their barbaritie, and want of ciuilitie, and partly through their corruption in Religion to breake foorth in rebellions. Yee know, how vnlooked for a Rebellion brake foorth there the last yeere, which could not but put mee to extraordinary charges. Besides I doe maintaine there continually an Armie, which is a goodly Seminarie of expert and old Souldiers. And I dare neuer suffer the same to be diminished, till this Plantation[889] take effect, which (no doubt) is the greatest moate that euer came in the Rebels eyes: and it is to be looked for, that if euer they will bee able to make any stirre, they will presse at it by all meanes, for the preuenting and discouraging this Plantation. Now it is trew, that besides all these honourable and necessary occasions of my charge, I haue spent much in liberalitie: but yet I hope you will consider, that what I haue giuen, hath bene giuen amongst you; and so what comes in from you, goes out againe amongst you. But it may be thought that I haue giuen much amongst Scottishmen. Indeed if I had not beene liberall in rewarding some of my old seruants of that Nation, ye could neuer haue had reason to expect my thankefulnesse towards any of you that are more lately become my Subiects, if I had beene ingrate to the old: And yet yee will find, that I haue dealt twice as much amongst English men as I haue done to Scottishmen. And therefore he that in your House was not ashamed to affirme, that the siluer and gold did so abound in *Edenburgh*, was very farre mistaken; but I wish him no worse punishment, then that hee should onely liue vpon such profit of the money there. But I hope you will neuer mislike me for my liberalitie, since I can looke very few of you this day in the face, that haue not made suits to mee, at least for some thing, either of honour or profit. It is trew, a Kings liberalitie must neuer be dried vp altogether: for then he can neuer maintaine nor oblige his seruants and well deseruing Subiects: But that vastnesse of my expence is past, which I vsed the first two or three yeeres after my comming hither: And, as I oft vsed to say, that Christmas and open tide is ended: For at my first comming here, partly ignorance of this State (which no man can acquire but by time and experience) and partly the forme of my comming being so honourable and miraculous, enforced me to extend my liberalitie so much the more at the beginning. Ye saw I made Knights then by hundreths, and Barons in great numbers: but I hope you find I doe not so now, nor minde not to doe so hereafter: For to conclude this point anent expences, I hold that a Kings expence must alwayes bee honourable, though not wastefull, and the charges of your King in maintaining those ancient honourable formes of liuing that the former Kings of *England* my Predecessours haue done, and his liuing to bee ruled according to the proportion of his greatnesse, is aswell for the honour of your Kingdome, as of your King. Now this cannot be supplied out of the ayre or liquid elements, but must come from the people. And for remouing of that diffidence which men may haue, that I minde not to liue in any wastefull sort hereafter, will you but looke vpon my selfe and my posteritie; and if there were no more but that, it will teach you that if I were but a naturall man, I must needs bee carefull of my expences: For as for my owne person, I hope none that knowes me well, can thinke me but as little inclined to any prodigall humours of vnnecessary things, as any other reasonable man of a farre meaner estate. Therefore since (as I haue said) I cannot be helped but from the people; I assure my selfe that you will well allow mee such measure of Supplie, as the people may beare, and support him with more Honourable meanes then others haue had, that (as I may say without vaunting) hath brought you more Honour then euer you had: For I hope there are no good Subiects either within, or out of the Parliament House, that would not be content for setting streight once and setling the Honourable State of their King, to spare so much euery one of them out of their purses, which peraduenture they would in one night throw away at Dice or Cards, or bestow vpon a horse for their fancies, that might breake his necke or his legge the next morning: Nay I am sure euery good Subiect would rather chuse to liue more sparingly vpon his owne, then that his Kings State should be in want.

For conclusion then of this purpose, I wish you now to put a speedie end to your businesse. Freenesse in giuing graceth the gift, *Bis dat, qui cito dat*;[890] The longer I want helpe, the greater will my debt still rise: and so must I looke for the greater helpes. And now I would pray you to turne your eyes with mee from home, and looke vpon forreine States. Consider that the eyes of all forreine States are vpon this affaire, and in expectation what the successe thereof will be; And what can they thinke, if ye depart without relieuing mee in that proportion that may make me able to maintaine my State, but that either ye are vnwilling to helpe mee, thinking me vnworthy thereof, or at least that my State is so desperate, as it cannot be repaired, and so that the Parliament parts in disgrace with the King, and the King in distaste with the Parliament, which cannot but weaken my reputation both at home and abroad? For of this you may he assured, that forreine Princes care the more one for an other, if they may haue reason to expect that they may bee able to doe them good or harme in Retribution. And ye know, that if a King fall to be contemned with his neighbours, that cannot but bring an oppression and warre by them vpon him, and then will it be too late to support the King, when the cure is almost desperate. Things foreseene and preuented, are euer easliest remedied: And therefore I would aduise you now so to settle your businesse, as ye may not take in hand so many things at once, as may both crosse my errand, and euery one of them crosse another. Yee remember the French Prouerbe, *Qui trop embrasse, rien estrient;*[891] We are not in this Parliament to make our Testament, as if wee should neuer meete againe, and that all things that were to be done in any Parliament, were to be done at this time: and yet for filling vp of your vacant houres, I will recommend to your consideration such nature of things, as are to bee specially thought vpon in these times. First I will beginne at GOD: for the beginning with him makes all other actions to bee blessed: And this I meane by the cause of Religion. Next I will speake of some things that concerne the Common-wealth. And thirdly, matters of Pleasure and ornament to the Kingdome.

As for Religion, we haue all great cause to take heed vnto it; Papists are waxed as proud at this time as euer they were, which makes many to think they haue some new plot in hand. And although the poorest sort of them bee (God be thanked) much decreased, yet doeth the greater sort of them dayly increase, especially among the foeminine Sexe; nay they are waxed so proud, that some say, no man dare present them, nor Iudges meddle with them, they are so backed and vpholden by diuers great Courtiers. It is a surer and better way to remooue the materials of fire before they bee kindled, then to quenche the fire when once it is kindled.

Nam leuius lædit quicquid præuidimus ante.[892]

I doe not meane by this to mooue you to make stronger Lawes then are already made, but see those Lawes may bee well executed that are in force; otherwise they cannot but fall into contempt and become rustie. I neuer found, that blood and too much seueritie did good in matters of Religion: for, besides that it is a sure rule in Diuinitie, that God neuer loues to plant his Church by violence and bloodshed; naturall reason may euen perswade vs, and dayly experience prooues it trew, That when men are seuerely persecuted for Religion, the gallantnesse of many mens spirits, and the wilfulnes of their humors, rather then the iustnesse of the cause, makes them to take a pride boldly to endure any torments, or death it selfe, to gaine thereby the reputation[893] of Martyrdome, though but in a false shadow.

Some doubts haue beene conceiued anent the vsing of the Oath of Allegiance, and that part of the Acte which ordaines the taking thereof, is thought so obscure, that no man can tell who ought to bee pressed therewith. For I my selfe, when vpon a time I called the Iudges before mee at their going to their Circuits, I mooued this question vnto them; wherein, as I thought they could not resolutely answere me: And therefore if there bee any scruple touching the ministring of it, I would wish it now to bee cleared. And since I haue with my owne pen brought the Popes quarell vpon mee, and proclaimed publique defiance to *Babylon* in maintaining it; should it now sleepe, and should I seeme (as it were) to steale from it againe?

As for Recusants, let them bee all duely presented without exception: for in times past there hath beene too great a conniuence, and forbearing of them, especially of great mens wiues, and their kinne and followers. None ought to be spared from being brought vnder the danger of Law, and then it is my part to vse mercie, as I thinke conuenient. To winke at faults, and not to suffer them to bee discouered, is no Honour, nor Mercy in a King, neither is he euer thanked for it; It onely argues his dulnesse: But to forgiue faults after they are confessed, or tried, is Mercie. And now I must turne me in this case to you, my Lords the Bishops, and euen exhort you earnestly, to be more carefull, then you haue bene, that your Officers may more duely present Recusants, then heretofore they haue done, without exception of persons; That although[894] it must be the worke of GOD that must make their mindes to bee altered, yet at least by this course they may be stayed from increasing, or insulting vpon vs.

And that yee all may know the trewth of my heart in this case, I diuide all my Subiects that are Papists, into two rankes: either olde Papists, that were so brought vp in times of Poperie, like old Queene *Mary* Priests, and those, that though they bee younger in yeeres, yet haue neuer drunke in other milke, but beene still nusled in that blindnesse: Or else such as doe become Apostats; hauing once beene of our Profession, and haue forsaken the trewth, either vpon discontent, or practise, or else vpon a light vaine humour of Noueltie, making no more scruple to seeke out new formes of Religion, then if it were but a new forme of Garment, or a new cut or courtsey after the French fashion.

For the former sort, I pitie them; but if they bee good and quiet Subiects, I hate not their persons; and if I were a priuate man, I could well keepe a ciuill friendship and conuersation with some of them: But as for those Apostates, who, I know, must be greatest haters of their owne Sect, I confesse I can neuer shew any fauourable countenance toward them, and they may all of them be sure without exception, that they shall neuer finde any more fauour of mee, further then I must needs in Iustice afford them. And these would I haue the Law to strike seuereliest vpon, and you carefullest to discouer. Yee know there hath beene great stirre kept for begging Concealements these yeeres past; and I pray you, let mee begge this concealment both of the Bishops, and Iudges, That Papists be no longer concealed.

Next, as concerning the Common wealth, I doe specially recommend vnto you the framing of some new Statute for preseruation of woods. In the end of the last Session of Parliament, ye had a Bill amongst you of that subiect; but because you found some faults therein, you cast out the whole Bil: But I could haue rather wished that yee had either mended it, or made a new one; For to cast out the whole Bill because of some faults, was euen as if a man, that had a new garment brought him, would chuse rather to go naked, then haue his garment made fit for him: But on my conscience, I cannot imagine why you should so lightly haue esteemed a thing, so necessary for the Common wealth, if it were not out of a litle frowardnesse amongst you at that time, that what I then recommended earnestly vnto you, it was the worse liked of. The maintenance of woods is a thing so necessary for this Kingdome, as it cannot stand, nor be a Kingdome without it: For it concernes you both in your *Esse*,[895] *Bene esse*,[896] and in pleasures. Your *Esse*:[897] for without it you want the vse of one of the most necessarie Elements (which is Fire and fewell to dresse your meate with; for neither can the people liue in these colde Countries, if they want fire altogether, nor yet can you dresse your meate without it; and I thinke you will ill liue like the Cannibals vpon raw flesh: for the education of this people is farre from that. As to your *bene esse*;[898] The decay of woods will necessarily bring the decay of Shipping, which both is the security of this Kingdome, since God hath by nature made the Sea to bee the wall of this Iland; and the rather now, since God hath vnited it all in my Person and Crowne; As also by the decay of Shipping will you loose both all your forraine commodities that are fit for this countrey, and the venting of our owne, which is the losse of Trade, that is a maine pillar of this kingdome. And as for Pleasure, yee know my delight in Hunting and Hawking, and many of your selues are of the same minde; and all this must needes decay, by the decay of Woods: Ye haue reason therefore to prouide a good Law vpon this Subiect.

Now as to the last point concerning matters of Pleasure, it consists in the preseruing of Game, which is now almost vtterly destroyed through all the Kingdome. And if you offer not now a better Law for this, then was made in the last Session of Parliament, I will neuer thanke you for it: For as for your Law anent Partridge and Phesant, you haue giuen leaue to euery man how poore a Farmour that euer hee bee, to take and destroy them in his owne ground how he list. But I pray you, how can the Game bee maintained, if Gentlemen that haue great Lordships shall breed and preserue them there, and so soone as euer they shall but flie ouer the hedge and light in a poore fellowes Close, they shall all be destroyed? Surely I know no remedie for preseruing the Game that breedes in my grounds, except I cast a roofe ouer all the ground, or else put veruels to the Partridges feet with my Armes vpon them, as my Hawkes haue: otherwise I know not how they shall bee knowen to be the Kings Partridges, when they light in a Farmours Close.

And by your Lawe against stealing of Deere or Conies, after a long discourse and prohibition of stealing them, you conclude in the end with a restriction, that all this punishment shall bee vnderstood to bee vsed against them that steale the Game in the night: Which hath much encouraged all the looser sort of people, that it is no fault to steale Deere, so they doe it not like theeues in the night. As was that Law of the *Lacedemonians* against theft, that did not forbid theft, but onely taught them to doe it cunningly, and without discouerie: Whereupon a foolish boy suffered a Foxe to gnaw his heart through his breast. And this doctrine is like that Lesson of the Cannon Law, *Si non caste, tamen caute.*[899] I knowe you thinke that I speake partially in this case like a Hunter; But there is neuer a one of you that heares mee, that cares the least for the sport, for preseruation of the Game, but he would be as glad to haue a pastie of Venison if you might get it, as the best Hunter would: And if the Game be not preserued, you can eate no Venison. As for Partridge and Phesant, I doe not denie that Gentlemen should haue their sport, and specially vpon their owne ground. But first I doe not thinke such Game and pleasures should be free to base people. And next I would euen wish that

Gentlemen should vse it in a Gentlemanlike fashion, and not with Nets, or Gunnes, or such other vngentlemanlike fashions that serue but for vtter destruction of all Game, nor yet to kill them at vnseasonable times, as to kill the Phesant and Partridges when they are no bigger then Mice, when as for euery one their Hawkes kill, ten will be destroyed with their Dogs and Horse feet; besides the great and intolerable harme they doe to Corne in that season.

And now in the end of all this faschious Speach, I must conclude like a Grey Frier, in speaking for my selfe at last. At the beginning of this Session of Parliament, when the Treasourer opened my necessities vnto you, then my Purse onely laboured; But now that word is spread both at home and abroad of the demaunds I haue made vnto you; my Reputation laboureth aswell as my Purse: For if you part without the repairing of my State in some reasonable sort, what can the world thinke, but that the euill will my Subiects beare vnto mee, hath bred a refuse? And yee can neuer part so, without apprehending that I am distasted with your behauiour, and yet to be in feare of my displeasure. But I assure and promise my selfe farre otherwise.

Thus haue I now performed my promise, in presenting vnto you the Christall of your Kings heart.

Yee know that principally by three wayes yee may wrong a Mirrour.

First,[900] I pray you, looke not vpon my Mirrour with a false light: which yee doe, if ye mistake, or mis-vnderstand my Speach, and so alter the sence thereof.

But secondly, I pray you beware to soile it with a foule breath, and vncleane hands: I meane, that yee peruert not my words by any corrupt affections, turning them to an ill meaning, like one, who when hee heares the tolling of a Bell, fancies to himselfe, that it speakes those words which are most in his minde.

And lastly, (which is worst of all) beware to let it fall or breake; (for glasse is brittle) which ye doe, if ye lightly esteeme it, and by contemning it, conforme not your selues to my perswasions.

To conclude then: As all these three days of *Iubile* haue fallen in the midst of this season of penitence, wherein you haue presented your thanks to me, and I the like againe to you: So doe I wish and hope, that the end of this Parliament will bee such, as wee may all haue cause (both I your Head, and yee the Body) to ioyne in Eucharisticke Thanks and Praises vnto God, for so good and happie an end.

A SPEACH IN THE[901] STARRE-CHAMBER, *THE XX. OF JVNE.* ANNO 1616.

GIVE Thy Ivdgements To The King, O GOD, And Thy Right-eovsnes To The Kings Sonne.[902]

These be the first words of one of the Psalmes of the Kingly Prophet *Dauid*, whereof the literall sense runnes vpon him, and his sonne *Salomon*, and the mysticall sense vpon GOD and CHRIST his eternall Sonne: but they are both so wouen together, as some parts are, and can onely bee properly applied vnto GOD and CHRIST, and other parts vnto *Dauid* and *Salomon*, as this Verse, *Giue thy Iudgements to the King, O God, and thy Righteousnesse to the Kings Sonne*, cannot be properly spoken of any, but of *Dauid* and his sonne; because it is said, *Giue thy Iudgements, &c.* Now God cannot giue to himselfe. In another part of the same Psalme, where it is said, that *Righteousnes shall flourish, and abundance of Peace, as long as the Moone endureth*, it signifieth eternitie, and cannot be properly applied but to GOD and CHRIST: But both senses, aswell literall as mysticall, serue to Kings for imitation, and especially to Christian Kings: for Kings sit in the Throne of GOD, and they themselues are called Gods.

And therefore all good Kings in their gouernment, must imitate GOD and his Christ, in being iust and righteous; *Dauid* and *Salomon*, in being godly and wise: To be wise, is vnderstood, able to discerne, able to iudge others: To be godly is, that the fountaine be pure whence the streames proceed: for what auailes it though all his workes be godly, if they proceed not from godlinesse: To bee righteous, is to a mans selfe: To bee iust, is towards others. But Iustice in a King auailes not, vnlesse it be with a cleane heart: for except he bee Righteous aswell as Iust, he is no good King; and whatsoeuer iustice he doeth; except he doeth it for Iustice sake, and out of the purenesse of his owne heart, neither from priuate ends, vaine-glory, or any other by-respects of his owne, all such Iustice is vnrighteousnesse, and no trew Iustice. From this imitation of GOD and CHRIST, in whose Throne wee sit, the gouernment of all Common-wealths, and especially Monarchies, hath bene from the beginning setled and established. Kings are properly Iudges, and Iudgement properly belongs to them from GOD: for Kings sit in the Throne of GOD, and thence all Iudgement is deriued.

In all well setled Monarchies, where Law is established formerly and orderly, there Iudgement is deferred from the King to his subordinate Magistrates; not that the King takes it from himselfe, but giues it vnto them: So it comes not to them *Priuatiue,*[903] but *cumulatiue,*[904] as the Shoolemen speake. The ground is ancient, euer sithence that Counsell which *Iethro* gaue to *Moses*: for after that *Moses* had gouerned a long time, in his owne person, the burthen grew so great, hauing none to helpe him, as his father in law comming to visite him, found him so cumbred with ministring of Iustice, that neither the people were satisfied, nor he well able to performe it; Therefore by his aduice, Iudges were deputed for easier questions, and the greater and more profound were left to *Moses*: And according to this establishment, all Kings that haue had a formall gouernement, especially Christian Kings in all aages haue gouerned their people, though after a diuers maner.

This Deputation is after one manner in *France*, after another here, and euen my owne Kingdomes differ in this point of gouernment: for *Scotland* differs both from *France* and *England* herein; but all agree in this, (I speake of such Kingdomes or States where the formalitie of Law hath place) that the King that sits in Gods Throne, onely deputes subalterne Iudges, and he deputes not one but a number (for no one subalterne Iudges mouth makes Law) and their office is to interprete Law, and administer Iustice. But as to the number of them, the forme of gouernement, the maner of interpretation, the distinction of Benches, the diuersitie of Courts; these varie according to the varietie of gouernment, and institution of diuers Kings: So this ground I lay, that the seate of Iudgement is properly Gods, and Kings are Gods Vicegerents; and by Kings Iudges are deputed vnder them, to beare the burden of gouernement, according to the first example of *Moses* by the aduice of *Iethro*, and sithence practised by *Dauid* and

Salomon, the wisest Kings that euer were; which is in this Psalme so interlaced, that as the first verse cannot be applied properly but to *Dauid* and *Salomon*, in the words, *Giue thy Iudgements to the King*, &c. So the other place in the same Psalme, *Righteousnesse shall flourish, and abundance of peace shall remaine as long as the Moone endureth*, properly signifieth the eternitie of CHRIST. This I speake, to shew what a neere coniunction there is betweene God and the King vpward, and the King and his Iudges downewards: for the same coniunction that is betweene God and the King vpward; the same coniunction is betweene the King and his Iudges downewards.

As Kings borrow their power from God, so Iudges from Kings: And as Kings are to accompt to God, so Iudges vnto God and Kings; and both Kings and Iudges by imitation, haue two qualities from God and his Christ, and two qualities from *Dauid* and his *Salomon*: Iudgement and Righteousnesse, from God and Christ: Godlinesse and Wisedome from *Dauid* and *Salomon*. And as no King can discharge his accompt to God, vnlesse he make conscience not to alter, but to declare and establish the will of God: So Iudges cannot discharge their accompts to Kings, vnlesse they take the like care, not to take vpon them to make Law, but ioyned together after a deliberate consultation, to declare what the Law is; For as Kings are subiect vnto Gods Law, so they to mans Law. It is the Kings Office to protect and settle the trew interpretation of the Law of God within his Dominions: And it is the Iudges Office to interprete the Law of the King, whereto themselues are also subiect.

Hauing now perfourmed this ancient Prouerbe, *A Ioue principium*;[905] which though it was spoken by a Pagan, yet it is good and holy: I am now to come to my particular Errand, for which I am heere this day; wherein I must handle two parts: First, the reason why I haue not these fourteene yeeres, sithence my Coronation vntill now, satisfied a great many of my louing subiects, who I know haue had a great expectation, and as it were a longing, like them that are with child, to heare mee speake in this place, where my Predecessors haue often sitten, and especially King *Henry* the seuenth, from whom, as diuers wayes before, I am lineally descended, and that doubly to this Crowne;[906] and as I am neerest descended of him, so doe I desire to follow him in his best actions.

The next part is the reason, Why I am now come: The cause that made mee abstaine, was this: When I came into *England*, although I was an old King, past middle aage, and practised in gouernment euer sithence I was twelue yeeres olde; yet being heere a stranger in gouernement, though not in blood, because my breeding was in another Kingdome; I resolued therefore with *Pythagoras* to keepe silence seuen yeeres, and learne my selfe the Lawes of the Kingdome, before I would take vpon mee to teach them vnto others: When this Apprentiship was ended, then another impediment came, which was in the choice of that cause, that should first bring me hither. I expected some great cause to make my first entry vpon: For I thought that hauing abstained so long, it should be a worthy matter that should bring mee hither. Now euery cause must be great or small: In small causes I thought it disgracefull to come, hauing beene so long absent: In great causes, they must be either betwixt the King and some of his Subiects, or betwixt Subiect and Subiect.

In a cause where my selfe was concerned, I was loath to come, because men should not thinke I did come for my owne priuate, either Prerogatiue or profit; or for any other by-respect: And in that case I will alwayes abide the triall of men and Angels, neuer to haue had any particular end, in that which is the Maine of all things, *Iustice*.

In a great cause also betweene partie and partie, great in respect either of the question, or value of the thing, my comming might seeme, as it were obliquely, to be in fauour of one partie, and for that cause this Counsellour, or that Courtier might be thought to mooue me to come hither; And a meane cause was not worthy of mee, especially for my first entrance: So lacke of choice in both respects kept mee off till now: And now hauing passed a double apprentiship of twice seuen yeeres, I am come hither to speake vnto you. And next as to the reasons of my comming at this time, they are these.

I haue obserued in the time of my whole Reigne here, and my double Apprentiship, diuers things fallen out in the Iudicatures here at *Westminster* Hall, that I thought required and vrged a reformation at my hands; whereupon I resolued with my selfe, that I could not more fitly begin a reformation, then here to make an open declaration of my meaning. I remember Christs saying, *My sheepe heare my voyce*,[907] and so I assure my selfe, my people will most willingly heare the voyce of me, their owne Shepheard and King; whereupon I tooke this occasion in mine owne person here in this Seate of Iudgement, not iudicially, but declaratorily and openly to giue those directions, which, at other times, by piece-meale, I haue deliuered to some of you in diuers lesse publike places; but now will put it vp in all your audience, where I hope it shall bee trewly caried, and cannot be mistaken, as it might haue bene when it was spoken more priuately: I will for order sake take mee to the methode of the number of Three, the number of perfection, and vpon that number distribute all I haue to declare to you.

First, I am to giue a charge to my selfe: for a King, or Iudge vnder a King, that first giues not a good charge to himselfe, will neuer be able to giue a good charge to his inferiours; for as I haue said, Good riuers cannot flow but from good springs; if the fountaine be impure, so must the riuers be.

Secondly, to the Iudges: And thirdly, to the Auditory, and the rest of the inferiour ministers of Iustice.

First, I protest to you all, in all your audience, heere sitting in the seate of Iustice, belonging vnto GOD, and now by right fallen vnto mee, that I haue resolued, as Confirmation in Maioritie followeth Baptisme in minoritie; so now after many yeeres, to renew my promise and Oath made at my Coronation concerning Iustice, and the promise therein for maintenance of the Law of the Land. And I protest in GODS presence, my care hath euer beene to keepe my conscience cleare in all the points of my Oath, taken at my Coronation, so farre as humane frailtie may permit mee, or my knowledge enforme mee, I speake in point of Iustice and Law; For Religion, I hope I am reasonably well knowen already: I meane therefore of Lawe and Iustice; and for Law, I meane the Common Law of the Land, according to which the King gouernes, and by which the people are gouerned. For the Common Law, you can all beare mee witnesse, I neuer pressed alteration of it in Parliament; but on the contrary, when I endeauoured most an Vnion reall, as was already in my person, my desire was to conforme the Lawes of *Scotland* to the Law of *England*, and not the Law of *England* to the Law of *Scotland*; and so the prophecie to be trew of my wise Grandfather *Henry* the seuenth, who foretold that the lesser Kingdom by marriage, would follow the greater, and not the greater the lesser; And therefore married his eldest daughter *Margaret* to *Iames* the fourth, my great Grandfather.

It was a foolish Querke of some Iudges, who held that the Parliament of *England*, could not vnite *Scotland* and *England* by the name of *Great Britaine*, but that it would make an alteration of the Lawes, though I am since come to that knowledge, that an Acte of Parliament can doe greater wonders: And that old wise man the Treasourer *Burghley*[908] was wont to say, Hee knew not what an Acte of Parliament could not doe in *England*: For my intention was alwayes to effect vnion by vniting *Scotland* to *England*; and not *England* to *Scotland*: For I euer meant, being euer resolued, that this Law should continue in this Kingdome, and two things mooued mee thereunto; One is, that in matter of Policie and State, you shall neuer see any thing anciently and maturely established, but by Innouation or alteration it is worse then it was, I meane not by purging of it from corruptions, and restoring it to the ancient integritie; Another reason was, I was sworne to maintaine the Law of the Land, and therefore I had beene periured if I had altered it; And this I speake to root out the conceit and misapprehension, if it be in any heart, that I would change, damnifie, vilifie or suppresse the Law of this Land: GOD is my Iudge I neuer meant it; And this confirmation I make before you all.

To this I ioyne the point of Iustice, which I call *Vnicuique suum tribuere.*[909] All my Councell, and Iudges dead and aliue, can, and could beare mee witnesse, how vnpartiall I haue beene in declaring of Law. And where it hath concerned mee in my owne inheritance, I haue as willingly submitted my interest to the Lawe, as any my Subiects could doe; and it becomes mee so to doe, to giue example to others: much lesse then will I be partiall to others, where I am not to my selfe. And so resolue your selues, Iustice with mee may bee moderated in point of clemencie: for no Iustice can be without mercie. But in matters of Iustice to giue euery man his owne, to be blinde without eyes of partialitie; This is my full resolution.

I vsed to say when I was in *Scotland*, if any man mooued mee to delay Iustice, that it was against the Office of a King so to doe; But when any made suite to hasten Iustice, I told them I had rather grant fourtie of these suits, then one of the other: This was alwayes my custome and shall be euer, with Gods leaue.

Now what I haue spoken of Law and Iustice, I meane by the Lawe kept in her owne bounds: For I vnderstand the inheritance of the King, and Subiects in this land, must bee determined by the Common Law, &c; and that is, by the Law set downe in our fore-fathers time, expounded by learned men diuers times after in the declaratory Comments, called *Responsa Prudentum*;[910] Or else by Statute Law set downe by Acte of Parliament, as occasion serues: By this I doe not seclude all other Lawes of *England*, but this is the Law of inheritance in this Kingdome.

There is another Law, of all Lawes free and supreame, which is GODS LAW: And by this all Common and municipall Lawes must be gouerned: And except they haue dependance vpon this Law, they are vniust and vnlawfull.

When I speake of that Law, I onely giue this touch, That Law in this Kingdome hath beene too much neglected, and Churchmen too much had in contempt; I must speake trewth, Great men, Lords, Iudges, and people of all degrees from the highest to the lowest, haue too much contemned them: And God will not blesse vs in our owne Lawes, if wee doe not reuerence and obey GODS LAW; which cannot bee, except the interpreters of it be respected and reuerenced.

And it is a signe of the latter dayes drawing on; euen the contempt of the Church, and of the Gouernours and Teachers thereof now in the Church of ENGLAND, which I say in my Conscience, of any Church that euer I read or knew of, present or past, is most pure, and neerest the Primitiue and Apostolicall Church in Doctrine and Discipline, and is sureliest founded vpon the word of God, of any Church in Christendome.

Next vnto this Law is the Law of Nations, which God forbid should bee barred, and that for two causes: One, because it is a Law to satisfie Strangers, which will not so well hold themselues satisfied with other municipall Lawes: Another, to satisfie our owne Subiects in matters of Piracie, Marriage, Wills, and things of like nature: That Law I diuide into Ciuil and Canon; And this Law hath bene so much encroched vpon, sithence my comming to the Crowne, and so had in contempt, that young men are discouraged from studying, and the rest wearie of their liues that doe professe it, and would be glad to seeke any other craft.

So, speaking of the Common Law, I meane the Common Law kept within her owne limits, and not derogating from these other Lawes, which by long⁹¹¹ custome haue beene rooted here; first, the Law of GOD and his Church; and next, the Law Ciuill and Canon, which in many cases cannot be wanting.

To conclude this charge which I giue my selfe, I professe to maintaine all the points of mine Oath, especially in Lawes, and of Lawes, especially the Common Law.

And as to maintaine it, so to purge it; for else it cannot bee maintained: and especially to purge it from two corruptions, Incertaintie and Noueltie: Incertaintie is found in the Law it selfe, wherein I will bee painefull to cleare it to the people; and this is properly to bee done in Parliament by aduice of the Iudges.

The other corruption is introduced by the Iudges themselues, by Nicities that are vsed, where it may be said, *Ab initio non fuit sic.*[912]

Nothing in the world is more likely to be permanent to our eyes then yron or steele, yet the rust corrupts it, if it bee not kept cleane: which sheweth, nothing is permanent here in this world, if it be not purged; So I cannot discharge my conscience in maintaining the Lawes, if I keepe them not cleane from corruption.

And now that I may bee like the Pastor, that first takes the Sacrament himselfe, and then giues it to the people: So I haue first taken my owne charge vpon me, before I giue you your Charge, lest it might be said,

Turpe est doctori, cum culpa redarguit ipsum.[913]

Now my Lords the Iudges for your parts, the Charge I haue to giue you, consists likewise in three parts.

First in generall, that you doe Iustice vprightly, as you shall answere to GOD and mee: For as I haue only GOD to answere to, and to expect punishment at his hands, if I offend; So you are to answere both to GOD and to mee, and expect punishment at GODS hands and mine, if you be found in fault.

Secondly, to doe Iustice indifferently betweene Subiect and Subiect, betweene King and Subiect, without delay, partialitie, feare or bribery, with stout and vpright hearts, with cleane and vncorrupt hands.

When I bid you doe Iustice boldly, yet I bid you doe it fearefully; fearefully in this, to vtter your owne conceites, and not the trew meaning of the Law: And remember you are no makers of Law, but Interpretours of Law, according to the trew sence thereof; for your Office is *Ius dicere*,[914] and not *Ius dare*:[915] And that you are so farre from making Law, that euen in the higher house of Parliament, you haue no voyce in making of a Law, but only to giue your aduice when you are required.

And though the Laws be in many places obscure, and not so wel knowen to the multitude as to you; and that there are many parts that come not into ordinary practise, which are knowen to you, because you can finde out the reason thereof by bookes and presidents; yet know this, that your interpretations must be alwayes subiect to common sense and reason.

For I will neuer trust any Interpretation, that agreeth not with my common sense and reason, and trew Logicke: for *Ratio est anima Legis*[916] in all humane Lawes, without exception; it must not be Sophistrie or straines of wit that must interprete, but either cleare Law, or solide reason.

But in Countreys where the formalitie of Law hath no place, as in *Denmarke*, which I may trewly report, as hauing my selfe beene an eye-witnesse thereof; all their State is gouerned onely by a written Law; there is no Aduocate or Proctour admitted to plead, onely the parties themselues plead their own cause, and then a man stands vp and reads the Law, and there is an end, for the very Law-booke it selfe is their onely Iudge. Happy were all kingdomes if they could be so: But heere, curious wits, various conceits, different actions, and varietie of examples breed questions in Law: And therefore when you heare the questions if they be plaine, there is a plaine way in it selfe; if they be such as are not plaine (for mens inuentions dayly abound) then are you to interprete according to common sense, and draw a good and certaine *Minor* of naturall reason, out of the *Maior* of direct Lawe, and thereupon to make a right and trew *Conclusion*.

For though the Common Law be a mystery and skill best knowen vnto your selues, yet if your interpretation be such, as other men which haue Logicke and common sense vnderstand not the reason, I will neuer trust such an Interpretation.

Remember also you are Iudges, and not a Iudge, and diuided into Benches, which sheweth that what you doe, that you should doe with aduice and deliberation, not hastily and rashly, before you well study the case, and conferre together; debating it duely, not giuing single opinions, *per emendicata suffragia*;[917] and so to giue your Iudgement, as you will answer to God and me.

Now hauing spoken of your Office in generall, I am next to come to the limits wherein you are to bound your selues, which likewise are three. First, Incroach not vpon the Prerogatiue of the Crowne: If there fall out a question that concernes my Prerogatiue or mystery of State, deale not with it, till you consult with the King or his Councell, or both: for they are transcendent matters, and must not be sliberely caried with ouer-rash wilfulnesse; for so may you wound the King through the sides of a priuate person: and this I commend vnto your speciall care, as some of you of late haue done very well, to blunt the sharpe edge and vaine popular humour of some Lawyers at the Barre, that thinke they are not eloquent and bold spirited enough, except they meddle with the Kings Prerogatiue: But doe not you suffer this; for certainely if this liberty be suffered, the Kings Prerogatiue, the Crowne, and I, shall bee as much wounded by their pleading, as if you resolued what they disputed: That which concernes the mysterie of the Kings power, is not lawfull to be disputed; for that is to wade into the weaknesse of Princes, and to take away the mysticall reuerence, that belongs vnto them that sit in the Throne of God.

Secondly, That you keepe your selues within your owne Benches, not to inuade other Iurisdictions, which is vnfit, and an vnlawful thing; In this I must inlarge my selfe. Besides the Courts of Common Law, there is the Court of Requests; the Admiraltie Court; the Court of the President and Councell of Wales, the President and Councell of the North; High Commission Courts, euery Bishop in his owne Court.

These Courts ought to keepe their owne limits and boundes of their Commission and Instructions, according to the ancient Presidents: And like as I declare that my pleasure is, that euery of these shall keepe their owne limits and boundes; So the Courts of Common Lawe are not to encroach vpon them, no more then it is my pleasure that they should encroach vpon the Common Law. And this is a thing Regall and proper to a King, to keepe euery Court within his owne bounds.

In *Westminster* Hall there are foure Courts: Two that handle causes Ciuill, which are the Common-pleas, and the Exchequer: Two that determine causes Criminall, which are the Kings-Bench, and the Starre-Chamber, where I now sit. The Common-Pleas is a part and branch of the Kings-Bench; for it was first all one Court; and then the Common-Pleas being extracted, it was called Common-Pleas; because it medled with the Pleas of Priuate persons, and that which remained, the Kings-Bench. The other of the Courts for ciuill Causes, is the Exchequer, which was ordeined for the Kings Reuenew: That is the principall Institution of that Court, and ought to be their chiefe studie; and as other things come orderly thither by occasion of the former, they may be handled, and Iustice there administred.

Keepe you therefore all in your owne bounds, and for my part, I desire you to giue me no more right in my priuate Prerogatiue, then you giue to any Subiect; and therein I will be acquiescent: As for the absolute Prerogatiue of the Crowne, that is no Subiect for the tongue of a Lawyer, nor is lawfull to be disputed.

It is Atheisme and blasphemie to dispute what God can doe: good Christians content themselues with his will reuealed in his word. So,[918] it is presumption and high contempt in a Subiect, to dispute what a King can doe, or say that a King cannot doe this, or that; but rest in that which is the Kings reuealed will in his Law.

The Kings-Bench is the principall Court for criminall causes, and in some respects it dealcs with Ciuill causes.

Then is there a Chancerie Court; this is a Court of Equitie, and hath power to deale likewise in Ciuill causes: It is called the dispenser of the Kings Conscience, following alwayes the intention of Law and Iustice; not altering the Law, not making that blacke which other Courts made white, nor *e conuerso*;[919] But in this it exceeds other Courts, mixing Mercie with Iustice, where other Courts proceed onely according to the strict rules of Law: And where the rigour of the Law in many cases will vndoe a Subiect, there the Chancerie tempers the Law with equitie, and so mixeth Mercy with Iustice, as it preserues men from destruction.

And thus (as before I told you) is the Kings Throne established by Mercy and Iustice.

The Chancerie is vndependant of any other Court, and is onely vnder the King: There it is written *Teste meipso*;[920] from that Court there is no Appeale. And as I am bound in my Conscience to maintaine euery Courts Iurisdiction, so especially this, and not suffer it to sustaine wrong; yet so to maintaine it, as to keepe it within the owne limits, and free from corruption. My Chancellour that now is,[921] I found him Keeper of the Seale, the same place in substance, although I gaue him the Stile of Chancellour, and God hath kept him in it till now; and I pray God he may hold it long; and so I hope he will. He will beare mee witnesse, I neuer gaue him other warrant, then to goe on in his Court according to Presidents, warranted by Law in the time of the best gouerning Kings, and most learned

Chancellours: These were the limits I gaue vnto him; beyond the same limits he hath promised me he will neuer goe.

And as he hath promised me to take no other Iurisdiction to him-selfe, so is it my promise euer to maintaine this Iurisdiction in that Court: Therefore I speake this to vindicate that Court from miscon-ceipt and contempt.

It is the duetie of Iudges to punish those that seeke to depraue the proceedings of any the Kings Courts, and not to encourage them any way: And I must confesse I thought it an odious and inept speach, and it grieued me very much, that it should be said in *Westminster* Hall, that a *Premunire* lay against the Court of the Chancery and Officers there: How can the King grant a *Premunire* against himselfe?

It was a foolish, inept, and presumptuous attempt, and fitter for the time of some vnworthy King: vnderstand mee aright; I meane not, the Chancerie should exceed his limite; but on the other part, the King onely is to correct it, and none else: And therefore I was greatly abused in that attempt: For if any was wronged there, the complaint should haue come to mee. None of you but will confesse you haue a King of reasonable vnderstanding, and willing to reforme; why then should you spare to complaine to me, that being the high way, and not goe the other way, and backe-way, in contempt of our Authoritie?

And therefore sitting heere in a seat of Iudgement, I declare and command, that no man hereafter presume to sue a *Premunire* against the Chancery; which I may the more easily doe, because no *Premunire* can bee sued but at my Suit: And I may iustly barre my selfe at mine owne pleasure.

As all inundations come with ouerflowing the bankes, and neuer come without great inconuenience, and are thought prodigious by Astrologers in things to come: So is this ouerflowing the bankes of your Iurisdiction in it selfe inconuenient, and may proue prodigious to the State.

Remember therefore, that hereafter you keepe within your limits and Iurisdictions. It is a speciall point of my Office to procure and command, that amongst Courts there bee a concordance, and musicall accord; and it is your parts to obey, and see this kept: And, as you are to obserue the ancient Lawes and customes of *England*; so are you to keepe your selues within the bound of direct Law, or

Presidents; and of those, not euery snatched President, carped now here, now there, as it were running by the way; but such as haue neuer beene controuerted, but by the contrary, approued by common vsage, in times of best Kings, and by most learned Iudges.

The *Starre-Chamber* Court hath bene likewise shaken of late, and the last yeere it had receiued a sore blow, if it had not bene assisted and caried by a few voyces; The very name of *Starre-Chamber*, seemeth to procure a reuerence to the Court.

I will not play the Criticke to descant on the name; It hath a name from heauen, a Starre placed in it; and a Starre is a glorious creature, and seated in a glorious place, next vnto the Angels. The *Starre-Chamber* is also glorious in substance: for in the composition, it is of foure sorts of persons: The first two are Priuie Counsellours and Iudges, the one by wisedome in matters of State; the other, by learning in matters of Law, to direct and order all things both according to Law and State: The other two sorts are Peeres of the Realme, and Bishops: The Peeres are there by reason of their greatnesse, to giue authority to that Court: The Bishops because of their learning in Diuinitie, and the interest they haue in the good gouernment of the Church: And so, both the learning of both Diuine and humane Law, and experience and practise in Gouernment, are conioyned together in the proceedings of this Court.

There is no Kingdome but hath a Court of Equitie, either by it selfe, as is heere in *England*, or else mixed, and incorporate in their Office that are Iudges in the Law, as it is in *Scotland*: But the order of *England* is much more perfect, where they are diuided. And as in case of Equitie, where the Law determines not clearly, there the Chancerie doeth determine, hauing Equitie belonging to it, which doeth belong to no other Court: So the *Starre-Chamber* hath that belonging to it, which belongs to no other Court: For in this Court Attempts are punishable, where other Courts punish onely facts; And also where the Law punisheth facts easily, as in case of Riots or Combates, there the Starre-Chamber punisheth in a higher degree; And also all combinations of practises and conspiracies; And if the King be dishonoured or contemned in his Prerogatiue, it belongeth most properly to the Peeres and Iudges of this Court to punish it: So then this Court being instituted for so great causes, it is great reason it should haue great honour.

Remember now how I haue taught you brotherly loue one toward another: For you know well, that as you are Iudges, you are all brethren, and your Courts are sisters. I pray you therefore, labour to keepe that sweete harmonie, which is amongst those sisters the *Muses*. What greater miserie can there bee to the Law, then contempt of the Law? and what readier way to contempt, then when questions come, what shall bee determined in this Court, and what in that? Whereupon two euils doe arise: The one, that men come not now to Courts of iustice, to heare matters of right pleaded, and Decrees giuen accordingly, but onely out of a curiosity, to heare questions of the Iurisdictions of Courts disputed, and to see the euent, what Court is like to preuaile aboue the other; And the other is, that the Pleas are turned from Court to Court in an endlesse circular motion, as vpon *Ixions* wheele: And this was the reason why I found iust fault with that multitude of Prohibitions: For when a poore Minister had with long labour, and great expence of charge and time, gotten a sentence for his Tithes, then comes a Prohibition, and turnes him round from Court to Court, and so makes his cause immortall and endlesse: for by this vncertaintie of Iurisdiction amongst Courts, causes are scourged from Court to Court, and this makes the fruit of Suits like *Tantalus* fruite, still neere the Suiters lips, but can neuer come to taste it. And this in deed is a great delay of Iustice, and makes causes endlesse: Therefore the onely way to auoyd this, is for you to keepe your owne bounds, and nourish not the people in contempt of other Courts, but teach them reuerence to Courts in your publique speaches, both in your Benches, and in your Circuits; so shall you bring them to a reuerence, both of GOD, and of the King.

Keepe therefore your owne limits towards the King, towards other Courts, and towards other Lawes, bounding your selues within your owne Law, and make not new Law. Remember, as I said before, that you are Iudges, to declare, and not to make Law: For when you make a Decree neuer heard of before, you are Law-giuers, and not Law-tellers.

I haue laboured to gather some Articles, like an *Index expurgatorius*, of nouelties new crept into the Law, and I haue it ready to bee considered of: Looke to *Plowdens* Cases, and your old *Responsa prudentum*:[922] if you finde it not there, then (*ab initio non fuit sic*)[923] I must say with CHRIST, Away with the new polygamie, and maintaine the ancient Law pure and vndefiled, as it was before.

To the Auditory I haue but little to say, yet that little will not bee ill bestowed to be said at this time.

Since I haue now renewed and confirmed my resolution to maintaine my Oath, the Law and Iustice of the Land; So doe I expect, that you my Subiects doe submit your selues as you ought, to the obseruance of that Law.

And as I haue diuided the two former parts of my Charge; So will I diuide this your submission into three parts; for orderly diuisions and methode, cause things better to be remembred.

First in generall, that you giue due reuerence to the Law: and this generall diuides it selfe into three.

First, not to sue, but vpon iust cause.

Secondly, beeing sued, and Iudgement passed against you, Acquiesce in the Iudgement, and doe not tumultuate against it; and take example from mee, whom you haue heard here protest, that when euer any Decree shall be giuen against me in my priuate right, betweene me and a Subiect, I will as humbly acquiesce as the meanest man in the Land. Imitate me in this, for in euery Plea there are two parties, and Iudgement can be but for one, and against the other; so one must always be displeased.

Thirdly, doe not complaine and importune mee against Iudgements; for I hold this Paradoxe to bee a good rule in Gouernment, that it is better for a King to maintaine an vniust Decree, then to question euery Decree and Iudgement, after the giuing of a sentence, for then Suites shall neuer haue end: Therefore as you come gaping to the Law for Iustice, so bee satisfied and contented when Iudgement is past against you, and trouble not mee; but if you finde briberie or corruption, then come boldly: but when I say boldly, beware of comming to complaine, except you bee very sure to prooue the iustice of your cause: Otherwise looke for *Lex Talionis*[924] to bee executed vpon you; for your accusing of an vpright Iudge, deserues double punishment, in that you seeke to lay infamie vpon a worthy person of that reuerent calling.

And be not tild on with your own Lawyers tales, that say the cause is iust for their owne gaine; but beleeue the Iudges that haue no hire but of me.

Secondly, in your Pleas, presume not to meddle with things against the Kings Prerogatiue, or Honour: Some Gentlemen of late haue beene too bold this wayes; If you vse it, the Iudges will punish you: and if they suffer it, I must punish both them and you. Plead not vpon new Puritanicall straines, that make all things popular; but keepe you within the ancient Limits of Pleas.

Thirdly, make not many changes from Court to Court: for hee that changeth Courts, shewes to mistrust the iustnesse of the cause. Goe to the right place, and the Court that is proper for your cause; change not thence and submit your selues to the Iudgement giuen there.

Thus hauing finished the Charge to my selfe, the Iudges and the Auditorie, I am to craue your pardon if I haue forgotten any thing, or beene inforced to break my Methode: for you must remember, I come not hither with a written Sermon: I haue no Bookes to read it out of, and a long speach, manifold businesse, and a little leasure may well pleade pardon for any fault of memorie; and trewly I know not if I haue forgotten any thing or not.

And now haue I deliuered, First my excuse, why I came not till now: Next, the reasons why I came now: Thirdly, my charge, and that to my selfe, to you my Lords the Iudges, and to the Auditory.

I haue also an ordinary charge that I vse to deliuer to the Iudges before my Councell, when they goe their Circuits: and seeing I am come to this place, you shall haue that also, and so I will make the old saying trew, *Combe seldome, combe sore*, I meane by my long deteining you at this time, which will bee so much the more profitable in this Auditorie; because a number of the Auditorie will be informed here, who may relate it to their fellow Iustices in the countrey.

My Lords the Iudges, you know very well, that as you are Iudges with mee when you sit here; so are you Iudges vnder mee, and my Substitutes in the Circuits, where you are Iudges Itinerant to doe Iustice to my people.

It is an ancient and laudable custome in this Kingdome, that the Iudges goe thorow the Kingdome in Circuits, easing the people thereby of great charges, who must otherwise come from all the remote parts of the Kingdome to *Westminster Hall*, for the finding out and punishing of offences past, and preuenting the occasion of offences that may arise.

I can giue you no other charge in effect, but onely to remember you againe of the same in substance which I deliuered to you this time Twelue-moneth.

First, Remember that when you goe your Circuits, you goe not onely to punish and preuent offences, but you are to take care for the good government in generall of the parts where you trauell, as well as to doe Iustice in particular betwixt party and party, in causes criminall and ciuill.

You haue charges to giue to Iustices of peace, that they doe their dueties when you are absent, aswell as present: Take an accompt of them, and report their seruice to me at your returne.

As none of you will hold it sufficient to giue a charge, except in taking the accompt, you finde the fruit of it: So I say to you, it will not bee sufficient for you, to heare my charge, if at your returne you bring not an accompt to the haruest of my sowing, which cannot be done in generall, but in making to me a particular report what you haue done.

For, a King hath two Offices.

First, to direct things to be done:

Secondly, to take an accompt how they are fulfilled; for what is it the better for me to direct as an Angel, if I take not accompt of your doings.

I know not whether misunderstanding, or slacknesse bred this, that I had no accompt but in generall, of that I gaue you in particular in charge the last yeere: Therefore I now charge you againe, that at your next returne, you repaire to my Chancellour, and bring your accompts to him in writing, of those things which in particular I haue giuen you in charge: And then when I haue seene your accompts, as occasion shall serue, it may bee I will call for some of you, to be informed of the state of that part of the countrey where your Circuit lay.

Of these two parts of your seruice, I know the ordinary Legall part of *Nisi prius*[925] is the more profitable to you: But the other part of Iustice is more necessary for my seruice. Therefore as CHRIST said to the Pharises, *Hoc agite*,[926] as the most principall: yet I will say, *Et illud non omittite:*[927] which, that you may the better doe, I haue allowed you a day more in your Circuits, then my Predecessours haue done.

And this you shall finde, that euen as a King, (let him be neuer so godly, wise, righteous, and iust) yet if the subalterne Magistrates doe not their parts vnder him, the Kingdome must needes suffer: So let the Iudges bee neuer so carefull and industrious, if the Iustices of Peace vnder them, put not to their helping hands, in vaine is all your labour: For they are the Kings eyes and eares in the countrey. It was an ancient custome, that all the Iudges both immediatly before their going to their Circuits, and immediatly vpon their returne, repaired to the Lord Chancellour of *England*, both to receiue what directions it should please the King by his mouth to giue vnto them; as also to giue him an accompt of their labours, who was to acquaint the King therewith: And this good ancient custome hath likewise beene too much slacked of late; And therefore first of all, I am to exhort and command you, that you be carefull to giue a good accompt to me and my Chancellour, of the dueties performed by all Iustices of Peace in your Circuits: Which gouernment by Iustices, is so laudable and so highly esteemed by mee, that I haue made *Scotland* to bee gouerned by Iustices and Constables, as *England* is. And let not Gentlemen be ashamed of this Place; for it is a place of high Honour, and great reputation, to be made a Minister of the Kings Iustice, in seruice of the Common-wealth.

Of these there are two sorts, as there is of all Companies, especially where there is a great number; that is, good and bad Iustices: For the good, you are to enforme me of them, that I may know them, thanke them, and reward them, as occasion serues: For I hold a good Iustice of Peace in his Countrey, to doe mee as good seruice, as hee that waites vpon mee in my Priuie Chamber, and as ready will I be to reward him; For I accompt him as capable of any Honour, Office, or preferment about my Person, or for any place of Councell or State, as well as any Courteour that is neere about mee, or any that haue deserued well of me in forreine employments: Yea, I esteeme the seruice done me by a good Iustice of Peace, three hundred miles, yea sixe hundred miles out of my sight, as well as the seruice done me in my presence: For as God hath giuen me large limits, so must I be carefull that my prouidence may reach to the farthest parts of them: And as Law cannot be honoured, except Honour be giuen to Iudges: so without due respect to Iustices of Peace, what regard will be had of the seruice?

Therefore let none be ashamed of this Office, or be discouraged in being a Iustice of Peace, if he serue worthily in it.

The Chancellour vnder me, makes Iustices, and puts them out; but neither I, nor he can tell what they are: Therefore wee must bee informed by you Iudges, who can onely tell, who doe well, and who doe ill; without which, how can the good be cherished and maintained, and the rest put out? The good Iustices are carefull to attend the seruice of the King and countrey, for thanks onely of the King, and loue to their countrey, and for no other respect.

The bad are either idle Slowbellies, that abide alwayes at home, giuen to a life of ease and delight, liker Ladies then men; and thinke it is enough to contemplate Iustice, when as *Virtus in actione consistit*:[928] contemplatiue Iustice is no iustice, and contemplatiue Iustices are fit to be put out.

Another sort of Iustices are busie-bodies, and will haue all men dance after their pipe, and follow their greatnesse, or else will not be content; A sort of men, *Qui se primos omnium esse putant, nec sunt tamen*:[929] these proud spirits must know, that the countrey is ordained to obey and follow GOD and the King, and not them.

Another sort are they, that goe seldome to the Kings seruice, but when it is to helpe some of their kindred or alliance; So as when they come, it is to helpe their friends, or hurt their enemies, making Iustice to serue for a shadow to Faction, and tumultuating the countrey.

Another sort are Gentlemen of great worth in their owne conceit, and cannot be content with the present forme of Gouernement, but must haue a kind of libertie in the people, and must be gracious Lords, and Redeemers of their libertie; and in euery cause that concernes Prerogatiue, giue a snatch against a Monarchie, through their Puritanicall itching after Popularitie: Some of them haue shewed themselues too bold of late in the lower house of Parliament: And when all is done, if there were not a King, they would be lesse cared for then other men.

And now hauing spoken of the qualities of the Iustices of Peace, I am next to speake of their number. As I euer held the midway in all things to be the way of Vertue, in eschewing both extremities: So doe I in this: for vpon the one part, a multitude of Iustices of Peace in the countrey more then is necessary, breeds but confusion: for although it be an old Prouerbe, that *Many handes make light worke*; yet too many make slight worke; and too great a number of Iustices of Peace, will make the businesse of the countrey to be the more neglected, euery one trusting to another, so as nothing shall bee well done; besides the breeding of great corruption: for where there is a great number, it can hardly bee, but some will bee corrupted. And vpon the other part, too few Iustices of Peace, will not be able to vndergoe the burthen of the seruice; And therefore I would neither haue too few, nor too many, but as many in euery countrey, as may, according to the proportion of that countrey, bee necessary for the performing of the seruice there, and no more.

As to the Charge you are to giue to the Iustices, I can but repeat what formerly I haue told you; yet in so good a businesse,

Lectio lecta placet, decies repetita placebit[930]

And as I began with fulfilling the Prouerbe, *A Ioue principium*;[931] so will I begin this Charge you are to giue to the Iustices with Church-matters: for GOD will blesse euery good businesse the better, that he and his Church haue the precedence. That which I am now to speake, is anent Recusants and Papists. You neuer returned from any Circuit, but by your accompt made vnto me, I both conceiued great comfort and great griefe: Comfort, when I heard a number of Recusants in some Circuits to be diminished: Griefe to my heart and soule, when I heard a number of Recusants to be in other Circuits increased.

I protest vnto you, nothing in the earth can grieue mee so much, as mens falling away from Religion in my dayes; And nothing so much ioyes mee, as when that Religion increaseth vnder mee. GOD is my witnesse, I speake nothing for vaine-glory; but speake it againe; My heart is grieued when I heare Recusants increase: Therefore I wish you Iudges, to take it to heart, as I doe, and preuent it as you can; and make me knowen to my people, as I am.

There are three sorts of Recusants: The first are they that for themselues will bee no Recusants, but their wiues and their families are; and they themselues doe come to Church, but once or twice in a yeere, inforced by Law, or for fashion sake; These may be formall to the Law, but more false to GOD then the other sort.

The second sort are they that are Recusants and haue their conscience misse-led, and therefore refuse to come to Church, but otherwise liue as peaceable Subiects.

The third sort are practising Recusants: These force all their seruants to bee Recusants with them; they will suffer none of their Tenants, but they must bee Recusants; and their neighbours if they liue by them in peace, must be Recusants also.

These you may finde out as a foxe by the foule smell, a great way round about his hole; This is a high pride and presumption, that they for whose soules I must answere to GOD, and who enioy their liues and liberties vnder mee, will not onely be Recusants themselues, but infect and draw others after them.

As I haue said in Parliament house, I can loue the person of a Papist, being otherwise a good man and honestly bred, neuer hauing knowen any other Religion: but the person of an Apostate Papist, I hate. And surely for those Polypragmaticke Papists, I would you would studie out some seuere punishment for them: for they keepe not infection in their owne hearts onely, but also infect others our good Subiects. And that which I say for Recusants, the same I say for Priests: I confesse I am loath to hang a Priest onely for Religion sake, and saying Masse; but if he refuse the Oath of Alleagiance (which, let the Pope and all the deuils in Hell say what they will) yet (as you finde by my booke and by diuers others, is meerely Ciuill) those that so refuse the Oath, and are Polypragmaticke Recusants; I leaue them to the Law; it is no persecution, but good Iustice.

And those Priests also, that out of my Grace and Mercy haue beene let goe out of prisons, and banished, vpon condition not to returne; aske mee no questions touching these, quit me of them, and let mee not heare of them: And to them I ioyne those that breake prison; for such Priests as the prison will not hold, it is a plaine signe nothing will hold them but a halter: Such are no Martyrs that refuse to suffer for their conscience. *Paul*, notwithstanding the doores were open, would not come foorth: And *Peter* came not out of the prison till led by the Angel of God: But these will goe forth though with the angel of the Diuell.

I haue giuen order to my Lord of *Canterbury*, and my Lord of *London* for the distinction, &c. of the degrees of Priests; and when I haue an accompt from them, then will I giue you another charge concerning them.

Another thing that offendeth the Realme, is abundance of Ale-houses; and therefore to auoyd the giuing occasion of euill, and to take away the root, and punish the example of vice, I would haue the infamous Ale houses pulled downe, and a command to all Iustices of Peace that this be done.

I may complaine of Ale-houses, for receipt of Stealers of my Deere; but the countrey may complaine for stealing their horses, oxen, and sheepe; for murder, cutting of purses, and such like offences; for these are their haunts. Deuouring beasts, as Lyons and Beares, will not bee where they haue no dennes nor couert: So there would be no theeues, if they had not their receipts, and these Ale-houses as their dennes.

Another sort, are a kind of Alehouses, which are houses of haunt and receipt for debaushed rogues and vagabonds, and idle sturdie fellowes; and these are not properly Ale-houses, but base victuallers, such as haue nothing else to liue by, but keeping houses of receipt for such kinde of customers. I haue discouered a strange packe of late, That within tenne or twelue miles of *London*, there are ten or twelue persons that liue in spight of mee, going with Pistols, and walking vp and downe from harbour to harbour killing my Deere, and so shift from hold to hold, that they cannot be apprehended.

For Rogues, you haue many good Acts of Parliament: *Edward* the sixt, though hee were a child, yet for this, he in his time gaue better order then many Kings did in their aage: You must take order for these Beggars and Rogues; for they so swarme in euery place, that a man cannot goe in the streetes, nor in the high wayes, nor any where for them.

Looke to your houses of Correction, and remember that in the chiefe Iustice *Pophams*[932] time, there was not a wandering begger to bee found in all *Somersetshire*, being his natiue countrey.

Haue a care also to suppresse the building of Cottages vpon Commons, which are as bad as Alehouses, and the dwellers in them doe commonly steale Deere, Conies, sheepe, oxen, horses; breake houses, and doe all maner of villanies. It is trew, some ill Iustices make gaine of these base things: take an accompt of the Iustices of Peace, that they may know they doe these things against the will of the King.

I am likewise to commend vnto you a thing very necessarie, Highwayes and Bridges; because no Common-weale can bee without passage: I protest, that as my heart doeth ioy in the erection of Schooles and Hospitals, which haue beene more in my time, then in many aages of my predecessours; so it grieues mee, and it is wonderfull to see the decay of charitie in this; how scant men are in contributing towards the amendment of High-wayes and Bridges: Therefore take a care of this, for that is done to day with a penie, that will not bee done hereafter with an hundred pounds, and that will be mended now in a day, which hereafter will not be mended in a yeere; and that in a yeere, which will not bee done in our time, as we may see by *Pauls* Steeple.

Another thing to be cared for, is, the new Buildings here about the Citie of *London*: concerning which my Proclamations haue gone foorth, and by the chiefe Iustice here, and his Predecessor *Popham*, it hath bene resolued to be a generall nusans to the whole Kingdome: And this is that, which is like the Spleene in the body, which in measure as it ouergrowes, the body wastes. For is it possible but the

Countrey must diminish, if *London* doe so increase, and all sorts of people doe come to *London*? and where doeth this increase appeare? not in the heart of the Citie, but in the suburbes; not giuing wealth or profit to the Citie, but bringing miserie and surcharge both to Citie and Court; causing dearth and scarsitie through the great prouision of victuals and fewel, that must be for such a multitude of people: And these buildings serue likewise to harbour the worst sort of people, as Alehouses and Cottages doe. I remember, that before Christmas was Twelue-moneth I made a Proclamation for this cause, That all Gentlemen of qualitie should depart to their owne countreys and houses, to maintaine Hospitalitie amongst their neighbours; which was equiuocally taken by some, as that it was meant onely for that Christmas: But my will and meaning was, and here I declare that my meaning was, that it should alwayes continue.

One of the greatest causes of all Gentlemens desire, that haue no calling or errand, to dwell in *London*, is apparently the pride of the women: For if they bee wiues, then their husbands; and if they be maydes, then their fathers must bring them vp to *London*; because the new fashion is to bee had no where but in *London*; and here, if they be vnmarried, they marre their marriages, and if they be married, they loose their reputations, and rob their husbands purses. It is the fashion of *Italy*, especially of *Naples*, (which is one of the richest parts of it) that all the Gentry dwell in the principall Townes, and so the whole countrey is emptie: Euen so now in *England*, all the countrey is gotten into *London*; so as with time, *England* will onely be *London*, and the whole countrey be left waste: For as wee now doe imitate the French fashion, in fashion of Clothes, and Lackeys to follow euery man; So haue wee got vp the Italian fashion, in liuing miserably in our houses, and dwelling all in the Citie: but let vs in Gods Name leaue these idle forreine toyes, and keepe the old fashion of *England*: For it was wont to be the honour and reputation of the English Nobilitie and Gentry, to liue in the countrey, and keepe hospitalitie; for which we were famous aboue all the countreys in the world, which wee may the better doe, hauing a soile abundantly fertile to liue in.

And now out of my owne mouth I declare vnto you, (which being in this place, is equall to a Proclamation, which I intend likewise shortly hereafter to haue publikely proclaimed,) that the Courtiers, Citizens, and Lawyers, and those that belong vnto them, and others as haue Pleas in Terme time, are onely necessary persons to remaine about this Citie: others must get them into the Countrey; For beside the hauing of the countrey desolate, when the Gentrie dwell thus in *London*, diuers other mischiefes arise vpon it: First, if insurrections should fall out (as was lately seene by the Leuellers gathering together) what order can bee taken with it, when the countrey is vnfurnished of Gentlemen to take order with it? Next, the poore want reliefe for fault of the Gentlemens hospitalitie at home: Thirdly, my seruice is neglected, and the good gouernment of the countrey for lacke of the principall Gentlemens presence, that should performe it: And lastly, the Gentlemen lose their owne thrift, for lacke of their owne presence, in seeing to their owne businesse at home. Therefore as euery fish liues in his owne place, some in the fresh, some in the salt, some in the mud: so let euery one liue in his owne place, some at Court, some in the Citie, some in the Countrey; specially at Festiuall times, as Christmas and Easter, and the rest.

And for the decrease of new Buildings heere, I would haue the builders restrained, and committed to prison: and if the builders cannot be found, then the workemen to be imprisoned; and not this onely, but likewise the buildings to bee cast downe; I meane such buildings as may be ouerthrowen without inconuenience, and therefore that to be done by order and direction.

There may be many other abuses that I know not of; take you care my Lords the Iudges of these, and of all other; for it is your part to looke vnto them. I heare say, robbery begins to abound more then heretofore, and that some of you are too mercifull; I pray you remember, that mercy is the Kings, not yours, and you are to doe Iustice where trew cause is: And take this for a rule of Policie. That what vice most abounds in a Common-wealth that must be most seuerely punished, for that is trew gouernment.

And now I will conclude my Speach with GOD, as I began. First, that in all your behauiours, aswell in your Circuits as in your Benches, you giue due reuerence to GOD; I meane, let not the Church nor Churchmen bee disgraced in your Charges, nor Papists nor Puritanes countenanced: Countenance and encourage the good Church-men, and teach the people by your example to reuerence them: for, if they be good, they are worthy of double honour for their Office sake; if they be faultie, it is not your place to admonish them; they haue another *Forum* to answere to for their misbehauiour.

Next, procure reuerence to the King and the Law, enforme my people trewly of mee, how zealous I am for Religion, how I desire Law may bee maintained and flourish; that euery Court should haue his owne Iurisdiction; that euery Subiect should submit himselfe to Law; So may you liue a happie people vnder a iust KING, freely enioying the fruite of PEACE and IVSTICE, as such a people should doe.

Now I confesse, it is but a *Tandem aliquando*,[933] as they say in the Schooles, that I am come hither: Yet though this bee the first, it shall not, with the grace of GOD, bee the last time of my comming, now my choice is taken away; for hauing once bene here, a meaner occasion may bring mee againe: And I hope I haue euer caried my selfe so, and by GODS grace euer will, as none will euer suspect, that my comming here will be to any partiall end; for I will euer bee carefull in point of Iustice, to keepe my selfe vnspotted all the dayes of my life. And vpon this my generall protestation, I hope the world will know, that I came hither this day to maintaine the Law, and doe Iustice according to my Oath.

A MEDITATION[934]
Vpon the 27. 28. 29. Verses of the XXVII. Chapter of Saint MATTHEW.
OR
A PATERNE FOR A KINGS INAVGVRATION:
Written by the KINGS MAIESTIE.

PSAL. 2. 10.

*Bee wise now therefore, O yee Kings; bee
instructed yee Iudges of the earth.*[935]

THE EPISTLE DEDICATORIE.

MY dearest and onely Sonne, *in the beginning of this same yeere,*[936] *I wrote a short* Meditation *vpon the* Lords Prayer, *and I told the reason, that now being growen in yeares, I was weary of Controuersies and to write of high questions, and therefore had chosen now a plaine and easie subiect to treat of: But of late it hath fallen out, that one day reading priuatly to my selfe the passion of* CHRIST, *in the end of S.* Matthewes *Gospell, I lighted vpon that part, where the Gouernors Souldiers mocked our* Sauiour, *with putting the ornaments of a King vpon him. Which appeared to me to be so punctually set doune, that my head hammered vpon it diuers times after, and specially the Croune of thornes went neuer out of my mind, remembering the thorny cares, which a King (if he haue a care of his office) must be subiect vnto, as (God knowes) I daily and nightly feele in mine owne person. Whereupon I apprehended that it would bee a good paterne to put inheritors to kingdomes in minde of their calling, by the forme of their inauguration; and so resolued to borrow some houres from my rest, to write a short Meditation vpon it. But on a time telling* Buckingham *this my intention, and that I thought you the fittest person to whom I could dedicate it, for diuers reasons following, hee humbly and earnestly desired mee, that hee might haue the honour to be my* amanuensis *in this worke. First, because it would free mee from the paine of writing, by sparing the labour both of mine eyes and hand; and next, that hee might doe you some peece of seruice thereby; protesting, that his natural obligation to you (next me) is redoubled by the many fauours that you daily heape vpon him. And indeed, I must ingenuously confesse to my comfort, that in making your affections to follow and second thus your Fathers, you shew what reuerent loue you carry towards me in your heart; besides the worthy example you giue to all other Kings eldest Sonnes for imitation, beginning heereby to performe one of the rules set doune to my sonne* HENRY, *that is with God, in my* ΒΑΣΙΛΙΚΟΝ ΔΩΡΟΝ.*[937] And indeede my graunting of this request to* Buckingham *hath much eased my labour, considering the slownesse, ilnesse, and vncorrectnes of my hand.*

As I dedicated therfore my Meditation *vpon the* Lords Prayer *to him, in regard aswell of the necessity that Courtiers haue to pray (considering that among great resort of people they cannot euer be in good company, besides the many allurements they haue to sinne) as also that short Prayers are fittest for them; for they haue seldome leisure to bestow long time vpon praying, as I told him in my Preface: euen so I can dedicate this my* Paterne of a Kings inauguration *to none so fitly, as to you, my dearest* Sonne, *both for the subiect and the shortnesse of it: the shortnesse, since you spend so much time abroad, as you can bestow but little vpon the Muses at home. And yet I will thus farre excuse you, that I would haue euery age be like it selfe: to see a yong man old, and an old man yong, is an ill-fauoured sight. Youth should bee actiue and laborious, or else (I feare) dulnesse wil come with age*: Imberbis iuuenis, tandem custode remoto, Gaudet equis canibusque & aprici gramine campi,[938] *but yet vpon the other part*, est modus in rebus,[939] *and* moderata durant.[940] *And as to the subiect, whom can a paterne for a Kings Inauguration so well fit as a Kings sonne and heire, beeing written by the King his Father, and the paterne taken from the King of all Kings?*

To your brother (now with GOD) I dedicated my ΒΑΣΙΛΙΚΟΝ ΔΩΡΟΝ, *wherein I gaue him my aduice anent the gouernement of* Scotland *in particular: this is but a short preparatiue for a Kings Inauguration, and a little forewarning of his great and heauie burthen. it is soone read and easily caried: make it therefore your* vade mecum, *to prepare you, and put you in a habit for that day, which (I dare sweare) you will neuer wish for, (as you gaue sufficient proofe by your carefull attendance in my late great sicknesse, out of which it pleased God to deliuer mee) and I hope I shall neuer giue you cause. But it will bee a great reliefe to you in the bearing of your burthen, that you be not taken* tarde;[941] *but that you foresee the weight of it before hand, and make your selfe able to support the same*: nam leuius loedit quicquid præuidimus ante;[942] *and it is a good old Scottish prouerbe, that* a man warned is halfe armed. *Looke not therefore to finde the softnesse of a doune-pillow in a Croune, but remember that it is a thornie piece of stuffe and full of continuall cares. And because examples mooue much, I will remember you, what some kings of olde thought of the weight of a Diademe.*

Antigonus, *one of* Alexanders *successors, told an olde wife, that was praising vnto him his happinesse in his raigne; shewing his Diademe, that, if shee knew how many euils that clout was stuffed with, shee would not take it vp, if shee found it lying on the ground.*[943] *And* Seleucus *another of them spake many times to the like effect.*[944] *And* Dionysius, *the first tyrant of* Syracuse, *though hee gouerned like a Tyrant all his life, and therefore onely cared for himselfe and not for his people; yet, when* Damocles *his flatterer recounted vnto him his great magnificence, wealth, power, and all his Kingly maiestie, affirming, that neuer any man was more happie, thinking therby to please his humour; the tyrant asked him (if he thought his life so pleasant) whether he would be contented to trie his fortune a little. And his flatterer answering him that hee was contented, hee made him to bee set in a golden bed, and in the middest of a rich and sumptuous feast, where no sort of princely magnificence was wanting; and while* Damocles *was in the middest of his happie estate (as hee thought) hee made a naked sword to bee hanged in a horse haire perpendicularly ouer his head with the point downward. Vpon the sight whereof neither could his meate nor all his glorious royall attyre delight him any more; but all turned into his humble begging of the Tyrant, that hee might haue leaue to bee gone: for he was now resolued that he would be no more happie.*[945] *And one of our owne predecessours,* Henrie *the fourth (called* Henrie *of* Bullenbrooke*) being in a traunce vpon his death-bed; his Sonne,* Henrie *the fift, thinking he had beene dead, a little too nimbly carried away the croune that stood by his Father: but the King recouering a little out of his fit missed his croune, and called for it; and when his sonne brought it backe againe, hee tolde him that, if hee had knowen what a croune was, hee would not haue beene so hastie: for hee protested that hee was neuer a day without trouble since it was first put vpon his head. It is true that hee was an vniust vsurper of the croune, but after hee gouerned both with iustice and valour. For you must remember that there been two sorts of tyrants, the one by vsurpation, the other by their forme of gouernment, or rather misgouernement. As for vsurpation you neede it not: you are like to succeede to a reasonable proportion: and certainely,* Conquerours are but splendide robbers. *And for tyrannous gouernement, I hope, you haue it not of kinde, nor shall euer learne it by me. All this I speake* *not to scarre you from cheerefull accepting of that place, when* God *shall bring you vnto it; but onely to forewarne you; that you deceiue not your selfe with vaine hopes. But as I wrote in my late Meditation, that a man should both examine himselfe, and then receiue the blessed* Sacrament; *but neither examine and not receiue, nor yet receiue and not examine: so I say to you, in this case prepare your selfe for the worst, and yet bee not discouraged for it,* sed contra audentior ito.[946] *Remember that,* difficilia quae pulchra,[947] *and that,* via virtutis est ardua.[948] *And for my part I will pray the Lord of heauen and earth so to blesse you (that are the sonne and heire of a King) with this paterne of the inauguration of a King, written by a King; as you may in the owne time be worthy of a heauenly and permanent Kingdome.* Amen.

Dat. 29. Decemb. 1619.[949]

ADVERTISEMENT TO
THE READER

CVrteous Reader, *I know that in this extremely short discourse of mine of the* Paterne of a Kings inauguration, *thou wilt bee farre from finding the office of a King fully described therein. And therefore I haue thought good to informe thee hereby, that I onely write this as a ground, whereupon I meane (if God shall spare mee dayes and leisure) to set downe at large (as in the descant) the whole principall points belonging to the office of a King. And if my leisure cannot permit (whereof I despaire) I intend (God willing) to set some other more nimble pen on worke with my instructions. In the meane time, I haue made this as a short forewarning to my Son, that he may in time prepare himselfe for the bargaine, and study his craft; that if it shall please God by course of nature to bring him to it, (which I pray God he may) hee may not make his entry in it like a raw Spanish* Bisogno,[950] *but rather like an olde souldier of a trained band, that needes no prompting nor direction to teach him how to vse his armes. So as mine end in this is rather a warning, then an instruction vnto him.*

And so farewell.

A PATERN
FOR A KINGS
INAVGVRATION

S. MATTHEW. Chap. 27. Vers. 27, 28, 29.
Then the souldiers of the Gouernour tooke Iesus into the Common Hall, and gathered vnto him the whole band of souldiers.

And they stripped him, and put on him a skarlet Robe.
And when they had platted a crowne of thornes, they put it vpon his
head, and a reed in his right hand, and they bowed the knee before
him and mocked him, saying, HAILE KING OF THE IEWES.

HEere haue wee in these three Verses, set downe the forme and
paterne of the Inauguration of a King, together with a perfect
description of the cares and crosses, that a King must prepare himselfe to indure in the due administration of his office. For the true
vnderstanding whereof, two things are to be respected and had in
consideration, the Person and the Paterne: the qualities of the Person
to bee applied to our comfort and saluation; the Paterne for our
imitation or example. The Person was our SAVIOUR IESVS CHRIST,
who was humbled for our exaltation, tortured for our comfort, des-
pised for our glory, and suffered for our saluation.

What belongs therefore to his Person in his passion, I distinguish,
in this my *Meditation*, from that which hee left as a paterne for imitation by all good Kings; the former seruing for the generall soules
health of all Christians, the later onely for the instruction of Kings.
But since my chiefe end in this discourse is to speake of the paterne,
as properly belonging to my calling; I will onely glaunce slightly at
that which alanerly concernes his Person, that part being already
sufficiently handled by a whole armie of Diuines. But heere it may
bee obiected that this wrong and iniurie done by the Gouernours
Souldiers to our SAVIOUR cannot fitly be drawne in example, and set
foorth as a paterne for the Inauguration of Kings, because they did
it but in a mockerie of CHRIST;[951] who hauing beene immediately
before accused for vsurping the title of King of the *Iewes*; they thought
his person and presence so contemptible, as if it had beene worthy
of no better Kingdome, then that scornefull reproach, which then
they put vpon him. To this I answere, that heere I consider not
their wicked and scornefull actions, but what vse it hath pleased the
Almightie and *All-mercifull God* to draw out of their wickednesse, and
turne it to his glorie. For it is ordinarie with *God* to bring light out
of darkenesse, as hee did at the Creation,[952] and to extract out of the
worst of things good effects, as was expressed by *Sampsons* riddle.[953]
And therefore I obserue and distinguish in this action betwixt the
part of *God*, that wrang his glory out of their corruption without their
knowledge; and their peruerse inclination. For, though the nobler
part of man, which is the soule, was vtterly corrupted in them, yet
God inforced their bodies (which is the vilest part of man) to doe that

homage to his onely Sonne, vnwitting of their soules; which both their soules and their bodies ought to haue performed: euen as hee made *Balaams* Asse to instruct her master.[954] And *Balaam* himselfe to blesse the people of *Israel*, when hee came of intent to curse them for filthy lucres sake,[955] and as hee made *Caiphas* the high Priest to prophesie, though quite contrary to his owne meaning.[956] It pleased therefore the *Almighty* to make those Souldiers worship *Christ* in their bodies with the reuerence due to a King, which their wretched soules neuer intended, thereby teaching vs, that we euer ought to worship him and his onely Sonne as well with our bodies (as they did) as with our soules, which no Christians denie; since he is the Creator and Redeemer of both. These therefore, that will refuse in any place or at any time to worship *Christ* aswell in body as in soule, are in that point inferiour to those prophane souldiers: which I wish were well obserued by our foolish superstitious *Puritanes*, that refuse to kneele at the receiuing of the blessed *Sacrament*. For, if euer at any time *Christ* is to bee worshipped, it is in time of prayer: and no time can be so fit for prayer and meditation, as is the time of our receiuing the *Sacrament*; and if any place can be more fit then other for worshipping of *God* and his *Christ* in, it is the *Church*, where is the ordinary assembly and meeting of his Saints. And now I returne to speake of the paterne.

Then the Souldiers of the Gouernour tooke IESVS *into the common Hall* (S. MARK. 15, 16. calleth it *Prætorium*, which was the *common Hall*, like our *Westminster Hall*, and serued for administration of Iustice, as the place of greatest resort) *and gathered vnto him the whole band of Souldiers.*

WEe see heere the Emperour of the whole world receauing the homage due vnto him, in that place, after that forme, and by that sort of persons, as it pleased him that many of the *Romane* Emperours (his shadowes and substitutes) should bee soone after his death inaugurated and inuested in the Empire, after that the gouernement of *Rome* was turned into a Monarchie, and ruled by Emperours. And it is worthy the obseruation (for proouing of the lawfulnesse of Monarchies and how farre that sort of gouernement is to bee preferred to any other) that as *Christ* himselfe was the Sonne and right heire by lineall descent of King *Dauid*; so was he borne vnder the first *Romane* Emperour, that euer established the *Romane* Empire.

For, though *Iulius Cæsar* was in a manner the first Emperour, yet as
he wan it by bloud, so ended hee in bloud: and therefore as *God*
would not permit King *Dauid* to build him a materiall temple, because
of his shedding of bloud;[957] but made him leaue that worke to his
sonne *Salomon*,[958] who was a King of peace: so had it not beene
fitting that the Sauiour of the World, the builder of his Church
(whose body was likewise the true Temple represented by that of
Salomon) should haue beene borne but vnder a King of peace, as was
Augustus, and in a time of peace, when as the Temple of *Ianus* was
shut, and when as all the World did pay him an vniuersall contribu-
tion, as is said in the second of Saint *Lukes Gospel*.[959] Of which
happy and peacefull time the *Sibyls* (though Ethnikes) made notable
predictions, painting forth very viuely the blessed Child that then was
to bee borne. Now as all publique solemnities haue a respect to these
three circumstances, of forme, place, and person (whereof I haue
already made mention) so in this action were all these three punctually obserued. First, the place, wherein this action was done, was the
common Hall, the publique place for administration of Iustice. And
although the *Romanes* did not precisely obserue any one place for the
inauguration of their Emperours, yet were all the places, where that
action was performed, places of most publique resort of the people,
as was this *common Hall*. For it is very fitting that he, that is to be
acknowledged the head of all sorts of people, should be inuested in
a place where all sorts of people may conueene and concurre to doe
him homage. And as to the qualities of the persons that performed
this action, they were *Romane* Souldiers; and not a small number of
them, but it was done by the whole band of the Gouernours Souldiers. And this was iust the forme of the election of a number of the
Romane Emperours: for the *Romane* Emperours were neither elected
by the Senate, nor by the people. For although the authoritie till the
time of the Emperours was in the Senate and people of *Rome*, yet
euer after the rising of the great factions in *Rome*, betweene *Iulius
Cæsar* and *Pompey*, things were brought to that confusion, that the
Senate and people retained but the shadow of authority: but in very
deede it was the armie that vsurped the power of electing of all
the Emperours, beginning at *Claudius*, who next *Caligula* succeeded
Tiberius, who reigned at the time of *Christs* death, and so continuing
still till after *Titus Vespasian*; and after *Commodus* almost all were thus
chosen for the space of many yeares, as all the best Writers of the

Romane history make mention. Now the *Prætorian cohorts* (who were indeed the very flowre and greatest strength of the *Roman* armie), had the chiefe sway in the election of the Emperors. The resemblance whereof we may at this day see in the *Turkish* Empire. For the great *Turks Ianisaries* are his *Prætorian cohorts*; and although that Empire be hereditary, yet haue the *Ianisaries* so great power in it (as it was lately seene) that by them, after the death of *Achmat*⁹⁶⁰ this great Turkes father, this Princes Vncle⁹⁶¹ was set vpon the throne and quickly after deposed by them againe, and this Prince *Osman*⁹⁶² set vp in his fathers place. And euen so after the long troubles that were in *Moscouia*, after the death of their Duke or Emperour *Iuan Vasiliwich*⁹⁶³ (who was the last Prince that gouerned that land in⁹⁶⁴ peace) the *Cosackes*,⁹⁶⁵ which are the very *Prætorian cohorts* in that countrey, elected this Duke or Emperour, *Michael Feodorwich*,⁹⁶⁶ which now reignes. I know there was many sorts of *Prætors* in *Rome*, one was *Prætor ciuilis*, who iudged but in ciuill causes, and another was *Prætor militaris*, who was indeed the Captaine of the Emperours guards: and of them I now make mention, not that I meane hereby to exclude the power of the rest of the armie in that action; but the *Prætorian cohorts* being the strength and floure of them (as I said already) the rest of the armie commonly followed, where they led the ring. Now the kingdome of the *Iewes* being, in the time of *Christ*, subiect to the Emperour of *Rome*, the Emperours gouernours band of souldiers, which had a resemblance to the Emperours *Prætorian cohorts* (euen as a Viceroy represents the person of the Emperour or King his master) brought *Iesus* to the *common Hall* or *Prætorium*, and there did inaugurate him as you shall hereafter heare. And as to the forme of his inauguration, the spirit of GOD, sets it downe very punctually: First, *they stripped him, and put on him a scarlet robe*; S. *Marke*⁹⁶⁷ and S. *Iohn*⁹⁶⁸ cals it a *purple robe*, which is one in substance, although⁹⁶⁹ they were of diuers ingredients. For the ancient *purple* was of a reddish colour, and both scarlet and purple were so rich and princely dyes of old, as they were onely worne by Kings and Princes, and that chiefely in their princely robes: but now these sorts of dyes are lost. This purple or scarlet dye may also admit a meta-phoricall allusion to the blood of *Christ*, that was shed for vs.⁹⁷⁰ For the robes of his flesh were dyed in that true purple and scarlet dye of his bloud, whose bloud must wash our sinnes, that wee may appeare holy and vnspotted before him in our white robes, washed in the bloud of the *Lambe*.[971] They first *stripped him* then, for it is thought (and not improbably) that his owne cloathes were after the auncient forme of a Prophets garment; onely his coate, without any seame in it, was to fulfill the prophecie of *Dauid*,[972] that *they should cast lots for it*; and did also signifie the indiuisible vnitie of the *Church*, which I pray God the true *Church* of *Christ* would now well remember. Now therefore, when they were to declare him a King, they tooke off his Prophets garment and put a royall robe vpon him.

Kings euer vsed to weare robes when they sate in their throne of Maiestie, and euen purple robes: for robes or long gownes are fittest to sit withall, and sitting is the fittest posture for expressing of grauitie in iudgment; standing signifies too great precipitation, which is chiefly to bee auoyded in iudgement, for no man can stand long without wearying; walking betokens a wandring lightnesse and distraction of the senses; leaning portends weaknesse, and lying inability. And therefore *God* himselfe is (*per* ἀνθρωποπάθειαν) described in his word to sit in his Throne,[973] and *Christ* to sit at his right hand;[974] nay, the foure and twenty Elders haue Thrones set for them to sit in,[975] for they are euen to be CHRISTS assistants in iudging of the world.[976] Kings therefore, as GODS Deputie-iudges vpon earth, sit in thrones, clad with long robes, not as laikes and simply *togati*[977] (as inferior secular Iudges are) but as *mixtæ personæ*[978] (as I said in my ΒΑΣΙΛΙΚΟΝ ΔΩΡΟΝ) being bound to make a reckoning to GOD for their subiects soules as well as their bodies. Not that they ought to vsurpe any point of the Priestly office, no more then the Priest should the Kings, for these two offices were deuided in *Aarons* Priesthood; but it is the Kings office to ouersee and compell the *Church* to do her office, to purge all abuses in her, and by his sword (as *vindex vtriusque tabulæ*)[979] to procure her due reuerence and obedience of all his temporall subiects. And that royall robes are of *purple*, it is to represent thereby as well the continuance and honor of their function, as that their iustice and equitie should be without staine or blemish. For the ancient purple, whereof we haue now but the counterfeit, was of extreame long lasting, and could not be stayned. And next,

> *When they had platted a croune of thornes, they set it vpon his head.*

HEere is set doune what thing they set vpon his head, of what stuffe it was made, and in what manner it was wrought. The thing they set vpon his head was a *croune*, in the greeke text called στεφανος. Anciently the Kings of the Gentiles wore diademes: it is a greeke compound word of διὰ & δέειν, which is *to binde about*, for it went about the head: but in case one would stretch it to διὰ & δῆμος, which is *the people* (though the greeke language will no way beare it) it wil serue for a good remembrance to a King; for the diademe or croune must put him in mind how he raignes by the loue and acknowledgement of his people. I will not heere play the linguist to contest with a sort of popular tribunes, whether that διὰ may in a greeke coniunction of wordes bee sometimes vsed as well for *for* as *from*: for I admit that sense, that it shall onely bee vnderstood *from the people*. For no question, though all successiue Kings receiue their crounes from GOD onely, yet the people at their inauguration giue a publike acknowledgement of their willing subiection to his person and authority, submitting themselues to the will of GOD, who is the onely giuer of it; which is signified by the putting of the diademe or croune vpon his head.

The *diademe* it selfe was a manner of garland which went about the head made like a wreath of silke ribban, or some such like thing; which signified, that as all such, as wan the prize in any match, had garlands put vpon their heads, in signe of the popular applause for their good deseruings; so Kings had diademes put vpon their heads, in signe of the peoples willing consent to bee subiect vnto them, that diademe or garland being a marke of their eminencie aboue all others: not that I meane that the forme of diademes was taken from the garlands (for I take the diademes to bee farre more ancient then the garland) but I onely speake heere of the resemblance beteweene them in some cases. Neither will I denie that many Kings of the nations had their diademes or crounes giuen them by the people, who translated and transferred by that act all their power into their Kings; but it followeth not that GOD therefore did not set those Kings vpon their thrones. For although those infidell nations knew not *God*, yet *God, qui disponit omnia suauiter*,[980] put it in the peoples hearts to acknowledge them for their Kings, and willingly to submit themselues vnto them, euen that *God*, who is not onely the searcher and knower, but euen the rule of all hearts.[981] But among the people of *God*, where *God* visibly ruled, the King of his people was immediately chosen by himselfe, and the people onely gaue obedience thereunto (as is more then plaine in the *old Testament*)[982] so as the only difference was, that, what God did directly by his word and oracle among his owne people in the election of Kings, he did it onely by his secret working in the hearts of other nations, though themselues knew not from whence those motions came, which God by his finger wrought in their hearts. And the latine word *corona* signifies also the same thing that *diadema* did. For the croune is set vpon the Kings head and compasseth it to shew, that as the croune compasseth the Kings head, so is hee to sit in the middest of his people. His wakerif care is euer to bee imployed for their good, their loue is his greatest safetie, and their prosperitie is his greatest honour and felicitie. For many times among the *Romans*, the word *corona* signified the people, as **Aliquid etiam coronæ datum.*[983] And Saint *Paul*, 1. *Thess*. 2. 19. calls them the *Croune of his reioycing* or glorying.

As to the stuffe wherof this Croune was made, it was made of thornes: and it is vulgarly well knowen that thornes signifie stinging and pricking cares. That King therefore, who will take his paterne from this heauenly King, must not thinke to weare a Croune of gold and precious stones only, but it must be lyned with *Thornes*, that is, thornie cares: for he must remember that hee weares not that croune for himselfe, but for others; that hee is ordayned for his people, and not his people for him. For he is a great watchman and shepheard, as well as Church-men are: and his eye must neuer slumber nor sleepe for the care of his flocke, euer remembring that his office, beeing duely executed, will prooue as much *onus*[984] as *honos*[985] vnto him. And as to the forme of making the croune of thornes, it is said, *they platted thornes and made a croune of them*. Now euery man knoweth, that where a number of long things, in forme of lines, shall bee platted through other, it makes a troublesome and intricate worke to finde out all the ends of them, and set them asunder againe, especially to set straight and eauen againe all the seuerall peeces that must be bowed in the platting: but aboue all, to set straight and asunder againe thornes that are platted, is a most vncomfortable worke. For though any one peece of thorne may be handled in some place without hurt, yet no man can touch platted thornes without danger of pricking. As a croune of thornes then represents the stinging cares of Kings, so a croune of platted thornes doth more viuely represent the anxious and intricate cares of Kings, who must not only looke to be troubled with a continuall care for the good gouernement of their people, but they must euen expect to meete with a number of crosse and intricate difficulties, which will appeare to bee so full of repugnances among themselues, as they can scantly be touched without smarting. And euen as a good and skilfull Physitian is most troubled with that sort of patient, that hath many implicate diseases vpon him (the fittest cure for some of them beeing directly noysome to others, and the antidote to one of his diseases proouing little better then poyson to another of them) so must Kings exercise their wisedome in handling so wisely these knotty difficulties, and with so great a moderation; that too great extremitie in one kinde may not prooue hurtfull in another, but, by a musicall skill, temper and turne all these discords into a sweet harmonie.

And they put a reede in his right hand.

THis reede represented the Kingly scepter, which is the pastorall rod of a King; and the straightnesse of the reed, his righteousnesse in the administration of iustice, without any partiality, as it is *Psal.* 45. 7. *The scepter of thy kingdome is a right scepter.* The scepter represents the Kings authority; for as the royall robes are first put on vpon a King, to shew the grauitie and dignitie of the person that is to bee inaugurated, and as the croune represents the loue and willing acknowledgement of his people, so the scepter is next put in his hand to declare his authoritie who is already found worthy to enjoy the same by his coronation. The authoritie of *God* himselfe is expressed in the 2. Psal. by a *rod of yron*,[986] wherewith he is to bruise the nations that rebel against him, which rod of yron signifies his scepter. But this scepter put in the hand of *Christ* was a reede. It is true that the reeds of those countreys, as those of India are, bee a great deale bigger, harder and more solid then ours; but though one may giue a great blow with them, yet are they much more brittle then solide timber is, and hard blowes giuen with them will easily make them breake: thereby teaching Christian Kings that their scepters (which represent their authority) should not be too much vsed nor stretched, but where necessity requires it. For many harde blowes giuen with a reede would make it quickly breake (as I haue sayd) and wise Kings would bee loth to put their prerogatiue vpon the tenter-hookes, except a great necessity should require it. For there is a great difference betweene the scepter (which represents the authority of a King toward all his subjects as well good as bad) and the sword, which is onely ordayned for the punishment of the euill. And therefore the scepter of a King should bee of a reede, that is, to correct gently: but the sword, which is ordayned for punishment of vice, and purging the land of haynous and crying sinnes, must bee a sharpe weapon. And also the scepter of a reede did not onely serue for a paterne to other Kings, but it fitted properly the person of *Christ*, who, being the true King of mercy, came to conuert sinners and bring them to repentance, but not to destroy them;[987] for as himselfe sayth, *his burthen is light and his yoke is easie.*[988] But although this scepter must bee put in the KINGS hand by some one of his subiects (for *God* will not come himselfe, nor by an Angel out of heauen deliuer it vnto him, for that were miraculous and is not to bee expected) yet I hope no Christian doubts but that the authority of a King, whereof the scepter is the representation, is onely giuen by *God*. *Per me reges regnant & domini dominantur.*[989] Kings are anoynted of *God* sitting in his seate and therefore called Gods: and all superior powers are of *God*;[990] nay the Prophet *Ieremie* cals that Ethnike Emperour, *Nebuchadnezar, the seruant of God,* and *S. Paul* calls the tyrant *Nero*, in his time, *the minister of God.*[991]

And that it was put in his right hand, it was because the right hand signifieth both honour and power: Honour, *Christ sits at the right hand of God.*[992] *Sit thou at my right hand, Psal.* 110.[993] Power, as the hand of action: *And thy right hand shall teach thee terrible things, Psal.* 45. and *Psal.* 118. 16. both are expressed, *The right hand of the Lord hath the preeminence, the right hand of the Lord bringeth mighty things to passe.*

And they bowed the knee before him, and (as Saint *Marke*[994] witnesseth) *they worshipped him.*

NOw though this kneeling and worship was in a mockery done by them; yet may wee learne heere that *God* thought it no Idolatry that his sonne should be kneeled vnto, euen in the time of his greatest humilitie, and entring in his passion. But I haue touched this point already. As for their worshipping him, it is true that both their kneeling and worship were intended as a ciuill homage done to a temporal King; and[995] in that sence the old word of *worship* was wont to be vsed in English, and as yet it is vsed here in the celebration of marriage. This ciuill worship is easily distinguished by them that please from diuine worship: for to reuerence an earthly creature, and do him respect in regard of the eminencie of his place, yea euen to make a request or prayer vnto him, is quite different from a diuine and spirituall worship. For in the former we onely doe reuerence or make our request to these temporall Kings or persons that are subiect to our senses; but we can vse no spirituall worship or prayer that can be auaileable vnto vs without faith. Let the schoole distinctions of δουλεία, ὑπερδουλεία and λατρεία deceiue them that list to be deceiued with them: for all prayer in faith is due to *God* onely.

And after their kneeling and worshipping him,

> *They mocked him, saying,* HAILE KING OF THE IEWES.

AS for their mocking him, I haue largely declared that point already: but as to the words which they vsed in saluting him, they are also vsed in the ordinary forme of the Inauguration of Kings; that, after all the actions of ceremony are vsed vnto him, the people that are more remote & cannot with their eies see the performance of those actions, may know they are performed by the publike proclaiming of him. And because the rest of this inauguration of *Christ*, is set doune in other places of the *new Testament*, I must here supply it: for I onely set doune, in the beginning, the Text of S. *Matthew*, as being the only place of Scripture which makes the longest and most particular relation of his inauguration. For this action stayed not here, but *Pilate* (who was both iudge and gouernour, vnder the *Romanes* of that part of the country) made him to bee sent forth out of the *common hall*, and shewed to all the people in that kingly attire:[996] and when as the bloudy and malitious *Iewes* cryed out to crucifice him, hee answered againe, *shall I crucifie your King?*[997] And after that, he sent him to *Herod* (who was Tetrarch and Viceroy of the fourth part of *Iewrie*) who put other gorgeous robes vpon him:[998] so as he was not onely inaugurated and proclaimed King of the *Iewes* by the Gouernours *Roman* Souldiers who represented the *Praetorian cohorts*; but hee was also so acknowledged by the iudge and gouernour *Pilate*, and by the Tetrarch *Herod*. But herein was the difference, that all this action performed by *Herod* and his Souldiers, was but a wicked mockery in their intention: whereas by the contrary, *Pilate*, being both iudge and gouernour, meant it not in mockery; but was in a great doubt and wist not what to make of it: as it appeares both by his questioning of *Christ*,[999] and also that hee brought him forth of the *common hall* and shewed him to the whole multitude in his royall robes and his croune vpon his head, saying vnto them, *Behold the Man*;[1000] thereby as it were confirming publikely his inauguration done by the Souldiers

before, and when the people cryed, *Away with him*, his answere was
(as I said already) *Shall I crucifie your King?*[1001] Both which words he
spake to strike a terrour into them, or at least to mooue them, to
commiseration, seeming to mocke him as they did: for both Christs
answere vnto him, and his Wiues message vpon a dreame she had,
put him in a great perplexitie; till the feare he had of offending the
Emperor in case CHRIST had prooued thereafter to haue beene the
righteous King of the *Iewes* (which *Herod* the great also apprehended
at his birth) enforced him to pronounce so iniust and detestable a
sentence; so as, that in his owne heart he meant no iest in it, is
clearely apparant in making his title to be written aboue his head
vpon the Crosse, as an honorable inscription, euen set in that place
aboue his head, and to the view of all the world. And to make it the
more publike, it was written in three languages, *Hebrew, Greeke and
Latine:*[1002] *Hebrew*, as the vulgar language of that people; and *Greeke*
and *Latine* as the most common and publike languages of all *Proselytes*
and strangers, that should come to see that spectacle: especially, these
two were the languages of all prophane learning. Euen as in this
kingdome it was the ancient custome and is still obserued to this day,
that vpon S. *Georges* day, and at other high festiuall times, the chiefe
Herald garter comes in the middest of the feast, and proclaimes my
titles in three languages, *Latine, French*, and *English*: *English*, because
it is the vulgar language of this kingdome; and *Latine* and *French*, as
the two strange tongues that maniest here do vnderstand. Especially
the time is to be obserued when the order of the *Garter* was first
instituted by *Edward* the third who as hee was Sonne to the daughter
of *France*, so at that time the *French* tongue was in a manner the
vulgar language of this Nation: and therefore they are proclaimed in
three languages heere, that it may bee vnderstood by the vulgar sort
(as *Pilates* inscription was) and not concealed from them. Now what
ground the *Papists* can haue heereby, to haue not onely their *Masse*
and seruice in an vnknowne tongue, but euen that ignorant people
shall bee taught their prayers in a strange tongue which they vnderstand not, I leaue it to the iudgement of the indifferent reader: for,
besides that it is directly prohibited by Saint *Paul*,[1003] it is flatly contrary to *Pilates* action in this case. For one of the three languages
wherein *Christs* title was written vpon the crosse, was *Hebrew*, which
was the vulgar language of that Countrie: and the other two were
these that were best vnderstood by the strangers and *Proselytes* there.

So as it is a flat contradiction betweene *Pilates* act (who by all meanes stroue to make *Christs* title so to be read and vnderstood by all men) and our *Papists*, that will haue their seruice and prayers to bee in an vnknowen tongue, that no ignorant countrey-man may vnderstand them. But it is ill lucke for the *Church* of *Rome*, that the best warrant they can bring for this their forme of the worship of *God*, is grounded vpon the example of *Pilate*. But to returne to our purpose; though it was the common fashion that great offendors, so executed, had the nature and qualitie of their crimes written aboue their heads; yet in my opinion it is cleare enough (as I said already) that *Pilate* gaue the title to *Christ* in earnest. Not onely for that hee made it so solemnely to be written aboue his head vpon the crosse, but euen after that the high Priest had wittily and maliciously requested him to correct that writing, and in place of IESVS OF NAZARETH KING OF THE IEWES, to say, IESVS OF NAZARETH THAT CALLETH HIMSELFE KING OF THE IEWES,[1004] he absolutely refused it, in these words, *quod scripsi scripsi*,[1005] which was a constant refusall, worthy of a iudge in maintenance of a iust decree. Happy had *Pilate* beene, if base feare had not made him pronounce a worse sentence before. So as, if there were no more but this action of *Pilate* so constant and absolute, it were enough to prooue (according to my first ground in the beginning of this discourse) that though the wicked people (both *Iewes* and *Romanes*) intended nothing in all this worke, but a malicious and blasphemous mockery, yet had *God* his worke to two ends heerein. First, that his onely Sonne might thus be put to the height of derision, that his passion might be fully accomplished for our saluation: and next, that (as I said in the beginning) he, that brings light out of darkenes, might wring from this malitiously blinded people a bodily externall acknowledgement of his Sonnes true title to that kingdome, prophecied of old, that *the scepter should not depart from Iuda, nor a law-giuer from betweene his feete till Shiloh came*:[1006] prophecied likewise by *Balaam*,[1007] which prophecie (as some[1008] learned writers thinke) instructed the wise Kings of the East, who were guided by the starre, to come and worship *Christ*. This title was likewise the occasion of great trouble to *Herod the greats* minde, whereupon came his murthering of the children,[1009] and is so carefully set doune in the genealogie of *Christ*, written by two *Euangelists*;[1010] and was not denied by *Christ* himselfe, when *Pilate* asked him the question. And so this forme of

Christs inauguration was left for a paterne to all Christian Kings thereafter.

Yet amongst all these *insignia regalia*,[1011] the *sword* is amissing, the reason is, his first comming was to suffer for our saluation from the sword of diuine iustice; and not to vse the sword, to take vengeance vpon euill doers: at his second comming he will come as a iudge, and vse his sword vpon the wicked. And therefore he came in the flesh, as a lambe, not once opening his mouth when hee was led to the slaughter:[1012] suffering without repining the highest outrages to the minde, which is, mockery with contempt, a kinde of persecution; and the greatest tortures in the body that could bee deuised, that the prophecie of *Ieremie* might bee accomplished, *non est dolor sicut dolor meus*.[1013] He was buffeted,[1014] and so made a slaue, he was spit vpon as a worme,[1015] and so, farre lesse then any humane creature; *he was beaten with his owne rod*, as the prouerbe is: for after that they had put a reede in his right hand, they pulled it out againe and smote him with it: hee was mocked in the highest measure, both before and after his nayling to the crosse. And[1016] as to the torture of his body, hee was extreamly scourged: the croune of platted thornes made innumerable bloudy wounds in his head: and he was nayled both through his hands and feete to the infamous death of the crosse; that the extremity of his anguish in mind, and torture in body, might serue as a full ransome, to satisfie his fathers iustice for our redemption. He came then at this time as a titularie King of that kingdome, but not to exercise any worldly iurisdiction, *regnum eius non erat huius mundi*,[1017] and so he taught his Disciples to follow him, *Reges gentium dominantur eis vos autem non sic*.[1018] He had no vse of a sword then, nay, he found fault with Saint *Peters* vsing it, telling him, *Hee that striketh with the sword shall perish by the sword*;[1019] leauing it belike to those that call themselues *Peters* successors, who come in the spirit of *Elias* with fire, adding gun-powder and the sword vnto it. But our *Sauiour* knew not how to set both croune and mitre vpon one head: nor yet was he acquainted with that distinction, that a Church-man may vse the temporall sword, to procure *bonum spirituale*.[1020]

But to returne to our purpose of *Christs* humilitie; it may bee obiected that it is not likely, that our *Sauiour* would in the very mid-dest of his passion (which was the action of his greatest humility) giue euen then a glance of his title to a worldly kingdome: for suffering of iniuries, especially such base abuses, is directly contrary to the maiesty of a King and the honour of his inauguration. To this I answere two wayes,[1021] *first*, it was necessary that *Christ* in the time of his passion should approue himselfe to bee lineally descended from *Dauid*, yea euen next heire to the croune of the *Iewes*; that he might in the sight of the world, before his going out of it, fulfill these prophecies which I lately made mention of, thereby to prooue himselfe the true *Messias* that was promised. And *next*, as hee was both *God* and *Man*, so shall ye finde that euen from his conception till his very expiring vpon the crosse, he euer intermixed glances of his glory, in the midst of his greatest humilitie. Was it not a glorious thing that the Angel *Gabriel*[1022] should be the messenger to the blessed *Virgin* of his conception? When *Ioseph* thought to put away his wife, thinking shee had beene vnlawfully with childe by a man, hee was prohibited by an Angel in a dreame.[1023] When the blessed *Virgin*, beeing with child, went to the hill countrey to visit her cousin *Elizabeth*, *Iohn* the *Baptist* sprang in the belly of his mother, which was a miraculous kinde of worshipping and congratulating[1024] our *Sauiour* in the belly of his blessed mother.[1025] He was borne in a poore stable, in a beasts cribb, and amongst beasts,[1026] but the Angels sung a glorious hymne of gratulation at his birth.[1027] His parents fled to *Egypt* with him, when hee was yet in the cradle;[1028] but, immediatly before that, three Kings of the East brought presents to him, and worshipped him.[1029] Hee was obedient to his parents during his minority; but, being but twelue yeeres of age, hee disputed publikely in the Temple with the Doctors of their Law, to the admiration of all the hearers.[1030] Hee was baptized in *Iordan* by *Iohn Baptist*,[1031] as many of the common people were: but at his baptisme the *Holy Ghost* descended vpon his head in the likenesse of a doue, and a voice was heard from his Father, saying, *This is my beloued* SONNE, *in whom I am well pleased.*[1032] And hee auowed to the *Scribes* and *Pharisees*, that *Abraham* longed to see his day and did see it, giuing the title to himselfe which *God* vsed in the fiery bush to *Moses*, *I am that I am*; for hee sayd vnto them, *before Abraham was, I am.*[1033] Hee fled diuers times from the fury of the *Iewes*, nay, *the sonne of man had not a hole to hide his head in:*[1034] and yet hee purged the temple twice, and like a great temporall magistrate scourged and thrust out those that bought and sold in the temple:[1035] yea hee rebuked the windes and commanded the seas.[1036] And, at his transfiguration, he made his body appeare a glorified body, by dispensation at that time;[1037] hauing (as the true *God*) the *Law* and the commentary and application thereof, which is the *Prophets*, to attend vpon him in the persons of *Moses* and *Elias*. He payed tribute, to shew, that neither *Christ* as man, nor S. *Peter* must bee exempted from giuing vnto *Cæsar* that which is *Cæsars*: but caused *Peter* to angle for it, and take it out of the mouth of a fish, to shew the power of his Godhead.[1038] Sometimes hee went vp priuately to the feast at *Ierusalem* for feare of the *Iewes*:[1039] but at his last *Passeouer* hee sent some of his Disciples, and by them commanded him, whom hee meant to make his host, to prepare his house for him, *for the Lord meant to keepe his Passeouer there.*[1040] He refused to be a King when the people would haue made him one:[1041] and yet hee commanded some of his Disciples to vntie an asse, telling her owner *that the Master had neede of her.*[1042] And then made a publike entrie vpon her through *Ierusalem* like a temporall King, euen with many solemnities belonging to a Kings riding in state. For his Disciples put their clothes vpon the asse and the colt, as it were to represent the garnishing with foot-clothes, as wel the horse he rode on as his led horse: the people also spread their garments in the way, and others cut downe branches and strawed them: all which is an vsuall forme that people vse to honour their King with, at such solemne times. He had also the acclamation of all the people crying *Hosanna to the sonne of Dauid, &c.*[1043] nay, euen hee himselfe tooke it vpon him as his due; for when the chiefe Priests and Scribes thinking that hee would not take such state vpon him, asked if hee heard what the people said, hee answered them out of that of the eight *Psalme, Out of the mouthes of babes and sucklings thou hast perfected prayse.*[1044] And as for his riding vpon an asse, it was not a contemptible thing for Kings and Princes in the East, especially among the *Iewes*, to ride vpon asses euen in the sight of the people.[1045] Hee washed his disciples feete, to teach them humility, immediatly before his last *Supper*:[1046] and yet a few dayes before that, he highly commended *Mary Magdalen* for breaking an alabaster boxe of oyntments vpon his feete, and suffered her to wipe them with the haire of her head.[1047] When the *Iewes* sent their officers with *Iudas* to apprehend him; though he suffered them at the last to carrie him away, yet at the first with a flash and cast of his eye (wherein, no question, the Diuinitie sparkled when he listed),[1048] he made them all fall backwards,[1049] so as they could not approch him againe till hee permitted them. The cast of his eye made likewise S. *Peter* goe forth and weepe when the cocke crew.[1050] And euen vpon the very crosse, though the death thereupon was accursed by the Law, he was exalted, as S. *Paul* saith;[1051] and there promised the penitent thiefe, he should be that day with him in *Paradise*,[1052] hauing that royall inscription (whereof I haue made mention already) written aboue his head in the three most publike tongues. Yea, euen after that his body was taken off the crosse, a principall man amongst the *Iewes*, *Ioseph* of *Arimathea*,[1053] begged his bodie of *Pilate*; and not onely imbaumed it (as kings and Princes bodies vse to bee) but put it in a new faire sepulchre, which had been prepared for himselfe. And thus you see, that, through all the course of our *Sauiours* life in this world he gaue vpon euery occasion some glances of his glory; for the conuersion or confirming of some of his elect, and for making the wicked and stubborne hearted inexcusable. For *hee thought it no robberie to bee equall with God.*[1054]

And now to conclude this paterne of a King, I will shortly summe vp these regall ornaments together with their signification, which before I handled. A King hath first great cause of contentment if the people of all sorts (especially those to whose place it belongs) doe willingly conueene and concurre to his publike inauguration. A King must looke to haue that action performed in publike, and in a publike place; that the loue of his people may appeare in that solemne action. Two things a King hath specially to looke vnto at his inauguration; *first*, that his title to the croune be iust, and *next* that he may possesse it with the loue of his people. For although a Monarchie or hereditary kingdome cannot iustly be denied to the lawfull successor, what euer the affections of the people be; yet it is a great signe of the blessing of *God*, when he enters in it with the willing applause of his subiects. Now the first ornament, that is to be put vpon him, are his robes, to put him in memory that in his sitting in iudgment he is to vse grauitie, great patience in hearing all parties, & mature deliberation before he pronounce his sentence. And the purple dye of his robe, should put him in memory not to prooue vnworthy of so ancient a croune and dignitie: and to take great heed to his conscience, that his iudgement may be without blemish or staine of whatsoeuer corrupt affections. For iustice must be blinde, and it is she *that establisheth the thrones of* KINGS.[1055] The setting of the croune vpon his head must put him in mind, that he is euer to walke in the middest of his people, that their loue is his greatest safetie, and their prosperitie his greatest glory and worldly felicitie. But he must not expect a soft and easie croune, but a croune full of thornie cares, yea, of platted and intricate cares: and therefore hee ought to make it his principall studie (next the safetie of his soule) to learne, how to make himselfe able to rid and extricate those many knottie difficulties, that will occurre vnto him; according to my admonition to my sonne HENRY in the end of my ΒΑΣΙΛΙΚΟΝ ΔΩΡΟΝ wherein I apply some verses of *Virgil* to that purpose. And therefore, in all other commendable things he may presse so farre to excell, as his inclination and leisure will permit him; but in the science of gouernment hee must presse to be an arts-master. And his Scepter made of a reede, must put him in minde to manage his authoritie boldly, and yet temperately, not stretching his royall Prerogatiue but where necessitie shall require it. Temporall Kings must not likewise be barred the sword, though it bee not in this paterne (as I told before) for it is to be drawne for the punishment of the wicked in defence of the good: *for a King carries not his sword for naught.*[1056] But it must neither bee blunt: for lawes without execution are without life;[1057] nor yet must it be euer drawne: for a King should neuer punish but with a weeping eye. In a word, a Christian King should neuer be without that continuall and euer wakeriffe care, of the account he is one day to giue to *God*, of the good gouernment of his people, & their prosperous estate both in soules and bodies; which is a part of the health of his owne soule. And then he shall neuer need to doubt of that happy and willing acclamation of his people, with an *Aue Caesar*, or *haile King*, (which was mentioned in this paterne) not onely to begin at his entry to the croune, but euen to accompany him all the daies of his life thereafter; and when they haue bedewed and washed his graue with their teares, his posteritie to bee well-commed by them, as a bright and sunne-shining morning after a darke and gloomie night.

HIS[1058]
MAIESTIES
DECLARATION,
Touching his proceedings in the
late Assemblie and Conuention
of Parliament.

HAuing of late, vpon mature deliberation, with the aduice and vniforme consent of Our whole Priuie Councell, determined to dissolue the Assembly and Conuention of Parliament, lately called together by Our Regall power and Authoritie, Wee were pleased by Our Proclamation,[1059] giuen at Our Palace of *Westminster* the sixt day of this instant *Ianuary*, to declare, not onely Our pleasure and resolution therein, but also to expresse some especiall passages and proceedings, moouing vs to that resolution: Wherein, albeit hauing so many yeeres swayed the swords and scepters of three renowned kingdomes, Wee cannot but discerne (as much as any Prince liuing) what apperteineth to the height of a powerfull Monarch: yet, that all men might discerne, that Wee, like Gods true Vicegerent, delight not so much in the greatnesse of Our place, as in the goodnesse & benignitie of our gouernment, We were content in that one Act to descend many degrees beneath Our Selfe: First, by communicating to all Our people the reasons of a resolution of State, which Princes vse to reserue, *inter arcana Imperij*,[1060] to themselues and their Priuie Councell: Secondly, by mollifying and mixing the peremptorie and binding qualitie of a Proclamation, with the indulgence of a milde and fatherly instruction: And lastly, leading them, and opening to them that forbidden Arke of Our absolute and indisputable Prerogatiue, concerning the calling, continuing, and dissoluing of Parliaments: which, though it were more then superabundant to make Our Subiects know the realitie of Our sincere intentions; yet Wee not satisfied therewith, but finding the bounds of a Proclamation too straight to conteine and expresse the boundlesse affection that Wee beare to Our good and louing people, are pleased hereby to inlarge Our Selfe, (as Wee promised in Our said Proclamation) by a more full and plaine expression of those Letters and Messages that passed from Vs to the Commons in Parliament, which by reason of the length of them, could not bee related at large, but briefly pointed at in Our said Proclamation. For, as in generall the great actions of Kings are done as vpon a stage, obuious to the publike gazing of euery man; so are Wee most willing, that the trueth of this particular, concerning Our owne honour, and the satisfaction of Our Subiects, should bee represented vnto all men without vaile or couering, being assured that the most plainnesse and freedome will most aduantage Vs, hauing in this, and all Our Actions euer affected such sinceritie and vprightnes of heart, as were Wee all transparent, and that men might readily passe to Our inward thoughts, they should there perceiue the self-same affections which Wee haue euer professed in Our outward words and Actions.

Hauing anticipated the time of reassembling Our Parliament to the twentieth day of *Nouember* last, (which Wee formerly appointed to haue met vpon the eighth of *February* next,) vpon the confidence that their noble and generous declaration at their parting the fourth of *Iune* put vs in,[1061] of their free and liberall assistance to the recouery of Our Childrens ancient inheritance;[1062] and hauing declared to them Our resolution of taking vpon Vs the defence of Our childrens patrimonie by way of Armes, the Commons very heartily and dutifully fell immediatly after their reassembling, to treat of a necessary supplie, and concluded, for the present, to grant a Subsidie to be paid in *February* next, (the last paiment of the latter Subsidie granted by them being not to come in vntill *May* following) whereby Wee were well and cleerly satisfied of the good intention of the Commons in generall, by whose vniforme vote & assent that Subsidy was resolued on, not without intimation of a more ample supplie to be yeelded in conuenient time.

But before this their resolution was reduced into a formall Acte or Bill, some discontented persons that were the cause of all that euill which succeeded, endeauouring to clog the good will of the Commons with their owne vnreasonable ends, fell to dispute in the House of Our high Prerogatiues, namely of the match of Our dearest sonne the Prince,[1063] of the making warre with forreigne Princes Our Allies, betweene whom and Vs there was a firme peace religiously made and obserued hitherunto: All which they couered with the cloake of

Religion, and with the faire pretence of a duetifull Petition to bee preferred to Vs. Wee vnderstanding right well, that those points were not disputable in Parliament, without Our owne Royall direction, being of Our highest Prerogatiues, the very Characters of Souereignty: & thinking, that when euery Subiect by nature, and the Lawes of the Realme, had the power of matching their children according to their owne best liking, none should denie Vs the like; especially Wee hauing at the beginning of the Parliament declared Our purpose concerning the matching of Our Sonne, the Prince, were fully perswaded, that those specious outsides of Religion and humble petitioning, were added onely to gaine passage vnto those things, which being propounded in their true colours, must needs haue appeared vniust and vnreasonable, as matters wherewith neuer any Parliament had presumed to meddle before, except they had bene thereunto required by their King; nay, not befitting Our Priuie Councell to meddle with, without Our speciall command and allowance; since the very consulting vpon such matters (though in neuer so priuate a maner) being discouered abroad, might at some time produce as ill effects, as if they were publikely resolued vpon. For as concerning the point of Religion, We aswell in the beginning of the Parliament, by a publike and open Declaration made to both Houses in the higher House of Parliament, as also shortly after, by a gracious answere vnto a former Petition of theirs, expressed to the full Our immutable resolution to maintaine true Religion, besides the vntainted practise of Our whole life in that point. And howsoeuer an humble Petition beare a faire shew of respect; yet if vnder colour of concluding on a Petition a way should bee opened to treat in Parliament of the mysteries of State, without Our Royall allowance, it were a great and vnusuall breach vpon the Royall power: Besides, who knoweth not that the preferring of a Petition, includes an expectation to haue it graunted? and therefore to nippe this springing euill in the beginning, Wee directed Our Letters to the Speaker of that House, the tenour of which Letters followeth.

MAster Speaker, *Wee haue heard by diuers reports to Our great griefe, That the farre distance of Our Person at this time from Our high Court of Parliament, caused by Our want of health, hath emboldened some fiery and popular spirits in Our House of Commons, to debate and argue publikely, in matters farre beyond their reach or capacitie, and so tending to Our high dishonour, and to the trenching vpon Our Prerogatiue Royall. You shall therefore acquaint that house with Our pleasurre, That none therein shall henceforth presume to meddle with any thing concerning Our gouernment, or mysteries of State; namely, not to speake of Our dearest Sonnes Match with the Daughter of* Spaine, *nor to touch the Honour of that King, or any other Our friends or Confederates: And also not to meddle with any mens particulars, which haue their due motion in Our ordinarie Courts of Iustice. And whereas We heare that they haue sent a message to* S^{ir} Edwin Sandys,[1064] *to know the reasons of his late restraint, you shall in Our name resolue them, That it was not for any misdemeanour of his in Parliament: But to put them out of doubt of any question of that nature that may arise among them hereafter, you shall resolue them in Our name, That We thinke our Selfe very free and able to punish any mans misdemeanours in Parliament, aswell during their sitting, as after; which We meane not to spare hereafter, vpon any occasion of any mans insolent behauiour there, that shalbe ministred vnto Vs. And if they haue already touched any of these points which Wee haue here forbidden, in any Petition of theirs which is to be sent vnto Vs, it is Our pleasure that you shall tell them, That except they reforme it before it come to Our hands, Wee will not deigne the hearing nor answering of it. And whereas Wee heare that they are desirous, that We should make this a Session of Parliament before Christmas, You may tell them, It shall be in their default if they want it: For if they will make ready betweene this and that time, some such Lawes as shall be really good for the Common-wealth, Wee will very willingly giue Our Royal assent vnto them: And so it shall thereby appeare, That if good Lawes bee not made at this time for the weale of the people, the blame shall onely and most iustly lie vpon such turbulent spirits, as shall preferre their particular ends to the weale of this Kingdome and Commonwealth. And so We bid you farewell. Giuen at Our Court at Newmarket, the third day of December,* 1621.

To Our trustie and welbeloued,
The Speaker of Our Commons
House of Parliament.

WHich Letters being publikely read in the House, they were so farre either from reforming their intended Petition, which conteined those points by Vs forbidden, or yet from going on cheerefully in propounding of good Lawes, for which they were called, and to which purpose Wee granted them in the end of Our said Letter to the Speaker, to make it a Session before Christmas, whereof Wee vnderstood them to bee very desirous, that they resolued to send the same

vnto vs together with another Petition iustifying the former, notwithstanding Our forbidding them in Our said Letter to send the former
Petition vnto Vs, as also sate euer silent thereafter, till they were
dissolued, as shall hereafter more largely be expressed.[1065]

Those petitions being sent from the Commons by a select number
of that House vnto Vs then being at *Newmarket* for Our health, the
House forbare to proceed in any businesse of importance, purposing,
as was apparantly discerned, and as the euent prooued, so to continue
vntill the returne of their Messengers with Our Answere; which wee
vnderstanding, and being desirous to haue the time better husbanded,
as was fit (the shortnesse thereof, by reason of the approach of
Christmas being respected) required Our Secretarie to deliuer a
Message vnto them for this purpose, which he did, first by word of
mouth, and after by appointment of the House set it downe in writing
in these words, viz.

> *HIs Maiestie, remembring that this House was desirous to haue a*
> *Session betweene this and Christmasse, whereupon it pleased Him to*
> *signifie vnto vs, that wee should haue contentment therein, and that*
> *there should bee a Session, if wee our selues were not in fault, taking*
> *now notice that the House forbeares to proceede with any Billes vntill*
> *the returne of the Messengers, lately sent vnto his Maiestie, hath*
> *enioyned mee to commaund the House in his Name not to lose time in*
> *their proceeding, for preparing of good Lawes in the meane while, in*
> *consideration of this so neere approach of Christmasse; And that his*
> *Maiestie hopes they will not take vpon them to make a Recesse in effect,*
> *though not in shew without his warrant.*

BVt this Message being deliuered, was so farre from working that
good effect, which Wee did most iustly expect, that contrariwise some
captious and curious heads tooke exception thereat, as tending to the
breach of their Priuiledges, by commanding them to proceede with
Bills, though We thereby, neither designed any particular Billes for
them to proceed with, nor yet forbade any other Parliamentary proceedings; And with those, and such other vndutifull straines of wit,
they spunne out the time vntill the returne of their Messengers, who
being come to *Newmarket*, presented both the Petitions vnto vs, who
well knowing beforehand the effect of the former, and then obseruing
the contents of the latter, and finding, that from both did reflect vpon
Our Person and gouernment sundry causelesse aspersions, and that
thereby Our Royall Prerogatiues were inuaded and assailed, after an

admonition to beware of medling therewith, Wee returned vnto them
Our Answere in writing, as followeth.

HIS MAIESTIES AN-
swere to the Apologetike
Petition of the House of
COMMONS,
Presented to his Maiesty by a do-
zen of the Members of that House,
by their directions.

WE*e must heere begin in the same fashion that We would haue done
if your first Petition had come to Our hands before Wee had made a
stay thereof, which is to repeate the first wordes of the late* Queene *of
famous memory, vsed by her in Answer to an insolent proposition, made
by a* Polonian *Ambassadour vnto her, That is,* Legatum expectab-
amus, Heraldum accepimus.[1066] *For We had great reason to expect
that the first Message from your House should haue beene a Message
of thanksgiuing for Our continued gracious behauiour towards Our
people since your last Recesse, not onely by our Proclamation of Grace,
wherein were conteined six or seuen and thirty Articles, all of seuerall
points of Grace to the people;[1067] but also by the labour Wee tooke for
the satisfaction of both Houses in those three Articles recommended vnto
Vs in both their names by the right Reuerend Father in God, the
Archbishop of* Canterbury, *And likewise for the good gouernement of*
Ireland *We are now in hand with at your request. But not onely haue
Wee heard no newes of all this, but contrary great complaints of the
danger of Religion within this Kingdome tacitely implying Our ill
gouernement in this point. And Wee leaue to you to iudge, whether it
be your dueties that are the Representatiue body of Our people, so to
distaste them with Our gouernement, whereas by the contrary it is your
duety with all your endeauours to kindle more and more a dutifull and
thankefull loue in the peoples hearts towards Vs for Our iust and
gracious gouernment. Now, whereas in the very beginning of this your
Apologie, you taxe Vs in faire termes of trusting vncertaine reports, and
partiall informations concerning your proceedings, Wee wish you to
remember, that We are an old and experienced King, needing no such
lessons, being in Our conscience freest of any King aliue from hearing
or trusting idle reports, which so many of your House as are neerest Vs
can beare witnesse vnto you, if you would giue as good eare to them,
as you doe to some Tribunitiall Orators amongst you. And for proofe
in this particular, Wee haue made your owne Messengers conferre your
other Petition, sent by you, with the copy thereof, which was sent Vs*

before, betweene which there is no difference at all, but that since Our receiuing the first Copie you added a conclusion vnto it, which could not come to Our hands till it was done by you, and your Messengers sent, which was all at one time. And if that Wee had had no Copie of it before hand, Wee must haue receiued your first Petition to Our great dishonour, before Wee had knowen what it conteyned, which would haue enforced Vs to haue returned you a farre worse Answere then now Wee doe. For then your Messengers had returned with nothing; but that Wee haue iudged your petition vnlawfull, and vnworthy of an Answere. For as to your Conclusion thereof, it is nothing, but Pro-testatio contraria facto.[1068] *For in the body of your Petition you vsurpe vpon Our Prerogatiue Royall, and meddle with things farre aboue your reach: And then in the conclusion*[1069] *you protest the contrary, as if a Robber would take a mans purse, and then protest hee meant not to rob him. For first, you presume to giue Vs your aduice concerning the match of Our dearest Sonne with some Protestant, We cannot say Princesse (for Wee know none of these fit for him,) and disswade Vs from his match with* Spaine, *vrging Vs to a present warre with that King: And yet in the conclusion, forsooth, ye protest ye intend not to presse vpon Our most vndoubted and regall Prerogatiue as if the Peti-tioning of Vs in matters that your selues confesse yee ought not to meddle with, were not a medling with them. And whereas yee pretend, that you were inuited to this course by the speeches of three Honourable Lords; Yet by so much as your selues repeat of their speeches, nothing can bee concluded, but that We were resolued by warre to regaine the* Palatinate, *if otherwise Wee could not attaine vnto it; and you were inuited to aduise forthwith vpon a supply for keeping the forces in the* Palatinate *from disbanding, and to foresee the meanes for the raysing and maintaining of the body of an Armie for that warre against the Spring. Now what inference can bee made vpon this, That therefore Wee must presently denounce warre against the King of* Spaine, *breake Our dearest Sonnes match, and match him to one of Our Religion, let the world iudge. The difference is no greater, then as if Wee would tell a Merchant, that Wee had great neede to borrow money from him for raysing an Armie, that thereupon it should follow, that Wee were bound to follow his aduice in the directions of the warre, and all things depending thereupon. But yet not contenting your selues with this excuse of yours, which indeed cannot hold water, yee come after to a direct contradiction to the conclusion of your former Petition, saying, That the Honour and safety of Vs and Our Posterity, and the* Patrimony *of Our Children, inuaded and possessed by their enemies, the welfare of Religion, and State of Our Kingdome are matter at any time not*

*vnfit for your deepest considerations in Parliament. To this generality
We answere with the* Logicians, *That where all things are contained,
nothing is omitted. So as this plenipotencie of yours inuests you in all
power vpon Earth, lacking nothing but the Popes to haue the keyes also
both of Heauen and Purgatory. And to this vaste generality of yours,
Wee can giue no other answer, for it will trouble all the best Lawyers
in the House to make a good Commentary vpon it: For so did the
Puritan Ministers in Scotland bring all kinde of causes within the
compasse of their iurisdiction, saying, That it was the Churches office
to iudge of slander, and there could no kinde of crime or fault bee
committed, but there was a slander in it, either against God, the King,
or their Neighbour. And by this meanes they hooked in to themselues
the cognisance of all causes, or like* Bellarmines *distinction of the Popes
power ouer all Kings,* in ordine ad Spiritualia,[1070] *whereby he giues
him all temporall iurisdiction ouer them. But to giue you a direct
answere to the matter of warre, for which you are so earnest, We
confesse We rather expected that you should haue given Vs great and
heartie thankes for the so long maintaining a setled peace in all Our
Dominions, when as all Our Neighbours about are in a miserable
combustion of Warre; but* Dulce bellum inexpertis;[1071] *and We
indeed find by experience, that a number of Our Subiects are so pam-
pered with peace, as they are desirous of change, though they know not
what. It is true that We haue euer professed, and in that minde, with
Gods grace, Wee meane to liue and die, That We will labour by all
meanes possible, either by treaty, or by force to restore Our Children
to their ancient Dignities and Inheritances: and whatsoeuer Christian
Princes or Potentates will set themselues against it, Wee will not spare
any lawfull meanes to bring Our so iust and Honourable purpose to a
good end; neither shall the Match of Our Sonne, or any other worldly
respect be preferred to this Our Resolution: For by Our credit, and
interuention with the King of* Spaine, *and the Arch-duchesse,[1072] and
her Husband now with God, Wee preserued the lower* Palatinat *one
whole yeere from any further conquering in it, which within any eight
dayes space in that time might haue easily been swallowed vp by* Spino-
laes[1073] *Armie, without any resistance; and in no better case was it
now, at Our Ambassadour, the Lord* Digbies *coming through* Heydel-
berge, *if he had not extraordinarily succoured it. But because Wee
perceiue that ye couple this warre of the* Palatinate *with the cause of
Religion, We must a little vnfold your eyes herein. The beginning of
this miserable warre, which hath set all Christendome on fire, was
not for Religion; but onely caused by our Sonne in law his hastie and
rash Resolution, following euill counsell, to take to himselfe the Crowne*

of Bohemia:[1074] *And that this is true, himselfe wrote Letters vnto Vs at that time, desiring Vs to giue assurance, both to the French King, and State of* Venice, *that his accepting of the Crowne of* Bohemia *had no reference to the cause of Religion, but onely by reason of his right by Election (as hee called it:) And we would be sorrie that that aspersion should come vpon Our Religion, as to make it a good pretext for dethroning of Kings, and vsurping their Crownes. And Wee would bee loath that Our people here should be taught that doctrine: No, let vs not so farre wrong the Iesuites, as to rob them of their sweet Positions and practise in that point. And vpon the other part, We assure Our selfe so farre of your charitable thoughts of Vs, that We would neuer haue constantly denyed Our Sonne in law, both the title and assistance in that point, if Wee had beene well perswaded of the iustice of his quarrell. But to conclude this point, This vniust vsurpation of the Crownes of* Bohemia *and* Hungaria *from the Emperour, hath giuen the Pope, and all that partie, too faire a ground, and opened them too wide a gate for the curbing and oppressing of many thousands of Our Religion, in diuers parts of Christendome. And whereas yee excuse your touching vpon the King of* Spaine *vpon the occasion of the incidents by you repeated in that place, and yet affirme that it is without any touch to his honor, We cannot wonder ynough, that ye are so forgetfull, both of your words and writs. For in your former Petition ye plainely affirme, that hee affects the Temporall Monarchie of the whole earth, then which there can be no more malice vttered against any great King, to make all other Princes and Potentates, both enuie and hate him. But, if ye list, it may be easily tryed, whether that speech touched him in honour or not, if We shall aske him the question, whether hee meanes to assume to himselfe that title or no; For euery King can best iudge of his owne honour. Wee omit the particular eiaculations of some foule mouthed Orators in your House, against the honour of his Crowne and State. And touching your excuse of not determining any thing concerning the Match of Our dearest Sonne, but onely to tell your opinions, and lay it downe at Our feet; First, We desire to know how you could haue presumed to determine in that point, without committing of high Treason. And next, you cannot deny, but your talking of his Match after that manner was a direct breach of Our commandement & Declaration out of Our own mouth, at the first sitting downe of this Parliament: where We plainely professed, that We were in treatie of his Match with* Spaine, *and wished you to haue that confidence in Our Religion and Wisedome, that We would so manage it, as our Religion should receiue no preiudice by it. And the same We now repeat vnto you, professing, that We are so farre ingaged in that Match, as*

We cannot in honour goe backe, except the King of Spaine *performe not such things as We expect at his hands. And therefore We are sorrie, that ye should shew to haue so great distrust in Vs, or to conceiue that We should be cold in our Religion: Otherwise We cannot imagine how Our former publike Declaration should not haue stopped your mouthes in this point. And as to your request, that We would now receiue your former Petition, We wonder what could make you presume that Wee would now receiue it; whereas in Our former Letter We plainely declared the contrarie vnto you; and therefore Wee haue iustly reiected that suit of yours: For what haue you left vnattempted in the highest points of Soueraigntie in that Petition of yours, except the striking of Coine; For it containes the violation of Leagues, the particular way how to gouerne a warre, and the Marriage of Our dearest Sonne, both negatiue with* Spaine, *nay with any other Popish Princesse; and also affirmatiue, as to the matching with one of Our Religion, which Wee confesse is a straine beyond any prouidence or wisedome God hath giuen Vs, as things now stand. These are vnfit things to be handled in Parliament, except your King should require it of you; For who can haue wisedome to iudge of things of that nature, but such as are daily acquainted with the particulars of Treaties, and of the variable or fixed connexion of affaires of State, together with the knowledge of the secret wayes, ends, and intentions of Princes in their seuerall negotiations; otherwise a small mistaking in matters of this nature, may produce more effects then can be imagined: And therefore,* Ne sutor vltra crepidam.[1075] *And besides, the intermedling in Parliament with matters of Peace or Warre, and Marriage of Our dearest Sonne, would be such a diminution to Vs and to Our Crowne in forreine Countreys, as would make any Prince neglect to treat with Vs, either in matters of Peace or Marriage, except they might be assured by the assent of Parliament. And so it prooued long agoe with a King of* France, *who vpon a tricke procuring his States to dissent from some treaty, which before he had made, was after refused treating with by other Princes, to his great reproach, vnlesse hee would first procure the assent of the three Estates to their proposition. And will you cast your eyes vpon the late times, you shall finde, that the late Queene of famous memorie was humbly petitioned by a Parliament to be pleased to Marrie; But her answere was, That shee liked their Petition well, because it was simple, not limiting her to place or person, as not befitting her liking to their fancies; and if they had done otherwise, shee would haue thought it a high presumption in them. Iudge then what Wee may doe in such a case, hauing made Our publique Declaration alreadie, as Wee said before, directly contrary to that which you haue now petitioned. Now to those*

points in your Petition, whereof you desire an answere, as properly
belonging to a Parliament; The first and greatest point is that of Religion, concerning which at this time Wee can giue you no other answere
then in the generall, which is, That you may rest secure, that Wee will
neuer be wearie to doe all Wee can for the propagation of Our Religion,
and repressing of Poperie; but the maner and forme you must remit to
Our care and prouidence, who can best consider of times and seasons,
not by vndertaking a publique warre of Religion through all the world
at once, which how hard and dangerous a taske it would prooue, you
may iudge. But this puts vs in mind, how all the world complained
the last yeere of plentie of Corne, and God hath sent vs a cooling card
this yeere for that heat; And so We pray God, that this desire amongst
you of kindling warres, shewing your wearinesse of Peace and Plentie,
may not make God permit vs to fall in the miseries of both. But as
Wee alreadie said, Our care of Religion must be such, as on the one
part We must not by the hote prosecution of Our Recusants at home
irritate forreine Princes of contrary Religion, and teach them the way
to plague the Protestants in their Dominions, whom with Wee daily
intercede, and at this time principally, for ease to them of Our profession
that liue vnder them; yet vpon the other part, We neuer meane to spare
from due and seuere punishment any Papist that will grow insolent for
liuing vnder Our so milde Gouernment. And you may also be assured,
We will leaue no care vntaken, as well for the good education of the
youth at home, especially the children of Papists, as also for preseruing
at all times hereafter the youth that are, or shall be abroad, from being
bred in dangerous places, and so poisoned in Popish Seminaries. And
as in this point, namely concerning the good education of the Popish
youth at home, We haue alreadie giuen some good proofe, both in this
Kingdome and in Ireland: So will We be well pleased to passe any
good Lawes that shall be made, either now, or at any time hereafter
to this purpose. And as to your request, of making this a Session, and
granting a generall Pardon, it shall be in your defaults if Wee make
not this a Session before Christmas, as in Our former Letter We notified
vnto you. But for the Pardon, yee craue such particulars in it as Wee
must be well aduised vpon, lest otherwise Wee giue you backe the double
or triple of that Wee are to receiue by your entire Subsidie without
Fifteens. But the ordinarie course Wee hold fittest to bee vsed still in
this case, which is, that Wee should of Our free grace send you downe
a Pardon from the Higher House, containing such points as We shall
thinke fittest, wherein We hope ye shall receiue good satisfaction. But
We cannot omit to shew you how strange We thinke it, that ye should
make so bad and vniust a Commentarie vpon some words of Our

former Letter, as if We meant to restraine you thereby of your ancient priuiledges and liberties in Parliament. Truly a scholler would bee ashamed so to misplace and misiudge any sentences in another mans booke. For whereas in the fore-end of Our former Letter We discharge you to meddle with matters of gouernment, or mysteries of State, namely matters of Warre or Peace, or Our dearest Sonnes Match with Spaine; *by which particular denominations We interpret and restraine Our former words; and then after We forbid you to meddle with such things as haue their ordinarie course in Courts of Justice: Yee couple together those two distinct sentences, and plainly leaue out these words,* of mysteries of State; *So as yee erre* a bene diuisis ad male coniuncta.[1076] *For of the former part, concerning mysteries of State, Wee plainelie restrained Our meaning to the particulars that were after mentioned: and in the latter We confesse Wee meant it by* Sir Edward Cokes[1077] *foolish businesse, because these heades he is accused of were before your meeting presented vnto Vs, and We had setled a legall course of proceeding therin. And therefore it had well become him, especiallie being Our Seruant, and one of Our Councell, if he had had any thing against it, to haue complained vnto Vs, which he neuer did, though hee was ordinarilie at Our Court, since that time, and neuer had accesse refused vnto him. And although We cannot allow of the stile, calling it,* Your ancient and vndoubted right and inheritance, *but could rather haue wished, that ye had said that your priuiledges were deriued from the grace and permission of Our Ancestours and Vs; (For most of them grow from precedents, which shewes rather a toleration then inheritance.) Yet We are pleased to giue you Our Royall assurance, That as long as you shall continue to containe your selues within the limits of your dutie and respect to Vs (as Wee assure Our selfe you will doe) Wee will bee as carefull to maintaine and preserue your lawfull liberties and priuiledges as euer any Our Predecessours were, nay as to preserue Our owne Royall Prerogatiue. So as your House shall onelie haue neede to beware to trench vpon the Prerogatiue of the Crowne, which would enforce Vs, or any iust King to retrench them of their priuiledges, that would pare his Prerogatiue and flowers of the Crowne. But of this We hope there shall neuer be cause giuen. To conclude then, since Wee haue now so largely expressed the sinceritie of Our meaning vnto you, We require you to goe on cheerfullie, and to vse all conuenient diligence for preparing such good Lawes for Vs to passe at this time, as the people may see the care, that both Wee and you haue for the good gouernement of the Kingdome; ending as We did in Our former Letter; If there be not a happie Session made at this time, it shall bee in your default. And aboue all, beware by your waywardnesse at this time, to giue Our*

Childrens Aduersaries cause to insult vpon them, vpon the rumour that *shall be spred abroad of a distraction betweene Vs and Our people,* *wherof ye are the representatiue bodie.* At Our Court at Newmarket the 11. day of December, 1621.

THis Answere being giuen at *Newmarket*, on Tuesday, the eleuenth of *December*, and returned to the house on Friday, the fourteenth of that moneth, some carping wits that were more inclinable to peruert and wrest Our words vnto a sence contrary to our meaning, then to doe any good office between Vs and Our people, began to take exception at some words concerning their priuiledges toward the end of Our sayd Answere, that thereby their Priuiledges were denied and infringed; And by their example others of more moderate and better temper were drawn into some doubts and iealousies, which occasioned much discontentment in the House, which comming to Our eares, and being willing to omit nothing on Our part, that might assure the Commons that Wee meant nothing lesse then to violate their Priuiledges, for explanation of Our true intent in the former, We wrote Our Letters directed to Our Secretary, which followe in these words.

> RIght trusty and Welbeloued Councellour, Wee greet you well. Wee are
> sorrie to heare, that, notwithstanding Our reiterated Messages to Our
> House of Commons, for going on in their businesses in regard of the
> shortnesse of time, betwixt this and Christmas, and of their owne earnest
> desire, that Wee should now conclude a Session, by making of good
> and profitable Lawes, they continue to loose time; And now of late,
> vpon Our gracious Answer sent vnto them, haue taken occasion to make
> more delay, in appointing a Committee to morrow, to consider vpon
> the points of Our Answer; and especially concerning that point in it
> which maketh mention of their priuiledges. Our pleasure therefore is,
> that you shall in Our name tell them, that We are so loath to haue
> time mis-spent, which is so pretious a thing, in the well vsing whereof
> Our people may receiue so great a benefit, as We are thus farre contented
> to discend from Our Royall dignity, by explaining at this time Our
> meaning in Our sayd Answer, touching that point, That all Our good
> Subjects[1078] in that House, that intend nothing but Our Honour, and
> the weale of the Common-wealth, may cleerely see Our intention.
> Whereas in Our sayd Answere We told them, that Wee could not allow
> of the stile, calling it their ancient and vndoubted right and inheritance;
> but could rather haue wished, that they had sayd their priuiledges were
> deriued from the grace and permission of Our Ancestors and Vs: (for

262

most of them grow from presidents, which shewes rather a toleration then inheritance) the plaine truth is, That Wee cannot with patience endure Our Subiects to vse such Antimonarchicall words to Vs concerning their Liberties, except they had subioyned, that they were granted vnto them by the grace and fauour of Our Predecessours. But as for Our intention herein, God knowes Wee neuer meant to deny them any lawfull Priuiledges that euer that House enioyed in Our Predecessours times, as We expected Our said Answere should haue sufficiently cleered them; neither in Justice what euer they haue vndoubted right vnto; nor in Grace what euer Our Predecessours or We haue graciously permitted vnto them: And therefore We made that distinction of the most part; *For whatsoeuer Priuiledges or Liberties they enioy by any Law or Statue, shall be euer inuiolably preserued by Vs; And Wee hope Our Posteritie will imitate Our footsteps therein. And whatsoeuer Priuiledges they enioy by long Custome, and vncontrolled and lawfull Presidents, Wee will likewise be as carefull to preserue them, and transmit the care thereof to Our Posteritie; neither was it any way in Our minde to thinke of any particular point wherein Wee meant to disallow of their Liberties. So as in Iustice We confesse Our selues to be bound to maintaine them in their rights; and in Grace We are rather minded to encrease, then infringe any of them, if they shall so deserue at Our hands. To end therefore as Wee began, let them goe on cheerefully in their businesses, reiecting the curious wrangling of Lawyers upon words and syllables; otherwise (which God forbid) the world shall see how often and how earnestly Wee haue pressed them to goe on, according to their calling, with those things that are fit to be done for the weale of Our Crowne and Kingdome; And how many curious shifts haue beene from time to time maliciously found out, to frustrate Vs of Our good purpose, and hinder them from the performance of that Seruice, which they ought to Vs and to Our whole Kingdome; whereof when the Countrey shall come to be truely enformed, they will giue the Authours thereof little thankes.*

Giuen at Our Court at Royston, the sixteenth day of December, 1621.

To Our right trustie and welbeloued Councellor, Sir *George Caluert*, Knight, one of Our principall Secretaries.

AND finding, that notwithstanding all this care taken by Vs for their satisfaction, & that Our thrice reiterated pressing them to husband well the shortnesse of time, in doing good businesse fit for a Parliament, Wee were so farre from preuailing with them, as to all those three admonitions of Ours, which are here related, First, by Our message deliuered by Our Secretary; Next, by Our conclusion of Our Answere to their Petition; And lastly, by the conclusion of Our explanation sent to Our Secretarie, We neither got answere, nor obedience; Yet the continuall care Wee had that this meeting should not dissolue without some fruit for the publike good of Our Subiects, made Vs addresse another Letter to the Speaker in these words.

MAster Speaker, *Whereas at the humble suit of Our house of Commons Wee condescended to make this meeting a Session before Christmas, to which purpose We gaue them vntill Saturday next, in case they would seriously applie themselues to that end; & likewise since, out of Our Grace, and to take away al mistakings, by Our Letters directed to Our Secretarie, Wee were pleased so fully and clearely to explane Our selues in the point of maintaining all lawfull Priuiledges to Our said House, which since Wee cannot heare hath had the wished effect, in making them spend this short time in preparing things most necessary for a Session, Wee haue thought good once more clearely by this to impart Our minde vnto them; which is, that in respect of the expectation after this so long a meeting in Parliament, as also that the generalitie, for the most part, rather iudge things by the outward effects then enter into the causes of them, Wee haue an earnest desire to make this a Session, to the end that our good and louing Subiects may haue some taste, aswell of Our Grace and goodnesse towards them by our free Pardon, and good Lawes to bee passed, as they haue had, both by the great, and vnusuall examples of Iustice since this meeting, and the so many eases and comforts giuen vnto them by Proclamation: And therfore calling to minde, that the passing of the Subsidie, an Acte for continuance of Statutes, and the Pardon, are the three most pressing businesses to be effected before the end of the Session, Wee wish them, that, as Wee haue giuen order for the Pardon to goe on with all expedition, so they presently goe in hand with the Acte for continuance of Statutes. As for the Subsidie, though time presseth much, yet if they finde it may not now conueniently be done, we will not make that any way an impediment to the good which Wee desire our people should feele by making this a Session. Thus much We thought good to giue them to vnderstand, and withall to assure them, that if they shall not applie themselues instantly to prepare the aforesaid things for Our Royall Assent against Saturday next, Wee will without expecting any further answere from them, construe by their slackenesse, that they desire not a Session; and in such case We must giue a larger time for their returning homeward, to such of both Houses as are to goe into their Countreys to keepe hospitalitie among their neighbours in this time of Recesse.*

Giuen at our Court at *Theobalds*, the 17. day of *December*, 1621.
To Our trustie and welbeloued, Sir *Thomas Richardson*,
Knight, Speaker of Our Commons House of Parliament.

ANd hauing at last (as Wee hoped) by these meanes scattered and
dispersed those mistes and vapours, which had beene thus raised
about their Priuiledges, the House hauing resolued on Tuesday, the
eighteenth of *December*, to returne thankes vnto Vs, and therewith an
excuse for not making a Session, and passing Bills, both conteined
in a Petition in writing, and dispatched the same vnto Vs, being by
that time come to *Theobalds*, the tenour whereof followeth.

May it please your most Excellent MAIESTIE.

*We your most loyall and humble Subiects, the Knights, Citizens and
Burgesses of your Commons House of Parliament, hauing this Morning,
to our great comfort, heard your Maiesties Letter sent to our Speaker,
full of Grace and Goodnesse to vs and all your people, haue thought
it our duetie foorthwith, to returne our most humble and heartie thankes
to your Sacred Maiestie, for so Royall a fauour vouchsafed vnto vs;
And we doe humbly beseech your Maiestie to be truely informed from
vs, that although we haue beene very desirous in our duetie to your
Maiestie, who called vs to this seruice, and to our Countrey for whom
we serue, to haue some good Lawes now to haue beene passed; and that
there might haue beene a Session before Christmasse, to which your
Maiestie vpon our humble Petition, was heretofore Graciously pleased
to giue way: yet entring now into a serious consideration of the nature
of those things, which must of necessitie be prepared for the finishing
of a Session, and the strait of time whereunto we are driuen, by some
vnhappy diuersions which haue fallen vpon vs, to our great griefe, wee
are enforced once againe to fly to your Maiesties Grace and fauour,
humbly submitting our selues to your Royall wisedome, what time will
be fittest for our departure, and for our reaccesse, to perfect those begin-
nings which are in preparation with vs; which time by Gods grace we
resolue to spend with that diligence and care, as shall giue good satisfaction to your Maiestie, to our Countrey, and to our owne consciences,
that we shall make good vse thereof.*

This Wee accepted graciously, and returned them an answere by
their owne Messengers in these words.

*That we were sorrie this could not bee made a Session, according to
their owne desire expressed in their late Petition preferred vnto Vs, to
which Wee had most willingly assented; that they knew there was no*

fault in Vs, who obseruing the needlesse impediments, vpon which they tooke occasion to stay their proceedings, had often admonished them not to lose time; first, by Secretary Caluert, *and afterwards by three sundry Letters and Answers. But since they conceiued the straitnesse of time (which they had drawne vpon themselues) was such, that it would permit nothing to bee done at this time, Wee had giuen order to adiourne the Parliament till the eighth of February next, which was the first day Wee had formerly appointed for Our meeting together.*

Wee were likewise pleased to say, that Wee could not omit to tell them, that we expected other thankes from them, then they had sent Vs at this time, namely for Our gracious promises to maintaine their Priuiledges, as Our owne Soueraigne Prerogatiue: First contained in our Answere to their Petition, and afterwards as clearely explaned and enlarged by Our next Letter to Secretarie Caluert, *as Our wits, for their safetie, satisfaction and aduantage, could possibly deuise; but of this We heard nothing, being slipt by, and wholly omitted by them.*

WHich message was accordingly deliuered the next morning in the House of Commons. But while We were busied at *Theobalds* in receiuing their Petition, and returning this answere agreeable to Our Grace and good intention towards them, these mutinous and discontented spirits, neuer giuing ouer their wicked purpose, began anew to stirre the coles of discontentment amongst them; and making them beleeue, that their Priuiledges were yet in danger (vpon what ground God knowes, Wee cannot imagine nor guesse) procured a Committee to be made for taking their Liberties into consideration; where a Protestation[1079] was made, to whom Wee know not, concerning their Priuiledges, which they pretended to bee violated by Our Letters and messages, and thereupon in an vnseasonable houre, being sixe of the clocke at night, and a very thinne House, scarcely comming to the third part of the full number, contrary to their owne custome in all matters of weight, they conclude and enter a Protestation for their Liberties, in such ambiguous and generall words, as might serue for future times to inuade most of those Rights and Prerogatiues annexed to Our Imperiall Crowne, as bee the very markes and Characters of Monarchie and Soueronomie, and whereof Wee found Our Crowne vndoubtedly possessed. For founding the claime of their Priuiledges vpon the words of Our Writt for assembling a Parliament, the contriuers of that Protestation craftily mentioned some words, *viz. Super arduis Regni negotijs*,[1080] but of purpose left out *quibusdam*,[1081] which restraines that generalitie to such particular Cases, as Wee are to consult with them vpon. And the very vncontrolled Custome of all times doeth manifestly prooue, that the King Himselfe, or His Chancellour in his name, doeth at the very beginning of the Parliament declare vnto them what things these *quibusdam* are, wherein hee craueth their aduice and assistance; And vse is euer the best interpreter of words in a case of this nature: Vpon which vnduetifull Protestation Wee were iustly occasioned to publish Our Pleasure for dissolution of the Parliament, as appeares by Our Proclamation.

Notes

1. This book was written in the summer or early autumn of 1598. The first draft, in the king's own hand, is B. L. Royal MS 18. B. xv. It is written in Middle Scots. In 1599 seven copies of an Anglicised version of the work were printed for private distribution. The outspoken Scottish cleric Andrew Melville read the book and found much in it which he disliked. At the Synod of Fife in September 1599 other ministers of the Kirk were also sharply critical of it. The first generally available edition was published at Edinburgh in March 1603. It included a new section 'To the Reader', replying to some of the criticisms which had been mounted against the book. A copy of this Edinburgh edition was sent to London not long before 24 March, the day on which Elizabeth I died. A few days later the book was printed in London and several further printings appeared during the next two or three weeks (see STC 14350–4). In unpublished work, Dr Peter Blayney has shown that at least nine versions came out in London in 1603, perhaps totalling some 12,000 copies. *Basilicon Doron* was reprinted once more in the *Workes* of 1616.

   The standard modern edition of the book is Craigie 1944–50. The first volume contains the texts of the manuscript and of the Edinburgh editions of 1599 and 1603. The second volume includes an introduction, notes and various supplementary materials. Useful information on the publishing history of *Basilicon Doron* is in Craigie's edition, vol. 2, 1–38, and in Wormald 1991 especially at 50–1.

   The 1603 text contains a substantial number of additions to the 1599 version and occasionally omits material which the latter includes. The text of 1599 is close to the manuscript though there are a few differences. A discussion of the text of the manuscript and of the Edinburgh editions of 1599 and 1603 is in Craigie's edition, vol. 2, 88–116; a table of textual variants between the manuscript and the 1599 edition is in the same volume, Appendix B, 280–2; Appendix C, 283–303, records variants between the Edinburgh editions of 1599 and 1603. Craigie's Appendix D, 303–4, contains an extract from MS Bodley 166, fol. 7; Craigie states that this section, which is written in English but begins 'Candido Lectori', is a 'supplement to the Preface of *Basilicon Doron*' (303), and asserts that there 'seems . . . no reason to doubt that the passage was part of the Preface as originally composed, but for some reason was never printed' (304). The section has not been included in this edition since it does not, in fact, belong to *Basilicon Doron* but to the Latin version of James' *A Premonition to all Most Mightie Monarches* of 1609; it is printed (in Latin translation) in the king's *Opera* (STC 14346), 1619, 349.

The present text of *Basilicon Doron* is based on that in the *Workes* of 1616 (reissue of 1620; STC 14345), which was itself copied (with a few errors and some corrections) either from the 1603 Edinburgh edition or from one of its London derivatives. The notes occasionally record variants in earlier editions. MS indicates the manuscript (B. L. Royal MS 18. B. xv), 1599 the edition of 1599 (STC 14348), 1603 the Edinburgh edition of 1603 (STC 14349), and 1616 the version in the *Workes* (reissue of 1620; STC 14345).]

2. [*THE DEDICATION* . . . a perfite King indeede. This passage is from 1599; a version of it is in MS, but it was omitted in 1603, 1616]

3. [*THE ARGVMENT* . . . your mightie King Diuine. This passage is omitted in MS, but is printed in 1599, 1603, 1616. The poem may not be by James]

4. [instructions to   1603, 1616
   the institution of   MS, 1599]

5. [labour]

6. [honour]

7. [Treatise   1603, 1616
   haill booke   MS
   whole booke   1599]

8. [never less alone than when he was alone: cf. Cicero, *De Officiis*, III, i, 1]

9. [contrary   1616
   contrair   1599
   contrare   1603]

10. [This preface 'To the Reader' occurs only in 1603, 1616, and their derivatives]

11. Luk. 12. [Luke 12: 2–3]
12. [sucke   1616
    suckes   1603]
13. [trew   editor
    trwe   1616
    true   1603]
14. [let him be unto thee as an heathen man and a publican: Matthew 18: 17. These words were commonly seen as the biblical basis of the ecclesiastical censure of excommunication]
15. [That the loue . . . thinke of it: there are quotation marks in the margin here]
16. [In 1 Kings 2: 5–6 David asks that after his death his son Solomon take revenge against Joab]
17. [*hes*   1603, 1616]
18. [as many opinions as there are heads]
19. [there is no God; Psalms 14: 1]
20. [the fool hath said in his heart]
21. [The fool hath said]
22. The trew ground of good gouernment.
23. Psal. 127. 1.
24. 1. Cor. 3. 6.
25. Double bond of a Prince to God.
26. The greatnesse of the fault of a Prince.
27. The trew glorie of Kings.
28. Prou. 9. 10.
29. The meanes to know God.
30. Iohn 5. 39.
31. 2. Tim. 3. 16, 17.
32. Deut. 17.
33. Rom. 10. 17.
34. Wherein chiefely the whole Scripture consisteth.
35. Two degrees of the seruice of God.
36. A regardable paterne.
37. Religion.
38. The methode of Scripture.
39. Of the Law.
40. [reward]
41. [punishment]
42. Of Grace.
43. Vse of the Law.
44. Vse of the Gospel.
45. How to read the Scripture.

46. Tit. 3. 9.
47. Faith the nourisher of Religion.
48. Philip. 1. 29. [Romans 5: 15]
49. Prayer, and whence to learne the best forme therof.
50. Seuerall exercise of prayer.
51. What rule or regard to be vsed in prayer.
52. What to craue of God.
53. [according to circumstance]
54. Rom. 14. 23.
55. How to interpret the issue of prayer.
56. Luke 18 [1603; this reference is omitted in 1616]
57. Conscience the conseruer of Religion.
58. The inuentarie of our life.
59. Reu. 7. 14.
60. The diseases of conscience.
61. 1 Tim. 4. 2.
62. [2 Samuel 12: 1–13]
63. Preseruatiue against leprosie of conscience.
64. [self-love]
65. 1 Cor. 11. 31.
66. Last account.
67. Horat. lib. 1. Epist. [Believe that every day that has dawned is your last; Horace, *Epistles*, I, iv, 13]
68. Trew fortitude.
69. Foolish vse of oathes.
70. Against superstition.
71. Difference of internall and externall things.
72. Account of things externall.
73. Conclusion.
74. Luke 17. 10. [1599
    Luke 10. 17.   1603 and 1616]
    [we are unprofitable servants]
75. The Office of a King.
76. *Plato in Polit.*
77. Isocr. in Sym.
78. *Plato in Polit.*
79. *Claudian in 4. cons. Hon.* [Claudian, *Panegyricus de Quarto Consulatu Honorii Augusti* lines 299–301]
    [The world arranges itself according to the king's example, nor can decrees influence people's minds as much as their ruler's life]
80. Difference of a King and a Tyran.
81. [opposites placed next to each other become more apparent]

82. *Plato in Polit.*
83. *Arist.* 5. *Polit.*
84. *Xen.* 8. *Cyr.*
85. *Cic. lib.* 5. *de Rep.*
86. [by lawful or unlawful means]
87. *Arist.* 5. *Polit. Tacit.* 4. *hist.*
88. The issue and rewards of a good King.
89. *Cic.* 6. *de Rep.*
90. The issue of Tyrans,
91. *Arist.* 5. *Polit.*
92. *Isocr. in Sym.*
93. Anent the making of Lawes.
94. [from evil customs good laws are born]
95. The authoritie and trew vse of Parliaments.
96. *L.* 12. *Tab.*
97. *Cic.* 3 *de leg. pro D. s. & pro Sest.*
98. Anent the execution of Lawes.
99. A iust seueritie to be vsed at the first.
100. [the (first) five years of the reign of Nero, when he ruled well]
101. *Sen. de cl.* [Would that I had not learned to write: Seneca *De Clementia*, II, i, 2; said by Nero when he was first asked to sign a warrant for the execution of some criminals]
102. *Ar.* 7. *pol.*
103. [on sufferance]
104. *Plato* 2. *&* 10 *de Repub.*
105. *Cic. ad Q. fr.*
106. A good mixture.
107. *Plato in Pol. &* 9. *de L. Sal. orat. ad Cæsar.*
108. A deare president.
109. Crimes vnpardonable.
110. Treason against the Prince his person, or authoritie.
111. Stayning of the blood.
112. Exod. 20. 12.
113. *Plat.* 4. *de Legib.*
114. Of oppression.
115. *Arist.* 5. *polit. Isocr. de reg. Cic. in Of. & ad Q fr.*
116. The trew glorie of Kings.
117. [James V]
118. A memorable and worthie patterne.
119. [mine and thine]
120. Deut. 1.
121. *Plat. in polit. Cic. ad Q. frat. Arist.* 1. *Ret. Plat. in Is.*

122. Of the Hie-lands.
123. Of the Borders.
124. A necessarie point in a good gouernment.
125. *Plato in polit.*
126. A consideration of the three estates.
127. The diseases of the church.
128. [Revelation 2: 5]
129. The occasion of the Tribunat of some Puritanes.
130. [Mary of Guise, 1515–60]
131. Such were the Demagogi at Athens.
132. [Tribunes of the people]
133. Their formes in the State.
134. Their razing the ground of the princely rule.
135. Their pretence of paritie.
136. An euill sort of seed-men in the State.
137. *Xantippe.*
138. Preseruatiue against such poison.
139. [An act passed by the Scottish parliament in 1587. It transferred ecclesiastical property to the crown and was intended to make episcopacy on the English model impossible in Scotland]
140. Parity incompatible with a Monarchie.
141. Generall aduice in behalfe of the Church.
142. Of the Nobiltie and their formes.
143. [in their common: indebted to them]
144. Remedie of such euils.
145. *Arist. 5. Polit.*
146. *Zeno in Cyr. Iso. in Eu. Cic. ad Q. fra.*
147. [James V's]
148. *Plat. in 1. Al. in pol. & 5. de l. Arist. 2. oecon.*
149. *Zeno in Cyr.*
150. Of Shirefdomes and Regalities.
151. *Ar. 2. pol.*
152. Laudable custome of England.
153. The third estate.
154. The formes of Merchants.
155. *Pl. 2. de Rep. 8. & 11. de leg.*
156. Aduice anent the coyne.
157. Of craftsmen.
158. *Plat. 11. de leg.*
159. A good policie of England.
160. *Plat. 9. de leg.*
161. A generall fault in the people.

162. *Sal. in Iug.*
163. *Arist.* 5. *Pol. Isoc. in paneg.*
164. Hor. de art. poet. [He has won all the applause who has combined the useful with the pleasurable; Horace *De arte Poetica* 343]
165. *Plat. in pol. & Min.*
166. *Tacit.* 7. *an. Mart.*
167. Protection from forraine iniuries.
168. *Xeno.* 8. *Cyr. Arist.* 5. *pol. Polib.* 6.
169. *Dion. Hal. de Romul.*
170. What formes to be vsed with other Princes.
171. *Isoc. in Plat. & Parag.*
172. *Arist. ad A. Varr.* 11. *de V.P.R.*
173. *Cic.* 2. *Of. Liu. lib.* 4.
174. *Liu. lib.* 1. *Cic. eod.*
175. Of warre.
176. *Prop.* 4. *Eleg. Lucan.* 7.
177. *Varro* 11. *de V.*P.R.
178. 1. *Sam.* 31.
179. *Deut.* 18.
180. [Jeremiah 27: 9]
181. *Plutar. in Sert. & Ant.*
182. Luke 14.
183. *Thuc.* 2. *Sal. in Iug.*
184. [The sinew of war]
185. *Cic. pro l. Man. Demost. olyn.* 2. *Liu. li.* 30.
186. *Veget.* 1.
187. *Caes.* 1. & 3. *de bel. ciuili.*
188. *Proh. in Thras.*
189. *Caes.* 1. *de bello ciu.*
190. *Liu. l.* 7. *Xen.* 1. & 5. *Cyr. & de discipl. mi.*
191. *Xen. in Ages.*
192. *Pol. l.* 5.
193. *Xen.* 1. *Cyr. Thuc.* 5.
194. *Isoc. ad Phil. Pla.* 9. *de leg. Liu. l.* 22. & 31. *Tac.* 2. *his. Plut. de fort.*
195. Of Peace.
196. *Isocr. in Arch.*
197. *Polib.* 3. *Cic.* 1. *Of. &* 7. *Phil. Tac.* 4. *his.*
198. A Kings life must be exemplare.
199. *Pl. in pol. &* 4. *de leg.*
200. *Plat. in Theæ. & Euth.*
201. *Arist.* 1. *Eth.*
202. *Cic. in Offic.* [For the whole merit of virtue lies in action: Cicero, *De Officiis*, I, vi, 19]

203. Of the Court.
204. Psal. 101.
205. *Cic. ad Q. frat.*
206. *Plat. 5. de Leg.*
207. [a second nature]
208. *Arist. 2. oecon.*
209. *Ouid. 5. de Trist.* [For it is more disgraceful to throw out than not to receive a guest: Ovid, *Tristia*, V, 6, 13]
210. Of the choise of seruants.
211. *Arist. 1. & 5. polit.*
212. [(relying) on the honesty (or faithfulness) of their parents]
213. [the soul does not come from transmission; i.e. the individual's soul comes not from his or her parents but from God]
214. *Cic. ad Q. frat.*
215. Witnesse the experience of the late house of *Gowrie*. [Both the Earl of Gowrie and his brother were involved in the alleged Gowrie Plot of 5 August 1600 against James. This comment is (of course) omitted in MS, 1599]
216. *Plat. 6. de Leg. Arist. 2. oecon. & 1. pol.*
217. *Plat. 6. de leg. Isocr. in pan. Arist. 5. pol.*
218. *Dem. 2. ph.*
219. *Plat. 7. de Rep. 3. et 12. de Leg. Arist. 5. et 6. polit.*
220. Psal. 101.
221. A transmission of hereditarie kindnes.
222. [The goods of fortune]
223. A domesticke and neere example.
224. [The Ruthven Raid of 1582]
225. *Arist. 2. Pol.*
226. [the common parent]
227. Of the offices of the Crowne.
228. *Plat. de repub. Cic. ad Q. frat. Isoc. in Panath. ad Nic. & de pace.*
229. *Thuc. 6. Plutar. in pol.*
230. *Plat. in Phedr. & Menex. Arist. 5 pol. Isoc. in Sym. Tacit. 3. hist. Curt. 8.*
231. Of publicke receiuers.
232. A speciall principle in policie.
233. *Arist. 5. pol. Cic. ad Q. frat.*
234. *Plat. in 1. Al. in pol. & 5. de legib. Arist. 2. oecon.*
235. Gouernment of the Court.
236. *Isocr. in Areop.*
237. *Idem in Panath.*
238. *Arist. 2. Pol.*

239. *Tacit.* 1. *hist.*
240. *Val. lib.* 2. *Curt.* 4.
241. *Demost.* 8 *phil. Sal. in Cat. Liu.* 22.
242. *Tacit. eod. &* 1. *An.*
243. [reward]
244. [punishment]
245. The ground-stone of good gouernment.
246. *Ar.* 5. *polit. Tacit. in Ag. Dion li.* 52. *Xeno. in Ages. Isoc. in Sym. et ad Ph.*
247. *Id. de permutat.*
248. *Cic. ad Q. frat.*
249. 1. King. 10.
250. Of Mariage.
251. Gen. 2. 23.
252. [*Heuah*; i.e. Eve]
253. Preparation to mariage.
254. 1. Cor. 6. 10.
255. Reuel. 22. 15.
256. The dangerous effects of lust.
257. [James V]
258. A domesticke example.
259. 1. Cor. 6. 19.
260. Mariage ordained for three causes.
261. *Arist.* 7 *pol.*
262. *Id. eod.*
263. Accessory causes of mariage.
264. *AEg. Ro.* 2. *de reg. pr.*
265. Math. 6. 33 [1599
     Math. 13   1603
     Matth. 13   1616]
     [and all these things shall be added unto you]
266. A special caution in mariage.
267. For keeping the blood pure.
268. *Pla.* 5. *de Rep. Cic.* 2. *de Diu. Arist. de gen. An.*
269. *Lucr.* 4.
270. *Pl.* 11. *de leg. Is. in Sym.*
271. *Cic.* 2. *de leg.*
272. [James V]
273. *Arist.* 8. *AEth. &* 1. *Pol. Xen. & Arist. in oeco.*
274. *Arist.* 1. *rhet. Plu. in Menon. AEgid. R. de reg. pr. Plu.* 5. *de Rep. &* 7. *de leg.*
275. A Kings behauiour towards his children

276. *Plu. in Thes.* 4 & 5. *de Rep.* & 6 & 7. *de l. Arist.* 7. *pol.*
277. A caution foreshewing future diuision.
278. *Polid.* 1. [Brutus was the mythical founder of Britain. He was said to have divided the island amongst his three sons, giving the south to Locrine, the north to Albanact, and Wales to Camber]
279. Crownes come not in commerce.
280. *Plu. in Pol. Cic. ad Q. frat.*
281. [justice, prudence, temperance and fortitude]
282. The right vse of temperance.
283. *Arist.* 5. *pol. Pol.* 6. *Cic.* 1. *off.* 2. *de inuen.* & *in Par.*
284. [taste and touch]
285. In holinesse.
286. Iniustice.
287. *Pla. 4. de Leg. Arist.* 1. *mag. mor. Cic.* 1. *off. pro Rab.* & *ad Q. frat. Seneca de cl.*
288. [Law pushed to extremes is extreme injustice: Cicero, *De Officiis*, I, x, 33]
289. *Arist.* 5. *aeth.* & 1. *rhet. Cicer. pro Caec.* `
290. [For reason is the soul of the law]
291. [For virtue lies in the middle: i.e. virtue is a mean between two extremes]
292. The false semblance of extremities.
293. Their coincidence.
294. [all things meet in the infinite]
295. The right extention of a kings craft.
296. *Plat. in pol.* 5. *de Rep.* & *Epist.* 7. *Cic. ad Q. frat.* & *de or.*
297. *Id.* 1. *de fin.*
298. *Id.* 1. *Offic.*
299. The Scripture.
300. *Deut.* 17.
301. [The keeper of both tables; i.e. of both the first and second tables of the decalogue or Ten Commandments. The first table – or first four commandments – related to duties towards God. The remaining commandments constituted the second table and were concerned with duties towards our neighbours]
302. Of the Lawes municipall.
303. *Plat.* 4. *de Rep.* & 6. *de Leg. Arist.* 1. *rhet.*
304. *Cic.* 1. *de Orat. Sen. in Lud.*
305. Resort to the Session.
306. *Plat. in pol. Arist.* 1. *Rhet. Cic. ad Q. frat. Plut. in Is.*
307. *Xen.* 1. *Cyr.*
308. But specially to the secret Counsell.

309. *Cic. ad Q. frat. Tac.* 1. *hist.*
310. *Plut. in Demet.* [or may you be no king]
311. Reading of histories.
312. [Lest you be a foreigner at home]
313. *Plat. in Menon.*
314. *Arist.* 1. *Rhet. Polit.* 1. *Plut. in Timo. Cic.* 2. *de Or.*
315. Eccles. 1. [there is no new thing under the sun: Ecclesiastes 1: 9]
316. Ezech. 1.
317. [in the wheel of Fortune]
318. Of the arts liberall.
319. *Sen. ep.* 84.
320. *Liu. l.* 24. *Plut. in Marc.*
321. Of Mathematickes.
322. *Pl.* 7. *de leg. Arist.* 2. *Meta.*
323. Iam. 2. 17.
324. Of magnanimitie.
325. *Arist.* 4. *eth. Sen de cl.*
326. *Cic.* 1. *off. Virg.* 6. *AEn.*
327. Prou. 20. [Proverbs 20: 2]
328. Of humilitie.
329. *Plat.* 4. *de Leg. Xen.* 2. *de dict. & fact. Soc.*
330. [who for ten months bore the long distress of pregnancy; this is an adaptation of Virgil, *Eclogues*, IV, 61, which the Latin edition of 1619 quotes more accurately]
331. Exod. 20.
332. Exod. 20.
333. [in the place of parents]
334. *Xen.* 1. *&* 3. *Cyr.*
335. *Cic. ad Q. frat.*
336. *Arist.* 5. *pol.*
337. Matth. 18.
338. Of Constancie.
339. [of an unconquerable mind]
340. *Arist.* 4. *aeth. Thuc.* 3. 6. *Cic.* 1. *Of. & ad Q. f. Brut. ad Cic.*
341. [stupiditie, wherewith many ... their profession. 1603, 1616 *stupiditie that proud inconstant* LIPSIUS *perswadeth in his Constantia.* 1599, MS]

   [Justus Lipsius was a famous Belgian humanist and classical scholar who revived Stoic ideas in his *De Constantia* (1584) and elsewhere. James calls him inconstant because he taught at the Protestant university of Leiden between 1578 and 1591 but from 1592 was a professor at Catholic Louvain]

342. Of Liberalitie.
343. *Cic.* 1. *&* 2. *Of. Sal. in Iug. Sen.* 4. *de ben.*
344. [so that you do not drain the fountain of liberality]
345. [inviolable and not to be traded]
346. *Isoc. epist.* 7. *Xen.* 8. *Cyr. Phil. Com.* 10.
347. Arist. 5. *pol.*
348. [a faithful trustee]
349. Anent reporters.
350. *Isocr. ad Ph. in Panath. & de per.*
351. *Cic. ad Q. fr. Plut. de curios.*
352. *Isoc. de pac. Cic.* 3. *Of.*
353. [you shall rather sin in the other direction]
354. *Cicer.* 3. *Tusc.*
355. *C. ph.* 8. 3. *de leg. Ouid. ad Liu.*
356. *Quin.* 4. *decl.*
357. [meanwhile the just man suffers]
358. *Arist.* 5. *pol.*
359. Indifferent actions and their dependancie.
360. *Plato in Phil. &* 9. *de leg.*
361. Two sorts of them.
362. First sort, and how they be indifferent.
363. Formes at the Table.
364. *Xen. in Cyr.*
365. *Xen.* 1. *Cyr.*
366. *Plut. in Apoth.*
367. *Sen. ep.* 96.
368. *Sen. de consol. ad Alb.*
369. *Iuuen. sat.* 2.
370. *Arist.* 4. *eth.*
371. *Xen. de dict. & fact. Socr. Laert. in Socr.*
372. [the best sauce is hunger]
373. *Cic.* 5. *Tus. Plat.* 6. *de Leg. Plin. l.* 14.
374. *Cic.* 1. *Off.*
375. Of sleepe.
376. *Pla.* 7. *de leg.*
377. Best forme of diet.
378. *Pla.* 6. *de leg.*
379. Formes in the Chalmer.
380. *Val.* 2.
381. *Cur.* 4.
382. *Pla.* 6. *de leg.*
383. Dreames not to be taken heede to.

384. Rom. 14. Titus 1. [Unto the pure all things are pure: Titus 1: 15; cf. Romans 14: 14]
385. Of apparell.
386. *Isocr. de reg.*
387. *Cic. 1. Offic.*
388. [between citizens and soldiers]
389. *Plat. de rege.*
390. [a citizen]
391. [a soldier]
392. [a mere layman]
393. [able to bear cold and heat]
394. [fear supplies wings]
395. *Cic. 1. Off.*
396. *Ar. ad Alex.*
397. [adorned youths]
398. What ordinarie armour to be worne at Court.
399. Of language and gesture.
400. *Arist. 3. ad Theod.*
401. *Cic. in orat. ad Q. frat. & ad Bren.*
402. *Cic. 1. Offic.*
403. [Nothing counterfeit is estimable]
404. *Id. eod.*
405. *Cic. ad Q. frat. & ad Brut.*
406. *Idem. 1. Off.*
407. *Phil. ad Alex. Cic. 2. Off.*
408. *Arist. 4. æth.*
409. *Cic. ad At.*
410. *Isoc. de reg. & in Euagr.*
411. *Cic. 3. Off.*
412. *Id. 1. Off.*
413. Formes in reasoning.
414. In iudgment.
415. *Isoc. ad Nic. Cic. ad Q. frat.*
416. Of writing, and what stile fitteth a Prince.
417. *Cic. 1. Off.*
418. *De arte Poetica.* [Let them be kept back until the ninth year; cf. Horace, *De Arte Poetica* 388.]
419. *Idem eod.* [because a word which has been sent out cannot return; cf. Horace, *De Arte Poetica* 390.]
420. *Ar. de art. Poet.*
421. Of the exercise of the bodie.
422. *Xen. 1. Cyr.*

423. *Plat. 6. de leg. Ar. 7. & 8. Pol. Cic. 1. Off.*
424. *Pl. eod.*
425. *Xen. in Cyr. Is. de iug.*
426. *Plut. in Alex.*
427. [Plutarch, *Life of Alexander*, 6, 8 in the Teubner edition of K. Ziegler, and in later editions; 6, 5 in earlier editions: Macedonia does not have room for you]
428. Of hunting.
429. *In Cyn. 1. Cyr. & de rep. Lac. Cic. 1. Offic.*
430. *Cyropædia.*
431. Of hawking.
432. *Arist. 10. Eth.*
433. Of house-games.
434. *Arist. 8. Pol.*
435. [because nothing can be empty; i.e. there can be no vacuum]
436. *Dan. de lus. al.*
437. [curiositie of some . . . games of hazard   1603, 1616
curiositie of DANAEVS *in his booke* De lusu aleæ, *and most of the French ministers* 1599, MS]
[Danaeus was the French Calvinist Lambert Daneau, who held a professorship at Leiden]
438. *Cic. 1. Offic.*
439. Rules in playing.
440. What choise of companie.
441. *Isoc. de reg. Cic. 1. Off.*
442. *Ar. 2. ad Theod.*
443. Men. [evil communications corrupt good manners; 1 Corinthians 15: 33, quoted by St Paul from the Greek playwright Menander]
444. [incitements to lust]
445. *Pl. 3. de rep. Ar. 7. & 8. pol. Sen. 1. ep. Dyon.*
446. *Suidas.*
447. [lead me back to the quarries; Philoxenus had been imprisoned in the stone-quarries of Syracuse but was released so that he could hear a poem by Dionysius II, the ruler of Syracuse. When asked for his opinion of the poem, this was his reply]
448. *Suet. in Ner.* [what an artist is dying: Suetonius, *Nero*, XLIX, 1]
449. [their wits fly out at their fingers' ends]
450. *1. Sep.* [*La seconde sepmaine*, deuxième jour, Les Colonies, line 579]
451. *Curt. 8.*
452. *Liu. 35. Xen. in Ages. Cic. ad Q. frat.*
453. A speciall good rule in gouernment,
454. The fruitfull effects of the vnion.

455. Alreadie kything in the happy amitie.
456. Conclusion in forme of abridge of the whole Treatise.
457. *Thuc.* 6.
458. *Dion.* 52.
459. *Hor. lib.* 1. *epist.* [Anger is a short-lived madness: Horace, *Epistles*, I, ii, 62]
460. Ephes. 4. [Be ye angry, and sin not: Ephesians 4: 26]
461. *Arist.* 5. *pol. Dion.* 52.
462. *Plat.* 9. *de leg.*
463. [the crime follows the head; i.e. actionability for a crime lies against the person under whose authority the criminal is (and so against himself, if he is a free man). This was a Roman law principle; cf. e.g. Gaius, *Institutes*, IV, 77; Julius Paulus, *Sententiae*, II, xxxi, 8].
464. [Happy is the person whom another's perils make wary]
465. *Plat. in pol. Cic.* 5. *de rep.*
466. *Virg.* 6. *AEn.*
467. [Others will more pleasingly beat out the breathing bronze (I do believe), will draw forth living faces from marble; will better plead cases, will mark the movement of the sky with a rod and proclaim the rising of the stars. You, Roman, be sure to rule peoples by your power (for these will be your arts), to add law to peace, to spare the humble and to subdue the proud: Virgil, *Aeneid*, VI, 847–53]
468. [The first edition of this book was published at Edinburgh in 1598 (probably in September; STC 14409). It was reprinted at least four times at London in 1603 (STC 14410, two versions of STC 14410.5, and STC 14411; details are discussed in Akihiro Yamada, 'The Printing of King James I's *The True Lawe of Free Monarchies* with special reference to the 1603 editious', *Poetica* 23 (1986), 74–80). The earliest printing perhaps appeared in April. The book was included in James' *Workes* of 1616. The standard modern edition is in *Minor Prose Works of King James VI and I*, edited by James Craigie and prepared for the press by Alexander Law, Scottish Text Society, 4th series, vol. 14, Edinburgh 1982; the text is at 57–82, with notes at 128–42; there is an introduction and a bibliography of early editions at 193–203. Craigie's edition records a small number of textual variants, most of which are errors or misprints and their corrections. The present edition is based on the text in the *Workes* of 1616 (reissue of 1620; STC 14345). Variants are occasionally recorded in the notes: 1598 is the edition of 1598 (STC 14409); 1603 is one of the editions of 1603 (STC 14410); 1616 is the version in the *Workes* (reissue of 1620; STC 14345)]
469. [TREW 1616.
TRVE 1598]

470. [sontentious   1616
     sententious   1598]
471. [A lover of his country]
472. [TREW   1616
     TRVE   1598]
473. Psal. 82. 6.
474. Psal. 101.
475. Psal. 101.
476. 2. King. 18. 2. Chron. 29. 2. King. 22. and 23. 2. chro. 34. & 35.
477. Psal. 72.
478. 1. King 3.
479. Rom. 13. [Romans 13: 4]
480. 1. Sam. 8.
481. Ierem. 29.
482. 1. Sam. 15.
483. 1. Sam. 24.
484. 2. Sam. 1.
485. [Exodus 22: 28]
486. Ier. 27.
487. Iere. 29.
488. Rom. 13. [1598
     Iere. 13.   1616]
489. [Prayers and tears are the weapons of the church]
490. [Lord of all goods]
491. [Direct lord of the whole dominion]
492. [thervnto   1598
     thereuneto   1616]
493. [law pushed to extremes be extreme injustice; cf. Cicero, *De Officiis*,
     I, x, 33]
494. [Father of the fatherland]
495. [Du Bartas, *La Seconde Sepmaine*, troisième jour, Les Capitaines,
     lines 1107–1110.]
496. [The first edition of this book was published at London in February
     1608 (STC 14400). It was soon attacked by Roman Catholics
     including Cardinal Robert Bellarmine and the English Jesuit Robert
     Parsons (or Persons). About 1 April 1609 a new edition of the
     work was published, along with *A Premonition to all Most Mightie
     Monarches* (STC 14401). Many changes were made in this edition,
     only a few of which are recorded below. Some of the changes
     were intended to meet the criticisms of Bellarmine and Parsons. A
     number of errors were soon discovered in the book and on 8 April
     it was called in again. A revised version appeared in May (STC

14402). The text included in the *Workes* of 1616 was based on this latter edition, but added some mistakes and corrections. The text of the present edition is based on the 1616 *Workes* (reissue of 1620; STC 14345), which has been compared with the first edition and with the second of the two editions of 1609. In the notes, 1607 is the first edition (which has 1607 on the title-page, and was published in 1607 old style; STC 14400); 1609 is the second of the two editions of 1609 (STC 14402); 1616 is the version in *Workes* of 1616 (reissue of 1620; STC 14345)]

497. [A triple wedge for a triple knot (in wood); the two breves of Paul V and the letter of Bellarmine to Blackwell are the triple knot; James' replies are the triple wedge which destroys the knot]

498. [And all the people then shouted, and said, Great is Truth, and mighty above all things: 1 Esdras 4: 41]

499. [*Tunc omnes . . .* ESDR. 3.   1607, 1609
    1616 omits]

500. [This refers to the Gunpowder Plot of 5 November 1605]

501. *Gen. 4. 10.

502. ['A Proclamation denouncing Thomas Percy and other his adherents to be Traitors', 7 November 1605; SRP1: 58]

503. [put his sickle in another's harvest]

504. [a single erasure]

505. The Pope his first Breue.

506. The Oath.

507. [lawfull King   1607, 1609, 1616
    lawfull and rightfull King   3 & 4 Jac. I, c. 4, in SR4: 1071]

508. [dispose   1607, 3 & 4 Jac. I, c. 4, in SR4: 1071
    dispose of   1609, 1616]

509. [12 September old style]

510. [and what (was there) not?]

511. [*sic* 1607, 1609, 1616]

512. [departed spirit]

513. [faithfullest   1607, 1609
    faithfulliest   1616]

514. ['A Proclamation commanding all Jesuits, Seminaries, and other Priests, to depart the Realme by a day appointed', 22 February 1604; SRP1: 34]

515. *Magno cum animi moerore, &c.* [with great grief of mind; this refers to the opening section of the first breve]

516. The intendement of this discourse.

517. [he says many things but proves few]

518. [he proves nothing at all]

519. Iosh. 1. 17.
520. Iere. 27. 12.
521. Exod. 5. 1.
522. Ezra 1. 3.
523. Rom. 13. 5.
524. *August. in Psalm.* 124.
525. *Tertull. ad Scap.*
526. *Iust. Martyr. Apol.* 2. *ad Ant. Imperat.*
527. *Amb. in orat. cont. Auxentium, de basilicis traden. habetur lib.* 5. *epist. Ambr.*
528. *Optat. contra Parmen. lib.* 3.
529. *Greg. Mag. Epist. lib.* 2. *indict.* 11. *Epist.* 61.
530. [while his term of military service had not yet been completed]
531. *Concil. Arelatense sub Carolo Mag. Can.* 26.
532. *Vide Epistolam generalis Conc. Ephes. ad August.*
533. Iohn 18. 36.
534. Matt. 22. 21.
535. [infallibility   1607
     infallibilitie   1609
     infabillity   1616]
536. Question.
537. 1.
538. 2.
539. Answere to the Popes exhortation.
540. *Fama vires acquirit eundo.* [Rumour gains strength as it spreads]
541. *Eusebius, Oecumenius* and *Leo* hold, that by Babylon, in 1. Pet. 5. 13. *Rome* is meant, as the *Rhemists* themselues confesse.
542. See the Relation of the whole proceedings against the Traitours, *Garnet* and his confederates.
543. [at one and the same time]
544. [in one and the same breath]
545. The Catholikes opinion of the *Breue.*
546. The second Breue.
547. [13 August old style]
548. [by,; 1607: by]
549. [24   1609, 1616
     42   1607]
550. [who   1609, 1616
     he who   1607]
551. [18 September old style]
552. A great mistaking of the state of the Question, and case in hand
553. The difference betweene the oath of Supremacie, and this of Allegiance.

554. [This oath was introduced in the Act of Supremacy of 1559 ('An Act restoring to the Crown the ancient jurisdiction over the state ecclesiastical and spiritual, and abolishing all foreign power repugnant to the same'), 1 Eliz. I, c. 1; SR4: 350–5]
555. 1.
556. 2.
557. 3.
558. 4.
559. 5.
560. 6.
561. 7.
562. 8.
563. 9.
564. 10.
565. 11.
566. 12.
567. 13.
568. 14.
569. Touching the pretended Councell of Lateran. See Plat. *In vita Innocen. III.*
570. [irreconciliable   1609, 1616
     irreconcilable   1607]
571. The Oath of Allegiance confirmed by the authoritie of ancient Councels.
572. The ancient Councels prouided for *Equiuocation.*
573. The difference betweene the ancient Councels, and the Pope counselling of the Catholiques.
574. *Concil. Tolet.* 4. *can.* 47. *Anno* 633.
575. *Concil. Tolet.* 5. *Can.* 7. *anno* 636.
576. *Synod. Tolet.* 4. *vniuersalis, & magna Synodus dicta, Synod. Tolet.* 5. *cap.* 2.
577. *Concil. Tolet.* 6. *Can.* 18. *Anno* 638.
578. *Concil. Tolet.* 10. *Can.* 2. *AEra* 694.
579. *Concil. Tolet.* 4. *cap.* 74.
580. *Concil. Tolet.* 4. *cap.* 74.
581. *Concil. Aquisgran. sub Ludo Pio, & Greg.* 4. *Can.* 12. *anno* 836.
582. *Campian* and *Hart.* See the conference in the Tower.
583. The Cardinals Charitie.
584. Mat. 5. 43.
585. [nor   1607, 1609
     or   1616]
586. Mat. 11. 17.

587. No decision of any point of Religion in the Oath of Allegiance.
588. [in express words]
589. *Bellar. de Rom. Pont. li. 4. cap. 6. Ibid. l. 2. ca. 12.*
590. [it is piously to be believed]
591. *Idem ibid. lib. 2. cap. 14.*
592. [like Peter]
593. The Cardinals weightiest Argument.
594. *Bellarm. de Rom. Pont. lib. 5. cap. 8. et lib. 3. cap. 16.*
595. *Gotfrid. Viterb. Helmod. Cuspinian.*
596. *Paschal. 2.*
597. See the Oration of *Sixtus Quintus*, made in the Consistory vpon the death of *Henry* the 3.
598. [In August 1589 Henry III of France was assassinated by Jacques Clement. An oration in praise of Clement, and purportedly by Pope Sixtus V, was published shortly afterwards; three editions of the oration appeared in English in 1590]
599. *Bellar. de Iustif. lib. 5. cap. 7.*
600. Contrary to all his fiue bookes *de Iustificatione.*
601. *Bellar. de amis. gra. & stat. pecca. li. 2. c. 13.*
602. *Ibidem paulo post.*
603. *Bellar. de clericis, lib. 1. c. 14.*
604. *Bellar. de Pont. l. 4. c. 25.*
605. *Bellar. de Pont. lib. 1. c. 12.*
606. *Bellar. de Iustif. lib. 3. c. 14.*
607. *Bellar. de gra. & lib. arbit. lib. 5. cap. 5.*
608. *Eodem lib. cap. 9.*
609. Bellar. *de Pont. lib. 4. c. 3.*
610. Bell. *de Iust. lib. 3. cap. 14.*
611. Bell. *de Rom. Pontif. lib. 3. cap. 14.*
612. *Ibid. ex sentent. Hypol. & Cyril. & cap. 12. eiusdem libri.*
613. Bell. *lib. 1. de missa cap. 27.*
    [27   1607, 1609
    17   1616]
614. Bellar. *de miss. lib. 2. cap. 12.*
615. Bellar. *de anim. Christ. lib. 4. cap. 5.*
616. Bellar. *de Pont. lib. 3. cap. 17.*
617. Bellar. *de Pont. lib. 3. cap. 13.*
618. Bellar. *ibid.*
619. Bellar. *de Pont. lib. 2. cap. 31.*
620. Bellar. *de Pont. lib. 4. cap. 24.*
    [*lib. 2.*   1616
    lib. 4.   1607, 1609]

621. [the lion by its claw]
622. Henry 4.
623. *Abbas Vrspergen. Lamb. Scaff. Anno* 1077. *Plat. in vit. Greg.* 7.
624. Frederick Barbarossa
625. *Naucler. gener,* 40. *Iacob. Bergom. in Supplem. chron. Alfons. Clacon. in vit. Alex.* 3.
626. Henry 6.
627. *R. Houeden in Rich.* I. *Ranulph. in Polycronico. lib.* 7.
628. *Abbas Vrsper. ad Ann.* 1191. *Naucl. gen.* 40. *Cuspin. in Philippo.*
629. *Abbas Vrsper.*
630. *Math. Paris. in Henr.* 3. *Petr. de Vineis, Epist. li.* 1. & 2. *Cuspin in Freder.* 2.
631. *Vita Frederici Germanice conscripta.*
632. Fredericke Barbarossa.
633. *Paul. Iouius. Hist. lib.* 2. *Cuspinian. in Baiazet.* 11. *Guicciard. lib.* 2.
634. *Houeden, pag.* 308. *Matth. Paris. in Henric* 2. *Walsinga. in Hypodig. Neustriae. Ioan. Capgraue.*
635. *Gomecius de rebus gest. Fran. Ximenij Archiepis. Tolet. lib.* 5.
636. Card. Allens Answere to Stan. letter, Anno 1587.
637. [It is your own safety which is threatened when your neighbour's wall is on fire: Horace, *Epistles*, I, xviii, 84]
638. [slaves]
639. [Henry Garnet (1555–1606), superior of the Jesuits in England, was executed for complicity in the Gunpowder Plot]
640. [others   1607, 1609
      other   1616]
641. *Nazianzen. in Iulian. inuectiua prima.*
642. [to be lame in one foot]
643. The disproportion of the Cardinals similitude.
644. [Those whom he wishes to destroy, Jupiter first makes mad]
645. [what is disputed for what has been acknowledged]
646. 2. Maccab. chap. 6. ver. 18.
647. An answere to the Card. example of *Eleazar.*
648. [inferiours   1607, 1609
      inferiour   1616]
649. 1. Sam. 14. 24.
      [24   1607
      25   1609, 1616]
650. [that   1607, 1609
      the   1616]
651. *Theodoret. lib.* 4. *cap.* 19.
652. An answere to the Card. example of *S.* Basil.

653. [He greatly valued the emperor's friendship if it could be had with piety; but without piety he regarded it as pernicious]
654. *Theodoret. lib. 4. cap. 19.*
655. *Modestus* as *Nazianzen* vpon the death of *Basill* calleth him in his oration.
656. Looke cap. 12. *eiusdem libri.*
657. [by enquiring into unimportant doctrines]
658. [*Eleazars* 1607, 1609
   Eleazarus 1616]
659. [*Peters* 1607, 1609
   Peter 1616]
660. The Cardinal assimilating of the Archpr. case to *S. Peters,* and *Marcellinus,* considered.
661. Looke *Platina in vita Marcellini.*
662. *Concil. Tom. 1. pag. 222.* Looke *Baronius, Ann. 302. num. 96.*
663. [*obreptitious* 1607, 1609
   obreptious 1616]
664. See *Tom. 1. Concil. in Act. Concil. Sinuess.*
665. [the chief See is subject to no one's judgement]
666. [pass judgement on your case: our decision will not be overridden]
667. [the chief See is subject to no one's judgement]
668. [Paolo Sarpi (1552–1623), a Servite friar who defended the Venetian position against Bellarmine and others during the controversy over the Interdict which Paul V imposed upon Venice, 1606–7.]
669. *Apol. Pat. Paul. aduersus opposit. Card. Bellar.*
670. [oppositions 1609, 1616
   propositions 1607]
671. An answere to the place alledged out of S. Gregory.
672. *Greg. lib. 11. cap. 42.*
673. *Beda Ecclesi. Hist. gen. Ang. lib. 1. cap. 25.*
674. *Beda Ecclesi. Hist. gen. Ang. lib. 1. cap. 4.*
675. [slaves]
676. *Greg. lib. 11. cap. 42.*
677. [the right to wear the pall]
678. [head of the faith]
679. Iohn of *Constantinople.* See *Greg. lib. 4. Epist,* 32. [universal bishop]
680. *Lib. 6. Epist. 30.*
681. *Greg. lib. 4. epist. 32. & 36.*
682. *Bellar. de Rom. Pont. lib. 2. cap. 10.*
683. [he spoke rather carelessly]
684. *Idem. lib. 2. de Missa, cap. 10.*
685. [he spoke through error]

686. *Greg. lib.* 7. *Epist.* 1.
687. An answere to the authoritie out of *Leo.*
688. *Leo Primus in die assump. suae ad Pont. serm.* 3. *Leo Epist.* 89. *ad Episc. Vien. Idem ibid. ca.* 2.
689. *Cic. in Hort.*
690. For so hee calleth himselfe *in serm.* 1. *in die assum.*
691. *Ex breuiario Romano.*
692. *Epist.* 89.
693. *Epist.* 52.
694. *Epist.* 89.
695. *In serm.* 2 *in die anniuer. assum. suæ.*
696. *Serm.* 3. *in die anniuer. assump. suæ.*
697. *Epist.* 24.
698. *Epist.* 4.
699. *Concil. Chalcedon. Act.* 16. *& Can.* 28.
700. *Epist.* 9. *Theodosio.*
701. *Epist.* 16. *Flau.*
702. *Epist.* 17. *Theodosio.*
703. [under one kind; i.e. by giving only the bread and not the wine to the laity in the eucharist]
704. *Bellar. de sacra Eucharist. lib.* 4. *cap.* 14.
705. [divine doctrines]
706. [Lord God the pope]
707. [by prayers or by threats]
708. Some of Sanders his worthy sayings remembred.
709. *Sand. de visib. Monar. lib.* 6. *cap.* 4.
710. *Sand. de clau. Dauid. li.* 6. *c.* 1.
711. [Kings   1607
     things   1609, 1616]
712. *Sand. de visib. Monar. lib.* 2 *cap.* 4.
713. *Ibidem.*
714. *Ibidem.*
715. *Ibidem.*
716. *Sand. de clau. Dauid. li.* 5. *c.* 2.
717. *Ibidem.*
718. *Sand. de clau. Dauid. li.* 5. *c.* 4.
719. The Cardinals paire of Martyrs weighed.
720. Called *Elizabeth Barton.* See the Act of Parliament.
721. *Histor. aliquot Martyrum nostri seculi, Anno* 1550.
722. [Published in 1537 and commonly known as the Bishops' Book]
723. The Supremacy of Kings sufficiently warranted by the Scriptures.

724. 2. Chron. 19. 4.
725. 2. Sam. 5. 6.
726. 1. Chron. 13. 12.
727. 2. Sam. 6. 16.
728. 1. Chron. 28. 6.
729. 2. Chron. 6.
730. 2. King. 22. 11.
731. Nehe. 9. 38. Dauid. Salomon.
732. 2. King. 18. 4.
733. 1. King. 15. 12. 2. King. 13. 4.
734. 2. Chron. 17. 8.
735. 1. King. 2. 27.
736. 2. Sam. 7. 14.
737. Psal. 82. 6. & exod. 22. 8.
738. 1. Sam. 24. 11. [1 Samuel 24: 10]
739. 2. Chro. 9. 8.
740. 2. Chro. 6. 15.
741. 2. Sam. 14. 20.
742. 1. Sam. 13. 14.
743. 2. Sam. 21. 17.
744. Isa. 49. 23.
745. Rom. 13. 5.
746. 1. Tim. 2. 2.
747. Rom. 13. 4.
748. 1. Pet. 2. 13.
749. Rom. 13. 7.
750. Mat. 22. 21.
751. Iohn 18. 36.
752. [My kingdom is not of this world]
753. Luk. 12. 14.
754. [Who made me a judge over you?]
755. Luk. 22. 25.
756. [The kings of the Gentiles exercise dominion over them . . . But it shall not be so among you: Matthew 20: 25–6]
757. [keepers of both tables]
758. *Euseb. lib. 3. de vita Constantini.*
759. *De laicis cap. 7.*
760. *De Pont. li. 1. cap. 7.*
761. *Ibidem.*
762. *Ibid. & de Cler. cap. 28.*
763. *De Pont. lib. 3. cap. 16.*

764. *De Rom. Pontif. lib.* 5. *cap.* 8.
765. *De laicis cap.* 18.
    [18   1607, 1609
    8   1616]
766. *De Pont. li.* 5. *cap.* 8.
    [8   1607, 1609
    18   1616]
767. *De Pon. lib.* 2. *cap.* 26.
768. *De Pont. lib.* 4. *cap.* 15.
769. *De Clericis, cap.* 28.
770. *Ibidem.*
771. *Ibidem.*
772. [So that from contraries placed next to each other the truth might shine out more brightly]
773. [irreconciliable   1609, 1616
    inreconcileable   1607]
774. [the chief priest; an ancient Roman official]
775. [The second king of ancient Rome, and founder of the Roman religion]
776. [head of the faith]
777. [This speech was delivered on 19 March 1604, and published shortly afterwards at London (STC 14390; STC 14390.3) and Edinburgh (STC 14390.7). It was printed again in the *Workes* of 1616. The text of the present edition is taken from the version in the *Workes* (reissue of 1620; STC 14345), which has been compared with one of the printings of 1604 (STC 14390.3). There are few changes of any significance and none have been recorded below]
778. [this refers to the plague in London in 1603]
779. [What, therefore, shall I give in return?]
780. 1
781. [England had been at war with Spain since 1585. James formally agreed to a peace treaty (the Treaty of London) on 19 August 1604]
782. [1 Samuel 17: 34–6]
783. 2
784. [The Lancastrian Henry VII united the roses by marrying Elizabeth of York. In 1489 he agreed to the Treaty of Medina del Campo with Spain]
785. Mars.
786. Loue and Peace.
787. 3
788. 4

789. [Psalms 127: 1]
790. [1 Corinthians 3: 6]
791. [Tobie Matthew (1546–1628), Bishop of Durham (1595–1606).]
792. [2 Timothy 4: 2]
793. The third reason of assembling the Parliament.
794. [In the worst commonwealth there are most laws: Tacitus, *Annals*, III, 27]
795. [I am an unprofitable servant; cf. Luke 17: 10]
796. [relatives]
797. [A sin that is committed by many is committed with impunity: cf. Lucan, *Pharsalia*, V, 260]
798. [This speech was delivered on 9 November 1605, four days after the discovery of the Gunpowder Plot. It was published shortly afterwards 'Together with a discourse of the maner of discouery of this late intended Treason, ioyned with the Examination of some of the prisoners' (STC 14392; quotation from title-page). Two other printings followed (STC 14392.5, 14393). The present edition is based on the version contained in the *Workes* of 1616 (reissue of 1620; STC 14345), which has been compared with the text of 1605 (STC 14392). There are few variants of any significance, and none have been recorded here]
799. [The mercy of God is above all his works]
800. [This refers to the Gowrie Plot of 5 August 1600 and the Gunpowder Plot of 5 November 1605.]
801. [(my) voice sticks in (my) throat; cf. Virgil, *Aeneid*, II, 774, III, 48, IV, 280, XII, 868]
802. Three miraculous euents be to be obserued in the Attempt.
803. 1. The crueltie of the Plot.
804. [Guy Fawkes]
805. Three wayes how mankind may come to death.
806. 1. By Man.
807. 2. By vnreasonable creatures.
808. 3. By insensible things.
809. 2. The small ground the Conspirators had to moue them.
810. [Thomas Percy (1560–1605), who was a leading figure in the Gunpowder Plot, was one of the king's gentlemen pensioners]
811. 3. Miraculous euent, the discouerie.
812. [They have fallen into the pit which they made: cf. Psalms 57: 6, 7: 15]
813. 1
814. 2
815. 3

816. 4
817. [for life]
818. [In the worst commonwealth there are most laws: Tacitus, *Annals*, III, 27]
819. [This speech was delivered on 31 March 1607 and published shortly afterwards (STC 14395). It was reprinted in the *Workes* of 1616. The present edition follows the text of the *Workes* (reissue of 1620; STC 14345), which has been compared with the edition of 1607 (STC 14395). There are few material differences. In the notes, 1607 is the edition of 1607 (STC 14395; setting with line 4 of sig. B2b ending 'when'), and 1616 is the version in the *Workes* of 1616 (reissue of 1620; STC 14345)]
820. [1 Corinthians 14: 1–5]
821. [Psalms 127: 1]
822. [1 Corinthians 3: 6]
823. [The king is a speaking law]
824. [clearer than light]
825. [A bill confirming ownership of certain lands was sent from the Lords to the Commons on 30 March 1607: C. J. 1: 357; Bowyer 252]
826. [Something that is to be decided once for all needs to be considered maturely and at length]
827. [with a slow foot, i.e. deliberately]
828. [to seek a knot in a bullrush; i.e. to find difficulties where there are none]
829. [one king]
830. [one society and one law]
831. [From the beginning it was not so: Matthew 19: 8]
832. [honey in the mouth, gall in the heart]
833. [This refers to the inflammatory speech against the Scots which Sir Christopher Pigott delivered in the House of Commons on 13 February 1607: C. J. 1: 333]
834. Secondly
835. [if the cause disappears, the effect disappears]
836. 3.
837. ['A Proclamation concerning the Kings Majesties Stile, of King of Great Britaine, &c.', 20 October 1604; SRP1: 45]
838. [honey in the mouth, gall in the heart]
839. Third. [1607]
840. [The bishopric of Durham]
841. [to grant citizenship]
842. [the king is judge]

843. [a speaking law]
844. Fourth.
845. [in terms]
846. [the power to interpret the law belongs to the person who makes it]
847. [On 13 February 1607 Sir Christopher Pigott delivered an abusive speech against the Scots in the House of Commons (C. J. 1: 333). The House committed him to the Tower of London]
848. [alter 1607
    altar 1616]
849. [hatred of a third party, i.e. England]
850. [unburden my mind]
851. [This speech was delivered on 21 March 1610 – 1609 old style – and printed shortly afterwards. It went through three printings in 1610 (STC 14396; STC 14396.3; STC 14396.7), and was included in the *Workes* of 1616. The present edition follows the text of the *Workes* of 1616 (reissue of 1620; STC 14345), which has been compared with one of the 1610 printings (STC 14396.3); in the notes, 1610 refers to that edition, and 1616 to the *Workes*]
852. [In 1610 Lent ran from 21 February to 8 April. On 19 March the Commons thanked the king for giving them permission to discuss his feudal rights (C. J. 1: 412–13; PP10, 2: 41, 193), and on the following day the Lords likewise met with James to give him their thanks: PP10, 1: 42–4]
853. [*Cor Regis . . . in manu Domini*: the king's heart (is) in the hand of the Lord: Proverbs 21: 1]
854. [the king's heart in the eyes of the people]
855. [recollection]
856. [to give an account of his faith]
857. [the parent of the fatherland]
858. [Samuel Harsnett, Bishop of Chichester, preached a sermon at Whitehall on 11 March 1610; it attracted adverse comment in the House of Commons: PP10, 2: 59–60, 60n4, 328]
859. [the abstract]
860. [fatherly power]
861. [the power of life and death]
862. [for edification, not destruction: cf. 2 Corinthians 10: 8, 13: 10]
863. [a speaking law]
864. [Genesis 8: 22]
865. [or may you be no king]
866. [you are gods: Psalms 82: 6]
867. [Psalms 82: 7]
868. [the greater the fall, the greater the pain]

869. [an undefined individual; i.e. before their power had been regulated]
870. [what God wants]
871. [from may be to is]
872. [mine and thine]
873. [mine and thine]
874. [the replies of the knowledgeable]
875. [From the beginning it was not so: Matthew 19: 8]
876. [Luke 12: 20]
877. [fitly and unfitly]
878. [On 24 February 1610 the House of Commons heard a complaint against Sir Stephen Proctor, who had been employed by the king in executing the penal laws and collecting fines (Winwood 3: 125). He was accused of abusing his position and on 21 March was examined by a committee of the House (PP10, 2: 63)]
879. [the workmen should handle the tools]
880. [by ancestral custom]
881. [Members of the High Commission, the highest of the English ecclesiastical courts and the only one which had the power to fine and imprison]
882. [votes obtained by begging]
883. [the parent of the fatherland]
884. [the fatherland itself]
885. [maintaine 1610
mainaine 1616]
886. [Henry was made Prince of Wales on 4 June 1610.]
887. [In 1609 there was a dispute over who should succeed to the territories of the childless John William, Duke of Cleves, Julich and Berg, who died in that year. James sent troops to Cleves to ensure that it would remain in Protestant hands]
888. [In 1585 Elizabeth made a treaty providing the Dutch with military assistance in their revolt against Spain. The towns of Flushing and Brill were placed in English hands (and occupied by English garrisons) as guarantees that the Dutch would eventually pay the Queen's expenses]
889. [In Ulster]
890. [he gives twice who gives quickly]
891. [someone who undertakes too much achieves nothing]
892. [For that does less damage which we have anticipated beforehand]
893. [reputation 1610
reputatiom 1616]
894. [although 1610
althought 1616]

895. [Being]
896. [Well-being]
897. [Being]
898. [well-being]
899. [if not chastely, at least cautiously]
900. [First   1610
     Frst   1616]
901. [This speech was delivered in the Star Chamber on 20 June 1616 and published shortly afterwards in quarto (there were three impressions: STC 14397, 14397.3, 14397.7). It was printed again in the *Workes* of 1616. There are a number of differences between the various versions, but few are of much importance. In the notes below 4to is one of the quartos (STC 14397) and Folio is the version in the *Workes* of 1616 (reissue of 1620; STC 14345)]
902. [Psalms 72: 1]
903. [by privation]
904. [by accumulation]
905. [the beginning is with Jupiter; i.e. I begin with Jupiter (or God): Virgil, *Eclogues*, III, 60]
906. [James' mother Mary Queen of Scots was the daughter of James V, who was the son of James IV and Margaret Tudor. James' father Henry Stewart (Lord Darnley) was the son of Matthew Stewart (Earl of Lennox) and Margaret Douglas. Margaret Douglas was the daughter of Archibald Douglas (Earl of Angus) and Margaret Tudor. So James was doubly descended from Margaret Tudor, the daughter of Henry VII]
907. [John 10: 27]
908. [William Cecil, Baron Burghley (1520–98), secretary and later treasurer under Elizabeth]
909. [to give everyone his own]
910. [the replies of the knowledgeable]
911. [long   4to
     longer   Folio]
912. [From the beginning it was not so: Matthew 19: 8]
913. [It is shameful for a teacher if his own faults contradict his teaching]
914. [to say what the law is]
915. [to make law]
916. [reason is the soul of the law]
917. [by votes obtained through begging]
918. [word. So   4to
     word. so   Folio]
919. [vice versa]

920. [with myself as witness: i.e. I personally attest it]
921. [Sir Thomas Egerton, Baron Ellesmere and Viscount Brackley]
922. [the replies of the knowledgeable]
923. [From the beginning it was not so: Matthew 19: 8]
924. [the law of retaliation in kind]
925. [unless beforehand; a writ commanding the sheriff of a county to provide a jury to try a legal case at Westminster, *unless* the judges of assize have visited the county *beforehand*; civil cases tried by the judges of assize]
926. [Do this]
927. [and do not neglect to do that]
928. [virtue consists in action]
929. [Who think themselves the foremost of men, but are not]
930. [the text pleases when read out, and will please if it is repeated ten times]
931. [the beginning is with Jupiter; i.e. I begin with Jupiter (or God): Virgil, *Eclogues*, III, 60]
932. [Sir John Popham, Chief Justice of the King's Bench 1592–1607]
933. [finally once]
934. [This work was printed in the 1620 version of the *Workes* of 1616 (with 1616 on the titlepage and a colophon dated 1620; STC 14345). There is also an 8vo edition of 1620 (STC 14381.5) and a 12mo of the same date (STC 14382). In addition, the book was included in 8vo in *Two Meditations of the Kings Maiestie*, 1620 (STC 14412). The present edition is based on the text in the *Workes*, which has been compared with STC 14382 and STC 14412. Both of these editions contain an inferior text, omitting words, phrases, and marginal notes that are included in the *Workes*, but also occasionally correcting mistakes in that version. In the notes, Folio refers to the *Workes* (reissue of 1620; STC 14345), 12mo to the 12mo (STC 14382), and 8vo to the text in *Two Meditations* (STC 14412)]
935. [PSAL. 2. . . . *earth.* 12mo]
936. [*in the beginning of this same yeere* Folio.
    the last yeere a little after this time 8vo. 12mo]
937. Lib. 2.
938. [the beardless youth, freed at last from his guardian, takes pleasure in the horses and dogs and the sunny grass of the Campus: Horace, *Ars Poetica* 161–2]
939. [there is a proper limit in everything]
940. [things which are kept within due bounds endure]
941. [(too) late]

942. [for that does less damage which we have anticipated beforehand]
943. Stob. serm, 47. & Val. Max. lib. 7. cap. 2.
944. Plutar. an seni gerenda sit Respub.
945. Cic. l.5. Tusc. quæst.
946. [but on the contrary you shall proceed more boldly]
947. τὰ καλὰ δύσκολα [things that are honourable are difficult]
948. [the path of virtue is arduous]
949. [Dat. 29 Decemb. 1619. 8vo, 12mo omit]
950. [recruit]
951. Matth. 27. 11.
952. Gen. 1. 23.
953. Iud. 14. 14.
954. Num. 22. 28.
955. Num. 6. 10. [Numbers 23: 6–11]
956. Ioh. 11. 49.
957. 2. Sam. 7. 5.
958. 2. Sam. 7. 13.
959. Luk. 2. 1.
960. [Ahmed I (1590–1617; Ottoman sultan of Turkey 1603–17)]
961. [Mustafa I (1591–1639), brother of Ahmed I; Mustafa was Ottoman sultan of Turkey 1617–18 and 1622–3.]
962. [Osman II (1603–22; Ottoman sultan of Turkey 1618–22)]
963. [*Iuan Vasiliwich* Folio
    Vasilij Iuanowich 8vo, 12mo]
    [Ivan IV Vasilievich (the terrible; 1530–84; tsar of Russia 1547–84)]
964. [in editor
    in in Folio
    (who was . . . in peace) omitted in 8vo, 12mo]
965. *The *Cosackes* are a sort of warlike people dwelling vpon the riuer *Borysthenes*, wherof a number serues the K. of *Poland* in his warres; and others the Duke of *Moscouia*: and of this latter sort, I speake here.
966. [Michael Fedorovich Romanov (1596–1645; tsar of Russia 1613–45)]
967. Mar. 15. 17.
968. Io. 19. 2.
969. *The purple was of the iuyce of a shell fish, named *purpura*, and the scarlet of the graines of a berry.
970. Esa. 63. 1, 2. 3. Reuel. 19. 13.
971. *Reu.* 7. 14. [12mo
    Reu. 7. 1. 8vo
    Folio omits]

972. Psal. 22. 18.
973. Reuel. 4. 2.
974. Mar. 16. 19.
975. Reuel. 4. 4.
976. *Saint Paul* 1. Cor. 6. 2. & 3.
977. [citizens]
978. [mixed persons]
979. [protector of both tables]
980. Wisd. 8. 2. [who arranges all things fittingly: Wisdom 8: 1]
981. Psal. 7. 9. Prou. 21. 1.
982. 1. Sam. 9. 16. 1. Sam. 16. 12.
983. *Cic. De finib. bon. & mal. lib.* 4. [Cicero, *De Finibus*, IV, 74; something was also given to the people]
984. [labour]
985. [honour]
986. Psal. 2. 9.
987. Matth. 9. 13.
988. Matth. 11. 30.
989. Prou. 8. 15. [By me kings reign, and princes decree justice]
990. Psal. 82. 6. Rom. 13. 1.
991. Iere. 34. 10. Rom. 13. 4.
992. Colos. 3. 1.
993. Verse 1.
994. [Mark 15: 19]
995. [King; and   8vo, 12mo
      King And   Folio]
996. Ioh. 19. 4.
997. Io. 19. 13. [John 19: 15]
998. Luc. 23. 11.
999. Io. 18. 33. & 37.
1000. Io. 19. 5.
1001. Io. 19. 15.
1002. Io. 19. 20.
1003. 1. Cor. 14. 15.
1004. Io. 19. 21.
1005. Verse 22 [what I have written I have written]
1006. Gen. 49. 10.
1007. Num. 24. 17.
1008. *Iust. mart. Epiphan. Basil., &c.*
1009. Mat. 2. 15.
1010. Matth. 2. & Luk. 3.
1011. [royal insignia]

1012. Isai. 53. 7.
1013. Lam. 1. 12. [there is no sorrow like unto my sorrow: cf. Lamentations 1: 12]
1014. Luc. 22. 65. [Luke 22: 63–4]
1015. Matt. 27. 30.
1016. [crosse. And   8vo
    crosse. and Folio,   12mo]
1017. Io. 18. 36. [his kingdom was not of this world: cf. John 18: 36]
1018. Matth. 20. 25. [The kings of the Gentiles exercised dominion over them . . . But it shall not be so among you: Matthew 20: 25–6]
1019. Matth. 26. 52.
1020. [the spiritual good; this refers to the theory expressed by Bellarmine and other Catholics that the pope may use temporal means to secure spiritual ends]
1021. [wayes,   8vo, 12mo
    wayes.   Folio]
1022. Luk. 1. 26.
1023. Matt. 1. 20.
1024. [congratulating   12mo
    congratuling   Folio]
1025. Luk. 1. 41.
1026. Luk. 2. 7.
1027. Cap. 2. 14.
1028. Matt. 2. 14.
1029. 2. 11.
1030. Luk. 2. 46.
1031. Matt. 3. 13.
1032. Matt. 3. 17.
1033. Io. 8. 58.
1034. Matt. 8. 20.
1035. Io. 2. 15.
1036. Matt. 8. 26.
1037. Matth. 17. 2.
1038. Matt. 17. 27.
1039. Io. 7. 10.
1040. Matt. 26. 18.
1041. Io. 6. 15.
1042. Matth. 21. 3.
1043. Matt. 21. 9.
1044. Psal. 8. v. 2.
1045. Iud. 10. 4. & 12. 14.
1046. Io. 13. 4.

1047. Io. 12. 7.
1048. Reuel. 1. 14.
1049. Io. 18. 6.
1050. Luk. 22. 61.
1051. Phil. 2. 9.
1052. Luk. 23. 43.
1053. Luk. 23. 50.
1054. Philip. 2. 6.
1055. Prou. 16. 12.
1056. *Rom.* 13. 4. [8vo, 12mo
    Rom. 3. 14. Folio, and a variant of 12mo in the Folger Shake-
    speare Library, STC 14382.2]
1057. [life; 8vo, 12mo
    life. Folio]
1058. [This work was published early in 1622 (STC 9241). STC records
    two settings; a copy with the second setting has been used in this
    edition, and is referred to below as 1622]
1059. ['A proclamation declaring his Majesties pleasure concerning the
    dissolving of the present Convention of Parliament', 6 January
    1622: SRP1: 223]
1060. [amongst state secrets]
1061. [The Commons' declaration of 4 June is printed in Rushworth 1:
    36]
1062. [James' daughter Elizabeth and her husband the Elector Palatine
    Frederick V were being driven out of Frederick's ancestral territ-
    ory, the Palatinate, in 1621]
1063. [The projected marriage of Prince Charles to a Spanish princess]
1064. [Sir Edwin Sandys (1561–1629) was imprisoned in the Tower of
    London from 16 June to 16 July 1621]
1065. [The two petitions are printed in Rushworth 1: 40–3, 44–6]
1066. [We were expecting an ambassador and have received a herald –
    i.e. someone declaring war]
1067. ['A Proclamation declaring His Majesties grace to his Subjects,
    touching matters complained of, as publique greevances', 10 July,
    1621: SRP1: 217]
1068. [a Protestation contrary to fact]
1069. [conclusion editor
    couclusion 1622]
1070. [for spiritual ends; Bellarmine held that popes possess no *direct*
    temporal power over kings since they cannot intervene in the
    affairs of states for temporal reasons, but that they may intervene
    in order to promote the spiritual good, and so have *indirect* tem-
    poral power]

1071. [war seems sweet to those who have not tried it]
1072. [The Archduchess Isabella ruled the Spanish Netherlands in conjunction with her husband the Archduke Albert, who died in 1621]
1073. [Ambrogio Spinola (1569–1630) was a Genoese soldier who commanded the Spanish army in the lower Palatinate and in the Netherlands]
1074. [In 1619 the Elector Palatine Frederick V accepted election to the crown of Bohemia]
1075. [the cobbler should stick to his last: i.e. people should stick to what they know about or are expert in]
1076. [by erroneously joining what should be separated]
1077. [Sir Edward Coke (1552–1634) had been deprived of his position as Chief Justice of the King's Bench in 1616. Thereafter he made efforts to regain royal favour, but his conduct in the Parliament of 1621 annoyed James, though it pleased many members of the Commons. A bill was preferred against him in Star Chamber accusing him of judicial malpractice. The Commons initiated proceedings against Coke's accusers]
1078. [Subiects   editor
    Subiests   1622]
1079. [The Protestation is printed in Rushworth 1: 53. It asserts (amongst other things) 'That the Liberties, Franchises, Priuiledges, and Iurisdictions of Parliament, are the antient and undoubted Birth-right and Inheritance of the Subjects of England; And that the arduous and urgent affairs concerning the King, State, and Defence of the Realm, and of the Church of England, and the maintenance and making of Laws, and redress of mischiefs and grieuances which daily happen within this Realm, are proper subjects and matter of Counsel and Debate in Parliament']
1080. [concerning urgent affairs of the kingdom]
1081. [certain]

Glossary

abilitie	habilitate, promote
adstipulation	adding (or acting as) a second receiving party in a bargain (Roman Law)
affectatlie	affectedly
agroofe (agrufe)	with face downward
alanerly	only
aliant	outcast
alluterly (allutterly)	wholly
anathema maranatha	the most serious form of excommunication; cf. 1 Corinthians 16: 22
anent	about, concerning, in respect of, regarding
Ante nati	people born in Scotland before James' accession to the crown of England
archibellouses	leading inciters
Arch-priest (Archpriest)	the head of the Catholic secular clergy in England, 1598–1623
arles-peny	money given to confirm a bargain
auaileable	effectual, beneficial, of advantage
auer	a cart-horse
ay(e)	ever
bairdes	ignorant wandering minstrels
baited	fed
balladine (baladine)	a theatrical dancer, mountebank, buffoon
bare	destitute, needy
begouth	began
blanch	tenure of land for a nominal rent (Scottish)
blew-blanket	the symbol of the craftsmen of Edinburgh and of their privileges

blocker	someone who stamps a title on the cover of a book
brangle	to cause to waver
breue	a papal brief; a letter written by the pope on matters of discipline
brooke	to enjoy
burreaux	executioners
byle	boil
caitch	tennis
caitife (caitiff)	basely wicked
Candie	Crete
carp	to discuss, chatter, reprehend, find fault with
chalmer	chamber
charet	chariot
chop	to strike
cogging	cheating
compeare	appear
concealments	the holding of land without proper title and contrary to the right of the crown; land held in this way
conies	rabbits
contrare	contradict
cooling card	something that cools or reduces a person's ardour or enthusiasm
corbies	ravens
courser	race-horse
craigges	necks
Crane-craig	crane's neck
cuffing	contending, opposing
dairned (derned)	hidden, concealed
danton(e) (daunton)	subdue, tame, intimidate
debosh	debauch
decern	judge, decide
disdiapason	a double octave in music
dite (dyte)	dictate
ditted	shut up
doazen	stupefy
dyte *see* dite	
ear(e)	to plough
eike	to add
empyring	ruling absolutely
engine (ingyne)	native wit, talent

Glossary

entresse	interest, benefit
ethnick(e), ethnik(e)	heathen, pagan
fairding	using facial cosmetics
faschious (fashious)	tiresome, vexatious
fashery	worry
fectlesse (feckless)	ineffective, futile
feide	feud, enmity
few	a perpetual lease for a fixed rent
fine	accomplished
fore-faltures	forfeitures
fra	from, from the time that
freets	superstitions
fro	from the moment when
gaigeour	wager
galliardest	most spruce
gar(re)	to make or cause something to be done
gate	got
glister	glitter
gust	taste, foretaste
hag-but	a portable gun
halfe marrow	equal partner
Hamper	the Hanaper, a department of the chancery which received fees for the enrolment of charters and other documents
hap	luck, chance, good fortune
hartly	cordial
hoord	hoard
horn(e), to be at the	to be proclaimed an outlaw
ingyne *see* engine	
instinction	natural impulse, prompting
intromission	management of another's property
iowking	bowing in greeting
kyth(e) (kith, kithe)	to make known, declare, indicate
laikes	laics, laity
lairdes	Scottish landowners
law-burrowes	legal securities required from a person that he will not injure another in person, family or property
lear	learn
leide	type of speech
lightlying	making light of, disparaging
liguers	members of the French League formed in

	1576 to prevent the succession of Henry of Navarre to the throne
lipening	trusting
liue-rentars	liferenters, people who have a right to use property for as long as they live, but not to bequeath it
liue Renter Barons	people (bishops) who hold their baronies for life but cannot bequeath them (*see also* liue-rentars)
lowable	desirable, commendable
mair(e)	more
maniest	most
marrow *see* halfe marrow	
meaned	lamented
meating (meting)	apportioning, assigning, dealing out
meet	suitable, fit, proper
menstrally	minstrelsy
mercate	market
middesses	means
mignarde	dainty
misprision of treason	the offence of concealing knowledge of treasonable activities
moate *see* mote	
moe	more
Momus	Greek god of ridicule; a fault-finder
morgue	haughty demeanour
mote (moate)	a particle of dust
moulture (multure)	a toll paid to a mill-owner for the use of the mill
moyen	means of living
nusled (nuzzled)	nurtured, educated
obreptitious	containing a falsehood used for the purpose of obtaining something
orbitie (orbity)	childlessness
ordinaries	eating houses, taverns, gambling houses
orping	muttering discontentedly
pall maillé	pall-mall; a game in which a wooden ball is driven through an iron ring
panse	think
pasquils	lampoons, libels
peart	ready
Pettibagge	an office in the court of chancery

Philosopher, the	Aristotle
pick	to peck
pistolet	a small gun, a pistol
polypragmaticke	meddlesome, officious
popple	tares
Post nati	people born in Scotland after James' accession to the crown of England
Powder-Treason	the Gunpowder Plot
praemunire *see* premunire	
præoccupied	prejudiced
preass(e) (press, presse)	to endeavour, strive, weigh down
premunire (præmunire)	a writ accusing a person of pursuing in a foreign court a lawsuit cognisable by English laws
press(e) *see* preass(e)	
prohibition	a writ terminating a lawsuit in a lower court and bringing it into a higher one
promulged	formally proclaimed
Pythagorist	believer in the transmigration of souls
quit(e)	behave
rathest	quickest, soonest
reaue	despoil, take by force
redacting	reducing
regrate	sorrow, regret
rehable	to reable, legitimise
Renter Barons *see* liue Renter Barons	
responsall	responsible
Rhemists	translators and annotators of the English New Testament published at Reims in 1582
Roffensis	of Rochester; i.e. John Fisher, Bishop of Rochester
roumth	room
royalties	royal rights granted by the king to a person or group
runnagates (runagates)	fugitives, vagabonds
ruse	boast
saltly	pungently
scant	lacking
scantly	sparsely, hesitantly
scar(re) (skarre)	to take a scare, to be alarmed; a scare
secrets	a concealed coat of armour
sen, sen-syne, sensyne	since

sententious	abounding in pointed maxims
sib	closely related, akin
sicker	secure, safe, sure
sith	since
skantly *see* scantly	
skarre *see* scarre	
sliberely	lightly, wantonly
sliddriest	most slippery
slow-bellies	sluggards, lazy people
smoared	hidden
snapper	stumble
sponke	spark
start-vps	upstarts
stayest	steepest
stomacked	angry
strait	to restrict in choice or freedom of action, constrain
syne	immediately afterwards
tack	leasehold tenure
tearm	term
temperature	temperateness
tent	attention, heed
thraw	extort
thrissels	thistles
tigging	meddling
tild	ensnared
timous(ly), (tymouslie)	in good time, timely
traist	trust
tratler	idle talker
trauell	work, bodily exertion
trunsh-men	interpreters
tuilyesome	quarrelsome
tyne	to lose, waste
vague	wander
vaike	fall vacant
vanterie (vauntery)	boasting
veruels (varvels)	metal rings
viue	alive, living, lively
vndanted	not broken in to harness
vnrehabled *see* rehable	
vnspeered	unquestioned
vnstaid	unsteady, capricious

wakerif (walkrife)	wakeful, vigilant
walkrife *see* wakerif	
ward	tenure of land for military service (Scottish)
ware	vigilant, alert
way-taking	violent removal
wracke	to punish, destroy; punishment, destruction
ynew	enough, sufficient

Index

Index

Index

Index

Index

319

Index

83, 163, 181, 182, 199, 202, 213,
215, 250, 253, 262, 267
plenipotency 257
plenty 168, 260
Plowden, Edmund 217
Plutarch 281 n. 427
poets xxi, xxxviii, xxxix, xl, 15, 44, 46,
55, 58, 61, 79, 149
poison 23, 27, 114, 183, 240
Pole, Reginald xlii, xliii, 127
policy xxv, 6, 7, 25, 27, 30, 45, 76, 96,
130, 138, 140, 169, 181, 183, 209,
227
politic 5, 26, 34, 42, 92
Polonian 255
polygamist 136
polypragmatic 224, 308
Pompey 235
pontifex maximus 130
Poole see Pole
poor, the xl, 24, 45, 48, 156, 227
popery xx, 7, 25, 86, 152, 200, 259,
260; see also Catholics; papistry;
papists; Roman Catholics; Rome
popes xxii, xxix, xxx, xxxvii, xxxviii,
xxxix, xl, xlii, 85–131, 140, 152, 200,
224, 257, 258
Popham, Sir John 225, 298 n. 932
popularity xxiv, 25, 26, 54, 174, 213,
219, 222, 238, 252
Post nati 167, 168, 171, 308
poverty 194
praemunire xx, xxiii, 215, 308
prayer xliv, 3, 7, 13, 16, 36, 79, 99,
102, 108, 124, 169, 179, 229, 230,
234, 242, 243, 244
preachers xv, xvii, 5–8, 41, 71, 149
precedents 162, 186, 187, 212–15, 262
preeminences 104, 241
preferment 144, 145, 170, 221
prejudice 154, 165, 171, 258
prerogative xx, xxiii, xxiv, xxvi, xxvii,
xxviii, xxxix, 124, 128, 129, 165, 167,
170, 171, 176, 184, 185, 207, 212–
14, 216, 218, 222, 240, 249–54,
256, 261, 266; see also absolute
prerogative
presbyterians xvi, xviii, xix, xxx, xxxviii
presumption xxiv, 15, 26, 72, 101, 106,
107, 122, 214, 223, 259
pride 2, 19, 24, 25, 27, 38, 41, 44, 47,

50, 83, 92, 101, 143, 199, 222, 223,
226
priests xx, xxxvi, xxxvii, 85, 86, 90, 92,
94, 98, 100, 107–9, 113, 117, 118,
120, 122, 125, 126, 128, 129, 186,
200, 224, 234, 237, 244, 247, 304
primacy 99–101, 110, 117, 124, 125
primitive church 15, 72, 210
privileges xvii, xxviii, xxxi, 25, 65, 69,
80, 104, 124, 136, 162, 172, 176,
254, 261–6, 304
Privy Chamber 144, 184, 221
Privy Council 194, 216, 250, 252
proclamations xii, xxv, xxxix, 55, 86, 92,
138, 167, 174, 177, 225, 226, 250,
251, 255, 264, 267
Proctor, Sir Stephen 190
prodigality 44, 48
prohibitions xxiii, 187, 188, 192, 217,
308
promises xix, 11, 16, 26, 32, 41, 78,
81, 82, 91, 92, 104, 110, 134, 142,
165, 178, 196, 203, 208, 215, 266
property see meum and tuum
prophecy 57, 67, 79, 154, 208, 237,
244, 245
prophets 12, 14, 15, 17, 32, 67, 70, 93,
107, 126, 204, 237, 241, 247
proroguing of parliament 153, 157
proselytes 243
prosperity 11, 20, 64, 71, 84, 143, 144,
158, 239, 249
Protestants xv, xvi, xxii, xxvii, xxviii,
xxxi, xxxiv, xxxvii, xl, xli, xlii, 256,
260
Protestation of 1621 xxviii, xxxi, 266,
267
proverbs 11, 34, 35, 56, 58, 82, 115,
163, 199, 206, 222, 223, 231, 245
Proverbs, book of 15
providence xl, 60, 83, 115, 135, 150,
221, 259, 260
provost 76
Psalms 10, 16, 151, 160, 183, 188,
204, 206, 247, 270 n. 19, 293 n.
812, 295 n. 866, 295 n. 867, 297 n.
902
Punic Wars 151
punishment xvii, xix, 6, 7, 22, 23, 29,
44, 45, 64, 65, 80, 81, 82, 83, 84,
86, 91, 93, 102, 106, 118, 135, 140,
148, 152, 153, 155, 197, 202, 211,

324

Index

Salomon *see* Solomon
salvation 19, 45, 88, 90, 93, 95, 97, 98,
138, 140, 152, 233, 244, 245
Sampson 233
Samuel xxv, 64, 66–8, 70, 71, 271 n.
62
sanctification 13, 128
Sander (Sanders, Saunderus), Nicholas
xliii, 102, 112, 125
Sandys, Sir Edwin 253, 302 n. 1064
Sarpi, Paolo 121, 289 n. 668
Satan 99, 100, 119; *see also* devils
satire 31, 71
satisfaction 4, 9, 14, 143, 156, 251,
255, 260, 263, 265, 266
sauces 50
Saviour, our 3, 15, 16, 108, 120, 229,
235, 245, 246
Saxons 136, 137
scarlet 113, 236
scarre 103, 232, 309
scarring 28
sceptre 1, 33, 74, 174, 240, 241, 244,
249
schisme 7, 140
schoolmaster 16, 60, 76, 83
schools 10, 15, 16, 60, 76, 105, 115,
152, 172, 242
sciences 44, 46
Scipio 3, 151
Scotland xii, xvi, xvii, xix, xxiv, xxx,
xxxii, xxxiv, xxxv, xxxviii, xxxix, xli,
xlii, 6, 25, 73, 110, 135, 137, 161–5,
167, 168, 171, 172–8, 185, 191,
205, 208, 209, 216, 221, 230, 257,
304, 308
Scots xii, xiii, xv, xvi, xviii, xxix, xxx,
xxxiii, xxxv, xxxviii, xl, xli, xliii, 8, 53,
161, 164–6, 168, 169–73, 175–7,
197, 231, 304, 306, 310
scribes 118, 246, 247
scripture xvii, xxi, xxii, xxvii, xxviii, 6,
10, 13, 14, 15, 18, 19, 32, 42, 44,
45, 54, 64, 66, 67, 70, 71, 80, 85,
93, 118, 120, 130, 131, 140, 143,
181, 242
Seal, the Great 166, 214
seas 89, 97, 99–101, 104, 110, 117,
122, 124, 125, 135, 136, 148, 175,
177, 188, 202, 246
seasons 52, 58, 260
secretary 176, 254, 264, 266

secrets 3, 4, 11, 15, 45, 51, 53, 89,
105, 138, 239, 259, 308
sects 6, 7, 48, 138, 152, 201
security xxvi, 17, 116, 159, 161, 175,
176, 178, 194
sedition xvii, xxv, xxvi, xliii, 27, 37, 71,
73, 98, 140, 156, 173, 184
Seleucus I 231
seminaries 27, 196
Seneca 272 n. 101
servants 4, 20, 28, 34, 35–8, 41, 42,
45, 54, 66, 69, 70, 94, 100, 102,
117, 123, 128, 143, 144, 150, 169,
197, 223, 241, 261
severity 22, 31, 109, 153, 199
sex 39, 42, 148, 199
shame 4, 18, 23, 52, 161
Sheba, the Queen of 38
sheep 66, 69, 96, 116, 207, 224, 225
sheriffdoms 29
Shiloh 244
shipping 201, 202
shires 137, 153, 162, 164, 186
Sibyls 235
Sicily 122, 172
sicknesses 10, 18, 41, 230
silver 30, 197
similitudes 17, 64, 76, 78, 110, 116,
117, 118, 135, 181
sincerity 5, 9, 11, 143, 146, 159, 251,
261
sins 6, 12, 14–19, 39, 48, 79, 85, 97,
113, 118, 140, 148, 149, 151, 230,
236, 241
Sinuessa, Council of 121
Sirens xvii, 62
Sisimus *see* Djem
Sixtus V xvi, 111, 287 n. 598
Skinner, Quentin x, xxxiii
slavery 141
sleep 17, 50, 51, 66, 200, 239
sliddriest 83, 309
sloth 33
slowbellies 222
Smith, A. G. R. xxxiii
snails 177
Socrates 27
sodomy 23
soldan *see* sultan
soldiers 33, 57, 93, 94, 196, 229, 232–
6, 242
Solomon 13, 15, 41, 64, 204, 206, 235

Cambridge Texts in the History of Political Thought

Titles published in the series thus far